Skagerrak

Skagerrak

The Battle of Jutland
Through German Eyes

Gary Staff

Pen & Sword
MARITIME

First published in Great Britain in 2016 by
Pen & Sword Maritime
an imprint of
Pen & Sword Books Ltd
47 Church Street
Barnsley
South Yorkshire
S70 2AS

Copyright © Gary Staff 2016

ISBN 978 1 78383 123 4

Typeset in Ehrhardt by
Mac Style Ltd, Bridlington, East Yorkshire
Printed and bound in the UK by CPI Group (UK) Ltd,
Croydon, CRO 4YY

Pen & Sword Books Ltd incorporates the imprints of Pen & Sword
Archaeology, Atlas, Aviation, Battleground, Discovery, Family History,
History, Maritime, Military, Naval, Politics, Railways, Select, Transport,
True Crime, and Fiction, Frontline Books, Leo Cooper, Praetorian Press,
Seaforth Publishing and Wharncliffe.

For a complete list of Pen & Sword titles please contact
PEN & SWORD BOOKS LIMITED
47 Church Street, Barnsley, South Yorkshire, S70 2AS, England
E-mail: enquiries@pen-and-sword.co.uk
Website: www.pen-and-sword.co.uk

Contents

Chapter 1	The War Year 1916	1
Chapter 2	Operational Plans	28
Chapter 3	Admirals Beatty and Hipper Engage	42
Chapter 4	Vizeadmiral Scheer Intervenes	71
Chapter 5	The Fleets Collide	102
Chapter 6	Vizeadmiral Scheer Attacks	125
Chapter 7	The Evening and Final Fleet Contacts	159
Chapter 8	The Night and Battle of the Destroyers	174
Chapter 9	1 June and Disengagement	211
Chapter 10	The Outcome	238
Notes		252
Appendices		259
Index		269

Chapter 1

The War Year 1916

On 8 January 1916 the hitherto Chief of the German High Sea Fleet, Admiral Hugo von Pohl, was taken seriously ill and was transferred to a hospital ship, and from there he was taken to Berlin for an operation. Unfortunately, Admiral von Pohl had been afflicted with cancer and he never recovered, passing away after a brief time on February 23. His temporary replacement was the Commander of the III Squadron, Vizeadmiral Reinhard Scheer, and his appointment began a chain of events that would culminate in what to that date was the greatest sea battle in history, to the Germans the Skagerrak Battle, and to the British the Battle of Jutland.

In the Fleet there were fears that Vizeadmiral Scheer would not succeed Admiral von Pohl as Fleet Chief, and Vizeadmiral Hipper, the Commander of Reconnaissance Ships or B.d.A., set out his thoughts in his *Nachlaß*, his diary or bequest:

January 9. Our Fleet Commander, Admiral von Pohl, is ill – a stomach ailment. It appears that he will take a long recovery time and therefore a new Fleet Commander must be appointed. Hopefully Scheer.

January 10. Vizeadmiral Scheer tentatively assumes command of the High Sea Fleet, in place of the ill Fleet Chief.

January 11. Heavy north storm, so that on the evening traffic with ashore is impossible. And so it goes day after day.

January 12. The risk that Admiral von Holtzendorff will get the Fleet, as I greatly feared, appears ended. Everything indicates that Scheer will take over. There are however, further changes in command necessary in the fleet, and from my cruiser commanders I will lose one or another.[1]

Vizeadmiral Scheer was appointed Chief of the High Sea Fleet on 18 January 1916, and held this post until August 1918. He was born on 30 September 1863 in Obernkirchen, Lower Saxony, and entered the navy on 22 April 1879, undertaking normal cadet training, the final year of which included a world trip aboard the training ship *Hertha*, which travelled to Melbourne Australia, Yokohama, Kobe and Nagasaki in Japan, and Shanghai in China. From 1884 to 1886 he served in East Africa where he became friends with the later Admiral Holtzendorff. After his return to Germany he served in various positions, including two periods at the RMA

(Imperial Navy Office), and as commander of the battleship *Elsass* from 1907 to 1909. When Vizeadmiral von Holtzendorff became Chief of the High Sea Fleet in 1909 Kapitän zur See Scheer was appointed his Chief of Staff. Promoted Kontreadmiral on 27 January 1910, Scheer took over as Director of the General Navy Department of the RMA in September 1911. In February 1913 he was appointed commander of the II Squadron and was promoted Vizeadmiral on 9 December 1913. Vizeadmiral Scheer took command of the III Squadron in December 1914 and held this post until assuming command of the Fleet.

After taking command as Chief of the High Sea Fleet, Vizeadmiral Scheer applied for, and was granted, the transfer of two of his trusted colleagues and friends to his Staff. Kapitän zur See von Trotha, formerly commander of SMS *Kaiser*, was appointed Chief of Staff, and Kapitän zur See von Levetzow was appointed Chief of the Operations Department. Vizeadmiral Hipper wrote:

> January 23–26. Meanwhile, one of my best commanders, Kapitän zur See von Levetzow of *Moltke*, was replaced as he was assigned to the Fleet Staff; replacement Kapitän zur See von Karpf. I entirely agree, although a new commander in the Unit must naturally first familiarise himself with the ship. Also the Commander of *von der Tann*, Hahn, was exchanged as an especially good artillerist is needed for the new dreadnought ship *Bayern*, which would enter service on 1 March.[2]

The triumvirate of Scheer-Trotha-Levetzow brought with it a new offensive spirit and work on new operations for the Fleet in an offensive direction began immediately. Early in February Vizeadmiral Scheer went to a conference in Berlin where he set out his program. Nevertheless, the very first point acknowledged one of the realities of the current situation. 'The currently existing balance of forces initially forbids us to seek a decisive battle against the assembled English Fleet. Our sea war Leadership must also prevent this decisive battle being forced upon us by the enemy.'[3] However, the program continued:

> Through planned, continuous exposure to the enemy we can force him from his waiting position to advance against us with certain forces which we can attack with favourable opportunities; but on the other hand we must avoid giving rise to a feeling of superiority by the enemy, whereby he would not be afraid to give us battle.
>
> The shallowness of our opponent offers us the advantage that our inferior force can always act as the aggressor.

To achieve this aim, Vizeadmiral Scheer proposed merchant warfare with U-Bootes, the mine war, merchant warfare to the north, the aerial war and lively activity by advancing the High Sea Fleet. He also saw U-Boot warfare as the quickest method of dissuading Britain from continuing the war. He wrote 'That might be expected if success could be achieved either by a blow at her sea power centred on her Navy, or at her financial life, preferably both.' And:

> The then prevailing conditions of strength kept us from seeking a decisive battle with the enemy. Our conduct of the naval war was rather aimed at preventing a decisive battle being forced on us by the enemy. This might perhaps occur if our tactics began to be troublesome to him that he would try at all costs to get rid of the German Fleet. It might, for instance, become necessary, if the U-Boot war succeeded again in seriously threatening English economic life.[4]

The interesting part of what Admiral Scheer said was that the U-Boot war was primarily aimed at damaging Britain's economic strength, not mounting a 'hunger blockade' as the British had done to Germany. In this the U-Bootes succeeded.

On 8 February 1916 the German Government announced that merchant ships carrying guns would be attacked without warning. Vizeadmiral Scheer objected to this half measure and went to Berlin on 16–17 February to make his disagreement known. Later that month, on 23 February, the Kaiser, his brother Großadmiral Prinz Heinrich, State Secretary Admiral von Tirpitz and Chief of the Naval Staff Admiral von Holtzendorff, visited the Fleet at Wilhelmshaven. At the Offizieres Club the Kaiser agreed to Vizeadmiral Scheer's program. Only the date for the commencement of the unrestricted U-Boot campaign remained to be fixed. Nevertheless, not all those present were convinced. Vizeadmiral Hipper wrote:

> 23 February. His Majesty was here, and held in the Offizieres club an address to the Offizier Corps and then distributed a number of Iron Crosses, which looked very well and there was an excited mood.
>
> The U-Boot War should now be pursued with all possible ruthlessness. Only the commencement date was to be decided but there was some ambiguity. I am not quite sure yet if at the last moment the Reich Chancellery Group will win and pull back.[5]

The first operation of the offensive campaign was to be an advance by torpedobootes, supported by airships. On 6 February the torpedobootes put to sea, however the airships were unable to ascend due to poor weather, as it had been since January. The torpedobootes could only proceed at slow speed, with look out from the crow's nests proving impossible and under these conditions, with a strong SW wind, the advance was broken off and the torpedobootes returned to Schillig Roads. On 10 February the torpedobootes, the II Flottille, VI Flottille and IX Flottille, once again put to sea, but as the moon was in its first quarter airship attacks were no longer possible. At dusk the Flottilles were 10nm north of Ameland and would advance into the area between Dogger Bank and the Swarte Bank mine fields. They were to perform reconnaissance and attack any enemy vessels encountered. The torpedobootes were escorted by a single small cruiser, SMS *Pillau*, with the I FdT (I Leader of Torpedobootes) Kommodore Hartog aboard.

At 2208hrs that evening the three Flottilles formed into a broad reconnaissance line approximately 25nm wide and steered to the west, whilst *Pillau* and two boats, *G42* and *G85*, followed about 20nm behind. Visibility to the west was 2000 to 3000 metres, but was less to the east. Meanwhile, the newly formed British 10 Sloop Flotilla (minesweeping sloops *Buttercup, Arabis, Alyssum* and *Poppy*) had been minesweeping in the vicinity of the Dogger Bank and because of strict wireless silence was not recalled when the British Admiralty detected increased German wireless activity, indicating some kind of operation. During the night *Arabis* stood near a light buoy which marked the sweep, whilst the other sloops cruised up and down nearby. Towards 2310hrs the right wing of the German reconnaissance line sighted a light ahead to port. Soon after, a second light was discerned and a large, darkened vessel could be made out. Further behind three more darkened vessels could be made out on a WNW course. Nevertheless, the German Half-Flottille Chief hesitated until at 2330hrs he thought he recognised the vessels as cruisers of the British *Arethusa* type. Thereon the attack signal was given and between 2330 and 2342hrs *G101* and *G102* launched three torpedoes at the line of three ships and then, together with *G104*, a further seven torpedoes at the individual ship near the light buoy. The group of three turned away, whilst the individual ship disappeared in smoke. The Germans gave chase to the line and at 2353hrs *G104* fired another two torpedoes at them but again the British turned away and the torpedoes missed. Only now did the Half-Flottille Chief give a wireless contact report as he renewed his attack on the single vessel, which in fact was *Arabis*. *G101* and *G102* each launched a further torpedo but *Arabis* again turned away, however at the same time the German torpedobootes switched on their searchlights and opened artillery fire. *Arabis* was hit in the forecastle and amidships, had a steam pipe shot through and her wireless disabled, but by 0020hrs the Germans had ceased fire, still believing that their opponent was a light cruiser of the *Arethusa* class.

After receiving the contact report the neighbouring torpedoboot group, *B97*, *B111* and *B112*, turned towards the reported position. About a quarter of an hour later they sighted three vessels to port, apparently light cruisers of the *Arethusa* type. A further vessel of this type could be made out in the distance behind this group. *B97* fired two torpedoes, both of which missed, and then the British turned away so that contact was lost.

Meanwhile, the adjacent torpedoboot groups, *B109*, *B110* and *G103*, and the VI Flottille Group *G41*, *V44*, *V43* and *S49*, had also noticed the gunfire but because of the confusing wireless message did not make contact with the enemy.

Towards 0100hrs the three Groups of the II Flottille assembled in Grid Square 080 delta and at 0110hrs the Flottille advanced to the NW at a speed of 25 knots. Soon after, at 0116hrs, a group of darkened vessels came in sight, but it was the

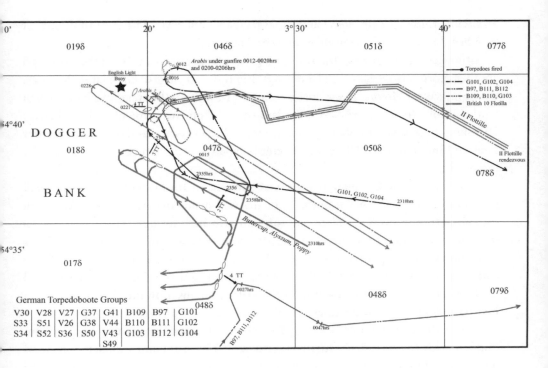

German Torpedoboote Groups

V30	V28	V27	G37	G41	B109	B97	G101
S33	S51	V26	G38	V44	B110	B111	G102
S34	S52	S36	S50	V43	B112	G104	
			S49				

VI Flottille. About 0148hrs the Flottille Chief, Korvettenkapitän Schuur aboard *B97*, recognized a clear light off the port bow. It was the previously observed light buoy, and nearby a darkened vessel with two funnels could be discerned, which soon turned away to the NE. *B97* closed to make a torpedo attack but the torpedo misfired and *B97* closed to just 400 metres and opened artillery fire. *B111* and *B112* also opened fire and several hits were observed resulting in smoke and steam emanating from the enemy ship. *Arabis* replied with four salvos, which passed over the bridge and bow gun of *B97*. Then *B111* launched a torpedo that struck the British minesweeper amidships and after that she lay stopped and unmanoeuvrable. Finally, at 0221hrs *B112* fired a further two torpedoes, which both hit *Arabis*, and she finally sank. Now the German torpedobootes launched boats to rescue the survivors. A total of three officers, including the commander and ship's doctor, three NCOs and 27 men were rescued from the cold waters. However, the doctor and four men perished from heart failure on the return trip. The Germans swept the entire area with searchlights for three-quarters of an hour before breaking off rescue operations.

Attempts to locate the other British vessels failed and at about 0300hrs Kommodore Hartog ordered his forces to a rendezvous 30nm north of Terschelling. Meanwhile, Vizeadmiral Hipper had put to sea with his I AG after receiving a report at 0115hrs and 20 minutes later the Panzerkreuzer were followed by the 1 Division of the I Squadron, which was on picket duty. The battleships on Wilhelmshaven Roads,

Westfalen, *Kaiser*, *König Albert* and *Markgraf*, also followed. The II AG followed at 0230hrs. After a fruitless advance the I AG anchored on the Jade at 1335hrs.

Although the sinking of *Arabis* was no great loss to the Royal Navy they suffered another more serious loss on 11 February when the flagship of the Harwich forces, the light cruiser *Arethusa*, was lost on the return journey to Harwich. Near North Cutler Buoy *Arethusa* struck a mine laid by *UC7* on the night of 9/10 February 1916 and after several failed towing attempts the cruiser was driven onto Cutler Reef and broke in two. All salvage attempts failed and the wreck was overtaken by her destiny.

As a result of the German torpedoboot advance on 10/11 February it was learnt that they required further training in tactics and manoeuvring together. Although the gunnery had been excellent the torpedo arm had not performed well. Of 19 torpedoes launched only three, or perhaps four, had hit. Whilst material failures contributed to this poor result, it was thought that the shallow draught of *Arabis* had also contributed. Nevertheless, on 12 February the I FdT and the VI and IX Flottilles departed for training in the Baltic, followed by the II Flottille on 14 February after they had completed boiler cleaning.

Part of the German operational plan was to continue the activity of merchant raiders, with the so-called Auxiliary Cruisers. The Auxiliary Cruiser *Möve* had put to sea in late 1915 and had laid mines off the Scottish coast, which had claimed the British battleship *King Edward VII*, but her return date remained unknown. In the meantime the Auxiliary Cruiser *Greif* put to sea on 27 February 1916 for a mission into the Atlantic. However, British Naval Intelligence, Room 40, was able to intercept and decipher German wireless signals, mainly because in 1914 the Russians had captured and passed on a copy of the German Naval Code book. With the help of this priceless aid, and the fact that German wireless discipline was lax, Room 40 was able to provide the British Admiralty and Admirals with advance knowledge of impending German operations. So it was when *Greif* put to sea, and several groups of British cruisers were sent to intercept the German cruiser. *Greif* was intercepted by the Auxiliary Cruiser *Alcantara* on 29 February and after a fierce fight both *Greif* and *Alcantara* sank, *Greif* after British reinforcements in the form of the auxiliary cruiser *Andes* and light cruiser *Comus* arrived and joined the battle.

On 3 March a wireless message arrived from *Möve* indicating she would arrive off Horns Reef the following morning. This message came as a complete surprise, however the available picket forces, the 2 Division of the I Squadron, *von der Tann*, the IV AG and V TBF immediately put to sea to welcome the raider home. They were followed by the II Flottille, *Seydlitz*, *Moltke* and *Derfflinger*, and the 1 Division of the I Squadron. Because of fog the following morning *Möve* was only found by *von der Tann* towards 0700hrs, but was then lost again. At 1700hrs *Möve* arrived safely in Wilhelmshaven.

The next offensive advance by the High Sea Fleet coincided with an airship attack on Britain. British light forces had frequently been reported in the Hoofden, the sea area between Holland and the Norfolk coast, and at 2030hrs on 5 March, in accordance with Operational Order 1180/0, the I AG ran out with *Seydlitz*, *Moltke*, *Derfflinger* and *von der Tann*, followed by the I and III Squadrons, with a total of 20 capital ships (*Rheinland* was in dockyard hands, *Bayern* and *Lützow* had yet to join the Fleet) to sweep through the Hoofden and surprise any British forces found there. The night was very dark with a light WNW wind and soon after the Fleet put to sea there was a snowstorm. During the morning the I and II AG continued south into the Hoofden, followed approximately 60nm behind by the Main Body. Vizeadmiral Hipper wrote:

> 5 March. 2030 in the evening I run out with the I AG. The weather was still and clear. During the night nothing occurred. Only a few fishing vessels were met. On investigation they were neutral. On 6 March the Panzerkreuzers and the light forces advanced deep in the Hoofden as far as the minefields known to us would allow. Of the enemy nothing was heard. In contrast during the morning a lively wireless traffic came in, whereby all enemy light forces were quickly called back into harbour. The English also followed the principle that

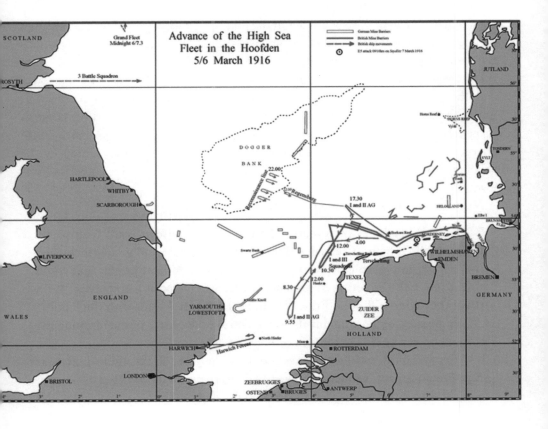

when their forces were not greatly superior in strength on the spot, then all were called back into harbour. During the night 3 airships which had ascended from the Hage, Tondern and Nordholz, had made attack on Hull and the surrounding area with good results. On the return journey they served as reconnaissance. Of the enemy forces nothing was seen.

About 10am at the latitude of Ijmuiden I made a turn and moved back on my Main Body, which stood north of Terschelling and I reached them about 2pm.

Then I received orders that during the night the three Flottilles II, VI and IX, under the II FdT,[6] should set in the direction of the Firth of Forth. The weather remained clear and still. About 4pm I detached the Flottilles and for the night went back to the German Bight, where the Main Body had marched about 2pm. The II AG should follow one hour later. During the rearmarch many drifting mines were sighted, which continually had to be avoided. Some were shot at. During the night I cruised in the inner German Bight and about 3.30am would run into the Jade when the torpedobootes were no longer in danger.[7]

During the evening the I AG cruised in the German Bight at a speed of 15 knots and sighted numerous drifting mines. The weather deteriorated and there was driving snow and a rough swell, strength 5. On the following morning, 7 March, at 0910hrs an enemy submarine was sighted from *Seydlitz* off the island of Juist. *Seydlitz*'s war diary reported: '9.10am. Grid Square 109ε. Submarine to port 500m. Ship turns away to starboard at 18 knots (a part of the darkly painted conning tower and the periscope were clearly made out).'[8] It was the British submarine E5, under the command of Lieutenant-Commander Edwards. The escorting German torpedobootes of the 9 Half-Flottille carried out an attack on the boat with depth charges but E5 probably survived as at 1130hrs a submarine was sighted by the small cruiser *Regensburg*. Nevertheless, E5 did not return from this patrol and was lost.

Vizeadmiral Hipper summed up what was a difficult day:

7 March. Already on the evening there was a strong east wind with partly snow squalls, which increased and on the morning the wind strength reached 6–8 with strong driving snow. The torpedobootes suffered heavily and could not steam with the ordered speed against the sea. Several had damage. With dawn they were still not off the Ems and for security I went with the I and II AG to a reception position off the Ems. During the course of the morning the torpedobootes gradually came in.

After the boats were safe I went back to the Jade. Suddenly to port near *Seydlitz* an enemy submarine dived and made an attack. With a hard turn away and an increase in speed we avoided the danger. In the driving snow and rough seas perhaps the submarine could not come to a shot quickly enough. Nevertheless it was a devilish situation.

In the afternoon we were again in the Jade. Stressful day.[9]

On 15 December 1915 the Russian observer and representative with the Grand Fleet, Captain 1 Rank Schoultz, drafted a memorandum to the British Admiralty in which, on behalf of the Russian Government and Navy, he requested that the Royal Navy penetrate the Baltic to open a supply route to Saint Petersburg, and Russia. Sea mastery of the Baltic would also allow a Russian advance on land to be secured on its vulnerable flank. The First Lord of the Admiralty, Lord Balfour, met with Captain 1 Rank Schoultz in late January 1916 and advised him that no assistance could be offered along these lines until the German High Sea Fleet had been decisively beaten. Nevertheless, spring 1916 did herald a new wave of British offensive activity.

The frequent air raids by German airships had been causing consternation in Britain and it was determined to attack the airships in their hangars with bomb laden seaplanes. Intelligence suggested the airship hangars were at Hoyer, but in reality they were at Tondern, a short distance away. The five seaplanes would be carried within range by the aircraft tender *Vindex*, which would be escorted by the Harwich Force, whilst the Battle Cruiser Fleet would act in support. Commodore Tyrwhitt's Harwich Force consisted of the 5th Light Cruiser Squadron: *Cleopatra*, *Penelope* and *Conquest*; two flotilla cruisers, *Aurora* and *Undaunted*; two flotilla leaders, *Nimrod* and *Lightfoot*; two divisions of the 10 Flotilla, *Meteor*, *Mastiff*, *Minos*, *Manly*, *Medusa*, *Murray*, *Mansfield* and *Morris*; and two of the 9 Flotilla, *Laforey*, *Liberty*, *Llewellyn*, *Laurel*, *Laertes*, *Lassoo*, *Laverock* and *Linnet*. Commodore Tyrwhitt and his forces set off at daybreak on 24 March and early on the morning of the following day were in the sea area off Vyl light vessel. The weather was very poor with frequent snow squalls. At 0530hrs *Vindex* was detached and proceeded closer towards Graa Deep light vessel. Soon afterwards a torpedo, which must have been launched by mistake by the British submarine *H7*, narrowly missed Tyrwhitt's flagship, *Cleopatra*. By 0630hrs *Vindex* had launched her floatplanes and began the wait until they returned. The first two aircraft returned about 0800hrs but had to report there were no airship hangars at Hoyer, but their base was further inland at Tondern. Of the other aircraft nothing could be found and they were lost, their crews being taken prisoner.

Meanwhile, the Germans had been planning an operation of their own. It had been planned that for the evening of 26 March the High Sea Forces would advance to the line Farn Island–Skagerrak and on the following night the II, VI and IX Flottilles would conduct merchant warfare west of the Dogger Bank mine field. Nevertheless, whilst preparations were underway for this operation, at 0945hrs on 25 March the FT Station at List reported: 'Vamdrup bombed by enemy aircraft in the early morning. Enemy aircraft drifts south of Hörnum.' At the same time the picket trawler *Braunschweig* reported enemy destroyers in sight. Commodore Tyrwhitt had ordered the Flotilla Leaders *Lightfoot* and *Nimrod* to take eight destroyers and sweep to the southward, whilst he himself would search for his missing aircraft. At 0938hrs the destroyer group was sighted from the Naval Intelligence Station at List, on the island of Sylt, which gave out a warning. This warning came too late for the picket trawlers *Braunschweig* and *Otto Rudolf*, which were attacked by the British destroyers and were quickly sunk. The destroyers saved most of the crews.

Whilst this battle was still underway the German aircraft 505, 541 and 291 took off for an attack and climbed above the clouds. Soon after 1000hrs approximately 15nm abeam of Rote Kliff aircraft 505 sighted the enemy from an altitude of 4000 feet. Descending to 2500 feet, the German aircraft sighted three large ships, which were thought to be light cruisers but were probably the destroyer leaders. About 1020hrs aircraft 505 attacked one of the larger ships with three bombs, and then bombed another destroyer with a further three bombs. Twenty to thirty minutes later aircraft 541 and 291 arrived and although 291 was hit on a float it dropped bombs and it was observed that two destroyers had to stop, whilst the others disappeared in a NW direction. What had occurred was that whilst taking evasive action the destroyer *Medusa* had been rammed by *Laverock*. The damage was so severe that *Medusa* could make no more than six knots. *Lightfoot* took *Medusa* in tow and the destroyers *Laertes* and *Lasso* remained with the tow unit as escort, as it slowly made its way to the west.

Also at around 1020hrs the German aircraft 508 and 553 alighted near the British aircraft adrift near Hörnum, and this aircraft, number 8040, was towed to shore by a boat of the Armee coast watch.

When he received news that *Medusa* had been crippled and the Harwich forces were still spread out in the outer German Bight, Vice Admiral Beatty pushed to the south to give his support and by 1300hrs his battle cruiser force was just 20nm west of Horns Reef. Perhaps Vice Admiral Beatty was hoping to repeat his success of August 1914 when he had trapped German light forces in the Helgoland Bight. In the meantime Commodore Tyrwhitt received an order from the Admiralty to immediately retire, as they had learned that German torpedobootes would attack during the night.

Despite the deteriorating weather Vizeadmiral Scheer ordered a riposte at 1345hrs. The I Squadron, I and IV AG and II FdT with the I, V, VI and VII TBFs were ordered to advance to the north, whilst the II AG and the I FdT with the III and IX TBFs were ordered to advance to the west, to reconnoitre off Terschelling in case a concurrent operation was underway against the airship base at Hage. The III Squadron would support this advance. About this time *Seydlitz*, *Moltke*, *Lützow* and the V TBF passed the outer Jade light vessel, but just as the worsening weather was making it difficult for the *Medusa* tow unit, the German forces were having a hard time of it. The two cruisers of the IV AG had a highest continuous speed of 20 knots so that the I FdT sent them back to *Regensburg*. The I Squadron and *Derfflinger* were further ahead and at 1500hrs were just 18nm behind *Regensburg*. Nevertheless, with the deteriorating visibility and increasing storm, and as there were no further reports about British movements, the German forces were ordered to turn about, the I Squadron to return to the Jade whilst the I AG would anchor for the night in Schmal Deep, off Amrum Bank. On the other hand there were still prospects of a successful night attack with torpedobootes and these light forces continued their advance.

The torpedobootes advancing to the west were under the command of the I FdT, Kommodore Hartog aboard *Rostock*, and were only advancing with great effort. At around 2130hrs one of the boats on the right wing, just 100m abeam *Rostock*, *S22*, struck a mine and a second detonation followed in quick succession. The forecastle ahead of the bridge was rent off and drifted aft, whilst fuel oil was ignited and apparently caused the second blast. After five minutes the remains of the torpedoboot sank, but the accompanying *S18* was able to rescue 16 men from the crew of 93. The commander, Kapitänleutnant Karl Galster, was not among them. However, the advance of the broad reconnaissance line continued to the SW at 12 knots before at 2300hrs a turn was made back to the NE.

Meanwhile, the advance of the I and VI Flottilles to the NW was having no better luck. By 2200hrs the British destroyer *Lassoo* had skilfully recovered the crew of *Medusa*, despite the stormy conditions, and she was abandoned at 2230hrs, although left at anchor in spite of orders to scuttle her in the hope of salvaging the destroyer the following morning. Not far away the German boats laboured against the heavy seas with waves breaking over their bridges, making the use of binoculars impossible and the gun and torpedo crews had to seek refuge below decks. The ready munition was washed overboard and the boiler rooms took on water and as it was impossible to clean the boiler fires sparks and flames shot from the funnels at speeds above 20 knots. The senior Flottille Chief, Korvettenkapitän Max Schultz, gave orders to reduce speed to 15 knots and finally at 2210hrs the II FdT, Kommodore Köthner, ordered the advance to be abandoned. However, part of the left wing had turned away to port to investigate trawlers and the following boats, *G193* and *G194*, lost contact with those ahead. When the order came to make a turn these two boats assumed the leading boats had already turned and turned themselves onto a SE course and at 2320hrs when approximately 40nm WNW of Horns Reef light vessel three darkened vessels were sighted ahead, 4 points to starboard. A collision between the leading *G193* and the leading vessel was averted with the order: 'Hard port, Utmost Power ahead.' The enemy cruiser missed by just 5 to 10 metres; however, *G194* was not so fortunate.

Commodore Tyrwhitt's force was steering north in three groups: ahead went *Nimrod* and the bulk of the destroyers; in the middle was the 5 Light Cruiser Squadron, the cruisers *Cleopatra*, *Undaunted*, *Penelope* and *Conquest*; aft at a greater distance were *Aurora*, *Lightfoot* and *Lassoo*. Aboard *Cleopatra* they recognized flames and sparks from the German torpedoboot funnels and she immediately steered out of line to ram one of them, however missed *G193* and then struck hapless *G194*. The boat was cut into two parts, which quickly sank in the rough seas. Unfortunately, the sudden course alteration brought *Cleopatra* beam on to the remainder of the line and she was rammed by *Undaunted*. Damage to *Cleopatra* was slight, but on *Undaunted* the bows were completely stove in and water pressure on her collision bulkhead only allowed a speed of just 6 knots. This situation was now worse than before *Medusa* had been abandoned. Neither was *G193* out of danger as she was taken under fire by British destroyers, but was able to escape undamaged. When the II FdT received a report from *G193* he ordered the I and VI Flottilles to the last reported position of *G193* at 2356hrs. However, because of the heavy seas the Kommodore soon had to abandon this advance.

In the meantime Vice Admiral Beatty and the Battle Cruiser Fleet had turned southwards to support the damaged cruiser *Undaunted*. As the British steamed to the south the I AG weighed anchor at 0115hrs and steered to the north, and would be supported by the III Squadron under Kontreadmiral Behncke, and the VII TBF, which weighed anchor so that they could meet the cruisers at dawn. At 0245hrs Vizeadmiral Scheer weighed anchor and advanced to the north with the I Squadron and Fleet flagship. When British Naval Intelligence learned of the German advance the Admiralty ordered the entire Grand Fleet to sea, but there was no chance of a general fleet action. At 0630hrs the German cruisers reported that the seas were so rough that engagement was impossible and accordingly the advance was given up as chanceless. The British forces retired later that same day for the same reasons.

During the night whilst at anchor some of the I AG had their anti-torpedo nets rent loose by the stormy weather. With the advance to the north, at 0915hrs, *Seydlitz* sighted an enemy submarine 25nm SW of Horns Reef light vessel at a distance of 800m to port. On the return journey *Lützow* was attacked by a submarine and the torpedo passed 50–100 metres behind the stern. This was most probably fired by the British submarine *E24*, which failed to return from this operation. The I AG anchored on Wilhelmshaven Roads at 2040hrs.

The plan of the German Fleet Leadership to conduct an advance to the north to the line Farn Island–Skagerrak with the High Sea Fleet on the evening of 26 March had been completely thwarted by the British seaplane attack.

Prior to this operation, on 20 March, Vizeadmiral Hipper had submitted a request for medical leave on the advice of his physician. Physically he was unwell with sciatica and mentally he was exhausted. After the operation of 25–26 March he was totally spent. He wrote:

26 March. Two terribly exhausting days that have probably finished my terribly weakened body. Shoulder pain. Tomorrow I will get off.

27 March. The Fleet Chief came aboard this morning to see me and speak about my representations and has ruled in my favour. The Leader of the II AG will represent me, and for him the Leader of the IV AG, as I had proposed. At noon I disembark and tomorrow will journey to Bad Nenndorf. Hopefully I will get back in order.[10]

Vizeadmiral Hipper remained on sick leave until 13 May.

In April 1916 the British were preparing three offensive plans: a Grand Fleet demonstration in the Kattegat for 21 April to draw attention away from the Russians, who were relaying their Baltic minefields after the spring thaw; an operation by Admiral Bacon from Dover to lay extensive minefields and antisubmarine nets off the Belgium coast on 24 April, and a second attack on the airship base at Tondern on 4 May. German intelligence believed Tondern would be attacked in about mid April and Vizeadmiral Scheer began taking defensive measures on 13 April. On the evening of 20 April a British cruiser force put to sea and proceeded towards the Kattegat with the intention of operating against trade. At dawn on 21 April the IV AG, supported by *Moltke* and *Derfflinger*, took station south of Amrum Bank, as an advanced picket. Then at 1600hrs the main deciphering station at Neumünster reported that intercepted wireless messages indicated that British units, including battleships and cruisers, had departed the Firth of Forth on the evening of 20 April and had taken course towards Horns Reef. Vizeadmiral Scheer believed this was the long awaited repeat attack against Tondern and the IAG and II AG, with two fast Flottilles, were dispatched to reconnoitre towards Horns Reef.

From intercepted wireless reports the British learned that the German forces were putting to sea, and the Kattegat operation was immediately cancelled. The entire Grand Fleet was ordered to sea and by early on 22 April the Grand Fleet was 100nm east of Aberdeen with the Battle Cruiser Fleet 40nm ahead. The 3 Battle Squadron and 3 Cruiser Squadron were in support. The Germans remained unaware of these movements.

Meanwhile, the advance of German forces in response to the supposed attack on Tondern was not without events. The flagship of the acting Leader of the II AG, Kommodore von Reuter, ran onto a mine 15nm SW of Amrum Bank. The official history times this event as towards midnight on 21 April, however *Graudenz*'s damage report and other KTBs give the time of the mine hit as 0025hrs on 22 April. This discrepancy could be accounted for by one report using summer time. The outer skin of compartment I was buckled and torn, and the compartment filled with water, whilst the rudder was blown off and the starboard propeller shaft was bent into an 'S' form with one propeller blade lost. The shock of the explosion caused the foremast to bend in two places, whilst the main mast was also slightly bent. There were no losses in men. The cruiser had to return to Wilhelmshaven, being towed by torpedoboot *S51* at first, and then later by *Frauenlob*. Kommodore von Reuter transferred his flag to *Pillau* as the I and II AG continued their advance to the north by passing to the east of Amrum Bank. In the meantime the airships *L20*, *L21* and *L9* ascended from Tondern, Nordholz and Hage respectively to reconnoitre the German Bight. Around 0525hrs *Elbing* sighted the periscope of an enemy submarine approximately 7nm SW of Vyl light vessel. The Panzerkreuzer *Seydlitz* also reported a submarine sighting about this time. By early morning the airships were able to report that there were no enemy forces inside the line Terschelling–Bovbjerg and a further advance with the prospect of submarine attack appeared unnecessary. Therefore at 0540hrs the recall order was given. During the rearmarch the cruiser *Frankfurt* was attacked by a submarine SW of Vyl light vessel. The assailant was the British submarine *E41*, but *E41*'s log gives the attack date as Saturday 23 April, when in fact the Saturday was the 22 April. Her commander, Lieutenant-Commander Hearn, relates how he spotted two cruisers of the *Friedrich Carl* type before later spotting a cruiser of the *Regensburg* class (it was *Frankfurt*) just 400 yards distant and he manoeuvred to make an attack. *Frankfurt* turned to ram the submarine and then two explosions were heard, as the cruiser had opened fire. Then a wire was heard scrapping down the starboard side of *E41*. The submarine survived and the German forces returned home, arriving on Schillig Roads around 1300hrs. Owing to the uncertain weather situation the airships were recalled.

When the British Admiralty learned from intercepted German wireless traffic that the German forces were at sea they suggested to Admiral Jellicoe that his light cruisers could sweep into the Skagerrak. The Grand Fleet would act in support. Accordingly the 4 Light Cruiser Squadron was detached for this purpose whilst the Battle Cruiser Fleet advanced to the SE. By 1900hrs on 22 April Vice Admiral Beatty had reached a point 75nm NW of Horns Reef. That evening there was a dense fog and at 1900hrs the battle cruisers *Australia* and *New Zealand* collided and both ships were badly damaged. They were detached back to Rosyth, whilst the remaining battle cruisers held their stations. Meanwhile, the Grand Fleet also encountered the thick fog and just after midnight the destroyers *Garland*, *Ambuscade* and *Ardent* came into collision with the latter being so badly damaged she had to be towed home stern first. The bad luck did not end there and shortly after the battleship *Neptune* was rammed by a neutral steamer and was considerably damaged. With the coming of morning the Grand Fleet began the return journey to Scapa Flow and Rosyth.

The events of 20–23 April caused Vizeadmiral Scheer to delay the next planned operation of his offensive, the bombardment of Yarmouth and Lowestoft, and it was postponed one day from its originally planned date of dawn on 24 April. The timing of this operation coincided with the uprising in Ireland against British rule. Vizeadmiral Scheer gave the following reasons for his attack on the coastal towns:

> On April 24, Easter Monday, the Fleet put out on an important operation which, like that at the beginning of March, was directed towards the Hoofden,

but was to be extended farther so as to force the enemy out of port. I expected to achieve this by bombarding coastal towns and carrying out air raids on England the night the Fleet went out. Both these actions would probably result in counter measures being taken by the enemy that would give our forces an opportunity to attack.[11]

The I Artillerie Offizier of *von der Tann*, Korvettenkapitän Mahrholz, gave a more insightful opinion:

The coastal bombardments, which were implemented by the German Naval Forces in the World War on the English coast and in the Baltic, I represent as more or less sleight of hand operations and demonstrations that had less purpose to destroy militarily valuable places, than to lure out enemy naval forces or make them become more active. The bombardment of the English east coast had still another aim, they should produce uneasiness in the population and promote war weariness. Through the pressure of public opinion, it should make the English leaders fortify the coastal towns, whereby personnel and materiel would be bound up in England, and would not reach the battle front on the mainland. Since the indirect results were the main purpose of these operations, then the fact that they took place at all was more important than the materiel effect and therefore no great artillerie value is placed on these coastal bombardments.[12]

At 1055hrs on 24 April the I and II AG and attached Flottilles weighed anchor and headed west, timing their advance so as to appear off the English coast at dawn the following morning. Towards 1215hrs the Main Body, consisting of the I, II and III Squadrons, together with the IV AG and accompanying torpedoboot Flottilles, put to sea. The Main Body would support the I AG by remaining in the Hoofden whilst the bombardment was carried out.

Meanwhile, Admiral Bacon had chosen this day to lay a mine and net barrier off the Belgium coast to impede U-Bootes operating from Zeebrugge in Flanders. The passage between Thornton Bank and the coast would be blockaded with a double row of mines and nets festooned with mines. Admiral Bacon had the four large minelayers *Orvietto*, *Princess Margaret*, *Biarritz* and *Paris*, and six minelaying trawlers available, supported by the monitors *General Wolfe* and *Prince Eugene* and a division of eight Harwich destroyers. The remainder of the Dover Patrol joined these forces off the coast. By 0730hrs on 24 April a 15-mile long double line of mines had been laid together with 13 miles of nets, and the minelayers had begun their return journey. Naval drifters had laid the nets and were detailed to keep a close guard on them.

The purpose of Admiral Bacon's operation was to hinder German U-Bootes from putting to sea from Zeebrugge and was timely as Admiral von Schröder, the chief of the Flanders forces, was to provide U–Boot support for the operation against Lowestoft and Yarmouth. Seven minelaying UC boats were to lay mines off Harwich and the Thames mouth, whilst four UB boats were to form a picket line SE of Southwold and two other UB boats would act as navigational fixes for the cruisers steering off the English coast. The UB boats *UB6*, *UB10*, *UB12*, *UB13*, *UB18* and *UB29* departed Zeebrugge on 23 April but *UB13* was mined and sunk. At dawn on 24 April the UC boats quit Zeebrugge and ran head on into the British forces. *UC5* almost completely discharged her batteries and was forced to return to Zeebrugge. *UC1* was attacked several times by patrolling trawlers with sweep gear and finished up between the nets, where she became intertwined and only escaped after several violent explosions. *UC10* likewise became entangled in the nets off Thornton Bank about 1320hrs and after heavy detonations sank to the bottom in a depth of 27 metres. Only when the sound of British propellers receded did *UC10* surface about 2135hrs. The boat again became caught in a net about 2330hrs before finally returning to Zeebrugge. *UC7* made several attempts to breakthrough and even ran aground off Zeebrugge, and only with the coming of darkness could she continue her journey. The only boat to successfully lay her mines in the planned area was *UC6*, which lay her mines off the northern exit from Harwich towards midnight, after passing some 20 destroyers. Of the UB boats only *UB6* occupied its allotted position on 24 April but was unaware the operation had been postponed one day and waited in vain for the coastal bombardment. Therefore Admiral Bacon's barrage had proved very effective on this important day.

Meanwhile, a lively air battle had developed over the Flanders coast. Around 0500hrs a British aircraft had dropped two bombs on the Zeebrugge locks, but without effect. When the British ships appeared off the coast six German seaplanes attacked them with bombs, likewise without success. The German seaplanes did not possess any machine gun armament and when confronted by allied land biplanes fitted with machine guns all they could do was dive away to evade their enemy. Towards midday the Friedrichshafen FF33E aircraft 503, piloted by Flugmeister Riedel, directed a 'Fernlenkboot' towards the British monitors (a 'Fernlenkboot' was an unmanned motorboat carrying a large explosive charge, directed from the coast or an aircraft by wireless control). After the boat had covered a distance of 12nm and was within 4nm of the British monitors the motor failed and the boat had to be blown up to prevent it falling into enemy hands. At the same time Friedrichshafen FF33E number 472 was shot down by a Nieuport land biplane. At 1340hrs the Tirpitz Battery, consisting of four 28cm cannon, straddled the monitor *General Wolfe* at the then portentous range of 29,200m with four salvos, however without hitting.

Towards midday three large German torpedobootes of the Z Flottille Flanders, *V67*, *V68* and *V47*, received orders to reconnoitre to the north and disrupt the British vessels, however without allowing themselves to be cut off. At around

1600hrs the three torpedobootes became involved in a lively battle with the British destroyers *Medea*, *Murray*, *Melpomene* and *Milne*, which were covering the trawlers from the north. Soon one of the monitors intervened and the German boats had to seek protection under the guns of the coastal batteries. These opened fire at 14.600m and each of the British destroyers was hit, with *Melpomene* struck in the engine room by a shell, which failed to detonate, but nevertheless the destroyer had to be towed away by *Medea*. The Z-Flottille renewed their attack and *Medea* had to slip the tow, but the monitors fire was so effective that the German boats were unable to get into a position for a torpedo attack and later retired back to Zeebrugge. One of the British drifters, *Clover Bank*, was lost on the mine barrier. Likewise, the French torpedoboat destroyer *Obusier* strayed into the mine field and was badly damaged, having her stern blown off.

The following day the boats of the Flanders Torpedoboot Flottille[13] ran out of Zeebrugge and began clearing the mine barriers. One boat, *A12*, was engaged in a brief battle with six British trawlers and one of their number, *Au Fait*, was brought to a halt by a shell hit and struck her flag. After taking off the crew the trawler was sunk. British losses amounted to one trawler and one drifter sunk, two destroyers damaged and one officer and seventeen men killed on *Clover Bank* and three dead from *Medea*.

In the meantime, at 1050hrs on 24 April, the I and II AG, under the command of Kontreadmiral Boedicker as BdA, put to sea to carry out Operational Order Number 5, the bombardment of Great Yarmouth and Lowestoft. Between 1315 and 1330hrs, with a light southerly breeze and very clear conditions, the III and I Squadrons weighed anchor and followed the cruisers. When the II Squadron joined the Main Body from the Elbe the entire High Sea Fleet was at sea and advancing to the west, consisting of 22 capital ships, five old battleships, twelve small cruisers and 48 torpedobootes. By around 1400hrs the Reconnaissance Forces had passed the Norderney gap and swung to starboard, taking one of the channels between the British and German mine fields and travelling 40nm from the coast, to avoid premature discovery from the Dutch islands. At 1535hrs the I AG resumed a WSW course but a short time later, at 1548hrs, the leading ship *Seydlitz* pushed onto a mine in grid square 104 epsilon. The detonation occurred on the starboard side at the level of the broadside torpedo room and the forecastle compartments XIV to XVI below the armoured deck filled with water. Approximately 1200 tonnes flooded into the ship and the draught forward increased 1.3 metres. Of the six torpedoes in the torpedo room none detonated even though three had their heads rent apart and the air flask of one blew up. A short time later a diving submarine was sighted from *Seydlitz*, whilst at 1630hrs *Lützow* sighted a torpedo track. Whilst *Seydlitz* was reckoned to be past the mine barrier the remainder of the I AG turned away to the east, and then steered to the south.

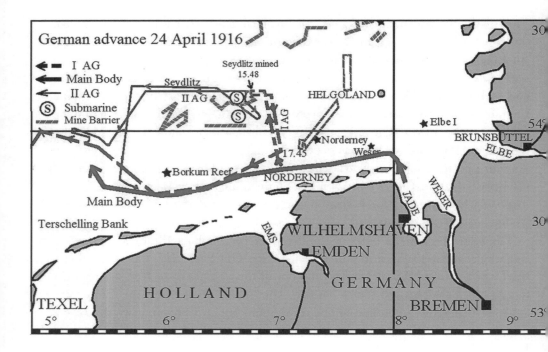

Seydlitz was escorted by the torpedobootes *V69*, *V45* and *V28*, the II AG and airship *L7*. Only at 1925hrs did Kontreadmiral Boedicker disembark from *Seydlitz* and board *V28* and it was not until 2040hrs that the BdA and his Staff boarded *Lützow*. Meanwhile, as the Main Body approached the Norderney gap towards 1700hrs the Panzerkreuzer, under the leadership of Kapitän zur See Hartog aboard *Derfflinger*, came in sight to the north. Vizeadmiral Scheer decided the northerly route was not safe and ordered the I AG to continue their advance along the East Friesian coast, despite the danger of being reported from the Dutch islands. About 2200hrs course was taken SW at 21 knots and the II AG divided into four groups each of two small cruisers and four torpedobootes, which formed a vanguard and flank cover as the strike force pushed into the Hoofden. The Main Body followed the same course at 14 knots, escorted by the IV AG and attached Torpedoboot Flottilles.

At 2130hrs an intelligence report arrived aboard the Fleet flagship, *Friedrich der Große*, stating that from intercepted British wireless signals all patrolling vessels had been recalled to harbour, a sign the British knew something was afoot. In fact, Admiral Jellicoe was informed by intelligence at 1900hrs that the I AG was 40nm west of Helgoland at 1600hrs, and shortly afterwards he ordered his forces to sea. At 2110hrs Jellicoe received a report about *Seydlitz* being mined and that the remainder of the I AG were 50nm NW of Borkum, which was their position at 2030hrs. The position of the III Squadron was also accurately reported. Therefore the British wireless direction finding stations and Naval Intelligence's Room 40 were working with great efficiency. The direction finding stations were able to correctly deduce the wireless bearings of the German ships, and Room 40 was able to decode the call signs of the concerned vessels. Therefore the British had the imponderable advantage of knowing where and who the German forces were. However, the Grand Fleet was somewhat tardy in its reaction on this day, probably because they had just returned from the operation off Little Fisher Bank on 22–23 April. The Battle Cruiser Fleet did not depart Rosyth until 2245hrs, about four hours after receiving orders. The 5 Battle Squadron left Scapa Flow at 2200hrs, followed at midnight by the Grand Fleet. The Admiralty also ordered submarines and the 5 Light Cruiser Squadron to put to sea from Harwich, and the submarines departed for ambush positions at 0010hrs on 25 April, followed by Commodore Tyrwhitt's cruisers and destroyers at 0130hrs. Prior to departure the Commodore was given the position and course of the German Reconnaissance Groups. Meanwhile Admiral Bacon was ordered to withdraw all his forces from the Belgium coast. During the night seven German airships crossed the English coast and were to carry out attacks on Norwich, Cambridge and Lincoln, but because of poor weather their missions remained largely undone.

From midnight on 25 April the two U-Bootes were in position south of the *Stralsund* mine barrier, which dated from 3 November 1914. *UB18*, Oberleutnant

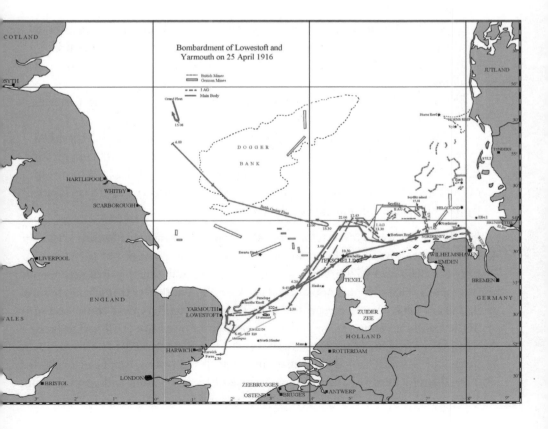

Bombardment of Lowestoft and Yarmouth on 25 April 1916

zur See Otto Steinbrinck, showed a red light and *UB29*, Oberleutnant zur See Pustkuchen, showed a green light to seaward to indicate the channel through which the arriving German forces should pass. At 0415hrs the attack force swept 1nm south of *UB18* and at 0455hrs Corton Reef light vessel was sighted ahead from *Lützow*. Off Lowestoft the conditions were good, with a slight SSE wind and good visibility. To the south the I AG were screened by *Rostock* and *Elbing*, and at about 0500hrs these small cruisers sighted Commodore Tyrwhitt's force to the south. At this time the I AG also turned south and before turning north to commence the bombardment they too sighted the three British light cruisers. Seeing this movement the *Rostock* group turned north to allow the Panzerkreuzer a free field of fire but at 0506hrs the I AG also turned north to open fire on Lowestoft at 0513hrs. The war diary of *Lützow* detailed the bombardment:

> 3 enemy light cruisers with several destroyers stand in the south, and turn away to the land.
>
> Fire opened on the batteries of Lowestoft.
>
> 5^{13}–5^{33} on north to NE course with 18 knots speed the batteries of Lowestoft and Great Yarmouth were bombarded. Batteries of Lowestoft answer the fire. Single salvos lie 400–500m ahead of the bow. One shot lays 30–50m ahead of the bow of the ship.
>
> 5^{22}. On NNE course to starboard lays a trawler, which appears to fire. About 5^{22} the medium artillery shoots a salvo on him, and the trawler catches fire.[14]
>
> 5^{33}. Turn away to starboard and go onto the reciprocal course, running at 21 knots.
>
> 5^{42} Lowestoft was taken under fire on the opposite course, the batteries replied to the fire without result.
>
> 5^{49} fire opened at 130hm on 3 light cruisers of the *Boadicea* class that stand in the south to starboard ahead. The cruisers go onto the opposite course and turn 12 points to port. After the turn fire opened on the lead ship, the first ship of the line. Third salvo hits behind the forth funnel. Observed with certainty. Apparently some ammunition exploded.[15]

The I AO of *Lützow*, Korvettenkapitän Paschen, noted that this occasion was the first time *Lützow* had fired her main armament with full charges.

Between 0517 and 0520hrs fire was ceased and then at 0524hrs fire was opened on Yarmouth. Visibility was not so good off Yarmouth and after firing a single salvo each *Lützow* and *Moltke* ceased fire with the heavy artillery and continued only with the medium calibre guns. *Von der Tann* did not open fire at all and preserved her ammunition. Only *Derfflinger* fired 14 × 30.5cm shells and 12 × 15cm shells at ranges of 110–130hm. By 0528hrs the allotted munitions had been expended and *Derfflinger*'s heavy artillerie likewise ceased fire. At 0520hrs and again at about 0540hrs attacking British fliers were taken under fire by *Lützow* and *Moltke* with their 8.8cm Flak, and one appeared to be shot down. At 0542hrs *Lützow* took Great Yarmouth lighthouse under fire with eight heavy projectiles at a range of 140 to 128hm, all the shells impacting ashore. During the bombardment the British submarine *H5* approached to within 2000m of the German cruisers.

Meanwhile, the 5 Light Cruiser Squadron, *Conquest*, *Cleopatra* and *Penelope*, had approached from the south. At 0530hrs Commodore Tyrwhitt opened fire on Kommodore von Reuter's II AG at great range, to which the German cruisers were unable to reply, but all the shots fell short. The battle continued and at 0547hrs the German cruisers were able to make reply. Just two minutes later the German Panzerkreuzer also opened fire on the British light cruisers. *Lützow* and *Derfflinger* opened fire on the light cruisers at ranges from 126 to 140hm with their heavy calibre cannon and soon obtained straddles against their opponents. Meanwhile, the medium-calibre artillery opened fire on British destroyers at 90 to 120hm and likewise straddled them. *Lützow* fired a total of 33 × 30.5cm calibre shells against *Conquest* and *Derfflinger* fired 27 × 30.5cm shells. The flagship *Conquest* was hit a total of five times and was severely damaged with hits on the superstructure and a funnel and suffered 23 dead and 13 wounded. Despite having her speed reduced to 20 knots she was able to escape to the south. A 15cm shell hit on the destroyer *Laertes* wounded five men and put a boiler out of action. When the I AG turned away to the east the last ship in line, *von der Tann*, fired 17 shots from 0555 to 0600hrs at the British destroyers at 140–158hm.

Of the German U-Bootes *UB1* made a mistake in navigation and positioned herself off Lowestoft, and could not follow quickly enough to the south when the Harwich Force appeared. She was attacked by British aircraft. *UB6* and *UB10* occupied their planned positions and *UB10* was also attacked by aircraft. However, the German U-Bootes were not the only submarines to be attacked with bombs, as at about 0540hrs both *V1* and *H10* were attacked with two and four bombs respectively, whilst later at 0645hrs *E37* was attacked with five or six bombs.

At 0555hrs Kontreadmiral Boedicker abandoned chasing the Harwich Force, although he could easily have caught *Conquest*, and took course to the east past *Stralsund*'s barrier. When he was 50nm from the Main Body Vizeadmiral Scheer allowed a turn towards the east at about 0620hrs. The airship *L9*, under the command of Hauptmann Stelling, was reconnoitring between the I AG and the Main Body and at 0538hrs was surprised by two British seaplanes when approximately 40nm east of Lowestoft, and at an altitude of just 2500 feet. With the sudden appearance of the aircraft *L9* was unable to ascend quickly enough to escape and she immediately made off to the NE. Whilst one aircraft turned away the second attacked *L9* with five bombs whilst the airship defended herself with a machine gun. The running battle brought them within sight of the Main Body, and fortunately *L9* was able to escape.

After concluding emergency repairs to his flagship, Commodore Tyrwhitt took course after the retiring German forces at 0640hrs, through 'K' channel at

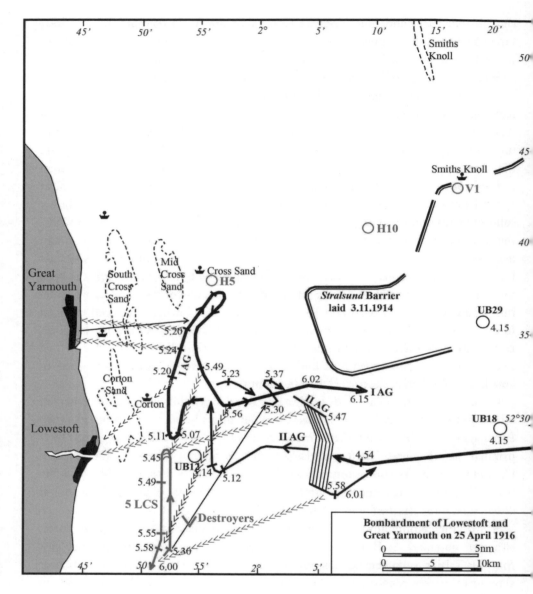

22 knots. The K channel was a swept channel that ran NE through the mined area. Meanwhile, the five British submarines, *E55*, *E29*, *E26*, *E22* and *D4*, which had departed Harwich with the destroyer *Melampus* at 2330hrs the previous evening were approaching their assigned positions. When the Submarine Flotilla Commander, Captain Waistell, who was aboard the destroyer *Lurcher*, heard gunfire at 0555hrs he ordered these submarines to run further north to cut off the German line of retreat. At 0712hrs the northern most boat, *E55*, sighted the Panzerkreuzers, led by *Rostock*, 5nm ahead steering ENE. Nevertheless, the submarine had no opportunity to attack. By 0945hrs Commodore Tyrwhitt only had the German smoke cloud

in sight and ten minutes later he was recalled by the Admiralty, thus precluding any chance of a night attack later with destroyers. Scarcely had the British cruisers turned for home than *Penelope* was struck by a torpedo.

The torpedo fired at *Penelope* was launched by *UB29*, Oberleutnant zur See Pustkuchen. Soon after 0500hrs, in accordance with their orders, *UB29* and *UB18* had quit their positions 20nm east of Yarmouth and had proceeded in an ESE direction. The two U-Bootes were therefore in the German line of retreat, Commodore Tyrwhitt's line of advance and the ambush position of *Melampus* submarines. At about 0700hrs *UB29* was forced to submerge by British aircraft, then acted as flank cover as the Panzerkreuzers passed by. An hour later the U-Boot again dived after sighting a British submarine ahead, and then sighted three British cruisers in the SW as they followed the German cruisers. Although it was already too late for an attack *UB29* followed the British cruisers on the surface, but at 0925hrs was forced to dive again by a group of about eight destroyers of the L class. Soon afterwards these and the British cruisers came in sight on the opposite course. *UB29* carried out an attack at long range and at about 1025hrs, 85 seconds after being launched, the sound of a torpedo detonation was heard. The torpedo blew off the rudder and wrecked the steering gear, but *Penelope* was still able to maintain 20 knots and Commodore Tyrwhitt's cruisers continued their withdrawal, reaching Harwich at 1600hrs.

At about 0645hrs *UB18*, Oberleutnant zur See Steinbrinck, was passed by two German small cruisers and torpedobootes and shortly afterwards sighted the destroyer *Melampus*, and north of her two submarines of the E class with their wireless antennas rigged. *UB18* immediately dived and closed to within 300m of a submarine and even passed beneath one boat, however, the torpedo shot of *UB18* missed when the target boat turned away. About 0900hrs several destroyers of the L class appeared in the south, on a northerly course at high speed. Then to the north *Melampus* was again sighted, at first with three submarines, and then only two. *UB18* began an attack attempt on *E26* when suddenly, as clearly observed, the watch officer on the conning tower of the English submarine swung the wheel and turned to ram *UB18*. The U-Boot dived and was only struck on the net cutter. Despite this the British submarines remained on the surface, perhaps misunderstanding Captain Waistell's order that they should remain surfaced to obtain a better view of the overall situation. He wrote:

> On this occasion, before they left, I ordered the submarines to patrol on the surface. I gave this order so that they should have full visibility, in view of the importance of their objective and so it should be possible to instruct them to proceed in accordance with any information received, believing that it was unlikely that an enemy submarine would be in the area in which they were to patrol. But it was never my intention that they should remain on the surface after an enemy submarine had been sighted....[16]

About 1240hrs the submarine *E22* was attacked from a range of 350m and after the torpedo detonation *E22* vanished. *E26* witnessed the explosion from 3nm away and dived. Despite the proximity of this boat Oberleutnant zur See Steinbrinck put his boat and crew at risk and surfaced to rescue the two survivors, whilst the commander, Lieutenant Dimsdale, and 30 of the crew perished.

Around this time *UB29* also carried out an attack on *E55*, however, despite stalking the British submarine for two hours and another two British submarines until 1600hrs there were no opportunities to shoot in the oily smooth sea.

During the retirement at around 0700hrs the Leader Boat of the VI Flottille, *G41*, captured a small trawler about 40nm east of Yarmouth. It was the trawler *King Stephen*, the crew of which had deliberately allowed the fifteen-man crew of the wrecked airship *L19* to drown on 2 February 1916. Commander Frost commented: 'It was this vessel that, contrary to all customs of honourable warfare on the sea, had deliberately allowed the crew of the wrecked airship *L19* to drown without any attempt at rescue.'[17]

Of the British heavy forces the Battle Cruiser Fleet reached a position approximately 45nm NW of Terschelling at 1330hrs, whereon Vice Admiral Beatty made a turn back to his base. The Grand Fleet never got nearer than 220nm to the homeward track of the Germans, before making a turn back to the north at 1500hrs. The High Sea Fleet returned to Wilhelmshaven around 1900 to 1930hrs that evening.

The material losses for this operation were for the Germans: one U-Boot sunk and one aircraft shot down. Most important was the mining and damage of SMS *Seydlitz*. The British lost one submarine, had two light cruisers severely damaged, five destroyers damaged, and five patrol craft sunk. The French had one destroyer damaged. What is interesting is that almost every arm had been utilized; battleships and battle cruisers, cruisers and destroyers, submarines, patrol craft and even remotely guided explosive boats. Aeroplanes and airships had also played big roles. All forms of weapons had an effect; shells, torpedoes and mines. There were two notable failures, one from each side. The British Admiralty had made futile attempts to direct tactical operations from a great distance, a policy that would always restrict the initiative of commanders at sea, and doom operations to a degree of mediocrity and even failure. The Germans were again careless in sending wireless messages, for even the most mundane orders, and the efficiency of British Naval Intelligence and its Room 40 meant that British commanders would know the position and course of German sea forces at regular intervals, and would also be aware of Vizeadmiral Scheer's plans many hours in advance.

As Vizeadmiral Scheer returned from the Lowestoft raid he received a telegram informing him of the German Governments decision to continue U-Boot warfare according to 'prize regulations', and not to the unlimited format that he desired. The reason for this was the reaction of the United States of America to the sinking of the French passenger steamer *Sussex* in the Channel. Vizeadmiral Scheer would not allow his U-Bootes to operate under these restrictions and he decided that instead of conducting merchant warfare the U-Bootes should be used to support the Fleet undertakings, and he subsequently received approval to operate in this fashion.

After the coastal bombardment there was a pause in the German operations. In addition to repairs to *Seydlitz* the battleships *Friedrich der Große*, *Ostfriesland* and *Nassau* went into the dockyard for planned overhaul work, and several ships of the III Squadron required minor engine repairs, mostly to condensers. To fully utilize this pause in operations the Chief of III Squadron, Kontreadmiral Behncke, went to the Baltic with *König*, *Kronprinz*, *Kaiser* and *Kaiserin* for training, and likewise the IV AG, the VI TBF and the 9 TBHF were also dispatched to Kiel. The II TBF, which had just changed their 8.8cm guns for 10.4cm pieces, also went to the western Baltic for training. Nevertheless, all these forces were to return to the North Sea by 6 May, as Vizeadmiral Scheer intended a large-scale operation in the Skagerrak.

Whilst the High Sea Fleet was drawing breath the Grand Fleet carried out a well planned operation. They would conduct another aircraft raid on the Tondern airship hangars, at the same setting a trap for the High Sea Fleet should it emerge on this occasion. The Battle Cruiser Fleet would be waiting off Horns Reef, supported by the Grand Fleet just to the north, in the Little Fisher Bank area. The mine layer *Abdiel* would lay mines in the northern exit from the German Bight, whilst *Princess Margaret* would do likewise in the western exit. A Light Cruiser Squadron would escort two seaplane carriers to Horns Reef where they would launch nine seaplanes to raid the hangars at Tondern. Seven submarines would occupy ambush positions off Horns Reef, *E53*, *E31*, *E34*, *G1*, *G2*, *G4* and *G5*, and three submarines, *E55*, *D4* and *D6* would lay in a line off Terschelling.

As Admiral Jellicoe prepared to put to sea the Germans launched an airship raid against coastal towns in England and Scotland, however the British plan proceeded on schedule. The minelayers had completed their allotted tasks by 0030hrs on 4 May and the 1 LCS with the aircraft tenders *Engadine* and *Vindex* arrived off the Danish coast just after 0400hrs. The Battle Cruiser Fleet and Grand Fleet were in their positions at 0500hrs. Now, however, things began to go awry for the British. Shortly after the nine seaplanes were lowered to the water to take off, seven of them received damage in the swell and had to abort their missions. Of the two that successfully took off one struck an aerial of the destroyer *Goshawk* and was destroyed. The last remaining aircraft failed to reach her objective, although the Germans did see her crossing the coast. Then at 1630hrs on 5 May the submarines *G5* and *G4* collided underwater, an incredible piece of bad luck. Although *G5* had a damaged periscope and steering gear, both boats were able to complete their patrols.

The German reaction was to immediately recall the forces in the Baltic and to dispatch the I AG, I Squadron, II Squadron and available battleships of the III

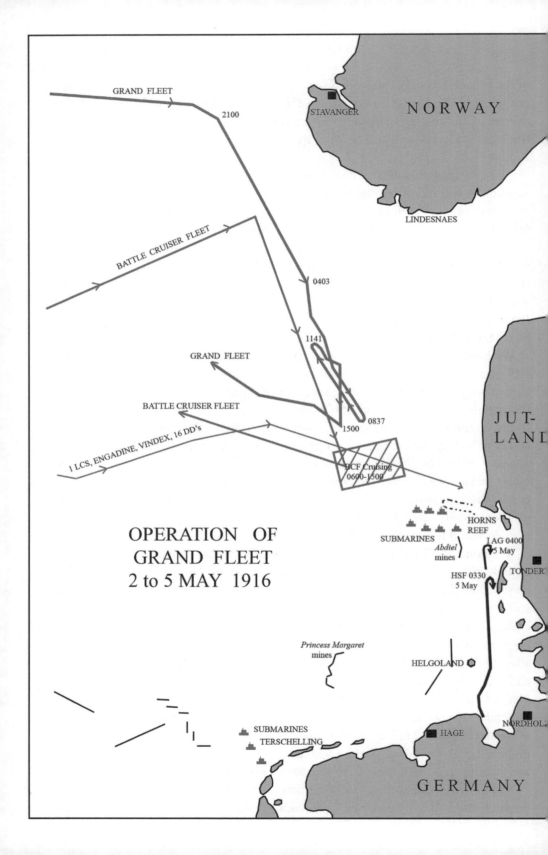

GRAND FLEET

2100

STAVANGER

NORWAY

LINDESNAES

BATTLE CRUISER FLEET

0403

1141

GRAND FLEET

BATTLE CRUISER FLEET

JUT-
LAND

1 LCS, ENGADINE, VINDEX, 16 DD's

0837

1500

BCF Cruising
0600-1500

SUBMARINES

HORNS
REEF

Abdiel
mines

I AG 0400
5 May

TONDER

HSF 0330
5 May

OPERATION OF
GRAND FLEET
2 to 5 MAY 1916

Princess Margaret
mines

HELGOLAND

SUBMARINES
TERSCHELLING

HAGE

NORDHOLZ

GERMANY

Squadron, together with the II AG and torpedobootes to sea. The III TBF and 1 TBHF made advances to the west, but found nothing and at 0330hrs and 0400hrs on 5 May the Main Body and I AG made turns back to the south. The Grand Fleet had begun its withdrawal at 1500hrs on 4 May.

At around 1130hrs on the morning of 4 May the British light cruisers *Galatea* and *Phaeton* had engaged the airship *L7* and after a lengthy chase brought the airship down in flames. Seven crew survived and were rescued by the submarine *E31*. At 0050hrs on the following morning *E31* was sighted by *Rostock* just 300m distant, 3 points to port. *Rostock* immediately attempted to ram the submarine, but *E31* evaded the German cruiser because of her tighter turning circle, and the cruiser missed by about 50m. When abeam of *E31 Rostock* illuminated a searchlight and in its beam could see the marking 'E31' on the conning tower and the white ensign. Independent fire was opened and a shell struck the conning tower of *E31*, but failed to explode. After that the submarine dived and lay on the bottom until dawn at a depth of 20m, then began the homeward journey.

The British plan had worked in essence; they had provoked a response from the High Sea Fleet but to have had any chance of an engagement Admiral Jellicoe should have returned to the advanced position on the following day, 5 May. The main significance of this operation was that it was the last time Admiral Jellicoe or the Grand Fleet made an advance into German waters in an attempt to entice the High Sea Fleet into putting to sea and engaging them.

Chapter 2

Operational Plans

The next operation to be undertaken in Vizeadmiral Scheer's spring offensive was to be the bombardment of the English coastal harbour of Sunderland. This town was less than 100 nautical miles from Vice Admiral Beatty's battle cruiser base at Rosyth. Vizeadmiral Scheer wrote:

> The order was issued on May 18th in this connection and was as follows: The bombardment of Sunderland by our cruisers is intended to compel the enemy to send out forces against us. For the attack on the advancing enemy the High Sea Fleet forces to be south of the Dogger Bank, and the U–Bootes to be stationed for attack off the east coast of England. The enemy's port of sortie will be closed by mines. The Naval Korps will support the operation with their U–Bootes. If time and circumstances permit, trade war will be carried out during the proceedings.[1]

He also said that this '....would be certain to call out a display of English fighting forces as promised by Mr. Balfour.'[2] Vizeadmiral Scheer was referring to a letter from the First Sea Lord, Arthur Balfour, to the Mayors of Lowestoft and Yarmouth, in which he stated that the home forces were about to be redistributed in a way such as to make a repetition of a raid against the East Coast highly dangerous to the Germans. In fact, on 12 May Admiral Jellicoe, Vice Admiral Beatty and First Sea Lord Balfour had held a conference at Rosyth. It was decided to redistribute the forces with Rosyth becoming a major base and it was agreed that it could maintain the 1 and 2 Battle Squadrons as well as the Battle Cruiser Fleet. Another squadron of Dreadnought capital ships could be based on the Humber. Then it was suggested that in the interim the 5 Battle Squadron, consisting of the latest 15-inch gunned *Queen Elizabeth* class battleships, could be based at Rosyth. Admiral Jellicoe disagreed, but when Vice Admiral Beatty pointed out that the 3 Battle Cruiser Squadron would soon travel north to Scapa Flow for training, Admiral Jellicoe agreed to a temporary transfer of the 5 Battle Squadron to Rosyth.

If Vizeadmiral Scheer held hopes that the order of 24 April 1916 concerning the employment of U-Boats would be rescinded, they were dashed on 4 May when Chancellor Bethmann-Hollweg issued a public note to the United States definitely renouncing unrestricted U-Boat operations and confirming the U-Boats would operate under existing prize regulations. Nevertheless, Vizeadmiral Scheer now believed he had two new advantages: Lord Balfour had announced the redistribution of British naval forces, and the U-Boats could now operate exclusively with the Fleet.

In the meantime Vizeadmiral Hipper had returned from sick leave. He wrote:

May 12. Today I have the first check-up from a nerve Specialist. Result: no question of a central nervous system disorder. Lord God, now I take heart. The mental depression has suddenly gone; in the evening I even go to an invitation from the Frau Princess Heinrich, then to the station.

May 13. For the first time in a long time I have slept well. Complaints significantly better, in the morning resume service aboard *Lützow*. The Fleet Chief gives me 8 training days for *Lützow* in the Baltic. Therefore in the morning my Staff and I again go aboard *Seydlitz*, even though the ship still lays in dock. If something is going on I must quickly board *Moltke*. This ship also lies in harbour.[3]

On 9 May Kontreadmiral Behncke, Chief of the III Squadron, returned from the Baltic with the battleships *König*, *Kronprinz*, *Kaiser* and *Kaiserin*, and was ready to begin the operation planned for 17 May. However, as some of the III Squadron ships were still having condenser repairs this date was moved back to 23 May, and it was expected that *Seydlitz* would also be ready on this date. In the meantime the II Squadron, I FdT with his flagship *Rostock*, the II and IX Flottilles, just as the 13 Half-Flottille, were sent for training in the Baltic. On 15 May *Lützow* followed, but all should be back in the North Sea on 23 May, ready for employment.

The operational plan supposed the English Fleet was distributed in the harbours of the Scottish northeast coast, the Channel and the Humber. The operational plan therefore said that on the determined day at dawn the I AG and II AG (Reconnaissance Groups), and the three fastest Flottilles would appear off Sunderland and bombard this militarily important town, thereby forcing the enemy to advance his forces. To attack these the I and III Squadrons, the IV AG and the remainder of the Flottilles would be between the southwest shallows of Dogger Bank and Flamborough Head, approximately 50nm east of the latter point in a reception position. Meanwhile the U-Bootes of the Fleet would take up attack positions off Scapa Flow, Moray Firth, the Firth of Forth, the Humber and north of Terschelling, and the U-Bootes of the Marine Korps would occupy attack positions off the Thames and mine the individual enemy harbours. In addition all airships should serve in this operation and apart from the immediate security of the battle cruisers, should reconnoitre in the direction of the Firth of Forth, the Humber, the Hoofden and the Skagerrak. During the advance of the Fleet originally the II Squadron was assigned for security of the German Bight, but it was eventually decided, after the urging of the II Squadron Chief, Kontreadmiral Mauve, that despite their low combat capability and lack of resistance of these obsolete ships, they could directly participate in the operation.

On 13 May the Leader of U-Bootes (FdU), Fregattenkapitän Hermann Bauer, proposed that the U-Bootes ready for operations be dispatched to sea to conduct reconnaissance in the northern North Sea, primarily in the area where the Grand Fleet had previously been observed. Vizeadmiral Scheer was in agreement and the 10 U-Bootes, *U52*, *U24*, *U70*, *U32*, *U66*, *U47*, *U43*, *U44*, *U63* and *U51* received orders to put to sea and on 17 and 18 May they complied and took up station in 20 by 120 nautical mile search areas in the North Sea. From 23 May these U-Bootes would take up stations off the British bases. It was of great importance that these bootes should not be discovered prematurely and they were only to use their wirelesses in urgent cases. The coded signal 'Reckon on enemy forces putting to sea', would be wirelessed to indicate the actual beginning of the operation by the High Sea Fleet, and in this way it was hoped the U-Bootes would be ready and on station in time. In addition, on 20 May *UB27* was sent to infiltrate the Firth of Forth and seek attack opportunities inside May Island.

Originally it was intended for *U46* to conduct reconnaissance off Sunderland, but as she was not ready in time *U47* was allocated this task. At the same time the large U-Boot minelayers *U72*, *U74* and *U75* would lay mines off the Firth of Forth, Moray Firth and to the west of the Orkney Islands, with each barrier being of 22 mines. The *U74* put to sea on 13 May, followed by the others on 23 and 24 May. The bootes *UB21* and *UB22* would keep the Humber under observation, and put to sea on 21 May. Finally, on 22 May *U67* and *U46* sailed and would operate off Terschelling. *U22* was also intended for this line but was not ready in time.

These German U-Boot operations did not remain unknown to the British for long. As early as 16 and 17 May there were indications of the departure of nine boats and as they took up their allocated positions east and west of the Dogger Bank they encountered British countermeasures. On the afternoon of 22 May the German U-Bootes moved their operations to the British coast and they continued to be sighted and reported.

In the meantime *UB27* proceeded to the Firth of Forth to conduct her special task. However, just after midnight of 23/24 May there were engine problems and *UB27*'s commander, Kapitänleutnant Dieckmann, decided to steer to St Andrews Bay to rectify these problems before continuing with his mission. Before he could carry out his intention of laying on the bottom in St. Andrews Bay, at about 0700hrs on 24 May he sighted four armoured cruisers at great range, apparently *Monmouth* class, coming out of the Forth. There was no hope of carrying out an attack, but an hour and a half later two cruisers were sighted, however these also steered out of range. It was probably the 4 Light Cruiser Squadron and destroyers, running out to head for the Norwegian coast. After laying submerged in St Andrews Bay and rectifying the engine problems *UB27* steered to May Island and then followed a steamer into the Firth of Forth. After running submerged for 18½ hours *UB27* surfaced in Largo Bay to recharge her batteries at 0245hrs on 25 May. As about

0500hrs Kapitänleutnant Dieckmann came to periscope depth to advance towards Inchkeith Island a grinding noise could be heard, as if hawsers and other heavy objects were being hauled across the deck. *UB27* was towing a large chain with large green glass balls behind herself. The U-Boot dived deep and attempted to release herself by going astern underwater, but hereby the net fouled the propellers and brought them to a stop. The only thing to do was to sink down to 40m depth onto the bottom and await the coming of darkness. *UB27* surfaced about 2230hrs that night in light foggy weather and after 20 minutes work the crew had cleared the nets. However, the port propeller remained stopped and therefore the mission could not be continued. Soon after midnight as the U-Boot passed between two guard vessels she suddenly jerked to a stop, obviously caught in a net being towed behind the two vessels. These soon began to burn flares but before they could approach the U-Boot she cut through the upper wires of the net and came free. On 26 May at about 0700hrs May Island was passed and at 1040hrs a large auxiliary cruiser was sighted, coming from the southeast. Despite the range being estimated at over 3000m a torpedo was fired, which nevertheless missed. Efforts to remove the steel line wrapped around the port propeller shaft failed and therefore on 27 May *UB27* began the trip home, reaching Helgoland on 30 May.

Likewise the large minelayer *U72* had to abandon her operation on 26 May as she stood 100nm east of Moray Firth. It was discovered that a leaky oil bunker was leaving a broad oil track behind the boot, betraying her presence. The *U74* was even more unfortunate and was lost with her entire crew. Only *U75* succeeded in laying her mine barrier off the west of Orkney Island on 29 May, between Brough of Birsay and Marwick Head. On 5 June 1916 this mine barrier claimed the armoured cruiser *Hampshire*.

Of the U-Bootes off Terschelling *U46* was surprised by the British submarine *E23* on 24 May. At 1315hrs *E23* fired two unobserved torpedo shots at *U46* before at 1317hrs *E23* was sighted 3000m away and the British boat managed to fire one artillery shot before *U46* dived. Between 1940hrs and 2000hrs that night *E23* fired another two torpedoes, this time at just 600m range, but the starboard torpedo broke the surface, and both torpedoes missed.

In the meantime a series of setbacks occurred which delayed the implementation of the German operation. On 23 May *Seydlitz* underwent a flooding test, which revealed that the repairs to the mine hit of 24 April were not water tight. The transverse and wing passage bulkheads leaked so much that it was necessary for the cruiser to return to the dockyard for further work which would continue until 28 May. On 28 May Vizeadmiral Hipper wrote:

> Today the weather is so bad, no air reconnaissance, that the fleet must still wait for their operation. Tomorrow or the day after tomorrow is the last date that the U-Bootes could support the operation, since they have been on their stations since 22 and should return on 31. One of the main purposes of our

cruisers in the North Sea is to get the English fleet to run out of their various harbours across our positioned U-Bootes which should bring about an attack. Whether this is successful is another question.[4]

Already on 28 May a decision was being undertaken in the Fleet command which would have great importance. Because their orders allowed the U-Bootes to remain in their ambush positions only until 1 June the High Sea Fleet would have to begin their operation by 30 May, however, an approach to the English coast so near the British bases meant the participation of airship reconnaissance was prerequisite. However, the weather was unsuitable for the employment of airships and if this situation did not change by 30 May then there would be no alternative other than temporarily postponing the Sunderland Operation. In place of this operation a substitute operation could be conducted against the Skagerrak and a corresponding Operational Order No.6 was issued the same day, 28 May. The purpose of the new Fleet Operation was the same as the planned Sunderland Operation, namely to cause the British to advance their naval forces. This would no longer be through appearing off the coast, but by the appearance of German cruisers off and in the Skagerrak. Vizeadmiral Hipper, the Commander of the Reconnaissance Ships, therefore had orders to quit the Jade early on the morning of 31 May with the I and II AG, the II Leader of the Torpedoboot aboard *Regensburg* and the II, VI and IX TBF, and to advance to the north out of sight of the Danish coast and still before darkness to show himself off the Norwegian coast. Thereby the English would receive news of the operation. During the late afternoon and the following night the German cruisers would conduct merchant warfare in the Skagerrak. In case Vizeadmiral Hipper met enemy forces, which had frequently been reported in this area, he would attempt to destroy them, but if they were superior, which could well occur without airship reconnaissance, he would withdraw on his own Main Body. Vizeadmiral Scheer intended to be 45nm south of Lindesnes at 0500hrs on 1 June to receive the cruisers with his I and III Squadrons, the IV AG, the cruiser *Hamburg*, the I FdT aboard *Rostock* and the remainder of the torpedobootes. The further course of the operation depended on the developing situation.

Towards midday on 29 May *Seydlitz* reported she was again combat ready, however, the following day the wind turned north-easterly, precluding airship reconnaissance, and it was expected to remain thus for several days. Therefore the operation against Sunderland finally had to be postponed, and the Skagerrak operation implemented in its place. Vizeadmiral Scheer made two important last minute changes. Because of the lack of airship reconnaissance the Main Body of the Fleet would follow the Reconnaissance Forces more closely, now departing just 1½ hours after them, and secondly Squadron II would now accompany the Main Body. Including this squadron was a mistake as the combat value of these second line battleships was little. Their broadside was half that of the dreadnought ships, and their armour was comparatively thinner. Most importantly they could only steam at 18 knots, rather than the 20 knots of the Main Body. At 1640hrs on 30 May the High Sea Fleet and Marine Korps were given the wireless signal '31 May Gg. 2490', the code for the new operation to take place on 31 May.

During the period prior to the German operation a group of young Offizieres devised a brilliant deception to disguise the fact the High Sea Fleet Main Body had put to sea. The FT (Wireless) Offizier of the Fleet and BdA conceived the idea of the Fleet flagship and the wireless station of the III Entrance at Wilhelmshaven exchanging call signs for the duration of the operation. In an article in the June 1961 edition of *Naval Offiziere Support – News Journal*, by Oberleutnant zur See a.D. Dr Hans Boetticher, he explained that it was unknown who first presented the idea and that the two then surviving Offizieres, Lt.z.S Harald Kienast, I FT Offizier on the BdA Staff, and Oblt.z.S Lensch, II FT Offizier on the Fleet Staff, could no longer recall the details. It seems the one who originally came up with the idea allowed others to develop it and then the Flaggleutnants (Oblt. z. S. Christ, BdA. and Kptlt. Bindseil, Fleet) presented the idea to the Fleet Command, who accepted the plan. When the British wireless direction finding stations took a bearing on the Fleet flagship call sign, 'DK', they would place it on Wilhelmshaven Roads. This is precisely what occurred, when just before noon on 31 May the British Director of Operations, Captain Jackson, visited Room 40 of Naval Intelligence and inquired where the direction finding stations placed call sign DK. He was given the answer 'in Wilhelmshaven'. With that he departed and later acting Vice Admiral Oliver, the Chief of the Naval War Staff, informed Admiral Jellicoe the German flagship was in the Jade river. The first Admiral Jellicoe knew of the High Sea Fleet being at sea was with the contact report from the light cruiser *Southampton*. Had he known earlier he might not have delayed his advance by steaming at economical speed and investigating neutral steamers, and could have come into action sooner with more daylight hours remaining. Secondly, when Jellicoe did encounter the German Main Body his faith in Admiralty Intelligence had been severely shaken. Therefore the plan devised by the young Offizier was a very successful subterfuge. However, claims the Germans frequently used this ploy are without foundation.

Nevertheless, there was one hint for the British. The war diary of the II FdT,[5] Kommodore Heinrich, records a wireless message from the evening of 30 May:

FT 1941. To Fleet.
The head of the III Squadron pass A of the Jade[6] at 5.30 in the morning. II Squadron take part in the operation from the beginning, and should follow the I Squadron.
High Sea Fleet conduct FT traffic in the German Bight via III Entrance Wilhelmshaven.
High Sea Chief.

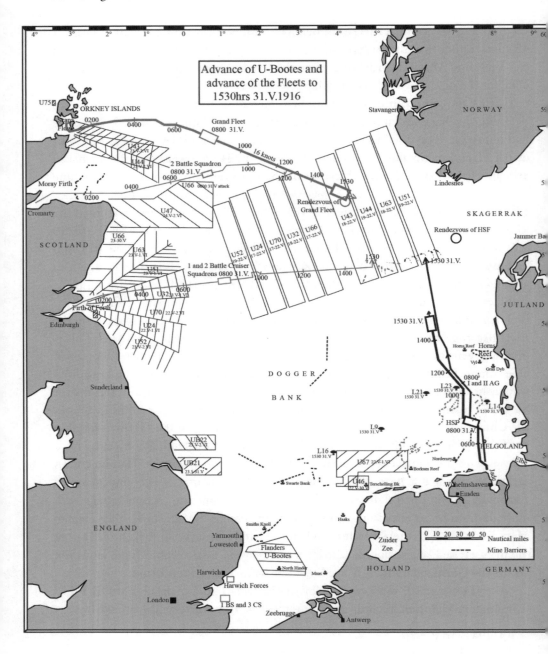

However, this signal was made with an entirely new encipher and could not be decoded until later the next day.

As the Germans had been using wireless for the communication of routine orders preparatory to the operation the British had been able to intercept and decode some of these signals. The signal '31 May Gg. 2490' was also intercepted and therewith the British Admiralty learned that some kind of significant German operation was underway. Wireless orders to minesweepers had also been intercepted and it was known that numerous German U-Bootes were active in the North Sea. Therefore at 1815hrs[7] on 30 May the Admiralty gave the Grand Fleet orders to raise steam, and finally at 1850hrs Admiral Jellicoe was ordered to concentrate his forces east of the 'long forties', that is more than 100nm east of Aberdeen. At 2230hrs on 30 May the Grand Fleet began departing Scapa Flow, whilst at 2300hrs the Battle Cruiser Fleet began leaving Rosyth whilst between 2300hrs and 2315hrs the 2 Battle Squadron departed Cromarty. Therefore the Grand Fleet departed their base 5 hours before the German High Sea Fleet, which put to sea at 0330hrs, whilst the I AG had departed at 0200hrs.

Already on 30 May the German U-Bootes began attacks on British vessels, thus revealing their presence. Towards 1230hrs *U43* sighted a group of twelve destroyers she thought to be of the *Foxglove* class. *U43* fired a torpedo at the considerable range of 2000–2500m, which missed its target. The torpedo was observed from the minesweeper *Gentian* and therefore more destroyers rushed out of Scapa Flow to help search for the U-Boot.

U66, under the command of Kapitänleutnant Bothmer, took up the northern sector off Peterhead but as unusually strong countermeasures were encountered Kapitänleutnant Bothmer reported by wireless that he intended to move further north. On 31 May *U66* was in her new guard position 60nm east of Peterhead when at 0200hrs she received the code word from Bruges indicating the commencement of the German Fleet operation. At around 0600hrs, when approximately 60nm east of Kinnaird, an armoured cruiser was sighted approximately 5000m away, travelling at 20 knots. It appeared to be of the *Duke of Edinburgh* class and *U66* immediately dived and readied all torpedo tubes. At this moment the cruiser abruptly turned away and vanished in the gloom. Then in the same direction a light cruiser with four funnels, *Boadicea*, was sighted, accompanied by destroyers in a broad line abreast. As *U66* prepared to attack a squadron of eight battleships, the 2 Battle Squadron, was sighted 1000m astern of the cruiser. *U66* immediately abandoned the attack on the cruiser and began an attack on the battleships. Nevertheless, an approaching destroyer forced the U-Boot to dive deep and the battle squadron passed overhead in two columns. At 0735 *U66* surfaced and reported these events by wireless.

U32, under the command of Kapitänleutnant Freiherr Spiegel von und zu Peckelsheim, was assigned the sector to the east of the Firth of Forth and after receiving the coded signal for the commencement of the operation arranged her speed so that with dawn on 31 May she was 80nm east of May Island. At around 0440hrs two warships came in sight from the direction of Firth of Forth, the light cruisers *Galatea* and *Phaeton*, and in the poor visibility these approached the U-Boot very quickly at a speed of around 18 to 19 knots, closing to within 900m. Kapitänleutnant Freiherr Spiegel von und zu Peckelsheim intended a double bow shot at the first cruiser and a stern torpedo shot at the second. However, just

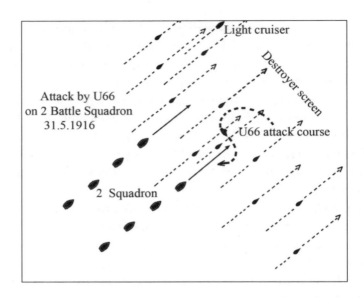

Attack by U66
on 2 Battle Squadron
31.5.1916

Light cruiser

Destroyer screen

U66 attack course

2 Squadron

after the first bow torpedo was fired at about 0450hrs the periscope jammed in the extended position, betraying the position of the U-Boot. Therefore with the second shot the leading cruiser turned hard away, whilst the second turned towards *U32*. One torpedo passed ahead of *Galatea*, and the other passed astern of the cruiser. As *Phaeton* closed to ram, *U32* quickly dived to 15m depth and heard the sound of propellers passing overhead. As towards 0510hrs *U32* went to periscope depth she sighted two battle cruisers on a SE course, surrounded by destroyers. It was the 2 Battle Cruiser Squadron, and *U32* immediately surfaced, rigged her wireless antenna, and reported what she had sighted.

Early on the morning of 31 May 1916 the weather on Schillig Roads was poor. The wind was from the NNW at strength 3; it was hazy and overcast, partly with rain, and the visibility was poor. At 0200hrs the I AG weighed anchor and ran out, preceded by the II AG and torpedobootes. The Group proceeded into the German Bight in the following order: *Lützow*, Kapitän zur See Harder; *Derfflinger*, Kapitän zur See Hartog; *Seydlitz*, Kapitän zur See Egidy; *Moltke*, Kapitän zur See von Karpf; and *von der Tann*, Kapitän zur See Zenker. The I AG was under the command of the BdA (Commander of Reconnaissance Ships) Vizeadmiral Franz Hipper. He was born on 13 September 1863 in Weilhein, Bavaria. Like most German Offizieres he joined the Imperial Navy at the age of 18, in 1881. After passing out Hipper served aboard SMS *Leipzig* (the older vessel) during a two-year world cruise, and then in the Mediterranean. He undertook courses in gunnery and torpedo training and served aboard SMS *Wörth* under Prinz Heinrich. He served aboard other battleships, and then commanded torpedobootes and cruisers, including *Leipzig* and *Gneisenau*. He was promoted to Kontreadmiral on 27 January 1912 and in October 1913 was appointed BdA. Promoted to Vizeadmiral on 17 June 1915, Hipper was known as energetic and hard working, and was liked by his subordinates. 'He was an active and quick man, who because of his cordial friendliness and personal modesty was much loved and admired by everyone.'[8] He was known to dislike paperwork and was happy to leave this task to his staff. For most of the war the BdA had responsibility for not only the I and II AG, but also the torpedobootes and minesweepers of the North Sea, and consequently was overworked with staff work at a time when he should have been concentrating more on just the operations of his cruisers.

Ahead of the I AG ran the II AG, under Kontreadmiral Boedicker, with *Frankfurt*, Kapitän zur See Thilo von Trotha; *Pillau*, Fregattenkapitän Mommsen; *Elbing*, Fregattenkapitän Madlung; and *Wiesbaden*, Kapitän zur See Reiß. They were escorted by the II, VI and IX Torpedoboote Flottilles, led by II FdT Kommodore Heinrich, aboard *Regensburg*, Fregattenkapitän Heuberer. At around 0300hrs the reconnaissance forces passed War Light Vessel A of the Jade and at 0915hrs, after passing the mined area of the German Bight, the II AG formed a broad reconnaissance line ahead of the I AG.

The advance went quietly during the morning and early afternoon and an Offizier aboard *Lützow* described it thus:

At first the weather was not exactly pretty and enticing for such an enterprise. We went to the north, and in addition the wind was from the north and whipped into my face as I stood in my position in the foremast, keeping watch for submarines. Near us went torpedobootes, likewise for submarine protection, ready to immediately ram them.... I had the early watch from 4 to 8 and was then relieved. On the entire horizon, far and wide, there was nothing to be seen. Therefore I went down the foremast, and in my heavy coat

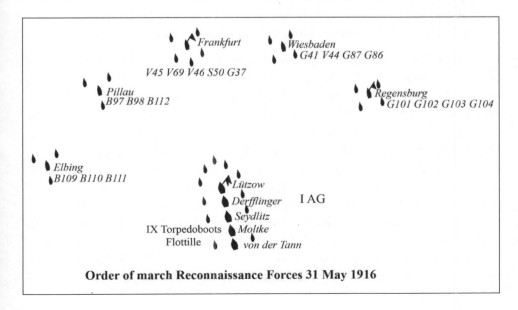

Order of march Reconnaissance Forces 31 May 1916

in the strong wind and with the narrow holes, which I had to crawl through, it was not easy. I then reported from watch and went to the infirmary, where we Offizieres slept together during an advance. The aft ship was cleared of all Offizieres, but nevertheless all our cabins were there. The object of this arrangement was as follows: in case we suddenly ran onto a mine or else were torpedoed, the compartments could not fill with water through inattention. After the rooms were quit, the bulkhead doors were closed tight and nobody was permitted to enter. Moreover, this arrangement had the advantage that if the alarm sounded we were quickly in our positions. Therefore, I went and washed myself. Then went to breakfast. This was nothing special, some bread, some butter, that one needed a magnifying glass to see as it was spread, and some jam.

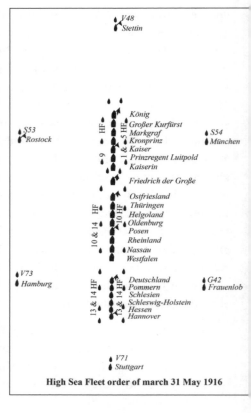

High Sea Fleet order of march 31 May 1916

So, it had meanwhile become 1030 and I again went to the infirmary, to sleep for two hours until 1230. At 1245 in the afternoon we had 7 sprigs of asparagus and 2 slices of ham, before soup. You see only too clearly they also give us nothing. This meal had to last over 26 hours, before I was to eat again.[9]

In the meantime the I AG were followed about 1½ hours later by the Main Body of the High Sea Fleet. The III Battle Squadron and the I Battle Squadron were joined from the Elbe River by the II Battle Squadron, consisting of the older pre-dreadnought battleships. The Main Body was escorted by the IV AG under the Command of Kommodore von Reuter and consisting of the small cruisers *Stettin*, Fregattenkapitän Rebensburg; *München*, Korvettenkapitän Böcker; *Frauenlob*, Fregattenkapitän Hoffmann; and *Stuttgart*, Fregattenkapitän Hagedorn, with *Hamburg* Korvettenkapitän von Gaudecker attached. *Hamburg* was the flagship of the Leader of U-Bootes, Fregattenkapitän and Kommodore Hermann Bauer, with his Asto Korvettenkapitän Friedrich Lützow. The Main Body torpedoboot forces were under command of the I FdT,[10] Kommodore Michelsen aboard *Rostock*, Fregattenkapitän Otto Feldmann, and consisted of the 1 TBHF, III Flottille, V Flottille and VII Flottille. Only the battleship *König Albert* was absent, remaining in harbour having condenser repairs, whilst the new battleship *Bayern* was still not worked up to operational status.

At 0637hrs the *U32*'s contact report was received by Vizeadmiral Scheer via *Arcona* and the III Entrance. Around one hour later, at 0740hrs, the wireless station at Neumünster, via the III Entrance, reported that 'two large warships or Units with destroyers departed Scapa Flow', and just 8 minutes later at 0748hrs the report from *U66* about eight enemy battleships in sight was received via *Arcona* and the III Entrance. Therefore Vizeadmiral Scheer had information about all three elements of the British forces putting to sea, but he was confused by *U66*'s report that the force was on a northerly course.

At 2230hrs Admiral Jellicoe and the Scapa Flow forces began departing and set course to the eastwards. A little later, between 2300hrs and 2315hrs, Vice Admiral Jerram left Cromarty with the 2 Battle Squadron and 1 Cruiser Squadron. This force rendezvoused with the Scapa force at around 1200 noon on 31 May. Vice Admiral Beatty with the 1 and 2 Battle Cruiser Squadrons and 5 Battle Squadron departed Rosyth at 2300hrs. This force likewise proceeded in an easterly direction across the North Sea and at 1530hrs turned north towards their planned rendezvous with the Grand Fleet.

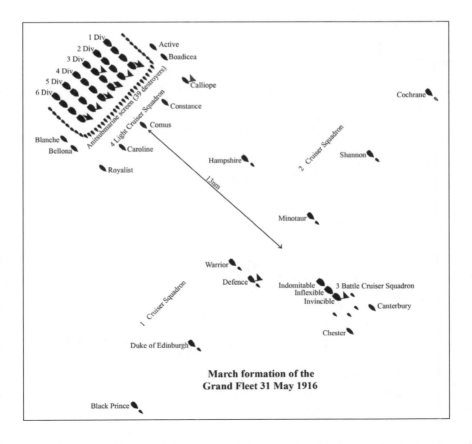

**March formation of the
Grand Fleet 31 May 1916**

The Grand Fleet was under the Command of Admiral Jellicoe. John Jellicoe was born on 5 December 1859 and joined the Royal Navy in 1872. He spent his early career aboard various battleships and specialized in artillery. In 1893 he was posted to HMS *Victoria* and was serving aboard this ship when she was rammed and sunk by HMS *Camperdown* off Tripoli on 22 June 1893. He was promoted Captain in January 1897 and commanded the battleship *Centurion*. He served in China during the Boxer rising and was badly wounded, but returned to Britain with his ship in August 1901. For his service in China he was awarded the German Order of the Red Eagle, 2nd Class. In February 1907 he was promoted Rear Admiral. In September 1911 he was promoted Vice Admiral and at the outbreak of World War One was appointed commander of the renamed Grand Fleet, being promoted to Admiral at the same time. In this role he sought to write orders to cover every contingency with his 'Grand Fleet Battle Orders', which effectively curtailed individual initiative.

The British battle cruisers were commanded by Vice Admiral Beatty. He was born in Cheshire on 17 January 1871 and joined the Royal Navy in January 1884. After passing out he served in the Mediterranean and after service on various ships

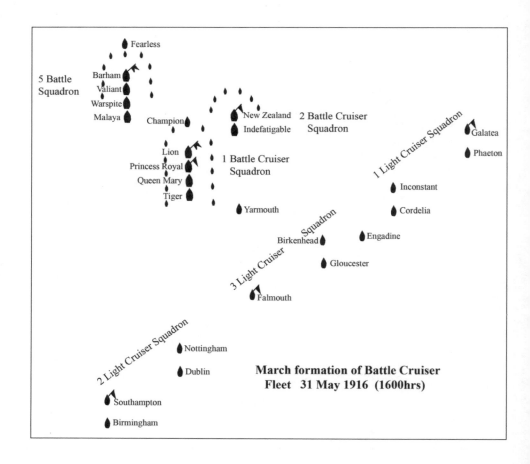

March formation of Battle Cruiser Fleet   31 May 1916 (1600hrs)

took part in the Khartoum campaign in 1898, where he commanded a gunboat. He saw further action in China during the Boxer Rebellion and was twice wounded. He was promoted Captain at age 29. Further shipboard appointments followed and in 1910 he was promoted Rear Admiral just short of his 39th birthday. A period on half pay followed and just when it looked like he would retire he was appointed secretary to the First Lord. In March 1913 he was appointed commander of the 1 Battle Cruiser Squadron, a post he still held at the beginning of the war. Beatty was known to be intelligent and energetic, and was an aggressive leader.

On the afternoon of 31 May the two fleets were approaching the Skagerrak. The German forces consisted of 16 modern battleships, 6 old pre-dreadnought battleships, 5 Große Kreuzer (battle cruisers), 11 small cruisers and 61 torpedobootes. Against these German forces was arranged the powerful Grand Fleet with 29 dreadnought type battleships, 9 battle cruisers, 8 armoured cruisers, 26 light cruisers and 79 destroyers and flotilla leaders. Therefore the Germans were outnumbered by almost 2:1, and their capital ships amounted to just 55 per cent of the British capital ship strength.

Chapter 3

Admirals Beatty and Hipper Engage

On the afternoon of 31 May 1916 the weather off the coast of Jutland and the Skagerrak was a light north-westerly breeze, strength 3, with a slight haze and partly cloudy skies. Towards 1500hrs the cruiser on the left wing of the reconnaissance line, *Elbing*, sighted the Danish steamer *N.J. Fjord* and dispatched the torpedobootes *B109*, leader boot of the 4 HF under Korvettenkapitän Dithmar, and *B110*, Kapitänleutnant Vollheim, to investigate. Almost at the same time the British cruisers *Galatea* and *Phaeton* on the eastern wing of the British reconnaissance line also sighted *N.J. Fjord* and turned to investigate. It was observed that the steamer had stopped and was blowing off steam, and nearby lay two warships. When the Battle Cruiser Fleet turned north about 1515hrs the Leader of the 1 LCS, Commodore Alexander-Sinclair, did not follow but took *Galatea* and *Phaeton* towards the Danish steamer, a movement followed by the second cruiser file, *Inconstant* and *Cordelia*. At 1520hrs *Galatea* signalled 'Enemy in sight' by wireless, immediately followed by a signal that two enemy cruisers were in sight.

At 1525hrs *B109* gave the FT message: 'Individual enemy forces in sight in 164 gamma', and then at 1528hrs: 'Enemy steers east'. On approaching the sighted ships it was seen that they were of the *Cleopatra* and *Arethusa* class on an easterly course at high speed. Both cruisers made the recognition signal 'P.S.', which was immediately reported by wireless by *B109*.[1] As *B109* neared these opponents to within 90hm she opened fire at 1528hrs, to which *Galatea* immediately replied. The two bootes then closed on *Elbing*. The war diary of *Elbing* reported the following about these events:

> *Elbing* sighted a smoke cloud in the direction of one of the torpedobootes and turned with high speed towards it. The vessels that appeared under the smoke clouds appeared to be battle cruisers, that at first steered east, then they soon turned onto a northern course and were now irreproachably made out as two light cruisers. The first enemy shell struck at quite a large distance from the ship. *Elbing* opened fire at 3.32pm at a range of 130–140hm in the brief passing battle, with the enemy bearing to starboard ahead. The enemy turned away to the west after the first straddling salvo. His number had meanwhile grown to 4 light cruisers. He obviously tries to draw us to the northwest. *Elbing* turns to starboard on approximately a northerly course to the running battle and took the enemy under fire from 3.48pm to 4.07pm several times, for short periods at great range. At 4.10pm a total of 7 light cruisers could clearly be made out at uneven distances from one another. At 4.12pm further smoke

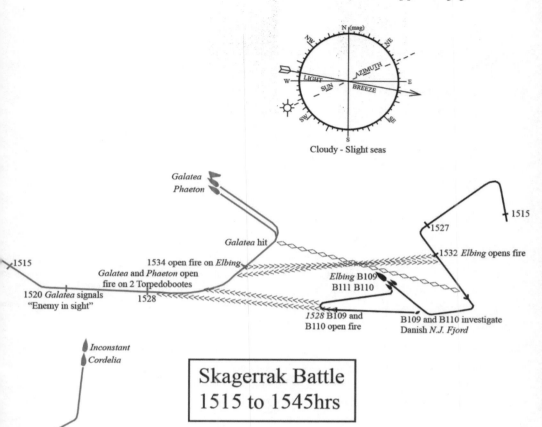

Cloudy - Slight seas

Skagerrak Battle
1515 to 1545hrs

clouds came in sight to the west. At 4.15pm *Frankfurt*, which had approached from the east with *Pillau* at high speed, signalled: 'Course 304°'. The enemy was now only poorly made out. At 4.20pm in the course taken by *Elbing* the first impacts of a heavy calibre were observed. From where the shots came was at first not known.[2] At 4.27pm the F.d.II.A.G. gave the signal: '*Elbing* join on', and immediately thereon: 'Z.O.[3] Course change to SE'. *Elbing* sheered into the II AG [line].[4]

The fire of *Elbing* was effective and soon after opening fire, at about 1537hrs, she obtained a hit on *Galatea* squarely under the bridge, which penetrated several decks, however the 15cm shell did not detonate. It was the first hit of the battle and immediately afterwards Commodore Alexander-Sinclair turned away to the NW. *Elbing* followed but due to their speed superiority *Galatea* and *Phaeton* gradually pulled ahead so that firing became intermittent. Meanwhile at 1525hrs *Galatea* broadcast an important message: 'Have sighted large amount of smoke as though from a Fleet bearing ENE.' As at this time the I AG was more than 20nm to the east the smoke more probably came from the II AG, but nevertheless the report created

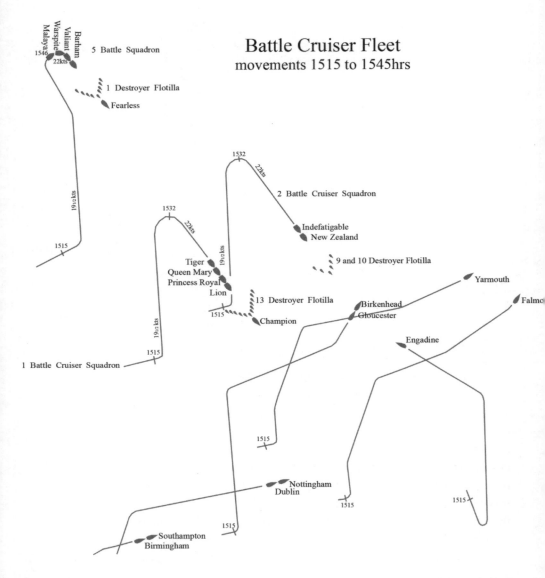

Battle Cruiser Fleet
movements 1515 to 1545hrs

the impression heavy German forces were in contact and Vice Admiral Beatty altered course from north to SSE and then ENE. The first movement was carried out by the battle cruisers at 1532hrs but Rear Admiral Evan-Thomas and *Barham* did not record the execution of the turn to SSE until 1537hrs, five minutes later. Another three minutes elapsed before the 5 Battle Squadron commenced the turn at 1540hrs, during which time the distance between *Lion* and *Barham* increased from 5 to 10nm. One reason for this failure of communication was that flags alone were used for the signal, and as they were flying almost directly in line with the ship they were difficult to read. The message should have been repeated by searchlight, as at this time *Falmouth* had signalled *Lion* by searchlight at a distance of over 8nm, but it was not. Finally, at 1540hrs Rear Admiral Evan-Thomas turned his 5 Battle Squadron after the 1 Battle Cruiser Squadron on his own initiative, Vice Admiral Beatty's signal for a change in course having never been received.

Soon after the first report from *Elbing* was received at 1526hrs Vizeadmiral Hipper turned his ships to course WSW and went to full speed to close on the light cruisers as quickly as possible. At 1534hrs aboard *Lützow* the order was given for clear ship for battle. This order brought great delight and Kapitänleutnant Jung, commander of A turret, wrote: 'On, Clear for action', drums and horns sounded through the decks. Those who have heard the call from the drums and horns will never forget how serious it was, but also the magic of the moment. In a few moments the last preparations were met, and the battle stations announce: 'Clear! Solemn silence surrounds those in their rushing colossus. There are no longer men to be seen on the upper deck.'[5] At 1535hrs *Lützow* reported to the High Sea Chief: Several smoke clouds of enemy forces in sight in 164γ. At 1620hrs speed was increased to 25 knots to chase the enemy light cruisers, but then large warships came in sight to port.

At 1620hrs the German battle cruisers sighted, in the WSW, the two columns of quickly approaching dreadnoughts, and at about 1622, at a range of 15nm two battle cruisers with tripod masts, the II BCS, were clearly sighted from *Seydlitz*. At 1625hrs *Princess Royal* made out five smoke clouds in the east by north. Whether the British ships were easier to make out against the clearer western horizon, or if the German measuring and observation equipment was better, or the light grey colour of the German ships was more favourable, a reason for the earlier German observation of the English ships remains unknown. In any case the German side continued to observe the composition and course of the sighted forces for some time.[6]

Leutnant zur See Kienast was on the Staff of Vizeadmiral Hipper and later wrote:

High tension dominates with all the crew, as after scarcely one hour after sighting British light forces smoke clouds and heavy masts of ships climb over the horizon. I hear more, as Admiral Hipper up the Admiral's bridge said to his Chief of Staff, in his Bavarian dialect: 'Raeder, I'll eat my broomstick if that is not Beatty again!'[7]

Korvettenkapitän Paschen, the I Artillerie Offizier of *Lützow* wrote:

With the sighting of the enemy heavy forces I could already see with certainty battleships behind the battle cruisers which were at least 26 kilometres distant, evidence of the excellent visibility to the west. When the battle cruisers took up a southern course these ships continued peacefully further to the north, whereby they found themselves in a position 10 nautical miles behind the battle cruisers, and at first could not interfere.[8]

Lützow now signalled for a speed of 18 knots and a distance between ships of 700 metres as the German line was now assembling into battle formation to begin the action on a northerly course. Vizeadmiral Hipper then signalled fire distribution from the right. This order meant that the German battle cruiser line would each take their opposite number under fire, ship against ship, beginning with *Lützow* taking the leading enemy ship as target. Vizeadmiral Hipper was happily beginning the battle against a superior enemy on a northerly course. The Krieg zur See explains further:

> Only this remained certain: the newly sighted force, including six dreadnoughts, steered north, and it was decided to choose this as a combat course. Indeed a battle on a northern course, away from the German main body, in no way agreed with the German operational plan, but, nevertheless, Admiral Hipper determined to use this direction for battle. This course would also bring him closer to the II AG, and therefore he ordered fire distribution from the right. However, around 1629hrs an enemy course alteration could be recognized.
>
> About this time Admiral Beatty swung onto an easterly course, ordered 'action stations', and ordered the 2 LCS, with the 9 and 13 Flotillas to take station at the head, and the 2 BCS to follow the 1 BCS on ESE course in battle line. At the same time the 5 Battle Squadron, that at this time was 8nm WNW, received an order to push east at high speed. The visibility was good, the sun in the rear, the wind WNW. Vizeadmiral Hipper remained on his hitherto course and the enemy stood between him and his bases. [In fact Vice Admiral Beatty lost the opportunity of interposing himself between the I AG and its base when he turned NE at 1615hrs.] Whether he received support or not, Vice Admiral Beatty's ships were of the same class and he would remain in contact and give battle, so long as the enemy numbers were not greatly superior. It appeared to him that he had a great opportunity, tactically and strategically, and the decision did not seem in doubt.[9]

Upon sighting the British forces Vizeadmiral Hipper prepared for a battle on a northerly course, even though he knew he was outnumbered by two to one, and was faced by the enemies most powerful ships, armed with 15-inch cannon. Vizeadmiral Hipper did not flinch, and should be commended for his resolve and bravery in the face of greatly superior odds.

Korvettenkapitän Mahrholz served as an Artillerie Offizier aboard *von der Tann* and *Hindenburg* from 1910 to 1918, and as I AO of the former he remembered:

> It dawned on some that the battle was beginning, but probably no one supposed the entire English fleet was on the spot. However, this time was completely different to earlier opportunities, because our entire Fleet stood only 50nm behind us and therefore gave a beautiful feeling of strength and power and everyone onboard desired a meeting with the enemy with their whole heart.

Many eyes full of expectation and tension looked with sharp glasses and periscopes to make out the details and soon the ships were recognized as battle cruisers from below [on deck], which in two columns drew towards the German ships. Whilst we still steered on a NW course, the English Admiral formed a line on course south and stated his intention of cutting off our Panzerkreuzers from our line of retreat. Admiral Hipper followed this movement, and gave the best opportunity of drawing the enemy forces onto our Main Body to the south. And now the two enemy columns neared one another with a converging course. Now at great range a further squadron was sighted, which as later turned out was the 5 Battle Squadron with 4 ships of the *Queen Elizabeth* class, the most powerful battleships in the world with an armament of 38cm guns. There was more than double the superiority on the English side, however, there was not a man onboard in which it did not burn to approach the enemy. There was tremendous tension in all minds which increased until the order to open fire, and which could not be released until fire was inaugurated.[10]

At 1630hrs Vizeadmiral Hipper ordered the II AG to close with the I AG and at 1632hrs he ordered a speed reduction to 18 knots to allow the II AG small cruisers to close with him. On observing the course change by Vice Admiral Beatty's battle cruisers to an easterly course at 1635hrs Vizeadmiral Hipper ordered a change in course to course SE, and then at 1639hrs he ordered fire distribution from the left. A minute later he renewed his order for a speed of 18 knots. At the same time, upon receiving the contact reports of Kontreadmiral Boedicker and Vizeadmiral Hipper, Vizeadmiral Scheer ordered his Main Body to increase speed to 'All Speed' (AF). At 1642hrs Vizeadmiral Hipper ordered a distance between ships of 500m and three minutes later a turn onto course SSE. At 1648hrs the awaited signal was hoist aboard *Lützow*: 'Jot Dora', or JD, the signal to inaugurate fire.

The American author Commander H.H. Frost had the following comments about these opening movements and summed up:

Beatty's claim that he was 'between the enemy and his base' was not correct as far as the German battle cruisers were concerned. In fact, the line of bearing between Hipper and Beatty was very nearly at right angles to the bearing of Horns Reefs light vessel. It is true that Beatty might have been able to cut off the line of retreat of the II AG. This fact might have, in some measure, induced Hipper to offer battle to his superior foe but, if so, it was certainly only a contributory cause. The facts demonstrate that Hipper was fighting of his own volition. He had prepared for a fight on the unfavourable north-westerly course. Then, after counter-marching, he had deliberately slowed to 18 knots as early as 16.40. Five minutes later he had headed sharply toward the enemy. Not only did he wish to fight, but he intended to do so at decisive ranges. Our hats are off to Hipper![11]

At the battle of the Dogger Bank on 24 January 1915 the artillery of the British battle cruisers was found to outrange that of their German opponents. Whilst the 12 inch pieces of *New Zealand* and *Indefatigable* could range to just 172hm, the 13.5 inch cannon of *Lion* and *Princess Royal* could range to 217hm, whilst those of *Tiger* and *Queen Mary* could reach slightly further. In contrast the 30.5cm cannon of *Lützow* and *Derfflinger* could range to 191hm, the 28cm pieces of *Seydlitz* and *Moltke* could reach 181hm, whilst the 28cm L/45 guns of *von der Tann* could reach the furthest with a range of 204hm. Vizeadmiral Hipper was mindful of being outranged as at the Dogger Bank and at 1645hrs allowed his Panzerkreuzers to turn two points[12] towards the enemy onto a course of SSE, in an en-echelon formation, to pass through the danger zone as quickly as possible. Nevertheless, the British guns remained silent. Vice Admiral Beatty should have been aware of his range advantage and with his 1 knot speed advantage he should have been able to choose his range, but he was busy issuing final manoeuvring orders to his ships, ordering fire distribution and giving a report to Admiral Jellicoe. Beatty ordered his six battle cruisers to turn together to ESE, 'to clear the smoke', whilst at the same time to take a line of bearing NW. It was a complicated double manoeuvre which was highly undesirable at such a critical moment and meant that the British ships were still manoeuvring into line when the Germans opened fire at 1648hrs.

Korvettenkapitän Paschen, of *Lützow*, recorded the opening of fire thus:

We had a good range on our rangefinders of 240 hectometres (hm), and it seemed an eternity, but in reality only 20 minutes, before they reached our effective range of 190hm. Then we also had to wait for the range to reduce for *Seydlitz*. Five points = 57°, that is where the enemy lay, moving into range. Estimated speed 26 knots, bearing 110°. That gives a closure of 4hm per minute. At 167hm according to our measurement, at about 4.48 hours, the first salvo crashed out from turrets A and B.

For the entire battle *Lützow* fired with turret salvo fire, forward and aft alternating, a method of fire which I cannot praise highly enough. Both guns worked as one, loaded as one and were directed by one man. After the loading all was quiet in the turret. The Gunnery Leader changed the direction, as and when required. The muzzle smoke collected at the end of the ship, which was most unfavourable for observation conditions. I only fired one salvo from all four turrets, but did not encourage a repetition of this. They fell short, or predominantly short, and concealed the entire target with water columns. The flight time was 22 seconds. Impact. 12/16 left, ahead of the bow. 12 to the right. Salvo! A shock from turrets C and D. Impact, over, amidships. 8 down, salvo! Over! 8 down, salvo! – straddle! A hit near the bridge! A sigh of relief, and then continue. This continues two minutes while the batterie has the aim. What is the range finders measurement? 160hm reducing. The range

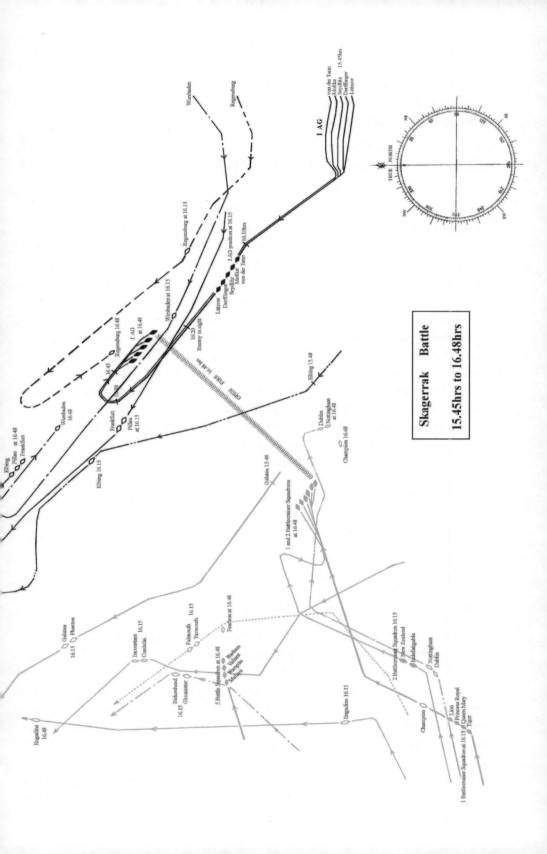

Skagerrak Battle
15.45hrs to 16.48hrs

difference cannot be wrong. These thoughts fill the time of flight. – With the opponent it is thus; with the opening of fire at 167hm range he shot over us by far, but after a while he came close.[13]

The last ship in the German line was *von der Tann*, and she took the last British battle cruiser, *Indefatigable*, as target. From the German perspective her I Artillerie Offizier described the opening of fire:

However, there was still time to leisurely regard the enemy through my periscope. Over there the ships pushed powerfully through the water, and I could clearly recognize each movement on the ships; the hoisting of signals and the following swings and turns, the traversing of the heavy turrets and the elevating of the barrels, which pointed threateningly at us, a sight which we were used to from many battle practices, only then the muzzle flash had been a harmless fire flashlight. Constantly the range finding Offizier was questioned, and he reported to me that the measured ranges were excellent, and there was only 100m difference between the devices. All the better for ranging in I thought, however, I would still form my 8hm Gabel,[14] as at such great range there were many influences. The E.U.[15] was determined and put on the estimate telegraph, in all calm the lateral deflection was reckoned and the corresponding orders were given to the guns, so that fire could be opened at any time. One really had the same feeling as at an important practice shoot, a long, constant approach without useless turns, favourable for all computations and estimations, a long series of comparative measurements must be good for giving the beginning range, no haste and over-estimation with the order transmitters or guns, an approach to gladden the heart of the artillerist. The loading of the guns was long ordered, and in the turrets the men had shoved semi-armour piercing (Panzersprenggranaten) into the barrels, on which a not too friendly greeting for the English had been written in chalk. The adjusted range was 162hm, when finally came the release: 'J.D. open fire!' and at the same second the first salvo crashed against the enemy.[16]

With the order 'fire distribution from the left' the German ships took the following targets: *Lützow* fired on *Lion*; *Derfflinger* fired on *Princess Royal*; *Seydlitz* fired on *Queen Mary*; *Moltke* fired on *Tiger*, whilst *von der Tann* targeted *Indefatigable*. One minute after the Germans inaugurated fire the leading British ships opened fire, however, *New Zealand* only opened fire at 1652hrs and *Indefatigable* at the same time or even later. Nevertheless, at first the British ships could only fire from their forward turrets. As the British had superiority in numbers Vice Admiral Beatty ordered the first two of his ships to fire on the German flagship, *Lützow*, as it was highly desirable to knock the enemy flagship out of action early in the battle. However, the British ships messed up their fire distribution and *Queen Mary* took the third German ship, *Seydlitz*, under fire instead of *Derfflinger*. This left *Derfflinger* unfired upon for the first ten minutes of the battle. So, *Lion* and *Princess Royal* fired on *Lützow*, *Queen Mary* fired on *Seydlitz*; *Tiger* and *New Zealand* fired on *Moltke*, whilst *Indefatigable* engaged in a one on one duel with *von der Tann*. Despite conditions being favourable, as described by Vice Admiral Beatty,[17] the British fire was poor, and at times *Regensburg*, 2000m in the fire lee of the I AG, was in danger of being hit by the British battle cruisers. On the other hand Captain Pelly of *Tiger* described the conditions as: 'weather was misty in patches with varying visibility.'

After commencing fire at 1648hrs the German fire soon became very effective. *Lützow* took the British flagship, *Lion*, under fire and already three minutes later, at 1651hrs, a shell hit on the British cruiser was obtained with the fourth salvo. *Lützow*'s I Artillerie Offizier had written: '22 second flight time. Impact. 12/16 left, ahead of the bow. 12 to the right. Salvo! A shock from turrets C and D. Impact, over, midships. 8 down, salvo! Over! 8 down, salvo! – straddle! A hit near the bridge! A sigh of relief, and then continue.'[18] The first hit struck between the forecastle and upper decks near the fore funnel, as described by Korvettenkapitän Paschen. A minute later at 1652hrs a semi-armoured piecing shell struck the base of the second funnel, causing extensive damage and D and B boiler rooms filled with smoke and fumes. At 1700hrs a shell struck on Q turret at the junction of the turret face and roof, which penetrated and exploded over the left 13.5 inch gun.

At 1700hrs *Lützow* received its first hit on the forecastle, followed closely by a second nearby. 'The *Lion*'s first salvo to straddle comes after 9 minutes, and therefore it was a surprise when we receive a soft hit in the forecastle, despite the fact that *Lion* and *Princess Royal*, the first two ships in the enemy line, are firing on *Lützow*.'[19] At 1657hrs Vice Admiral Beatty turned his ships away 2 points to increase the range. Two minutes later Vizeadmiral Hipper also turned away, 1 point to port.

The second ship of the British line, *Princess Royal*, fired on *Lützow* during the first part of the battle, before changing target to *Derfflinger*. Nevertheless, despite being unfired upon, it was not until 1652hrs that the fire of *Derfflinger*, under the control of I Artillerie Offizier Korvettenkapitän von Hase, obtained its first straddle. He wrote:

> ....like thunder our first salvo crashes out. The splashes are well together, but 'over,' that is behind the target and to the right. 'Deflection 2 more left! down 400! continue!' Those were the orders for the next salvo.... The second salvo crashed out. Again it was over. 'Down 400,' I ordered. The third and fourth salvoes were also over in spite of the fact that after the third I had given the order, 'Down 800.' 'Good God, Stachow! there's something wrong' I cursed. 'Down 800!' It appeared later from the gunnery-log that the Fähnrich had probably not understood the first 'down 800', or, at any rate, it had not been acted upon. This time, however, the 'down 800' was effective. The sixth salvo,

fired at 4.52, straddled, three splashes over the target, one short! We had meanwhile reached a range of 11,900m, as the elevation clock had shown a rate of 200 closing and then 300 closing per minute, and I had already gone down 1,600. We had already been in action four minutes and only now had we straddled our target.... Our first rounds had been well over. This was due to inaccurate determination of the opening range and a delay in the first reports of the measured range. I explain the serious error of calculation as follows: The Bg. men were completely overwhelmed by the first view of the enemy monsters. Each one saw the enemy ship magnified twenty-three times in his instrument! Their minds were at first concentrated on the appearance of the enemy. They tried to ascertain who their enemy was. And so when the order suddenly came to open fire they had not accurately fixed the estimated range.[20]

Korvettenkapitän Mahrholz gave a more technical explanation for *Derfflinger*'s inaccurate fire: 'The Artillerie Offizier of *Derfflinger* allowed himself a 4hm fork under the favourable conditions, repeated this three times, and then went to forming an 8hm fork, in order to impact in front of the target. The result was that with the seventh salvo *Derfflinger* straddled the target.'[21] Therefore it was not until 1558hrs that *Derfflinger* struck *Princess Royal* with two armoured piercing shells. One shell penetrated the 6 inch armour around frame 74–76 and detonated in a coal bunker. The second hit burst on the 6 inch armour and the shock of these two impacts temporarily put the fire control tower out of action so that control had to be from B turret. At about 1700hrs a shell struck at frame 84 about four feet above the upper deck, through a rectangular skylight, and then through the Ward Room bulkhead and an adjacent coaling trunk. The shell detonated against the armour of B turret barbette, forcing the armour ¾ inch. There was severe damage to light structures and several small fires started. Eight men were killed and 38 were wounded, mostly from burns and toxic gas. On the other hand *Derfflinger* remained undamaged during this period.

The Panzerkreuzer *Seydlitz* took *Queen Mary* as her target from the beginning of the battle. The I Artillerie Offizier of *Seydlitz*, Korvettenkapitän Foerster, wrote the following about the approach of the British ships:

Behind the English battle cruisers we observed battleships, which we recognized as being of the *Malaya* class, and therefore from the beginning we were outnumbered two to one. On a southerly course the two lines of battle cruisers came ever nearer. My range 200hm, 190hm, 180hm, 170hm 160hm; well does no one want to open fire? On our side I could understand it, we preferred to deal with the enemy at low range where the results of our guns on the comparatively weak armour of the English ships would be greater, but why were the English so reticent until now?

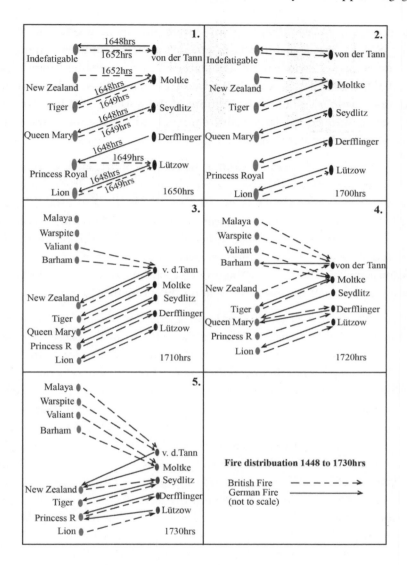

At 150hm the flagship signalled 'open fire!' 'Drauf Seydlitz!'[22] the old battle parole of the Rittergeneral, which we had adopted as our battle parole. Then the command 'salvo fire', and 'ruummms!' out rushed the 28cm shells from our barrels.

Our target was the tactical position corresponding to that of us in the line, the third ship in the enemy line that I recognized as *Queen Mary*. There we spoke of our English sistership; built at the same time, put into service on almost the same day, approximately the same size, and the pride of the English fleet.[23]

It is uncertain if *Queen Mary* was hit during the opening phase of the battle, however, *Seydlitz* was struck twice. At 1655hrs a shell struck near frame 116 and caused the starboard switch room and starboard turbo-dynamo room to fall out, and at 1657hrs a shell struck the barbette of C turret. This shell penetrated the 230mm thick armour and ignited munitions in the working chamber. Turret C was immediately enveloped in a large yellow smoke cloud and the turret was burnt out. Korvettenkapitän Foerster wrote:

> Then, approximately ten minutes after the opening of fire, Habler[24] reported to me by telephone, 'Turret Caesar does not give any answer; from the speaking tube of turret Caesar smoke is penetrating the artillerie central.' This was exactly the same report that I had received on January 24 on the Dogger Bank, also at the beginning of the battle. I therefore knew what this report signified. The cartridges were in flames, and the turret was put out of action.
>
> Almost mechanically I gave the order: 'Flood magazine of turret C.' This would put the chamber under water, and prevent further [damage].[25]

The fire of the forth German Panzerkreuzer, *Moltke*, was under the direction of Kapitänleutnant Schirmacher, and during the first part of the battle a devastatingly accurate fire was rained down on her opposite number, HMS *Tiger*, which was hit a total of nine times prior to 1700hrs. *Moltke* opened fire at 1648hrs at a range of 140hm, but was unaware of the effectiveness of her fire and only recorded the observation of a hit at 1706hrs. Nevertheless the first hit on *Tiger* struck at 1650hrs, just two minutes after the opening of fire. This hit struck far aft at station 292–298 on the belt armour to port, between the main and middle deck, but only dented the armoured plate and pushed it in about 3 inches. The internal frames were generally distorted. Just one minute later a shell struck forward at station 21 and caused damage to light structures. At 1652, or perhaps 1651hrs, a shot struck that caused considerable damage at the base of the second funnel on the starboard side. But again the damage was to light structures. At 1653hrs a shell entered *Tiger* through a sidelight in the C.P.O.'s mess at station 46 to port, between the forecastle and upper decks. The mess was wrecked and a hole was made in the upper deck. There were two hits just a minute later at 1654hrs. One shell penetrated the port side plating at station 54 at the lower edge of a sidelight and struck the armour of A barbette. The barbette plate was pushed in by 6 inches at its lower edge and the A turret handling room was severely affected by smoke and gases, but the turret machinery was not affected. At 1655hrs another shell penetrated the port side 5 inch belt armour at station 70, at the main deck into the Stokers' Mess, leaving a calibre sized hole. The main deck was holed with a 10ft × 4ft hole, and much damage was done to light structures. At 1654 or 1655hrs the roof of Q turret was struck by a heavy shell which pierced the crown plate abreast of the sighting hood, which was shot away, with considerable damage being done to the sighting equipment and both centre sights and training wheels were destroyed, along with the turret dynamo. The right gun hoists were damaged and the air cocks for the run in and run out cylinder of the right gun were broken. Three men were killed and five were wounded and Q turret was put out of action, and although later repaired only fired a total of 32 shots during the entire battle. At 1656hrs a 28cm shell struck the 9 inch thick barbette armour of X turret at the line of the upper deck on the port side, blowing a hole 2½ ft × 1ft in the armour and bending down the deck plating in the vicinity. The revolving structure inside was holed 4ft × 4ft. The shell entered the turret, but did not detonate, although the explosive filling burnt. The centre training shaft was smashed and the firing circuits were cut, and the turret was put out of action, so that *Tiger*'s effective broadside had thus been halved. The turret was later brought back into action, but the damage to the director training equipment meant that it was firing 19° off target.

At 1658hrs a hit occurred that could have had fateful consequences for *Tiger*. This 28cm shell struck just above the armoured deck at station 204 and penetrated the 6 inch armour, leaving a calibre-sized hole. The base of the shell penetrated the upper deck and then the armoured deck and punched a hole in the bracket supporting the main steam pipe in the port engine room. If the pipe had been struck instead of the bracket the ship would have been disabled. The shell itself detonated in the ammunition passage and killed a dozen men and set fire to ready use cordite in the passage, necessitating flooding the midships 6 inch magazine. The engine room was immediately filled with dense smoke and gases, whilst fractured water mains allowed water to penetrate.

During this time *Moltke* remained unhit, despite being under the concentrated fire of both *Tiger* and *New Zealand*. Only at 1702hrs did a near miss cause some flooding forward to starboard.

At the end of the respective lines were *Indefatigable* and *von der Tann*. Whilst the fire of *Indefatigable* was over and wide, that of *von der Tann* was up to the normal German standard, that is there was a straddle and hit with the third or fourth salvo. The I Artillerie Offizier of *von der Tann*, Korvettenkapitän Mahrholz, wrote:

As our first salvo was out, I put all my energy into my eyes, so that no movement of the enemy, no fall of shot of my batterie, escaped my view. Accurately the middle of the sixteenth division lay under the middle funnel of the battle cruiser *Indefatigable*, the name I did not know at the time, only recognizing the type. I concentrated, as I was familiar with during firing exercises, my main attention on the bow part of the opponent, because any alteration in course is recognizable at the bow and by the bridge, and laterally displaced impacts collapse perhaps onto the ship, making a longer observation possible. The bow of the opponent must therefore be specially observed by the Artillerie Offizier. With the sound of the impact reporting clocks four enormous fountains sprayed over there, the lateral deflection was correct, and the aft superstructure lay in line with the fall of shot. '8 back, 4 more left, one salvo!' was my correction. During the flight time I allowed the measurements to be given to the E.U., which accurately agreed with the indicator. With the quality of the measurement I now expected the 'Fork', and over there four water columns jumped high, and for a moment the entire middle part of the target was covered, all four were clearly on the water surface, but doubtlessly short. '4 forwards, one salvo', and after the flight time another struck near the enemy, two impacts short, one over, the fourth was not seen, probably a hit, as the [Shooting] List Leader assured me that four shots had fallen in the salvo. The semi armoured piercing shell only exploded inside and therefore a hit result could only be seen when the interior was clearly destroyed. I guarded myself against observing hits, and adhered strictly to observing the fall of shot. My young Leutnant in the mast also reported a hit. 'Straddling, good rapid!' followed the order after the impact and now followed salvos in brief intervals, salvos following salvos into the air. The enemy fired slowly, you could clearly see the flash of the salvos, and those who had time could use a stopwatch to determine the enemy fall of shot near the ship. Still the enemy did not shoot well, and many salvos came nowhere near the target, probably over there they had poorer visibility than us, and our clear ship colour made it difficult in the hazy weather. According to the observation of the small cruisers the enemy continually shot over the target, and the fall of shot lay partly so far, that the vessels travelling in the fire lee were threatened by this fire. In the beginning you could not mistake the enemy muzzle flashes with our own hits in the good visibility, and the red and yellow fire flash was followed by a yellow–brown smoke cloud, whilst our own hits, which were not swallowed up by the ship, appeared clearly as bright lights, nothing else. Meanwhile the fire of *von der Tann* was extraordinarily successful, and the enemy disappeared completely sometimes in the surrounding columns of water. As *Indefatigable* was so covered seemingly he ceased fire and attempted to withdraw from the deadly fire by a zigzag course, but thanks to the good glasses each movement could clearly be recognized. The enemy turned away and despite the straddles I changed 1hm ahead, and he turned nearer, 1hm back and changed the deflection a little to the side, to the bow of the enemy. Whilst the salvo was underway, a new position for the direction indicator was ordered, and I immediately received the new position for the ordered indicators. I immediately received the new movement and deflection ahead for the new position of the enemy. Usually the deflection ahead was struck freehand. The Offizier in the transmitting stations worked excellently, the estimate telegraph gave, after each course alteration of the enemy, the new E.U.; it allowed no escape, the batterie remained on the target and the rapid salvo fire was scarcely interrupted. Sometimes my impatience came out with the salvo fire, and I had in the peacetime training a private command that was not in the firing regulations; 'faster!' That meant the E–Uhr man was taken out of the batterie for a brief time, without consideration of the clear reports of the guns. That command was now given, and the salvos crashed out at speed. Then 14 minutes after the opening of fire the enemy caught fatal wounds. In the direction indicator periscope briefly after the impact of a salvo I saw a giant explosion in the aft gun turret, a bright flash flame pushed out and ship debris was thrown in a wide arc in the air, seemingly it was the turret roof, that through the pressure of the explosion inside had been thrown out. The next salvo gave the ship the rest, it hit further forward and had the result that soon after the impact a tremendous black smoke cloud climbed from the ship, reaching double the mast height and the enemy totally disappeared from sight. Probably an oil bunker was hit and burned. For the sake of certainty still another salvo was fired into the smoke cloud, which scarcely would have reached the target as they had already vanished in the waves.

At 1703hrs it was observed that *Indefatigable* was struck by two or three shells from one salvo around the aft gun turret. A small explosion occurred and *Indefatigable* swung out of line to starboard, probably to throw off the German aim. She appeared to be settling by the stern when two projectiles from the next salvo struck her, one on the forecastle, one on the forward A turret. After a further 30 seconds there was a tremendous explosion forward and the ship lay over to port and capsized. It is thought that the aft magazines of X turret exploded and then the forward magazines of A turret followed suit. A total of 57 officers and 960 men perished with the explosion, whilst two survivors were later picked up by the German torpedoboot *S16*. During the engagement *von der Tann* fired 52–28cm shells and 38–15cm shells at ranges of 162–123hm.

Throughout this phase of the battle *von der Tann* was not hit.

During the first 15 minutes of the battle Vice Admiral Beatty's battle cruisers were having a hard time of it. Vice Admiral Beatty wrote: 'the visibility at this time was good, the sun behind us and the wind SE. Being between the enemy and his base, our situation was both tactically and strategically good.'[26] Actually Beatty was wrong on two counts, the wind was from the west and he was not between the Germans and their base. In spite of his assertion the British were at a disadvantage. They were to windward and the breeze blew the funnel and gunfire smoke downrange, into the line of fire. Added to that six destroyers of the 9th and 10th Flotillas, which were steaming hard for the head of the British line, were passing down range and their smoke was likewise fouling the range.

At 1657hrs Vice Admiral Beatty turned away to starboard two points, to increase the range, and two minutes later Vizeadmiral Hipper turned away one point. Nevertheless, the effective German gunfire continued unabated. At 1700hrs *Lion* was struck by a 30.5cm shell from *Lützow*, which nearly had fateful consequences. After firing only twelve shots Q turret was struck by a semi-armoured piercing shell that hit the junction of the 9 inch thick face plate and the 3½ inch thick roof. A piece of 9 inch armour was broken off and entered the turret, whilst the shell also penetrated and detonated above the left gun. The detonation caused the deaths of all the occupants of the turret and most of those in the working chamber below, and this and ensuing cordite fire caused the deaths of around 60 men. The front roof plate was blow off and lay upside down on the engaged side deck, whilst the centre front plate was also blown off and landed on deck aft of the turret. Luckily the officer of the turret quickly ordered the magazine doors in the handling room to be closed and the magazine to be flooded. This was prudent as at 1728hrs there was a further cordite fire and flames towered above the masts, with Q turret magazine bulkheads being considerably buckled and bulged inwards. Those men remaining in the handling room and some of the fire party were killed, but if the magazine doors had been open or had been blown open *Lion* would have doubtlessly gone the way of the other battle cruisers which blew up.

The I Artillerie Offizier of *Lützow* recorded: 'Red flames climb up from the third turret, and a large part, a half of the turret roof, flies in the air. After a pause, suddenly flames shoot out of the turret, however, the turret commander has in death closed the magazine. This rescues the *Lion* and the Admiral.' However, Korvettenkapitän Paschen lamented:

It is to my sorrow today, that during the first hour of the battle, on the basis of the general instructions and reinforced to me briefly before by the advice given from the manual page, I had not fired one armoured piercing shell, but only high explosive shells. Otherwise *Lion* and her Admiral would scarcely have survived. It is nevertheless observed, that one of these shells struck a turret roof of *Lion* at a shallow striking angle and did not rupture, but detonated.[27]

However, he need not have worried, as the semi-armour piercing shell had done all that was required of it.

The records for *Lion* do not give a chronological order for the hits suffered during the early part of the engagement, but hits were suffered at 1651, 1652, 1700, two at 1701, 1703 and two at 1724hrs. Apart from those already mentioned the following damage was done, beginning in the bows: a hit struck about 115 feet from the bows, causing some damage and passing overboard without detonating; a ricochet passed through the blast screen of the middle funnel and fell unexploded between the funnel and screen; a shell struck the joint between two plates in line with the forward edge of Q turret barbette, the surfaces of both being splintered and flaked over a considerable area, while the plates were set in 2½ inches at the top and 1½ inches at the lower edge. A shell passed through the roof and side of unarmoured after 4 inch control without bursting. Finally two 30.5cm shells struck about 6 feet apart aft of the aft 4 inch gun battery. They passed through the aft superstructure before detonating and were responsible for the deaths of 19 men,

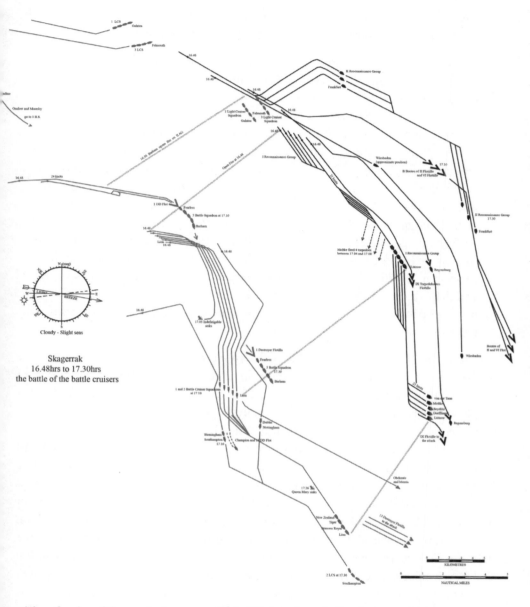

Skagerrak
16.48hrs to 17.30hrs
the battle of the battle cruisers

Cloudy - Slight seas

with a further 35 men being wounded. Of the nine shells that struck *Lion* during this period a total of four shots failed to detonate, a poor performance indeed, and in many respects *Lion* had been let off the hook. Between 1705 and 1730 *Lion* fired two torpedoes at *Derfflinger*.

At 1715hrs the German flagship, *Lützow*, was struck by another two 13.5 inch shells, this time fired by *Princess Royal*, as the British flagship, *Lion*, had sheered out of line at 1705hrs and had disappeared from view. One shell struck the belt armour on the waterline beneath the aft conning tower, but failed to penetrate and caused no damage, but caused a heavy vibration. The other hit struck between the barbettes of A and B turrets, in the forward battle dressing station.

17 minutes after the opening of fire the *Lion* turned hard away, until they disappeared aft and *Princess Royal* slid into view. I have counted 6 hits over there, from 31 salvos. We have received 3, including one which detonated between A and B barbettes and cleared the forward dressing station. There all are killed, including the friendly young doctor, Unterarzt Dr. Schönitz. Hit No.3 seems to have struck somewhere aft on the belt; there are strong vibrations but no loss. The obvious observation that *Lion* sheered out of line is not mentioned in the reports from the other side... The *Lion* later again assumed the lead position, but I cannot indicate when this occurred. At about 5.08pm we changed target to *Princess Royal*. The opponents worked with strong course changes and were difficult to see in the smoke. The range quickly changed from 151 to 130hm, then quickly out to 190 and then back to 150hm. In the fire lee of the enemy somewhat ahead are some destroyers, and their thick smoke conceals the target. The fire director of the enemy in the mast remains clearly visible and I suppose it is a good trick of the enemy to place his fire director there.[28]

Because the British flagship, *Lion*, had temporarily sheered out of line the fire distribution of the German line became somewhat confused for a time, and after initially firing on *Princess Royal* the second German ship, *Derfflinger*, changed target to *Queen Mary* for sometime before changing back to *Princess Royal* about 1727hrs. The fire was immediately effective and at 1727hrs *Princess Royal* was hit on the muzzle of the right gun of Q turret by a 30.5cm shell which was deflected and detonated in the air about 3 metres away, causing damage to the deck below. The inner gun tube was cracked but the gun continued to fire. Two minutes later, at 1729hrs, a shell passed through the second funnel and out the other side without detonating. A third shell at 1732hrs burst on the junction of the 6 inch and 9 inch armour at the level of the fore-funnel. In addition, the stud axis crank pinion of the left gun of A turret sheared with the breech closed and put the gun out of action for eleven hours. The right gun of this turret suffered misfires because of a bent retractor lever. Once again *Derfflinger* remained unhit during this period and it is uncertain if she was in fact fired upon by any British ships.

The third ship in the British line, *Queen Mary*, had *Seydlitz* as her direct opponent and engaged her until at least 1717hrs before changing target to *Derfflinger*. During the earlier part of the battle *Queen Mary* was hit a number of times by *Seydlitz*. One shell struck the aft 4 inch battery and caused an ammunition fire, whilst a further hit at around 1721hrs struck the right side of Q turret and put the right gun out of action. After *Lion* disappeared from view *Derfflinger* changed target to *Queen Mary* and was firing at a range of 132hm whilst *Queen Mary*'s opposite number, *Seydlitz*, was firing at her at 135hm. At 1726hrs three projectiles of a four-shell salvo were seen to strike *Queen Mary* but the only result appeared to be a small smoke and dust cloud, and then from another salvo of four shells two struck the ship and a tremendous yellow flame erupted and the ship disappeared in a huge smoke cloud. Witnesses reported some of the hits struck near Q turret and this is substantiated by a survivor, Midshipman Storey:

> The fire was maintained with great rapidity till 5.20, and during this time we were only slightly damaged by the enemy's fire. At 5.20 a big shell hit Q turret and put the right gun out of action, but the left gun continued firing. At 5.24 a terrific explosion took place which smashed up Q turret and started a big fire in the working chamber and the gun house was filled with smoke and gas. The Officer on the turret, Lieutenant Commander Street, gave the order to evacuate the turret. All the unwounded in the gun house got clear and, as they did so, another terrific explosion took place and all were thrown into the water.[29]

There was also a huge explosion forward, thought to be from B turret magazine. The I Artillerie Offizier of *Derfflinger*, Korvettenkapitän Hase wrote:

> And so the *Queen Mary* and the *Derfflinger* fought out a regular gunnery duel over the destroyer action that was raging between us. But the poor *Queen Mary* was having a bad time. In addition to the *Derfflinger* she was being engaged by the *Seydlitz* and the gunnery officer of the *Seydlitz*, Korvettenkapitän Foerster, was our crack gunnery expert, tried in all the previous engagements in which the ship had taken part, cool-headed and of quick decision. The *Seydlitz* only carried 28-cm. guns. These could not pierce the thickest armour of the *Queen Mary*, but every ship has less heavily armoured places which can be pierced with great damage even by a 28-cm. shell.... About 5.26 p.m. was the historic moment when the *Queen Mary*, the proudest ship of the English fleet, met her doom. Since 5.24 p.m. every one of our salvoes had straddled the enemy. When the salvo fired at 5h. 26m. fell, heavy explosions had already begun in the *Queen Mary*. First of all a vivid red flame shot up from her forepart. Then came an explosion forward which was followed by a much heavier explosion amidships, black debris of the ship flew into the air, and immediately afterwards the whole ship blew up with a terrific explosion. A gigantic cloud of smoke rose, the masts collapsed inwards, the smoke-cloud hid everything and rose higher and higher. Finally nothing but a thick, black cloud of smoke remained where the ship had been. At its base the smoke column only covered a small area, but it widened towards the summit and looked like a monstrous black pine. I estimated the height of the smoke column at from 300 to 400m.[30]

The I Artillerie Offizier of *Seydlitz*, Korvettenkapitän Foerster, wrote:

Suddenly on our opponent I saw a flash in the aft ship, that grew visibly, and this offered to the eye a scene that could move one deeply, but this could not be thought of. In a giant smoke cloud the ship seemed to lift itself from the water, shattered in the middle, with debris flying all around, the whole picture is framed in a blue-red fire glow. In my battle protocol I find written: '5.22hrs, our opponent has blown up, direction 88, 130hm.' After a moment of hesitation, the report was passed everywhere in the ship through telephone and speaking tubes; 'Our opponent has blown up.' 'Drauf Seydlitz!' was the reply, and with doubled enthusiasm they went to work. 'Target change right, on the next ship in the enemy line,' I commanded, and the two way fight continued with a new opponent.[31]

Queen Mary broke in two and the aft part was still afloat bottom up as *New Zealand* passed. A total of 18 survivors were picked up by the destroyers *Laurel* and *Petard* and two were saved by the German torpedoboot *V28*, whilst 1266 men perished.

What is interesting to note is that Korvettenkapitän von Hase seeks to denigrate the role played by *Seydlitz* in the destruction of *Queen Mary*, by saying that her 28cm shells could not penetrate the British battle cruiser's thickest armour, however, he ignores the fact that *Moltke*'s identical 28cm pieces had penetrated *Tiger*'s 9 inch barbette armour at even greater ranges.

Seydlitz was hit at 1718hrs by a 13.5 inch shell from *Queen Mary*, which struck the starboard VI 15cm casemate. The shell exploded in penetrating the 150mm armour and pieces of armour and shell splinters penetrated the casemate, killing the entire serving crew of the 15cm cannon with the exception of the squadron minister, Pastor Pfenger, who escaped the devastated casemate.

The next ship in the German battle line, *Moltke*, meanwhile continued to engage *Tiger*, but this ship was actually firing on *von der Tann* for some time and scored two hits. At 1705hrs *Tiger* was again hit by *Moltke* with a shell that struck far forward and caused severe damage to light structures and holed the upper deck. At 1720hrs *Moltke* hit with a shell that passed through the middle funnel. Then at 1730hrs a further two 28cm shells from *Moltke* struck *Tiger*, which hit the 6 inch side armour and the 9 inch side armour just aft of the forward engine room. The armour was pushed in but the shells did not penetrate. At 1735hrs *Seydlitz* hit *Tiger* with a shell that struck the forecastle causing damage to light structures.

Meanwhile, *Moltke* had launched four torpedoes towards the British and at 1711hrs *Lion* sighted a torpedo track in her wake whilst *Princess Royal* reported a torpedo had passed underneath her. A third torpedo passed between *Tiger* and *New Zealand*. Vizeadmiral Hipper wanted to press his advantage and at the same time as he turned towards the enemy he increased speed to 23 knots.

Nevertheless help was close at hand for Vice Admiral Beatty's sorely pressed battle cruisers. The British 5 Battle Squadron, under the command of Rear Admiral Evan-Thomas, was approaching at its best speed, probably not in excess of

24 knots.[32] Just 10 minutes after the commencement of action *Barham* was able to open fire on German units. The 5 Battle Squadron sighted the II AG and at 1658hrs heavy impacts arrived 300m from *Frankfurt*.

> The heavy impacts from the English battleships now lie continuously in the vicinity of the ships, somewhat short 80 to 100m, therefore artificial fog apparatus employed. The impacts in the vicinity of the ship cease after a short time; it was then observed that the impacts started in the vicinity of a smoke buoy thrown by *Frankfurt*. Therefore during this battle phase the artificial fog apparatus has served to allow the withdrawal of the 3 small cruisers from the well laying fire of the heaviest artillery of the enemy battleships.[33]

The II AG turned sharply away to the NE before continuing their course SE, under the cover of smoke. At 1706hrs the 5 Battle Squadron altered course to SE by S and two minutes later turned two more points to starboard to S by E. At approximately 1706hrs *Barham* opened fire on *von der Tann* at a range of 174hm. Soon *Valiant*, *Warspite* and *Malaya* also joined in, with *Barham* and *Valiant* concentrating on *Moltke* and *Warspite* and *Malaya* firing on *von der Tann*. Now Vizeadmiral Hipper's ships were outnumbered two to one, although his 28cm and 30.5cm pieces were pitted against 34.5cm and 38cm pieces and he was at a severe disadvantage. The German Große Kreuzer, or battle cruisers, were designed with the view that once battle was joined with the enemy they should join the battle line and be capable of fighting the enemy's battleships, but now they faced the most modern and powerful battleships in the world, armed with 15 inch cannon, and were outnumbered two to one. The German Panzerkreuzer would surely be tested to the limit.

At 1716hrs *Moltke* was by a 15 inch shell from *Barham* on the citadel armour below the V casemate 15cm cannon, which penetrated the upper coal bunker, where it detonated. The explosion put the V casemate 15cm cannon out of action and killed the 12 serving crew. Four stokers in the coal bunker were killed and one man in the munition chamber below was wounded and died a few days later. At 1723hrs a 15 inch shell struck near the water line beneath the forward funnel and detonated on the side armour. Although the armour was not penetrated a plate was displaced and the hull skin below the waterline was torn so that some wing passage and protective bunker compartments were flooded. A few minutes later at 1726hrs there was an underwater hit aft, which passed transversely across the ship before detonating and causing further flooding right aft. Finally at 1727hrs a 15 inch shell detonated on the armoured belt below the aft superstructure and caused some flooding in the wing passage and protective bunker. As a result of these hits 1000 tonnes of water entered the ship and she took a 3° list to starboard but was brought back to an even keel with counter flooding.

The battleships of the 5 Battle Squadron remained unfired on and could lob salvo after salvo at the last two German ships undisturbed.

Meanwhile the English 2 Battleship Squadron (*King George* class) had steamed ahead and joined with the English battle cruisers, however, it was later found out that they were really the *Warspite* class. From an aft position they obtained a good fire effect against the I AG, with close together lying salvos, fired by director with a great rapidity of fire. With the intervention of this squadron the situation changed to our disadvantage. As the aft ship of our line was SMS *von der Tann* sometimes the fall of shot completely surrounded us, which could partly be alleviated with changes in course and speed. The ship's hull vibrated and roared owing to the close fall of shot about the ship and in the immediate vicinity of the hull side. The overall effective fire of the battleships could not be replied to, as they were too far aft.[34]

Von der Tann was surrounded by high water columns from the impact of shells of the heaviest calibre and at 1709hrs she suffered her first heavy hit. A 15 inch shell struck the ship to starboard aft on the joint between two armoured plates and detonated during penetration. Several pieces of broken armour penetrated the ship and several rooms flooded.

> With the powerful impact of this shell the hull vibrated violently lengthwise, and the ship's end whipped up and down 5 to 6 times. After a brief interruption the rudder worked again without further disruption, but the rudder engine ran hot owing to the trim of the rudder spindle.[35]

In total 600 tonnes of water entered the ship, but there were no casualties. At 1720hrs a 15 inch shell penetrated the barbette of A turret and put the turret out of action and then at 1723hrs a shell penetrated the battery deck and struck the barbette of turret C, causing this turret to jam for the time being. A serious danger was caused by this hit as the torpedo net was torn loose and hung over the side, threatening to foul the propellers until secured.

Korvettenkapitän Mahrholz wrote:

> A new opponent had entered the battle: the 5 Battle Squadron approached from aft, and fired on *von der Tann*, and the salvos lay close together with 'director firing', their unpleasant clank clearly audible over the remaining battle noise. Luckily the spread of the enemy salvos was small, and the impacts lay sometimes ahead, sometimes behind the ship with no straddles, otherwise things would have gone badly for *von der Tann*. The nearby torpedobootes reported that during this phase of the battle the ship could scarcely be seen among the many impacts, and when the veil parted it was a wonder the ship was seen afloat. I had always held the opinion that some longitudinal dispersion of the shooting was necessary for our observation and that therefore the longitudinal dispersion of the batterie not to be allowed to be too small. To me a dispersion of 50–100m appears quite necessary for success. The shooting of the 5 Battle Squadron in the phase of the battle shows my opinion was correct.

In the course of further battle the ship was hit twice which robbed half the heavy artillerie. A powerful blow shook the forward conning tower, so that I believed the tower lifted, so I believed the tower was hit. Soon came the report from the Artillerie Transmitting Station 'turret Alsen gives no answer'. I looked through the vision slit to ahead, with raised barrels the turret stood fast, no turning, no movement of the barrels was to be seen. Immediately afterwards a further hard metal blow: 'turret Culm gives no answer'. And briefly afterwards the report: 'hit in the turret substructure, smoke and gas danger, munitions chamber flooded!' The Order Transmission Offizier reported to me later that the reports about the battle losses arrived in the transmitting station just as like peacetime training, concise and brief, exactly as in the regulations. One could see the great value of mechanical training and writing down reports. In the serious cases, especially where the battle excitement is added, the recording of losses and pedantic wording of messages is all the better. So within a few minutes two turrets had been put out of action, and only two impacts would lay in the fall of shot of each salvo on the target, and the shooting would be difficult. It became more hazy and the enemy battle cruisers were scarcely visible, and for a brief time fire went over onto the 5 Battle Squadron. However soon this target had to be quit because of the small training angle of the side turrets, and only slow, interrupted fire was possible. In this instant, when the old battle cruiser target had been gone over to, the ship suffered its first heavy loss during the battle. Turret Bautzen fired no more and reported that both barrels no longer returned to the firing position, because they were wedged in the gun cradle. So I only had one turret, which only shot now and then, how despairing![36]

Nevertheless *von der Tann* began hitting back, and at 1723hrs she hit *Barham* on the belt armour, displacing the plate slightly. Then at 1726hrs she struck *New Zealand*, her target after *Indefatigable* blew up, with a 28cm shell which punched out a large piece of armour from the X turret barbette. This turret was jammed for some time. Then at 1730hrs *von der Tann* changed targets back to the 5 Squadron, however with only the midship turrets, B and D. With their restricted training arc the target had to be changed back to the battle cruisers at 1737hrs, but just prior to this at 1735hrs both guns of B turret failed to run out so that *von der Tann* had only one serviceable turret.

Shooting conditions were good for the 5 Battle Squadron and *Barham* reported that *Moltke* was a fair target and was frequently straddled. *Valiant* and *Malaya* reported good results from their 15 foot rangefinders and both reported straddling their target.

At 1738hrs Vizeadmiral Hipper turned SSE and at 1741hrs turned S by W to again close with the opponent, despite the fact the German cruisers were outnumbered two to one. Soon after the smoke cloud of the High Sea Fleet was sighted and the support that had been absent on 16 December 1914 and at the Dogger Bank was close at hand. The British light cruiser *Southampton* signalled the sighting to Vice Admiral Beatty, who was surprised as up until now he had supposed the German Fleet to be on the Jade. Nevertheless, he sent a contact report to Admiral Jellicoe and the Grand Fleet and hoist the recall for his destroyers. At 1746hrs the British battle cruisers turned north at high speed to close on their own battle fleet. However, Beatty once again failed to inform Rear-Admiral Evan-Thomas until he passed on the opposite course so that the 5 Battle Squadron did not turn north until 1754hrs. At 1744hrs Vizeadmiral Hipper ordered his ships to change target to the battleships and two minutes later *Valiant* was heavily shaken by a near miss, and at the same time *Barham* received a hit from *Lützow* adjacent to the aft conning tower, which caused much damage to light structures. At 1751hrs and again at 1755hrs Vizeadmiral Hipper signalled for course north. As his cruisers turned *Seydlitz* was hit at 1757hrs by a torpedo fired by one of the British destroyers, either *Petard* or *Turbulent*. Aboard *Seydlitz* they had observed two torpedoes approaching and only one could be avoided. The torpedo struck in compartment XIII, directly below the turret A in the bow. A large hole was torn in the hull below the armoured belt but although bowed the torpedo bulkhead held firm, and only the wing passage and protective bunker filled with water. For the damage control personnel it was a repeat performance of the events of 24 April, and *Seydlitz* could hold her place in the line at the unit speed.

Korvettenkapitän Foerster wrote:

Towards 5.30hrs the English destroyers broke through their line and rushed to attack us. Thereon the II Artillerie Offizier, Axel Lowe, allowed his medium artillerie to shoot and many of *Seydlitz* shells landed among the advancing destroyers. To repulse the English destroyer attack our torpedobootes counter attacked and a wild melee developed between the two cruiser lines, a wonderfully beautiful picture of a modern sea battle. However, there was no time in battle to ponder; suddenly there was a gigantic bang in the vicinity of the command tower, I flew high and bashed my head against something above; red appeared before my eyes. The ship put itself hard over and only slowly righted itself. What had happened? At first I believed that a heavy shell had struck near the command tower and thought of the sheep, as the managing Offizieres who assembled in the command tower were referred to in our peacetime shooting training. In this training events were called thus; 'Damage so and so, the sheep live.' We lived also, and this was a comforting feeling, but I feared for myself because I had received a sharp blow in the area of my eyes. In a moment I confirmed through the observation glasses that both by eyes were in order, but the red glimmer of blood ran down my forehead straight into my eyes. I could continue. The English battleships had meanwhile arrived within range and could intervene in the battle; the first 38cm shell rushed at us and we lay in the concentrated fire of double the number of ships as us, with considerably heavier artillery, which was uncomfortable. Then in the south the dead straight line of big ships came in sight, and with 'utmost power' the battle line steamed nearer to intervene. At this moment the English fire paused, as they turned away to the north. We turned before the head of our main body and took up the battle on a northerly course.

I learned later that the great crash had been caused by a torpedo hit in the foreship. It had not caused us much damage, only the outer hull side was penetrated; inside the so called torpedo bulkhead had successfully kept the damage away from the ship's interior, so that no water invaded; our battle capability was not impaired in the least.[37]

As early as 1709hrs Vice Admiral Beatty conveyed a signal for the Flotilla Leader *Champion*, via *Princess Royal* as *Lion*'s wireless telegraphy station was out of order: 'Attack the enemy with torpedoes.' By way of explanation he signalled a minute later to *Princess Royal*: 'Main W/T out of action...' *Champion* logged reception of this signal at 1816hrs, but nevertheless at 1715hrs the British destroyers were steaming out ahead of their battle cruisers in order to gain an attacking position. Unfortunately, in doing so they became scattered and disorganized. After ordering the attack *Champion* made no attempt to lead or support the attack with her 6 inch cannon but the commander of the 2 LCS, Commodore Goodenough, did order *Nottingham* to support the attack at 1715hrs, but this resulted in the light cruiser 'barging' through the flotillas, causing more confusion. The order of the 10th and 13th Flotillas was *Nestor*, *Nomad*, *Nicator*, *Narborough*, *Pelican*, *Turbulent*, *Nerissa* and *Termagent*, with *Moorsom* catching up quickly. *Obdurate* had fallen behind and *Moresby* and *Onslow* were still catching up after being escorts for *Engadine*. *Nottingham* barged through between *Pelican* and *Petard* and the rear four destroyers had to manoeuvre to avoid being rammed.

On seeing the British destroyers making for the head of their line the II Leader of Torpedobootes (II FdT), Kommodore Heinrich, aboard the small cruiser *Regensburg*, ordered a counter attack by the IX TBF. At 1726hrs on *Regensburg* the red pennant 'Z' was hoist, the signal for the torpedobootes to attack, and at the same time the optical signal was given: 'IX Flottille Ran!' At the same moment the *V28* made the optical signal 'Torpedobootes to the attack!' The word 'Ran' simply means attack, or go at it, and was used frequently in battle. When the Imperial Navy was in its infancy many Offizieres were drafted from the Armee, and they brought with them the term 'Ran!', which simply meant 'have at them'. As the British destroyers approached Vizeadmiral Hipper altered course away to the SE and reduced speed, then ESE, then east, before at 1741hrs orders were given for course SW.

A vicious destroyer-torpedoboote engagement followed. *Nomad* was hit once and brought to a stop by a shell in the engine room, whilst *Obdurate* was hit twice. At about 1734hrs the German *V27* was hit twice and unluckily the main steam pipe was ruptured. The *S36* was damaged by splinters whilst *V29* was hit by a torpedo fired from *Petard*. About 1738hrs two torpedoes passed under the crippled *Nomad*. Soon the *Regensburg* and four G–Bootes of the 3 HF joined the battle, whilst on the British side *Nottingham* fired five 6 inch gun salvoes at long range.

Kommodore Heinrich, the II Leader of Torpedobootes (II FdT) wrote:

1726hrs. With a brief clearing a reasonably accurate measurement of the enemy head could be carried out. The distance to the line was found to be 100hm. The range was transmitted to the IX Flottille with searchlight and cone signals and with searchlight and the flag signal 'Z Vor' the IX Flottille was ordered to the attack.

The Flottille Chief[38] had at the same moment recognized the necessity of the attack and gave up an unobtrusive attack and with the 'Z vor' signal ran out. The attack was made under heavy enemy fire.

1730hrs. As the running out of the IX Flottille began, ahead of the enemy head lay enemy destroyers (15–20) in a curve from E to N. Their intention was to repulse the IX Flottille or else an attack on the I AG. For the first aim there was an abundance.

To cover the attack of the IX Flottille I ordered *Regensburg* to push forward. The 3 Half Flottille accompanied.

The enemy light cruisers turned away to the NW, after they received some hits and fires. At the head of the running out destroyers one was badly damaged by the fire of *Regensburg*, so that it remained lying still. (1 mast, 4 funnels, forward completely fine, the boat appeared to be especially long). Another destroyer was damaged by the artillerie fire of the IX Flottille (*S52*) and was destroyed by a torpedo shot. In addition a further destroyer was thought to have been destroyed by the artillerie fire of the IX Flottille.

With *Regensburg*, *G101* and *G104* I pushed so far forward to the SW that the damaged bootes of the IX Flottille could withdraw from the greater part of the enemy fire. It was therewith possible that *V26* and *S35* could close with the bootes *V27* and *V29* and take over the entire crews.

1737hrs. The battle was concluded. The light forces of the enemy turned away to the NW and I went onto a NE course with *Regensburg*, *G101* and *G104*.[39]

Korvettenkapitän Goehle, commander of the IX Flottille, wrote:

Several large ships (4–5) come in sight in the NW, which intervene in the battle. At the same time the I AG moves nearer en-echelon, and it was assumed a decision against the battle cruisers was to be brought about, so intend an inconspicuous attack, each boot launching 2 torpedoes. Approximately 3 English light cruisers and 20 destroyers run out against the Flottille. Turn away at 95hm: immediately thereon there was a battle with the cruisers and destroyers. One destroyer was destroyed by *S52* with a destroyer shot.

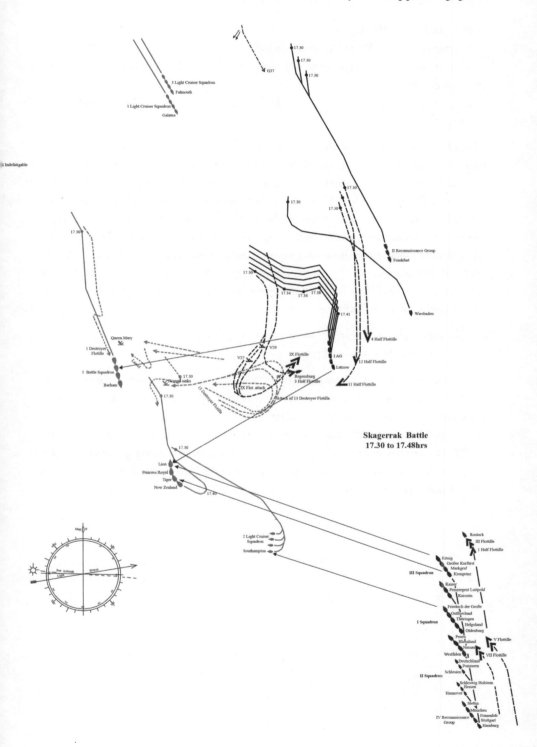

3 Light Cruiser Squadron
Falmouth

1 Light Cruiser Squadron
Galatea

G57

17.30
17.30
17.30

Indefatigable

17.30

17.30

17.30

17.30
17.30

II Reconnaissance Group
Frankfurt

Wiesbaden

17.30

17.34 17.36 17.38

17.41

4 Half Flottille

Queen Mary

1 Destroyer
Flotilla

V29

V27

IX Flottille

1 AG
Lützow

12 Half Flottille

5 Battle Squadron

Barham

17.30

Wiesbaden sinks

13 Destroyer Flotilla

IX Flot. attack

Regensburg
3 Half Flottille

11 Half Flottille

Attack of 13 Destroyer Flotilla

17.30

**Skagerrak Battle
17.30 to 17.48hrs**

17.30

Lion
Princess Royal
Tiger
New Zealand

17.40

Mag N

Sun Azimuth
Light

Bearing

2 Light Cruiser
Squadron

Southampton

Rostock
III Flottille
1 Half Flottille

König
Großer Kurfürst
Markgraf
Kronprinz

III Squadron

Kaiser
Prinzregent Luitpold
Kaiserin
Friedrich der Große

Ostfriesland
Thüringen
Helgoland
Oldenburg

I Squadron

Posen
Rheinland
Nassau
Westfalen

V Flottille

Deutschland
Pommern
Schlesien

VII Flottille

II Squadron

Schleswig Holstein
Hessen
Hannover

Stettin
München

IV Reconnaissance
Group

Frauenlob
Stuttgart
Hamburg

V29 and *V27* fall out.

Numerous torpedo tracks were sighted.

The result of the torpedo attack was not observed: the enemy line swung away after the shots.

Our own Main Body comes in sight in the SE, and the battle develops again to the NW.[40]

The rescue work of *V26* and *S35* was one of the finest exploits of this great battle… *V26*, skilfully handled by Kapitänleutnant Köhler, came alongside *V27* and rescued her entire crew, including two badly wounded men. Then, about 1738hrs she sank *V27* with gunfire, proceeded alongside *V29* and took off part of the crew of that vessel. The *S35*, Kapitänleutnant Ihn, rescued the remainder in an equally gallant manner at about 1748hrs. Their rescue work was performed while under heavy gunfire from the British destroyers, in particular *Obdurate, Morris, Nerissa* and *Termagant. Regensburg* and II Flottille covered *V26* and *S35* in fine style, scoring two 10.5cn hits on *Obdurate*, which had closed to within 3000m.[41]

The German torpedobootes were also supported by the heavy ships, as Korvettenkapitän Paschen describes:

After the blowing up of *Queen Mary,* which I could not see because of the limited field of vision of my periscope (our target was the leading ship), a violent torpedoboote battle developed between the two lines, and the II Artillerie Offizier finally had the opportunity to join the hot activity, but my target was usually completely concealed. At this time seemingly *Lion* has again assumed the lead, and presently we also again take him under fire, as we always fire on the foremost ship.[42]

Chapter 4

Vizeadmiral Scheer Intervenes

Even as the destroyer versus torpedoboat battle raged between the lines Commodore Goodenough was pushing ahead to the SE with his 2 Light Cruiser Squadron. At 1730hrs his position as an advanced reconnaissance unit paid a handsome dividend as he reported: 'Urgent: one enemy cruiser bearing SE, steering NE,' followed by his position. Two minutes later *Birmingham* reported by semaphore to Goodenough that she had sighted a four-funnelled cruiser, which *Southampton* immediately challenged, however getting no response. It was *Rostock*, the flagship of the I FdT, Kommodore Michelsen, which was the vanguard of the High Sea Fleet. Then at 1738hrs *Southampton* sent the electrifying signal: 'Urgent. Priority. Have sighted the enemy battle fleet bearing approximately SE, course of enemy N. My position Lat. 56°34′ N, Long 6°20′ E.' In the same instant the cruiser *Champion* gave a more detailed report: 'Course of enemy's battle Fleet is ENE, single line ahead. Van dreadnoughts. Bearing of centre SE. My position Lat. 56°51′ N, Long 5°46′ E.'[1] This news came as a great surprise to Vice Admiral Beatty and Admiral Jellicoe, who up until that moment had supposed the whereabouts of the High Sea Fleet to be in Wilhelmshaven, as reported by Room 40 and Naval Intelligence. During the morning the Director of Operations, Captain Thomas Jackson, had enquired where the direction finding stations placed the call sign DK, the call sign of Vizeadmiral Scheer's flagship. He was informed that DK was in Wilhelmshaven and the Chief of the Admiralty War Staff, acting Vice Admiral Oliver, signalled Admirals Beatty and Jellicoe to that effect at 1330hrs, saying '… directional's place flagship in Jade at 11.10am GMT' (1210hrs MEZ).

At 1742 *Lion* remarked that the enemy battle fleet had been sighted ahead, and at 1745hrs directed *Princess Royal* to report to Admiral Jellicoe 'Urgent. Priority. Have sighted enemy's battle fleet bearing SE. My position Lat. 56°36′ N, Long 6°04′ E.' In the meantime, at 1740hrs, Vice Admiral Beatty had ordered his battle cruisers to alter course in succession 16 points to starboard, that is 180°, and hoist the recall for the destroyers. By 1746hrs the British battle cruisers had turned north at 22 knots speed, and would close on Admiral Jellicoe's Grand Fleet. At 1748hrs *Lion* signalled the 5 Battle Squadron with flags to turn 16 points to starboard. As Beatty turned north the Flotillas and 1 and 3 Light Cruiser Squadrons followed the turn and formed a vanguard ahead of the battle cruisers. The 2 LCS pushed further south to the SW to determine the speed, course and composition of the German forces, and if possible deliver a torpedo attack. In the event only *Nottingham* fired one torpedo at 1740hrs at 140hm range. When the German ships opened fire at 1748hrs Goodenough's 2 LCS finally turned away to the north.

Meanwhile, at 1750hrs *Lion* remarked: 'Passed 5 Battle Squadron on opposite course.' The reason for this was that *Lion* did not haul down the 1748hrs signal, therefore the executive order, to the 5 BS until after the two flagships had passed, and therefore Rear Admiral Evan-Thomas' 5 BS did not turn until at least between 1754 and 1758hrs. Once again there had been a mistake in *Lion*'s signalling department and procedures. At 1744hrs Vizeadmiral Hipper ordered his ships to change target to the battleships and 2 minutes later *Valiant* was heavily shaken by a near miss, and at the same time *Barham* received a hit from *Lützow* adjacent to the aft conning tower which caused much damage to light structures. At 1751hrs and again at 1755hrs Vizeadmiral Hipper signalled for course north. As the I AG turned north *Seydlitz* was struck by a torpedo, as related previously.

As the Panzerkreuzer of Vizeadmiral Hipper were proceeding down the Jade into the North Sea the battleships of High Sea Fleet were making final preparations to put to sea. At 0315hrs *König*, *Kaiserin* and *Großer Kurfürst*, among others, weighed anchor, followed at 0320hrs by *Ostfriesland*. The official time the Main Body put to sea is given as 0330hrs, Middle European Time (MEZ). The III Squadron, under the command of Kontreadmiral Paul Behncke aboard *König*, led the long line of battleships, followed by the I Squadron, under the command of Vizeadmiral Ehrhard Schmidt, aboard *Ostfriesland*. At 0500hrs the I and III Squadrons were joined by the II Squadron, which had come from the Elbe river and were under the command of Kontreadmiral Mauve, aboard the pre-dreadnought battleship *Deutschland*, which had previously been the fleet flagship. Aboard *Hessen* was Seekadett Günther Schütz, who wrote the following about the putting to sea of the II Squadron:

> On the next day at about 0445hrs we were awakened by the Bootsmann Sturm. After we got up we were told that we should go on watch in the fore- and main mast. Of course we were very pleased, because from up there we got to see a whole lot more than from anywhere else. We had already run out about 0330hrs and as we climbed the mast about 0515hrs we were abeam of Neuwerk. About 0545hrs Helgoland was in sight. It was the first time in my life that I had got to see this island, which had become so important in the war. We got closer and closer, and the outline got clearer and finally about 0645hrs Helgoland was abeam and we could quite clearly see the entire island. In our observation position a fairly strong wind was blowing, but today everything was indifferent to us. They felt almost nothing as they were busy with important tasks, because now we joined with the III and the I Squadrons, that came in an endless long line ahead from Wilhelmshaven.
>
> About 0700hrs finally all three Squadrons were in line ahead and *Hessen* found herself as the 'rope' of the German Fleet, we were in total 22 battleships

and were in the series III Squadron, I Squadron and II Squadron. Of the cruiser squadron and other reconnaissance ships nothing could be seen because of the great range.[2]

Although *Hessen* found herself as 'rope', or last in line, later the positions changed and *Hannover*, flagship of the 2 Admiral of the II Squadron, Kontreadmiral Freiherr von Dalwigk zu Lichtenfels, took up the position of last in line.

The mood aboard the German battleships was somewhat sombre, as on many occasions they had put to sea in anticipation of encountering the enemy, but had always been disappointed. Korvettenkapitän Studt, Navigation Offizier of SMS *Kaiser*, had the following to say:

The Fleet Chief, Vizeadmiral Scheer, had scheduled an advance for the entire fleet into northern waters of the German Bight for that day. We had already repeated such operations in the hope of encountering the enemy but they had always been blows in the air. The English had got wind of our plan and perhaps did not have the intention to come out to battle. We had often bombarded their coastal towns, infested their channels with mines without once ever encountering a reaction! Would it be different this time? We could quietly confess: Nobody onboard, not even the highest lookout, could know that this time it was serious. The crew made their own conclusions from the little touches, they recognized that the peace steering position, a rain shelter with glass windows built around the forward conning tower, was not rigged because of the splinter danger in battle. The service on deck moved in the usual way, the chefs peacefully prepared in the kitchens, the mess stewards set the tables with the fragile plates and glasses on the white table clothes. No, it did not look like a serious case. Even during the afternoon, as the ship passed Amrun Bank, an idle peace and quiet dominated on board. Half of the crew found themselves on war watch stations, just as with all happenings outside the river mouths, owing to the submarine and mine danger. From all gun positions, from the masts and command position the Offizieres and lookouts scanned the surface of the water, and frequently nothing had been sighted during all the past months, but caution had its place as the enemy could not be underestimated....

The watch and duty free crew were for the greater part on deck, where it was pleasant in the occasional sunshine, despite the fresh northwest breeze, more so than in the artificially lit accommodation rooms below deck. Even the stoker watch had ventured out of their spacious accommodation on the armoured deck into the daylight. In the positions protected from the wind, where the funnel mantel exuded a cosy warmth, a colourful band of people had assembled. Beautiful uniforms, such as in peacetime, were no longer worn by these people. The patched jerkin, the worn cloth caps, and many stained blouses and pants would not exist if soap had not had to be saved. However, the mood did not suffer because of this, just as with the food supply, which diminished month after month, and was also felt on the menus of the warships, just as felt in the Fatherland... Now they stood on deck, smoking their pipes and surveying the scene.[3]

At 1610hrs the High Sea Chief gave the order to 'clear ship for battle' and ordered 'all speed', course north. This order brought joy aboard SMS *Kaiser*. Korvettenkapitän Studt wrote:

> It was 4.06pm as on the flagship the memorable signal went high: 'Clear ships for battle.'
> Now everyone knew: it was serious and the two yearlong battle would come to the outbreak of blows.
> 'Clear ship for battle' was called, piped and shouted through the whole ship. That was enthusiasm! 'Men, this time it is happening.' A pat on the back that could almost crack a bone and then he goes to his battle station. The musicians came not now, to blow the often practised clear ship signal, the torrent of men, swirling through one another, rushed to their stations. It continued only a few minutes and already the first reports came from the individual battle stations: 'Artillerie is clear', 'middle bulkhead crew in position', 'Torpedo arm clear', 'Combat dressing station established', reported the heads to the conning tower and from here also to the Central Command Position, where the I Offizier collected the incoming reports and messages. After 12 minutes the report was given to the Commander: 'Ship is clear for battle'.
> *Kaiser* is ready.[4]

At 1711hrs *Friedrich der Große* signalled optically for the fleet to close up to a distance between ships of just 500m. Vizeadmiral Scheer was assembling his battleships into combat formation. At 1730hrs the leading ship of the line, SMS *König*, sighted battling ships in the NNW and the situation soon became clear; to starboard were German Panzerkreuzers, and to port were two groups of enemy ships on a southern course, being brought to the German Main Body. Destroyers and torpedobootes were battling between the lines whilst cruisers could be seen pushing on ahead. The battle fleet increased speed from 15 to 17 knots at 1738hrs and soon the report arrived from *König*'s foretop that the British ships had turned onto a northerly course. At 1742hrs the signal was given for the Divisions to turn 2 points to port to bring the enemy closer. Three minutes later at 1745hrs *Friedrich der Große* ordered 'fire distribution from the right, ship against ship'. Then after a further minute came the order 'open fire'.

The leading German battleship, *König*, opened fire at 1748hrs on *Lion* at a range of 188hm. After a few salvos fire was ceased because the range was too great at 192hm and the target was changed to *Tiger*. From 1800hrs a destroyer was taken under fire with the medium calibre artillery at a range of 120hm. Then at 1810hrs *König* opened fire on a British battleship at a range of 170hm.

The next ship in line was *Großer Kurfürst* and she opened fire at 1749hrs on the second ship from the right, *Princess Royal*, at a range of 188hm. From 1756hrs the medium artillery fired on one of the light cruisers of the 2 LCS at a range of 120hm. At 1758hrs *Großer Kurfürst* changed target to *Valiant* at a range of 174hm. At 1809hrs *Großer Kurfürst* received her first damage when a 15 inch shell from *Malaya* landed short and splinters struck the ship forward. At 1816hrs *Großer Kurfürst* ceased fire as the range was too great.

SMS *Markgraf* was the next ship in the German line and opened fire at 1748hrs, firing at *Tiger* at a range of 170hm. However, the British ships were quickly running out of range and at 1756hrs the range was already 183hm. At 1803hrs a heavy shell impacted just 50m away, shaking *Markgraf* with a heavy vibration. At 1825hrs *Markgraf* ceased fire on this target.

Kronprinz opened fire on a light cruiser with one mast and four funnels at 1751hrs, at a range of 170hm. At 1800hrs she ceased fire on this target but from 1808 to 1821hrs fired on the last ship of 5 Battle Squadron, *Malaya*, at a range of 170hm, using semi-armoured piercing shells and then armoured piercing. At 1821hrs the range was 195hm, and hits were thought to have been observed.

The next astern was *Kaiser* and at 1747hrs she opened fire on *Southampton*, but already ceased fire at 1756hrs.

The Artillerie Offizier counted, still there are four units, one, two, three, four. That was just enough for the four ships of the 5 Division standing ahead of us. However, soon further targets appeared, their 4 low sloping funnels and masts in the same direction gave the impression of speed. 'On the light cruiser with 4 funnels and one mast, 146 hundred, defection right, fire!' The cannon had already been swung in the expected direction, now it only lacked the push of a button…. The first salvo crashed towards the enemy, a loud hurrah accompanied from all gun positions. Through clever turns and speed changes the enemy cruisers targeted by us avoided being hit.[5]

Astern of *Kaiser* came *Prinzregent Luitpold*, and at 1749hrs she opened fire on a *Lion* class battle cruiser.

1747hrs. At this time the enemy still stands 200hm away. The individual ships can still not be clearly made out. They rise against the setting sun on the hazy horizon and only later were recognised as battle cruisers of the *Indefatigable* and *Lion* classes.

1749hrs. Fire was opened with semi-armoured piercing shells against the best recognisable target at a range of 204hm.

At 1752hrs the enemy turned onto a NW course to a running battle.

1758hrs. Signal: 'Division wise battle turn 2 points to port, onto NW.'

At 1804hrs cease fire, as the enemy stood out so poorly against the hazy horizon that it was impossible to see the impacting shells. During the course of the battle the enemy was recognised as a battle cruiser of the *Lion* class.

The impacts lay predominantly short, hits were not observed. In total 8 salvos were fired at 204 to 195hm.

At 1808hrs fire was renewed on a battle cruiser of the *Indefatigable* class at 175hm.[6]

The fact that *Prinzregent Luitpold* was able to fire at a range of 204hm means that she must have already had her gun mountings modified to allow an elevation of 16 degrees, giving an increase of maximum range from 191hm to 204hm.

At 1750hrs the battleship *Kaiserin* opened fire on the battleship furthest to the left.

Fire opened on the battleship furthest left at 295°, at the great range of 192hm. In a straddling salvo a hit was observed.

1758hrs. Fire was again ceased, as the range was too great. Through two battle turns by Division each of 2 points to port it was attempted to close nearer the enemy en-echelon. This succeeds only for a brief time, as the enemy moved away more en-echelon.[7]

Therefore at 1758hrs *Kaiserin* had already ceased fire. As reported in the war diary of *Friedrich der Große* this battleship opened fire on the 2 Light Cruiser Squadron, at 1748hrs, however fire was ceased just three minutes later at 1751hrs because the enemy had moved out of range at 190hm.

The first battleship of the I Squadron was SMS *Ostfriesland*, flagship of Vizeadmiral Ehrhard Schmidt, and at 1751hrs she opened fire on the leading light cruiser, *Southampton*, at a range of 180–172hm. From 1812hrs to 1817hrs fire was also undertaken on the second and third light cruisers at a range of 180–188hm.

At 1745hrs *Thüringen* opened fire on the second cruiser from the right, *Dublin*, at a range of 192hm. However, at 1758hrs fire ceased because the range was too great.

Helgoland opened fire at 1750hrs at a range of 190hm on the second cruiser from the left, *Birmingham*, but by 1755hrs had ceased fire as the cruiser had turned away to the west and was out of range.

At 1752hrs the next battleship in line, *Oldenburg*, opened fire on a light cruiser of the 2 Light Cruiser Squadron, and thought she had seen an explosion cloud aboard the target. The range quickly increased and *Oldenburg* ceased fire. Nevertheless, *Oldenburg*'s combat report states that she also took the leading battleship under fire about this time, but this target also moved out of range.

The battleship *Posen* opened fire on the light cruiser furthest to the left, therefore *Nottingham*, at 1752hrs at a range of 160–170hm. After a few salvos fire was ceased because several ships were firing on *Nottingham* at the same time and *Posen* did not want to disrupt the observation of the fall of shot. And as *Posen*'s war diary said: 'The cruiser understandably attempted to throw off the fire and withdraw by using a zigzag course.'

At 1746hrs *Rheinland* opened fire on *Birmingham*. *Rheinland*'s war diary recorded the following:

1746hrs. The heavy artillerie opens fire on the third cruiser (198–204hm), 4 salvos. The enemy made energetic course alterations. Secure shooting in was difficult because of the smoke concealment and the numerous impacts of the other ships.

1750hrs. Cease fire, the enemy is out of range.

1805hrs. Open fire on the same target (192–197hm). Two salvos straddle. Effective shooting was made difficult through enemy movements and smoke development.[8]

The following ship, *Nassau*, opened fire on a light cruiser at 1750hrs. Fire was continued for 20 minutes with the heavy artillery at a range of from 185 to 209hm, and was finally ceased at 1810hrs as the range had become too great.

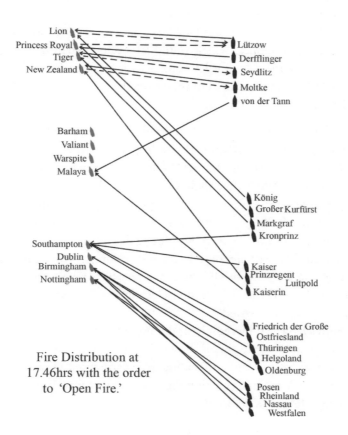

Fire Distribution at
17.46hrs with the order
to 'Open Fire.'

At 1750hrs the tail ship of the 2 Division, *Westfalen*, opened fire on the second ship from the left, a light cruiser with four funnels, *Birmingham*. At a range of 155hm to 165hm *Westfalen* fired a total of six 28cm armour-piercing shells. Three minutes later *Westfalen* received a signal to operate on the last enemy ship, and at 1758hrs changed target to the left. Thirty-eight 28cm armour-piercing shots were fired at ranges between 168hm to 194hm. It is noteworthy that *Westfalen* was yet to be fitted with RW (Direction Indicator) equipment. The single result of all this firing on the 2 Light Cruiser Squadron was a 28cm shell hit on *Southampton* at 1750hrs, to port aft.

As the range from the II Squadron to the enemy totalled approximately 250hm the pre-dreadnought battleships were unable to intervene in the battle.

After the I AG had made a 16-point turn to starboard, that is towards the enemy, at 1757hrs Vizeadmiral Hipper signalled optically for 'fire distribution from right, ship against ship'. Therefore *Lützow*, *Derfflinger*, *Seydlitz* and *Moltke* renewed their fire on the British battle cruisers, which were already under fire from *König*, *Großer Kurfürst*, *Markgraf* and *Prinzregent Luitpold*. The artillery battle continued with increasing ferocity. Already at 1750hrs *Seydlitz* had been hit by a 15 inch projectile, probably fired from *Barham*, which struck the forecastle deck making a large hole. Then at 1806 and 1808, and then again at 1810hrs *Seydlitz* was struck by three more 15 inch calibre shells. The first two shells also struck the forecastle and made further large holes in the deck, which would later allow much flooding, whilst the hit at 1810hrs struck right forward face of turret Bertha. An Offizier, Leutnant zur See Kurt Goebel, was stationed in turret Bertha and wrote the following in his unpublished *Experiences and Memories*:

> The battle pause did last for long, then briefly after the turn the fire was again opened at a range of 160–184hm. Battle to port in direction 280°. We shot through the gap between the funnels. The most difficult time for our ship was still yet to come. Shell after shell left the heavy barrels at the target which was invisible to us in the turret.... At the same time we lay in the barrage of hundreds and hundreds of 34 and 38cm shells of the most modern English Battle Cruiser Squadron. We were also hit again. Several times we could feel the heavy concussion with a strong burst and splinters. Three powerful shells penetrated in the foreship briefly after one another. There was unbelievable destruction and the earlier mentioned electrical station in the foreship was hereby finally totally destroyed.
>
> Two minutes later: An incredibly deafening burst next to me, fire appeared, a fearful concussion in the turret, it shook and vibrated. It was dark. I was violently thrown. Smoke and suffocating gas surrounded everyone, we could no longer breath. With a reflex action the new gasmask was ripped on. We only received them a few days before the battle. They were still alien to us.

A noiseless silence in the turret followed the fearful crash, then suddenly the nerve straining cries of the wounded…It was still dark in the turret. The smoke took the breath and prevented sight. Only weakly could I recognise the red glow of an electric bulb…Now the munition must detonate! Turret Cäsar was flooded. Again the crying…Then again quiet. Some wanted to throw open the turret hatch, to expel the gas and allow fresh air, but also certain death. … Then correctly the turret Offizier ordered: 'No one to leave the turret.' The order was followed.

The right tube of our gun barrel seemed to be shot through. It would no longer move. The situation itself was not yet clear. With machine power the turret turned towards the enemy with our barrels. An English 38cm shell had penetrated the front wall of our gun turret and exploded in the penetration opening. There was a great deal of devastation.

Involuntarily one fumbled to the next frame or caisson, perhaps only with the conviction to obtain something of the surroundings. The order not to quit the turret was repeated, loud so it could be heard through the gasmasks. We standing inside had the impression that at any moment the munitions in the turret would detonate and all would be blown up. However, thank God, no explosion occurred. The smoke cleared only slowly. The lamps were clearly visible… The situation in the turret was still uncertain. The left barrel would again shoot. No orders came from the Artillerie Direction Position. Was the telephone shot through? I groped my way back to the turret hood, where the telephone was. The Order Transmitter appeared to be wounded, he was not at his post. I attempted to listen to the service but could perceive not one sound…. The insane noise of the turret hit had completely stunned my ears. They failed to respond to the fine sounds of the telephone.

Only a few minutes had passed since the explosion of the English shell. It was again bright in the turret as the smoke moved more and more, and damage was not to be seen from the place I stood. The pumps to elevate the right gun had failed. They were changed over to the other gun and the gun could again be forcibly elevated. At the moment of the hit it was in its cradle and was about to be loaded. For our gun the position was a dangerous situation, as without elevating the guns the turret could not be swung past the forward funnel. If the battle went over to the right side of the ship we could no longer shoot, and also offered only our weakly armoured rear wall as a target for the enemy. At least the left barrel could continue to shoot.[9]

Seydlitz had taken the third ship in the British line, *Tiger*, as target and at 1758hrs scored a hit with a shell which passed through the aft funnel near the top. Around this time aboard *Tiger* the right gun of A turret broke down.

When the I AG resumed fire on the British battle cruisers *Lützow* took *Lion* as target once again and obtained shell hits at 1759, 1801 and 1802hrs. The first shell struck the aft superstructure and detonated in the galley. The upper deck was holed and some 4 inch gun cordite was set on fire. Of the next two hits one struck the sick bay skylight at station 283 and exploded against the port side armour inside the sick bay. The sick bay was wrecked and there was much damage to light structures, and there was much smoke development. The other shell passed through the main mast without exploding and the mast was then in danger of toppling.

After the turn to the north there is some confusion about the target of *Derfflinger*. The notes of the port Transmitting Station report the following for this period:

1751 to 1753hrs. Ship turns hard to starboard. Quickly change for battle to port. Deflection +-0, on the second battle cruiser to the left. Deflection left 40. Fire distribution from the right, 180hm, deflection left 10, 170hm, 176hm, deflection 1, fire, 172hm, 180hm fire, fire, 188hm fire. Train on the waterline, 178hm, fire. Medium artillerie deflection +-0, fire.

1800hrs. Ship runs at 21 knots. Medium artillerie on a destroyer 130hm, with bearing indicator, fire. Training point, waterline.

1807hrs. 120hm, 130hm, training point upper edge of bridge, fire. Deflection 4, fire, fire, deflection 4 to the left, training point upper edge of the funnels, fire.

1811hrs. Port medium artillerie hold, 174hm, heavy artillerie fire, medium artillerie on the destroyer 130hm, fire.

1813hrs. Medium artillerie hold. Heavy artillerie fire, fire, fire. Medium artillerie follow, fire.

1816hrs. Ship runs at 21 knots. Heavy artillerie, fire, fire, fire. 183hm, fire, 197hm. Target is second battleship from the right, fire.

1818hrs. Fire pause.[10]

So after the turn to the north *Derfflinger* continued to shoot at the British battle cruisers, but at some time later changed target to the 5 Battle Squadron, possibly *Valiant*.

After the turn to the north the next ship in line, *Moltke*, took *New Zealand* as a target, but reported that due to unfavourable visibility conditions the range could not be measured accurately.

The last ship of the I AG, *von der Tann*, took the ship furthest to the left under fire, the battleship *Malaya*, whilst the medium calibre guns took a destroyer as target. At this time *von der Tann* only had two 28cm cannon in action. Turret A had been jammed by a shell hit, turret C was likewise jammed because of damage from the hit at 1723hrs and then at 1736hrs both guns of turret B had failed to run out because of overheating. Unfortunately, at 1818hrs the two guns of turret D failed to run out shortly after one another. Now *von der Tann* had no heavy artillery remaining in action, but Kapitän zur See Zenker held his ship in line to draw the fire of the British and prevent them doubling up on any of the other ships.

The I AO, Korvettenkapitän Mahrholz reported:

> The intervention of our battleships in the battle caused great enthusiasm, and came at the right time, and with a swing turn the Panzerkreuzers placed themselves at the head of the High Sea Fleet. With the only turret firing I decided to target the last ship of the 5 Battle Squadron. I adhered closely to the measurements, as only now and then had I observation, whereby I watched sharply for the fall of shot, and only made an improvement when I observed the impacts perfectly. Soon after 6 o'clock, with the sound of the fall of shot indicator, I saw flames spring up from my target, not so high as with *Indefatigable*, but heavy fires on the ship followed and this success again gave me hope, that I could contribute some success with my one remaining turret. For the hundredth time turret Bautzen was asked whether the barrels would soon be delivered to the firing position, and still the same answer in the negative came. Because of the smoke there was nothing more to be seen of the enemy. Then suddenly came destroyers, which the medium artillerie opened fire on and I directed my turret onto them and fired. Finally, further shooting where the fall of shot could be securely observed. Then after a few shots instead of the clang of the fire bells there was nothing but the report that also in turret Düppel the barrels would no longer return to the firing position. With a heavy heart I reported to the Commander the falling out of the entire heavy artillerie for an indefinite time, and a short council of war took place through the vision slits. Result: the ship remains in the unit, in order to relieve the other ships of fire distribution from the enemy. Since our own artillerie had no effect, no consideration had to be made to take a steady course and the ship was manoeuvred to the impacts of the enemy heavy shells and was protected against further hits.[11]

After sighting the German Main Body and turning away to the north Vice Admiral Beatty ran off at a speed of 24 knots, and as the I AG was proceeding at 21 knots the British battle cruisers soon passed out of range and disappeared in conditions of poor visibility.

> Gradually the visibility becomes worse. The sun becomes a hindrance and occasionally also artificial smoke. In the north salvos come from the grey on grey, however, no glasses or cannon can hold the muzzle flashes (as targets). There is nothing to be seen of the enemy![12]

At 1802hrs Vizeadmiral Hipper called for a speed reduction, repeating this order at 1806hrs. The German battle cruisers, in German parlance Panzerkreuzer or Großer Kreuzer, had been designed to a different conceptual model to their British counterparts in that they were designed so as to be able to take their place in the line and fight against enemy battleships. If the British battle cruisers had attempted to engage battleships they would have been destroyed in short order. Nevertheless, now the Panzerkreuzer of the I AG found themselves engaging the newest and most powerful battleships in the world, the 15 inch gunned *Queen Elizabeth* class. There could be no severer test for the I AG. At 1805hrs Rear Admiral Evan-Thomas signalled: 'Engage enemy's right 1 to 4.' Vizeadmiral Hipper commented:

> Now the III Squadron also attacked, but only the five forward most ships since the others could not intervene. The enemy now used his old trick to conduct the battle at the longest possible range, where our guns could not reach, at over 180hm. This succeeded because of his superior speed. So I had to move en-echelon, whereby gradually I came more astern and in the vicinity of the four fast *Malaya*s, and now they afflicted difficulties on me. Temporarily I had to cease fire on the battle cruisers and concern myself with the battleships. Now the enemy gradually turned our head around.[13]

Due to the gunfire smoke, smoke from destroyers, torpedobootes and water spray the haze between the two battle lines had thickened and Vice Admiral Beatty's battle cruisers could no longer be seen from the I AG. Between 1805hrs and 1810hrs fire erupted between the II AG and the 1 LCS, which was to starboard ahead of the 1 and 2 BCS, at a range of 116 to 140hm, before the latter turned away. By 1812hrs *Lion* had ceased fire. Of the battle cruisers *Lion* had been hit 10 times and *Tiger* had been struck 13 times. However, none of the remaining battle cruisers or battleships had been rendered unmanoeuvrable or had their speed reduced, although *Tiger* had been lucky in this regard, and *Lion* had nearly gone the way of *Queen Mary*. By 1810hrs Vice Admiral Beatty was outside effective gunfire range and Vizeadmiral Hipper's ships had to change target to the 5 Battle Squadron.

The ships of Rear Admiral Evan-Thomas' 5 Battle Squadron were showing clearly against the western horizon whilst the German ships were in haze and against the darker eastern horizon. Only when the sun shone through did the German ships stand out and then the German gunnery Offizieres were dazzled. The battleships of the 5 Battle Squadron were in an unenviable position of fighting the Panzerkreuzer of the I AG and some of the German battleships. At 1827hrs *Lützow* was firing on *Barham*, *Derfflinger* was firing on *Valiant*, *Seydlitz* was firing on *Warspite* and from 1800hrs *von der Tann* had been firing on *Malaya*.

When *König* resumed firing at 1810hrs it was against one of the battleships of the 5 Battle Squadron at a range of 170hm. At 1817hrs it was believed a hit was observed near the forward turret group and at 1828hrs a further hit was believed to

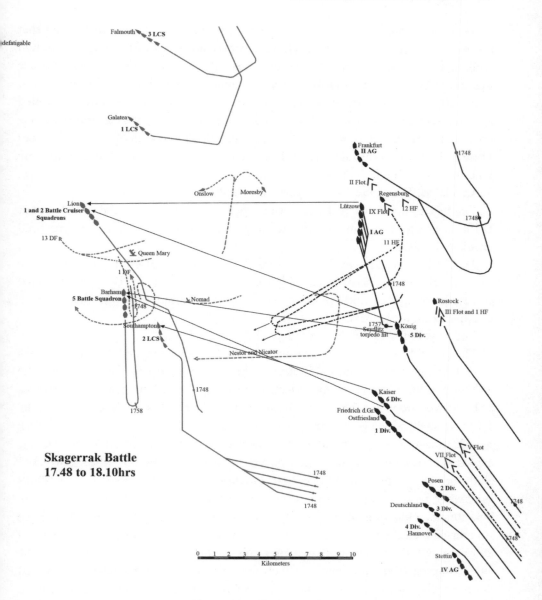

Skagerrak Battle
17.48 to 18.10hrs

have been observed. By 1830hrs *König* was firing with only the two forward turrets A and B and was pursuing at her highest speed, making 240 to 245 revolutions and from 1804hrs the supplemental oil firing was in use. At 1839hrs the first fall of shot arrived near *König* and just one minute later she had to cease fire as the range was too great. *König*'s targets had included *Lion*, *Tiger* and *Barham*.

At 1822hrs the heavy artillery of *Großer Kurfürst* again opened fire on the hitherto target, *Valiant*, at a range of 182 to 189hm with turrets A and B. Nevertheless fire was ceased a short time later at 1830hrs and there was a battle pause.

At 1825hrs *Markgraf* had ceased fire on *Tiger*, and it was not until 1853hrs that fire was again opened, on a battleship identified simply as of the *Queen Elizabeth* type, at a range of 170hm. Observation was difficult and after a short time fire was interrupted. At 1810hrs *Markgraf* was struck by a 15 inch shell to port aft at frame 20, which penetrated the joint of two armoured plates. Splinters travelled transversely across the ship and impacted against the starboard side, and there was flooding to port and starboard, but the shell hole was closed with a leak mat. Another 15 inch shell passed through the starboard derrick post without detonating and one other passed through the foremast.

As related, *Kronprinz* was firing on *Malaya* during this period.

The battleship *Kaiser* had been firing upon a light cruiser of the 2 LCS but at 1810hrs changed target to the last battleship in line. After 1835hrs *Kaiser* again fired on a light cruiser.

At 1808hrs *Prinzregent Luitpold* renewed fire on a battleship, thought to be *Malaya*, although noted as an *Indefatigable* class in her KTB, and continued at a range of 175hm until 1838hrs, when fire was ceased, after the British ships disappeared into the haze.

The target of *Kaiserin* during this period was *Barham*.

The fire of the German ships during this period was effective, and the I AG obtained several hits against Vice Admiral Beatty's battle cruisers, as related. The fire against the 5 Battle Squadron was even more effective during this time. After being hit by *Lützow* at 1746hrs *Barham* was struck another four times. At 1758hrs *Barham* was struck by a 30.5cm shell, which had a very destructive effect. The shell struck the upper deck outside the starboard 6 inch battery at 70–72 stations, making a hole 2ft 6in × 1ft 6in. It exploded on reaching the main deck, blowing a hole in it 7 feet in length and wrecked all fittings etc. in the vicinity. The dwarf bulkhead here was blown towards the ship's side, while fragments pierced the deck around the hole wrecking the medical store beneath, the bulkheads of this compartment being riddled by fragments. One large splinter pierced the longitudinal bulkhead just below the main deck, and penetrated down through the middle deck making a hole of similar dimensions and entered the lower conning tower, the floor of which was pierced by two fragments that passed down into the 6 inch magazine. The shell had a marked incendiary effect. The port and starboard 6 inch hoists were holed and flash flames passed to the No.2 casemate causing a serious fire and putting the gun crew out of action. The flash also passed down into the dynamo room on the platform deck and burned all the men there.

At 1801hrs a shell struck the aft superstructure abaft the main mast at station 176 to starboard. The shell exploded in the officers' WC and there was severe damage to light structures and the main wireless station was put out of action.

At 1808hrs a shell struck far aft at station 240 between the upper and main decks, detonating on contact with the main deck blowing a hole 7ft ×3ft 6in. A large hole 7ft × 2ft 6in was blown in the middle deck and fragments caused extensive damage to the main, middle and lower decks. Fire broke out in the cabins on the port side of the main deck and gutted them between 237 and 245 stations.

The last shell to hit struck at 1810hrs on the upper deck 50lbs (1¼ inch) plating outside the starboard 6 inch battery between 60 and 62 stations. The deck was holed 3ft 6in × 1ft 9in, the shell exploding between the upper and main decks, blowing a large hole in the latter. The dwarf longitudinal bulkhead was blown towards the ship's side, hinging about its lower edge. The main deck in the vicinity of the explosion was generally perforated by fragments of the shell, one large piece piercing the provision room bulkhead between the main and middle decks at 68 station.

Despite being targeted by several ships during this period *Valiant* remained unhit, although she was continuously straddled and was showered with water from short and over shots.

Warspite was hit three times during the turn to the north. A heavy calibre shell penetrated the upper strake of the armoured belt just below the waterline and detonated in the aft capstan flat. The explosion blew down bulkhead 237 and flooded both flats on the middle deck. The second hit struck near the stern on the waterline, below the Admiral's day cabin. A 4 ft ×3 ft hole was blown in the hull and a 20 foot long split was caused in the hull plates. This caused some flooding. Hit number three at this time penetrated the 6 inch upper strake of the armoured belt, just ahead of the foremost 6 inch gun on the starboard side. One large shell fragment came to rest in the magazine flooding cabinet thirty feet from the explosion of the shell. Some of these shells are thought to have come from *Seydlitz*.

During the subsequent run to the north *Warspite* was hit another six times. A heavy calibre shell struck the upper deck, port side, mid way between X and Y barbettes. A hole 7 feet 6 inches by 1 foot 8 inches was torn in the deck and the shell detonated in the aft casemate lobby. X magazine cooler was damaged and water from burst fire mains caused some flooding. Hit number five penetrated the port side upper belt at station 190, between the upper and main decks. The shell failed to detonate and broke into two pieces, one piece striking the 4 inch armour of X barbette tearing off a piece of armour, before deflecting downward into the Engineers' Workshop, where it killed three men of the number 5 fire brigade. The Executive Officer, Commander Walwyn, believed two shells might have struck because of the extent of the damage. The sixth hit struck the side plating just below the upper deck in line with the after part of Y barbette. The shell detonated 40 feet from impact on the main deck, blowing a hole 4ft 6in × 3ft. There was severe damage to internal structures and a hole 7ft × 3ft was blown in the side of the commander's cabin. The escape trunk to the steering compartment was badly damaged, allowing water into the trunk and flooding the steering compartment to a depth of 4 feet. Hit seven exploded on the centreline stanchion, wrecking the lobby. Hit number eight detonated in the Captain's pantry and hit nine apparently detonated right aft on the waterline, without causing much damage. It is not possible to determine which German ships were responsible for the majority of these hits.

The popular target *Malaya* also suffered badly during this time and during a seventeen–minute period she was hit a total of seven times. The first hit at 1820hrs is thought to have detonated just short of the 8 inch lower belt armour, just abaft A turret between stations 48 and 56. The armour was driven in slightly and the hull plating behind the armour was also driven in.

At 1827hrs X turret was struck on the roof. The projectile struck the 4¼ inch armour and detonated on impact. Although there were some small holes in the armour and the armoured roof was started up, clear of the turret walls, with many securing bolts sheared, the other damage was restricted to putting the range finder out of action.

Then at 1830hrs a projectile struck the lower boom stanchion and caused damage to the starboard forward superstructure.

Another shell at 1830hrs, probably from the same salvo, struck the forecastle deck between stations 92 and 95 to starboard immediately above the No.3 6 inch cannon. The deck planking was torn up and a hole made in the deck 5ft × 3ft with the adjacent superstructure being pierced in eight places by splinters. The forecastle deck beams at stations 90, 92 and 94 were broken and distorted, while the surrounding deck was set up to a maximum of 4 inches over an area of 10 square feet, all voice pipes and ventilation trunking beneath being carried away by the explosion of the shell, the upper deck also being set down a distance of 7 inches between 86 and 100 stations above the 6 inch battery where extensive damage was done generally, this being further increased by fire. The gun was completely carried away. The 1½ inch (60lb) bulkhead between No.2 and No.3 6 inch guns was pierced by a shell fragment, and the longitudinal bulkhead enclosing the canteen, cook's kitchen, vent to the boiler room, galley and drying room, was severely damaged for a length of 12 feet, and was holed in the boiler room vent by the nose of the projectile, which struck the armoured grating inside the vent and glanced off, piercing the bulkheads to the canteen and cooks kitchen. The top of the No.3 gun mounting was damaged, the right gun trunnion smashed and sights destroyed, while all electrical instruments and circuits for fire control, director firing etc. to this gun were destroyed. The instruments and circuits of the remaining guns in this battery, including several motors and their circuits were damaged by fire. The entire starboard side 6 inch casemate was put out of action by the ensuing fire and there were 102 casualties. The flash from the cordite fire passed down into the 6 inch shell room and only prompt action by the magazine crew prevented this magazine blowing up, which was adjacent to a 15 inch magazine and the detonation of which would have caused the loss of the ship. *Malaya* had had a very lucky escape indeed, just as *Lion* and *Tiger*.

Nevertheless, the next two hits at 1835hrs were also very damaging. Two 30.5cm shells struck the outer bottom plating between stations 92 and 95, and stations 95 and 100, to starboard immediately below the armour shelf. One shell detonated after impact with the inshot hole being 7 feet by 4 feet in extent and a small piece of armour was chipped out at the lower edge of the belt. The inner bottom was pierced by several large holes and the plate frames were badly torn and buckled. The torpedo bulkhead was bulged in between stations 91 and 100, but was not holed and the inner bulkhead was distorted.

The other 30.5cm shell made a large hole in the outer skin, however, it failed to explode and passed out through the double bottom, making another large hole. Flooding of the inner and outer oil bunkers between stations 82–100 and wing compartments 82–109, resulting from these two hits, caused *Malaya* to take up a 4° list to starboard within 10 minutes.

The hit for which the time is unknown was on the 6 inch side armour, between 48 and 56 stations, just above the main deck and between A and B turrets. The shell detonated on impact and pushed the armour in without penetrating and caused cracking and scalloping of the plate.

Malaya suffered a total of 65 dead, which included four civilians, and approximately 41 wounded.

At 1830hrs Rear Admiral Evan-Thomas signalled his ships for 'utmost speed'.

At 1750hrs *Lion* had passed the 5 Battle Squadron on the opposite course and two minutes late Vice Admiral Beatty signalled for a speed for his battle cruisers of 25 knots. Vizeadmiral Hipper had turned onto a northerly course at 1755hrs and only at 1758hrs did Rear Admiral Evan-Thomas' 5 BS likewise make the turn onto a northerly heading. At 1802hrs Vizeadmiral Hipper ordered a speed reduction to allow a closer connection with Kontreadmiral Behncke's battleships. In contrast to the fire of the 1 and 2 Battle Cruiser Squadrons during the first phase of the battle, the fire of the 5 Battle Squadron was accurate and was quickly effective. Several of the German war diaries comment on this. At 1825hrs two shells of 15 inch calibre struck *Lützow* between the funnels and destroyed the main and reserve wireless rooms, thereby severing Vizeadmiral Hipper's connection with the High Sea Fleet Chief. Vizeadmiral Hipper now had to rely on optical signals. At 1830hrs *Valiant* struck *Lützow* with a 15 inch shell between the No.4 and No.5 casemates. Then at 1845hrs, from out of the haze *Princess Royal* struck *Lützow* with a shell below the conning tower.

At 1819hrs *Derfflinger* was also hit on the hull forward, and then at 1855hrs a hit detached two 100mm armoured plates far forward in the bows. This allowed some flooding.

In addition to the previously mentioned hits *Seydlitz* was struck by two further hits at 1855hrs that hit the side armour forward and the port windlass. Despite hitting *Warspite* at least twice, conditions for shooting aboard *Seydlitz* were poor, as her I Artillerie Offizier reported:

When the mist cleared some dreadnoughts were sighted to port, the ships of the *Malaya* class with 38cm guns. After à short pause we again went to the guns; the lighting had become very unfavourable for us, and the outlines of ships with the gradually darkening eastern heavens were hardly recognizable, and only when they fired could we see the muzzle flash of their guns, although now the range was quite low. Many 38cm shells landed on and around us and we could hardly fight back as we couldn't observe them. The heavy shells that struck close beside us in the water showered the ship with mountainous fountains. Time after time I had to send Obermatrosen Lange out of the command position to clean the object lenses of my rangefinder, and he would climb on top of the conning tower, unconcerned about the whizzing and crashing shells, and for a time at least observation was possible.[14]

Moltke remained unhit, as was *von der Tann*.

The German cruisers, and their battle line, were in an unfavourable position as with the low lying sun and haze observation and fire direction were practically impossible. Vice Admiral Beatty and his forces gradually swung north then NNE to come across the head of the German line. For this reason at 1819hrs Vizeadmiral Scheer ordered Vizeadmiral Hipper to pursue Beatty and report his position as he was out of sight. Because *Lützow*'s wireless had been destroyed Vizeadmiral Hipper did not receive this message until 1826hrs whereon he turned NW, however, he was soon forced back onto course NE.

The Official German History commented:

Meanwhile the hitherto favourable visibility conditions for the German line had turned into the opposite. The opponents, who now stood in the direction of the setting sun, were hardly recognizable when this broke through the clouds. The observation of the fall of shot was impossible, and sometimes the German Panzerkreuzers only ran as targets, whilst the distance between them and their own Main Body increased, just as the distance between the 5 and 6 Divisions of battleships increased despite the pursuit being taken up with the utmost power of the engines (A.K.). Because of the reduced visibility conditions the German fire was reduced and Vice Admiral Beatty immediately took advantage to gradually, and at first with his light forces, take a northerly course and then NNE course around the head of the German forces, encircling them. Therefore about 6.21pm Vizeadmiral Hipper received orders to take up the pursuit with his ships, so the enemy would not run out of gun range, just as the Leader of the German Panzerkreuzer was about to report that the enemy was initiating an outflanking manoeuvre, which was obviously not yet apparent to the flagship standing to the rear. However, unfortunately this FT (wireless) message could not be delivered because just at that moment onboard *Lützow* the main and reserve FT stations were knocked out and could no longer be utilized. Therefore nothing remained for Vizeadmiral Hipper but to obey the order, and despite the unfavourable conditions at around 0627hrs he turned the Panzerkreuzers to the northwest so that, when possible, he could again approach the enemy battle cruisers with highest speed. However, this encircling movement of the enemy was only relieved for a moment, and already at about 0639hrs Vizeadmiral Hipper had to swing back to the northeast. Even Kontreadmiral Behncke aboard *König* had meanwhile observed that the enemy forces had moved away en-echelon and had gradually moved around to the north. It was this movement which the 5 Division followed and slowly turned to starboard, likewise followed by the remaining battleships. Because of this the German Battle Fleet soon came into an extended line ahead seven nautical miles behind the forces of Vizeadmiral Hipper, whilst to port ahead in the failing light of the setting sun the squadrons and flotillas of Beatty were chased to the north, and at times were completely covered by the huge columns of smoke, which concealed his connection with the Grand Fleet.[15]

The war diary of *Seydlitz* reported:

For the I AG the lighting gradually became worse. It was very hazy, so that usually only the muzzle flash of the enemy ship was visible, not the ship itself. The combat range against the *Malaya*'s reduced from 180hm to 130hm. From the NW to the NE there was an additional firing line, ahead of the I AG, and from time to time only their muzzle flash could be seen in the haze. A horribly powerful impression. A reply to this fire was not possible. By moving away en-echelon the battle was temporarily broken off, however, with the signal: 'Take up the pursuit', and 'R. Ran an den Feind',[16] it was renewed. Thereby the Panzerkreuzer already quite battered in the previous battle were placed in a very disadvantageous situation by the approach of considerably stronger enemy battleships. Meanwhile the enemy battle cruisers had moved across the head of the I AG and simultaneously swept the Unit from ahead. Nevertheless, the fire of the *Malaya* ships was considerably more accurate than the shooting of the enemy battle cruisers, which was bad laterally. By manoeuvring hits from the salvos were made more difficult.[17]

It is very important to note here that *Seydlitz*'s war diary says Vizeadmiral Scheer used the term '*Ran an den Feind*', or 'have at the enemy'. This term was used frequently during the battle, to both Panzerkreuzer and torpedobootes. It appears that when Vizeadmiral Scheer wanted to hurry up his Panzerkreuzers he used this term, as if he was losing patience. However, when he used it later in the battle many writers seized upon this order as a sign of panic, but in the instance here, and also later, this was clearly not the case. This order is discussed further in Chapter 6.

The American author Commander H. Frost was very critical of Vice Admiral Beatty for his running off at 25 knots speed during this battle phase, and said:

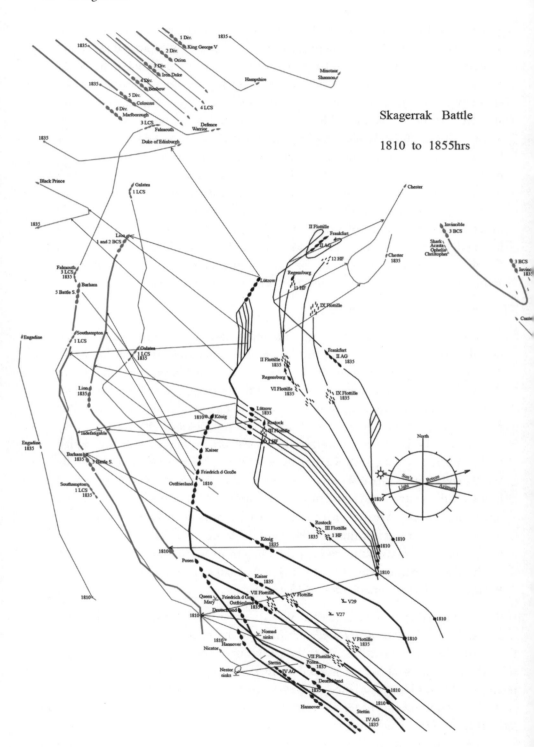

Skagerrak Battle

1810 to 1855hrs

It will be noted that Beatty was entirely out of the fight for this critical period. Evan-Thomas had been told to prolong the line astern and then had been left to fight it out alone against four effective battle cruisers and four battleships. Had Beatty remained in the action, the forces engaged would have been about equal. The most charitable explanation of this amazing situation is that Beatty felt that his battle cruisers were no longer able to stand up against their German opponents, at least without a period of rest. They had been decisively defeated by an [numerically] inferior force.[18]

Earlier during the afternoon the British destroyers *Nestor* and *Nomad* had been heavily engaged with the German IX Flottille and the small cruiser *Regensburg*, and had both been disabled, *Nomad* by a hit in the engine room. Now as the High Sea Fleet came up both were taken under fire by the multitude of battleships with their medium calibre armaments, as the war diaries of one after another battleships show:
Kaiser: '6.22. A destroyer with the number *G31* on the port side, slacks aft.'[19]
Prinzregent Luitpold:

6.24 to 6.30. An enemy destroyer shot at with the medium artillerie with high explosive shells at 48 to 35hm. The destroyer apparently was damaged and lagged behind. Under the forward funnel it carried the marking 'G31'.[20] Several hits were definitely observed. The destroyer sank stern first after the 8th salvo.

6.35 to 6.37. An enemy Destroyer Leader taken under fire with the medium artillerie at 87 to 80hm. Several hits were definitely observed. With the 8th salvo the enemy received a hit in the aft ship. It immediately resulted in a violent explosion and the destroyer leader sank.'[21]

Kaiserin: '6.12. An enemy destroyer was taken under fire with the medium artillerie, he sank at 6.25pm and was fired on by several ships.'[22]
Friedrich der Große:

Towards 6.30hrs the destroyer *G31* was shot at with the medium calibre artillerie at 111 to 72hm. It was necessary to totally destroy him, as he could possibly utilize his very favourable opportunity for a torpedo shot. At 6.31hrs *G31* sank over the stern. In his vicinity a ship's boat and two floats were observed.[23]

Kapitänleutnant Oldekop, serving in a turret of *Friedrich der Große*, described the scene thus:

Finally we came so far ahead that I could see a destroyer. He lay still in the water. Three small black shadows are nearby, rescue boats. The crew have abandoned ship. One can clearly read: *G31*. A completely new ship. It lists to port and slowly lays further and further over. Now it lays flat on the water. Water runs into the funnels; thick white steam clouds push out. With a jerk it capsizes and drifts keel up. Now the stern goes under, the bow rises until it extends vertically into the air. It is getting shorter and shorter. Still a few metres and then it will also vanish. But then suddenly it remains stopped, probably because the boat rests on the bottom. After a brief time it leans to the side. Then just swirling water and gurgling water indicate the grave of *G31*.[24]

Ostfriesland:

Behind these light cruisers several destroyers appeared (3 funnels) with course on our line. About 6.25pm the medium artillerie took a destroyer under fire at 108hm, and with the 3 salvos a hit was obtained; the destroyer turned away, and in the following two salvos received 3 hits behind the funnel; he began to sink.

Ostfriesland ceased fire at 84hm about 6.34pm.

And further: '6.20. Torpedoboat *G31* sinks between the lines. It has put out 2 boats.'[25]

Thüringen: '6.17. Torpedo boat lying still 18.6km. 6.20: Torpedo boat lying still burns. 6.23: Torpedo boat lying still 11.1km. 6.24 1 salvo, 10.6km.'[26]

Helgoland:

The destroyer *G31*, shot at by the ships ahead, sinks.

6.31 to 6.33. A second destroyer to port, also already fired on by the other ships, however not so heavily damaged as to be certain of sinking, was taken under fire by *Helgoland* with the heavy and medium artillerie and sank. Range 92hm.[27]

Oldenburg:

6.15. One enemy destroyer, apparently unmanoeuvrable and burning, in sight 1 point to port. 3 funnels (the foremost is broad).

6.19. Range to the enemy line increasing.

6.20. The enemy turns en-echelon approximately 4 points away to port.

6.27. The destroyer lays over to port; it carries the number 31 (*G31*).

6.35. Destroyer sinks with stern first

6.38. Open fire on a second unmanoeuvrable destroyer; the first salvo hits and the destroyer capsizes and sinks.

The destroyer was brought to sinking with 3 salvos in order to prevent a torpedo shot on our line.[28]

In addition *Posen*, *Rheinland* and *Nassau* also took one or other of the destroyers under fire and likewise at least *Schlesien* and *Hannover* of the II Squadron.

Torpedoboats of the VII Torpedoboot Flottille rescued survivors from the hapless *Nestor* and *Nomad*:

No picture could be obtained of the enemy forces engaged by the I AG and III Squadron, neither course, number of ships, nor accurate position. The smoke from the guns and funnels made a view impossible. The destruction of two English destroyers to port of the line by gunfire of the I Squadron was observed towards 7hrs in the evening. The Flottille detached *S20* and *V189* to one, *S16* and *S17* to the other, to rescue survivors. From the boats 5 Officers and approximately 75 survivors of the destroyer *Nestor* were rescued.[29]

Despite the withering fire to which these two destroyers were subjected *Nestor* suffered only six dead and 80 were saved from her, whilst *Nomad* suffered eight dead and had 72 saved.

At 1705hrs the Grand Fleet commander, Admiral Jellicoe, had ordered the 3 Battle Cruiser Squadron, under the command of Rear Admiral Hood, to 'Proceed immediately to support BCF. Position Lat. 56°53′N., Long. 5°31′E., course S. 55°E at 4.50pm.' It was extremely fortunate for the British that the position given was 7½ nautical miles too far to the east, and this, in conjunction with the German course being given by Commodore Goodenough as north when in reality it was NNW, meant that Rear Admiral Hood took course to the east of the advancing High Sea Fleet and would appear unexpectedly in an outflanking position to the east of the Germans and would change the entire complexion of the battle, even allowing the Grand Fleet to arrive undetected on the battle field.

Rear Admiral Hood was already 25nm SE of Admiral Jellicoe and was still to sight Vice Admiral Beatty's battle cruisers when at 1827hrs the light cruiser *Chester*, stationed 5nm head and to the west, heard the sound of gunfire to the southwest. In this direction visibility varied from 130hm to 50hm, but sometimes was reduced to 20hm in thick smoke. *Chester* turned to starboard to investigate, and soon the flash of gunfire was seen, and then at 1836hrs the outline of a cruiser with three funnels and an accompanying torpedoboot could be dimly made out steering northwards. Meanwhile at 1832hrs the cruiser stationed to port ahead of Rear Admiral Hood's 3 BCS, *Canterbury*, reported to Hood by searchlight that gun flashes had been sighted ahead. Aboard *Chester* they believed they had part of Beatty's vanguard in sight but nevertheless gave the recognition signal, which, however, was correctly answered by the II AG as the torpedoboot *B109* had passed the English recognition signal to the German ships after the first contact earlier in the day. At 1838hrs *Frankfurt* opened fire on *Chester* at a range of 79hm, followed closely by *Pillau*, *Elbing* and *Wiesbaden*. The surprise was complete and the German ships fired three or four salvos before the hapless *Chester* could get one away.

Almost immediately Kontreadmiral Boedicker ordered *Elbing* and *Wiesbaden* to cease fire to allow *Frankfurt* and *Pillau* to more accurately observe their fall of shot. With the third salvo the German cruisers began registering hits on *Chester*. One shell struck the belt armour at Station 128, making a hole and a large dent in the plate, which allowed some flooding. Another shell struck the protective plating at station 59 to port, making a hole 4ft × 3ft 6in and badly buckling the framing and allowing flooding below deck. A hit on the port side at station 149 holed the plating and opened the space below deck to the sea. Another hit at station 72 to port damaged the armoured plate and internal bulkheads and structure. At station 101 the side plating was penetrated and cabin bulkheads were wrecked. Far forward the forecastle deck was hit on the starboard side and was badly holed, whilst the port bow plating was badly riddled and the wooden deck was splintered over a considerable area. The upper deck was pierced in the vicinity of the funnels, and the funnel coamings were damaged. The engine room skylight and ventilator were shot away and the screen bulkhead at 147 station was badly lacerated, the watertight door on it being destroyed.

The aft rangefinder position was completely wrecked, the single range transmitter, belt pushes and electrical fittings were carried away. The ends of the fore bridge were carried away, the bow lights, both 24 inch searchlight projectors, starboard motor sounding signalling apparatus, transmitters, mechanical searchlight controls, navigating fittings and instruments were all badly damaged, while the chart house was holed.

The forward wing shelters were completely riddled by splinters, the stays to the foremast were shot away and the topmast badly splintered. The whole of the wooden deck was badly splintered over about two thirds of its area. The guest warp boom, sounding booms and derricks were badly damaged, and all boats damaged by splinters, the gig, cutter, whaler, balsa raft and four Carley floats beyond repair.

The A1 and A2 boilers were slightly damaged, while 'A' stokehold fan was shifted on its seating, the holding down bolts being sheared. The No.1 funnel was pierced on the port side by a shell, which exploded blowing a hole 6 feet in diameter in the starboard side. The remaining funnels were closely perforated and the coamings to all funnels holed and buckled. All waste steam pipes were perforated and the guys and chains shot away.

The No.1 starboard 5.5 inch gun was damaged, the breech mechanism being thrown out of alignment. The No.2 starboard 5.5 inch gun breech mechanism was also damaged and jammed, the gun being loaded at the time, whilst the No.4 starboard 5.5 inch gun received a direct hit 3ft from the muzzle, which badly strained the mounting, and damaged the shield. Many of the gun crews were killed or wounded so that only the bow gun remained in action after the first few salvos came aboard.

When fire was ceased at 1855hrs *Chester* had been hit by a total of seventeen 15cm calibre shells and suffered a total of 35 dead and 42 wounded.

When the German II AG opened fire on *Chester* Captain Lawson immediately turned his ship away and ran off to the NE at high speed, zigzagging as he went. This caused the Germans considerable difficulties in holding her as a target as related in the combat report of *Pillau*:

About 6.37 an enemy cruiser of the *Gloucester* class came in sight to starboard about 80° at 80hm range, which was called with the enemy recognition signal. The II AG went on a NW course with 24 knots speed. Fire was opened by SMS *Frankfurt* at 79hm, and after a short time *Wiesbaden* and *Elbing* fell in, but then received the signal from the F.d.II AG: 'Cease fire'. On joining in fire on the target with SMS *Frankfurt* the impacts, or fall of shot, of our ship could not perfectly be made out, because our fire could not be differentiated from that of the next ship ahead. A hit was observed from the third salvo. In the course of further fire two more hits were observed and finally a full salvo hit in the aft ship which caused a powerful explosion on our opponent. At the opening of fire the enemy answered from all guns, but apparently within a few minutes all his guns, with the exception of a 5.5 inch gun on the stern, were put out of action, and only this gun fired. The guidance of the enemy to avoid the artillerie fire was very skilful. The enemy cruiser immediately turned away and showed only his stern, moving here and there, so that salvo on salvo had to be corrected for deflection. However, during the course of the fire it was found that his movements were too regular, so that the deflection recurred as red 6, zero and green 4. The range was at first 79 to 69hm, and then 59hm. Shooting was without E-Clock[30] (E-Uhr) because the rate of change continuously changed. Because the shooting at the enemy was mainly in a lengthwise direction and the range soon totalled over 80hm, high explosive shells were fired. In total 22 salvos of 90 shots were fired on this target.[31]

At 1840hrs the flashes of gunfire could be made out from the battle cruisers of the 3 BCS and Rear Admiral Hood turned his ships to starboard without signal to bring *Chester* and the II AG off the port quarter. At 1855hrs *Invincible*, *Inflexible* and *Indomitable* all opened fire on the cruisers of the II AG at a range of about 91hm or less. The fire of the English battle cruisers was soon effective: '18.55hrs. Impacts lay very near. 18.56hrs. *Frankfurt* turns away to starboard, I have swung to avoid this turning point, so that the enemy cannot shoot on the turning point. *Wiesbaden* has seemingly not made the turn, but holds north, and is running into the fire of the heavy ships.'[32] At 18.58hrs *Pillau* was hit by a 12 inch projectile that struck from port as she turned and detonated in the Offizieres' wash room below the bridge. Initially a lubricating oil fire and damage to the boiler room flues caused the six forward coal fired boilers to be closed down, and then an auxiliary condenser was found salted so that *Pillau*'s speed was temporarily reduced to 24 knots, however, later the boilers could be relit. The chart house, upper and lower bridges were wrecked and four men were killed.

The II AG also came under fire from the NW. At 1847hrs the advanced guard of the Grand Fleet, Rear Admiral Arbuthnot's I Cruiser Squadron, sighted the II AG and after opening fire on *Wiesbaden* at 1850hrs he turned towards the German cruisers with his cruisers *Defence* and *Warrior* as his salvos had fallen short. However, it is generally thought that either *Indomitable* or *Invincible* hit *Wiesbaden* and disabled her engines so that at 1901hrs she reported 'Both engines unclear, am unmanoeuvrable.'[33] Therefore she did not follow Kontreadmiral Boedicker's turn away to the south under the cover of a smoke screen.

To Vizeadmiral Hipper aboard *Lützow* it appeared the situation was deteriorating with the surprise appearance of ships armed with heavy calibre guns in the east. The 1 and 2 BCS had resumed fire on the I AG and at 1845hrs *Princess Royal* had hit *Lützow* with a 13.5 inch shell that struck the superstructure side to port just below the conning tower, and *Seydlitz* and *Derfflinger* were both hit at 1855hrs, *Derfflinger* by a hit which detached two 100mm armoured plates far forward in the bows and allowed some flooding and *Seydlitz* by two further hits on the side armour forward and the port windlass. Another shell, which struck at an undetermined time, struck below the waterline near frame 114 to port. On the other hand the Germans could not see their assailants, but only the muzzle flashes of the firing. Therefore at 1858hrs Vizeadmiral Hipper signalled optically 'Torpedobootes to the attack.' As at this time the only enemy forces Hipper had any sight of were the 1 and 2 BCS and the 5 Battle Squadron it must be assumed that these were the intended targets for the torpedoboot attack. At 1859hrs Vizeadmiral Hipper ordered the I AG to make a battle turn to starboard into their own wake. However, it appears with the exception of *von der Tann* the Panzerkreuzers only turned onto a southerly course before steadying.

When the II AG had turned towards the east the 12 HF turned with them and the Half Flottille Chief, Kapitänleutnant Lahs, had determined on an attack on the heavily damaged *Chester*. At 1855hrs however, the large shapes of the 3 BCS were sighted from the torpedobootes and Kapitänleutnant Lahs decided to attack this target, realizing that they represented a great danger to the II AG. Behind these capital ships were the destroyers *Shark*, *Acasta*, *Ophelia* and *Christopher*. The first group of the 12 HF, *V69*, *S50* and *V46* fired a total of four torpedoes at the 3 BCS when the II AG warned that they had also fired torpedoes, so that the 12 HF turned away to the west under a heavy fire. Of the second group only *V45* fired one torpedo at the 3 BCS whilst *G37* loosed one torpedo at the English destroyers at a range of 50 to 60hm, as the destroyers had advanced to meet the German attack. Meanwhile, the bootes of the IX TBF, under Korvettenkapitän Goehle, advanced to make their attack. Nevertheless, of these bootes only *V28*, *S52* and *S34* launched one torpedo each at the enemy capital ships at a range of 60hm. The 3 BCS was only sighted as dim, dark shapes in the mist and smoke. The remaining bootes became involved in a battle with the British destroyers, which they had mistaken for light cruisers.

The II TBF, under Fregattenkapitän Schuur, also advanced to the attack. They had joined the II AG firing on *Chester* and had followed the movements of the II AG. Then the four 'G' Bootes, *G101*, *G102*, *G103* and *G104*, had followed the IX Flottille into the attack. However, *G101* and *G102* were unable to see the 3 BCS and only *G103* and *G104* were able to develop an attack. Now, however, the returning bootes of the 12 HF masked *G103*'s aim and only *G104* was able to lose a torpedo at the second capital ship, *Inflexible*, at 60 to 70hm at 1855hrs.

The flagship of the II FdT, Kommodore Heinrich, *Regensburg*, gathered the remaining bootes of the II TBF, *G41* and the 11 HF and advanced to the attack. Between 1904 and 1908hrs *Regensburg* hit an English destroyer at a range of 68 to 26hm, which stopped and was on fire. *Regensburg*'s war diary reported:

> Some enemy destroyers and a 4 funnelled cruiser (apparently *Attentive* class) attempt to break through to the west ahead of *Regensburg*. They were advanced on at highest speed, and the enemy route was blocked and fire was opened on the next destroyer. The destroyer had the No.04 [*Shark* H04] painted in white on the hull. He was straddled with some salvos at a range of 26hm, and remained motionless and sank under the fire. Then the light cruiser was taken under fire and was likewise hit. Range 71hm. He turned away to the east.
>
> The Leaderboot of the VI TBF, *G41*, joined in this fire and then launched a torpedo on the stopped destroyer, *Shark*.[34]

The war diary of *G41* reported:

> The 12 Half Flottille attacks. *G41* and 11 Half Flottille pass some destroyers. Fire was opened on the next group at 7.01pm. After the 4 salvos, which straddled, a flash flame and strong smoke development were observed on a destroyer, which turned away and lay stopped.
>
> As long as it was visible it was fired on. After this destroyer, a second, apparently stopped destroyer was fired on with the artillerie at 80hm. After the first straddling salvo fire was ceased.
>
> 1906hrs. A torpedo was fired against him at approximately 60hm at a depth setting of 1.5m, as our own Main Body was approaching and eventually he would have an opportunity to shoot a torpedo at them. A detonation was observed on the stern of the destroyer. Sinking could not be seen.
>
> *Regensburg* was followed with various courses and speeds.[35]

The bootes of the II Flottille had varying degrees of success. *B97* hit *Shark* with several shells and then fired on a light cruiser. *B98* was hit by an enemy shell at 1907hrs.

> During the turn *B98* was hit on the aft tube pair. Both aft torpedo tubes fell out. Two dead, four badly wounded, seven slightly wounded. The mast went overboard; turn to starboard near the II AG. *Regensburg* signals 'F2' Z 0 [follow the leader].[36]

Now *Regensburg* had to take evasive action to avoid the cruisers of the II AG. *B112* fired 82 10.5cm shells against the enemy, but *B110* fired just two or three salvos before finding the enemy had turned away.

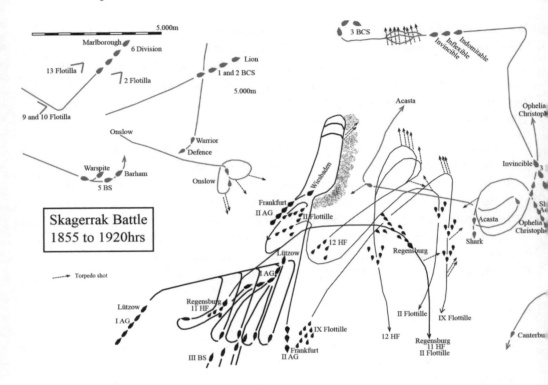

Skagerrak Battle
1855 to 1920hrs

Shark, under the command of Commander Jones, had fired two torpedoes at *Regensburg*, which missed and then had her fuel oil suction lines shot away and came to a stop. Her steering gear was also disabled along with two of her 4 inch cannon. The destroyer *Acasta* was also taken as a target and was hit by *Regensburg* in the port bow and in the starboard quarter. The light cruiser *Canterbury* was struck by a 10.5cm shell, which hit aft and passed through two bulkheads, the main deck and penetrated the fresh water tank without exploding.

At 1904hrs Rear Admiral Hood's 3 BCS made a turn onto a westerly course and about 1913hrs the German torpedoes approached the British line. *Invincible* turned away to avoid the torpedoes but her helm jammed and she stopped, blowing off steam. *Inflexible* turned towards the torpedo tracks but one track was seen to run beneath the ship and emerge on the other side. A second torpedo passed close astern and a third torpedo, travelling slowly, passed down the port side just 20 feet away. *Indomitable* sighted five torpedo tracks and turned away whilst at the same time increasing to full speed. From the fore top the first torpedo track was seen to pass under the ship amidships, and continue its run, whilst three other torpedoes approached, two passing close to the stern and another running just 20 yards past the port side. These three torpedoes were all travelling at slow speed. Rear Admiral Hood's battle cruisers had narrowly missed a catastrophic outcome by good luck, but would soon achieve a success out of all proportion to their numbers.

Meanwhile at 1900hrs, even as Vizeadmiral Hipper was carrying out his battle turn, the Leader of the II AG, Kontreadmiral Boedicker, signalled to him: 'Am fired on by enemy battleships.' He repeated this signal two minutes later, addressing both Admirals Hipper and Scheer, and then at 1910hrs he signalled Vizeadmiral Scheer: 'Enemy battleships stand in 025 epsilon. Leader of II Reconnaissance Group.' This was a serious and fateful mistake, leading Admirals Scheer and Hipper to the conclusion that there were heavy British forces to the east in an encircling position. The German official history commented:

> The unimportant loss to the British here [*Shark*] bore no relation to the gains. The surprise appearance of the 3 Battle Cruiser Squadron on the free flank of the German forces raised the possibility that they were either a separate unit or part of the main battle fleet. The diversion of the Flottilles from their prospective attack against Beatty and the likely discovery of the wing columns of the Grand Fleet were important results. Now the German I AG and III Battle Squadron were heading into the deploying enemy fleet.... However owing to Beatty's overlapping the Germans were already in a tactically untenable position.[37]

Vizeadmiral Hipper had intended his Flottilles to attack Vice Admiral Beatty's 1 and 2 Battle Cruiser Squadron, but what had resulted was a fruitless blow in the air against the 3 BCS.

In the meantime, two British destroyers made individual torpedo attacks against the German line. The *Onslow* sighted *Wiesbaden* about 1905hrs in a favourable position to launch torpedoes at the 1 BCS. *Onslow* advanced against the German cruiser and opened fire with her 4 inch guns before at 1910hrs she sighted the I AG. Now *Onslow* steered to a firing position off the German ship's port bow and fired a torpedo from a range of approximately 7300m, which however, missed. Writing in the early 1930s the insightful Commander H.H. Frost said: 'This was *Onslow*, Lieutenant-Commander J.C. Tovey, a name well worth remembering.'[38] *Lützow* opened fire on *Onslow* with his medium calibre artillery and made three hits. One shell struck aft, and two others exploded in the No.2 boiler room and badly damaged the main feed water tank. *Onslow* launched a torpedo at *Wiesbaden*, which is thought to have struck the unmanoeuvrable German cruiser beneath the conning tower. Then, proceeding at slow speed, *Onslow* fired her last two torpedoes at the German battle line, one surface runner passing ahead of *Kaiser* at 1925hrs. 'Torpedo track to port (shallow runner). *Kaiser* turns to port for a brief time to reduce the interception angle. Torpedo passes ahead, probably from the light cruiser.'[39] *Onslow* was hit a further two times by 10.5cm shells from *Rostock* but was later taken in tow by *Defender* and safely reached port.

Shortly after *Onslow*'s attack the destroyer *Acasta* made a torpedo attack from the starboard bow of the German line. One torpedo was launched at *Lützow* at a range of approximately 4100m, whilst that ship and *Derfflinger* opened fire on *Acasta* with their medium artillery. Two 15cm shells hit in the engine room and the steering gear was shot away, but the destroyer was able to escape and made port with the assistance of *Nonsuch*.

As the II AG were pursuing *Chester* they were sighted by Rear Admiral Arbuthnot and his 1 Cruiser Squadron, as related, which opened fire on the Germans at 1853hrs. The salvos fell short so that *Defence* led *Warrior* to starboard and cut across the approaching *Lions* bows, forcing the latter to take evasive action so that she passed just 200m astern of *Warrior*. The two British armoured cruisers then continued firing on the hapless *Wiesbaden*. The third ship of the squadron, *Duke of Edinburgh*, also opened fire on *Wiesbaden* but could not follow *Defence* because the 1 BCS were in the way. *Wiesbaden* replied with her 15cm cannon and obtained a hit against *Warrior*'s forward turret. There was only one survivor from *Wiesbaden*, Oberheizer Zenne, and he related:

> On 31 May I was on watch from 4 o'clock. Between 5 and 5½ there was the alarm. My station was on the Zwischendeck. First came the signal: 'Achtung starboard.' *Wiesbaden* went as last ship together with *Elbing*, *Pillau* and *Frankfurt*. At first only our Panzerkreuzer were in battle. I saw *von der Tann* curve out of line and signal: enemy submarine. Then suddenly: Battle to port. A vibration occurred through the ship and the order: Smoke and gas danger compartment VI. *Wiesbaden* had begun to shoot before. Through a chain of guards came the order: both engines utmost power ahead. Then no answer came: port engine utmost power ahead. The reply: port engine gives no answer. Now: great steam danger, compass telephone again in order. The next hit struck compartment IX on the oberdeck. The shell struck through the deck, the armoured deck was not penetrated. Later there were many hits, and aft in compartment II apparently a torpedo hit. Then the ship vibrated and was lifted. Thereon receive the order: All men from the ship. I went to above through compartment VI. On the Oberdeck (Upper deck) I saw a waste. The starboard hammock box was completely shot through and the hammocks were in tatters. The gun crews lay dead by their guns. The deck was torn up and holed. There was a fire pause at about 7½ hrs. I got a life jacket and ran to the aft guns. Only the starboard side was passable. Now shells struck quickly after one another again. We were wet with showering water, that smeared us with gas and we became quite yellow.[40]

From the German perspective the first part of the battle had been tremendously successful. The British opponents had lost two battle cruisers and several destroyers for the German loss of two torpedobootes. The other British battle cruisers had been damaged, as had the 5 Battle Squadron. Against this *Seydlitz* had been torpedoed but could still maintain the unit speed, but *Wiesbaden* now lay unmanoeuvrable between the converging fleets. Vizeadmiral Hipper had shown calm and resolute leadership against overwhelming odds, and had achieved a great success, but had his communication link with his Chief severed. His deputy, Kontreadmiral Boedicker, had not showed the same spirit and had flinched at the very time he needed to press ahead and discover the Grand Fleet battle squadrons. His II AG would play no further part in the day battle. Vizeadmiral Scheer had willingly taken up the pursuit of the British forces, but aboard his flagship he was pondering what lay ahead.

> While this encounter with the advance guard of the English main fleet was taking place, we, on our flagship, were occupied debating how much longer to continue the pursuit in view of the advanced time. There was no longer any question of a cruiser advance against merchantmen in the Skagerrak, as the meeting with the English forces which was to result from such an action had already taken place. But we were bound to take into consideration that the English Fleet, if at sea, which was obvious from the ships we had encountered, would offer battle the next day. Some steps would also have to be taken to shake off the English light forces before darkness fell in order to avoid any loss to our Main Body from nocturnal destroyer attacks.... There was never any question of our line veering round to avoid an encounter. The resolve to do battle with the enemy stood firm from the first. The leaders of our battleship squadrons, the 5 Division, turned at once for a running battle, carried out at about 13.000m.[41]

Both Vizeadmiral Scheer and Vizeadmiral Hipper believed that the British battleships bore more to the northeast, an erroneous impression based on Boedicker's exaggerated reports. Nevertheless, Vizeadmiral Scheer showed full confidence in the Leader of the 5 Division and III Squadron, Kontreadmiral Behncke, and his ability to deal with the developing situation, as he allowed his flagship *König* to proceed in precisely the direction of the reported enemy. The two fleets were converging for a giant collision, albeit that their positions were unknown to one another.

Chapter 5

The Fleets Collide

A dmiral Jellicoe approached the scene of the action with his fleet still in cruising formation of six parallel columns each of four battleships, and he remained in ignorance of the situation, even though he was expecting to sight *Lion* and Beatty's battle cruisers at any moment. At 1855hrs he signalled the leading ship of the western column, *Marlborough*, 'What can you see?' to which he received the answer five minutes later: 'Our battle cruisers bearing SSW, steering east, *Lion* leading ship,' and another message five minutes after this, at 1905hrs: '5 Battle Squadron bearing SW.' Admiral Jellicoe now had two options: to deploy his squadrons into battleline based on the western column, or to deploy on the eastern column. If he deployed on the western column he would engage in a passing battle with the German line, with the Battle Cruiser Fleet and 5 Battle Squadron in the van, and he would be well placed to cut off the German forces from their line of retreat. More importantly, the visibility conditions favoured firing eastward. If the Germans reversed course, to engage in a running battle to the southward, then their van would be composed of the old pre-dreadnoughts, old obsolete cruisers and the oldest torpedobootes, however Jellicoe was not to know this, and this supposes the fleet continued on a south-westerly course. On the other hand, deployment on the port wing column would allow the British line to come across the head of the German line, a manoeuvre that would allow them to concentrate the fire of their squadrons against the van of the German line. Jellicoe's deployment is still a point of controversy to this day, and he had many critics. The British Naval Staff Appreciation wrote:

> If the object of deployment is to bring all guns to bear at an effective range, that object does not appear to have been fulfilled, for the fleet, when deployed, under the prevailing conditions of visibility, was not at effective range.... Deployment on the port wing no doubt carried with it lesser risk, but it increased the range of the enemy by at least 4000 yards at a time when every 1000 yards of range was of value, and every ten minutes of daylight was beginning to weigh in the scale of victory.[1]

On the other hand the official German history supported Admiral Jellicoe's decision:

> The first and natural thought of the British fleet chief was to deploy into battle line on the western wing column, as this was closest to the enemy. With

this decision however, even as the heavy shells began impacting between the battleship columns, the weakest Division, consisting of the least battle worthy and oldest ships in the fleet, would lay in the concentrated fire of the best German ships and be exposed to the danger of a mass attack by German torpedobootes. The other battleship Divisions would have to swing to starboard to form the line behind the 6 Division, which would have to turn to port to form the battle line, and in this case the turning point would lie in the heaviest fire before their own fire could become effective. Finally, with this decision Admiral Jellicoe would be within range of the German battleship torpedoes from the outset, and this would have contradicted his views about the importance of the stronger torpedo armament of the German ships. One must agree with the British leader that such a decision would in fact have brought his fleet into a situation that could only be desirable for the Germans. The second possibility would have been for the flagship to take over as guide with the centre column, but this manoeuvre, although possible and practised, was complicated for the moment when the enemy already stood close at hand. Therefore there was nothing remaining but to deploy on the eastern wing division to form the line of battle and therewith accept the disadvantage that this movement would mean the fleet was at a greater range from the enemy.[2]

Admiral Jellicoe vacillated because he had no certain knowledge of precisely where the German fleet was and at 1901hrs he signalled Vice Admiral Beatty: 'Where is enemy's B.F.?' A reply was received five minutes later: 'Enemy's B.C. bearing S.E.' This was not the reply Admiral Jellicoe had desired, the whereabouts of the enemy battle cruisers. Nevertheless at 1902hrs he had ordered a course alteration from SE to south, before returning to course SE at 1906hrs. At 1908hrs Admiral Jellicoe ordered his destroyers to take up destroyer disposition 1, a signal that concentrated two flotillas to the eastward and one flotilla to the westward, so that it would appear that from this moment on he had decided to deploy on the easterly wing column. Things were happening very quickly for Admiral Jellicoe and he needed to make quick decisions based on the available knowledge, or risk being caught by the German battleships in his cruising formation. Although he had issued the preparatory order for deployment Jellicoe still wanted concrete information about the position of the German battle fleet and at 1910hrs he reiterated his signal to Beatty: 'Where is the enemy's B.F.?' In the same instant *Barham* signalled to the Commander in Chief: 'Enemy battle fleet SSE.' Then finally at 1915hrs Admiral Jellicoe issued the order to deploy his fleet on the eastern wing column.

If Admiral Jellicoe had been poorly served by his light cruiser reconnaissance forces during this critical phase of the battle, with Commodore Goodenough reporting at 1903hrs that he had lost sight of the German battle fleet and then adding the misleading report that he was engaging the enemy battle cruisers, then Vizeadmiral Scheer was even more poorly served by his reconnaissance units. He had placed great value in airship reconnaissance, and continued to do so over a long period during the war. And yet not once did the airships provide timely or accurate information to the fleet, and often provided inaccurate reports that misled Scheer. Perhaps Vizeadmiral Scheer's confidence was due to the energetic and confident approach taken by the Leader of Airships, Fregattenkapitän Strasser. On the 31 May three airships were in the vicinity of the High Sea Fleet, *L14*, *L21* and *L23*, and whilst they gave position reports during the course of the afternoon and evening there was no other communication with the High Sea Fleet leader, nor were any directions given to them. It could be said that airship reconnaissance failed completely on this day.

Likewise, the II AG under Kontreadmiral Boedicker failed to provide any useful reconnaissance. After their encounter with *Chester* and the 3 BCS they continued to circle in the lee of the IAG and then the High Sea Fleet, and seemingly Kontreadmiral Boedicker had completely lost his nerve. Nevertheless, at 1923hrs the II AG engaged the solitary cruiser *Canterbury*, and *Frankfurt* was hit at 1926hrs by two 6 inch shells and twice by 4 inch shells. The two 6 inch struck near the main mast whilst one 4 inch struck far forward and the other near the stern, slightly damaging the propellers. *Frankfurt* led the II AG around in a circle for a brief passing battle and then kept circling, whilst *Canterbury* made off.

During this time the fire fight between the opposing forces had continued. *Defence* and *Warrior* were firing at *Wiesbaden* whilst they themselves were straddled by heavy calibre salvos beginning at 1913hrs. The *Duke of Edinburgh*, also of the 1 Cruiser Squadron, opened fire on *Wiesbaden* at 1908hrs, but could not follow Rear Admiral Arbuthnot because of Beatty's battle cruisers. The fourth cruiser of this Squadron, *Black Prince*, had been briefly taken under fire by the German line at about 1845hrs. At 1905hrs *Lion* was hit again by *Lützow*. The shell struck the starboard hull side just forward of A turret and burst on the port side, which was holed. A small fire ensued.

Admiral Jellicoe had only just deployed in the nick of time and as Vice Admiral Burney's 6 Division turned to port to follow this movement the last two ships of the Division, *Agincourt* and *Hercules*, were straddled by heavy shells which threw huge fountains of water over both these battleships. The flagship, *Marlborough*, was able to open fire at 1917hrs at a range of 119hm on a ship of the *Kaiser* class, however after seven salvos she ceased fire at 1921hrs.

One of the main tasks of the armoured cruisers was to meet and defeat the reconnaissance forces of the enemy and Rear Admiral Arbuthnot understood this perfectly well, and therefore had boldly and fearlessly advanced against the small cruiser *Wiesbaden* when he had sighted her. Unfortunately, this brought his cruisers *Defence* and *Warrior* within visual range of the German line. *Markgraf* had opened fire on *Defence* at 1912hrs, followed by *Großer Kurfürst*, which opened fire at 1914hrs, and then changed target to *Warrior* at 1923hrs. Next to join in was *Kronprinz* at 1915hrs:

After a battle pause we fired on two cruisers from 7.16hrs, one of which stopped with her stern on fire. The opportunity to completely destroy the wounded cruiser was favourable for us. Already with the second salvo we obtained a hit on his forecastle. The immediate consequence was a powerful explosion. The entire ship burst apart with enormous flash flames, so that the ship quickly sank. For me it was the first time that I could precisely observe such an explosion at the relatively short range of 8 kilometres. Also when this success was conveyed through the ship there was great rejoicing.[3]

For some time virtually nothing could be seen from *Lützow* of the British forces through the smoke and haze. Kapitänleutnant Schumacher described the frustration aboard *Lützow*:

The medium artillerie fired here and there, however, the heavy guns remained silent – there was nothing to be seen of the enemy. The Artillerie Offizieres stood behind their telescopes gnashing their teeth, the ship impotent against the enemy.[4]

Then at the head of the German line *Lützow* could also recognize the British cruisers, however there was some doubt as to the identity of ship they were dealing with. Korvettenkapitän Paschen wrote:

Then something unexpected happens. From right to left a ship passes through the field of view of my periscope, improbably large and near. From the first glance I make out an older English armoured cruiser and give the necessary commands. Someone pulls me by the arm: 'Don't shoot, that is the *Rostock*!' But I clearly see the turrets on the forecastle and stern. – 'Passing battle. Armoured cruiser, 4 funnels. Bow left. Left 30. Measurement! 76hm, salvo!' Five salvoes fall in swift succession, of them three straddle, then the sight seen with the battle cruisers was repeated, and the ship blew up in full view of both fleets. The English main body also has him in sight at this time, although to us they are invisible and remain so. – Behind him comes a second such ship, but we leave him for our next astern, as the English battle cruisers require our entire attention.[5]

Lützow had fired five salvos in rapid succession and one torpedo.
Lützow's II AO confirmed the series of events, writing:

Suddenly a shadow in the haze. '310 degrees', commanded Paschen. 'On the armoured cruiser midway between the lines, salvo!'... 'Halt, halt Paschen, don't shoot, that is our *Rostock*!' – 'Fire!' is the answer. After one salvo other ships join in. Two further salvos. 'Hurrah, he blows up, he is destroyed with man and mouse.' However, just who was destroyed they question – an enemy? – a German ship – what was it? Just as on *Lützow* the next astern was suspicious and did not shoot. In a fraction of a second the Artillerie Offizier had decided the fate of this ship and crew. Paschen's sharp view, his quick decision, his accurate salvos, they have not destroyed the German *Rostock*, but the British *Defence*.[6]

The next astern of *Lützow* was *Derfflinger*, however her I AO, Korvettenkapitän von Hase, was not as confident about the identity of the four funnelled cruiser.

At this moment Kapitänleutnant Hausser, who had been engaging destroyers with his secondary armament, asked me: 'Is this cruiser with four funnels German or English, sir?' I examined the ship through the periscope. In the misty grey light the colours of the German and English ships were difficult to distinguish. The cruiser was not very far away from us. She had four funnels and two masts, like our *Rostock*. 'She is certainly English,' Kapitänleutnant Hausser shouted. 'May I fire?' 'Yes, fire away.' I was now certain she was a big English ship. The secondary armament was trained on the new target. Kapitänleutnant Hausser gave the order: '6,000!' Then, just as he was about to give the order: 'Fire!' something terrific happened: the English ship, which I had meanwhile identified as an old English armoured cruiser, broke in half with a tremendous explosion. Black smoke and debris shot into the air, a flame enveloped the whole ship, and then she sank before our eyes. There was nothing but a gigantic smoke cloud to mark the place where just before a proud ship had been fighting. I think she was destroyed by the fire of our next ahead, Vizeadmiral Hipper's flagship, the *Lützow*. This all happened in a much shorter time than I have taken to tell it. The whole thing was over in a few seconds, and then we had already engaged new targets. The destroyed ship was the *Defence*, an old armoured cruiser....

At 7.24 p.m. I began to engage large enemy battleships to the north-east. Even though the ranges were short, from 6,000 to 7,000 m, the ships often became invisible in the slowly advancing mists, mixed with the smoke from the guns and funnels. It was almost impossible to observe the splashes. All splashes that fell over could not be seen at all, and only those that fell very short could be distinguished clearly, which was not much help, for as soon as we got nearer the target again it became impossible to see where the shots fell. I was shooting by the measurements of the Bg. man in the fore-control, Obermatrosen Hänel, who had been my loyal servant for five years. In view of the misty weather these measurements were very irregular and inexact, but as no observation was possible I had no alternative. Meanwhile we were being subjected to a heavy, accurate and rapid fire from several ships at the same time. It was clear that the enemy could now see us much better than we could see them. This will be difficult to understand for anyone who does not know the sea, but it is a fact that in this sort of weather the differences in visibility are very great in different directions. A ship clear of the mist is much more clearly visible from a ship actually in the mist than vice versa. In determining visibility an important part is played by the position of the sun. In misty weather the ships with their shady side towards the enemy are much easier to see than those lit by the sun. In this way a severe, unequal struggle developed.[7]

At 1918hrs the battleship *König* also opened fire on *Defence* and a torpedo was loosed at 1921hrs. Then at 1922hrs *König* changed target to *Warspite* with the heavy and medium artillery.

Previously *Kaiser* had opened fire on *Defence* at 1914hrs and claimed two heavy calibre hits from 10 salvos fired. Korvettenkapitän Studt wrote:

> The clock showed 7.20pm. Suddenly from the smoke cloud which concealed the enemy on the port side the outline of a ship appeared travelling towards our head at high speed. The English 1 Cruiser Squadron! Achtung all! That is dashing! Admiral Jellicoe probably intended a powerful reconnaissance to the south, but this attack could only be described as foolhardy. The Artillerists of our battleships wait until they have a specific, clear target in the telescope line and threw themselves on the new opponent, who seemed surprised. Our target is the forward most ship of the enemy squadron, the *Defence*, and salvo on salvo hit. Soon they could see burning, but this was extinguished, only to erupt more violently again a short time later. Starting from the forecastle a yellow sea of flames spread quickly across the deck. Another salvo. A house high column of flame came from the enemy ship, which soon burst into two parts and vanished beneath the water's surface. The news of the success of our artillerie, the destruction of an enemy armoured cruiser – and *Defence* was even an Admiral's Flagship – brought a huge cheer from us. All speaking tubes and telephones brought these glad tidings even to the remotest corners of our ship, an incentive to all of us to preserve and continue to do our duty, even if for most the great events were for the most part invisible.[8]

Defence was hit several times which caused many fires when suddenly a salvo struck aft and it was thought the aft magazine exploded, but a short time later another salvo struck forward and the forward magazine detonated and *Defence* disappeared in a huge smoke cloud. There were no survivors.

The *Warrior* was closely following *Defence* and also came under a concentrated fire, likewise being set on fire in two or three places. One shell wrecked the bridge, whilst other hits caused the eventual disabling of both engines. The electrical and hydraulic power to the turrets failed. According to *Warrior*'s own report she was struck by at least 15 heavy shells, and 6 medium calibre shells. However, despite both engine rooms being flooded the engines continued to turn enabling a speed of 10 to 12 knots and *Warrior* escaped in the thick smoke. After that the seaplane carrier *Engadine* took *Warrior* in tow. *Warrior* continued to sink lower by the stern and the following morning, with the rising seas breaking over the stern and a list of 6°, she was abandoned and sank.

After ceasing fire on *Defence*, *Markgraf* changed target to *Princess Royal* and at 1922hrs struck her with two projectiles from the same salvo. One heavy shell struck the 9 inch armour of X barbette at the upper deck, splitting the plate at its lower edge and setting it up 6 inches at the middle line. The shell broke off a large fragment of armour measuring 6 feet by 20 inches whilst a hole 14 feet × 6 feet across was blown in the deck adjacent to the barbette, carrying away three deck beams. The 9 inch armour fragment was driven through the turntable into the gunhouse and damaged the left gun. All the crew of the left gun were killed and the turret was put out of action.

The other shell penetrated the 6 inch armour just above the main deck a little forward of X barbette. The shell passed athwartships and detonated on the port side. There were many casualties among the aft 4 inch gun crews and salvage party and flash flame ignited some cordite on the main deck. Both aft engine rooms filled with thick smoke, which also penetrated the starboard, forward engine room. These two shells killed eleven and wounded 31.

When Rear Admiral Evan-Thomas sighted *Marlborough* and the 6 Division he assumed that the Grand Fleet was deploying on the western column, and he, just as Vice Admiral Beatty, swung his 5 Battle Squadron round onto an easterly course to take up his disposition at the head of the fleet, in accordance with the Grand Fleet Battle Orders. However, Admiral Jellicoe had determined to deploy on the eastern column and although the battle cruisers could press on ahead across the line of fire of the battleships the 5 Squadron lacked the speed to follow Vice Admiral Beatty and was forced to turn to port onto a northerly heading at 1918hrs to take up a position at the tail of the battleship columns. During the turn back to starboard and whilst under a heavy German fire, *Warspite*'s helm jammed and she swung out of line to starboard, narrowly missing a collision with the ship next ahead, *Valiant*. Some authors say that the loss of control of the ship was not as the result of damage from German battleships, but it was. Either hit number 1 or number 7 damaged the bulkhead to which the steering engines were attached and as a result the thrust bearing and shaft overheated and later jammed, with 15° of port rudder, that is a turn to starboard. Rather than become a stationary target Captain Philpotts ordered full speed and *Warspite* completed two circles towards the German line, the first from 1920 to 1930hrs and the second from 1930 to 1935hrs. During this time she came under a violent German fire and was hit at least 20 times by heavy and medium calibre shells.

Whilst a number of German battleships had taken *Defence* as a target many others had opened a no less effect fire on the British battleship *Warspite*. At 1915hrs

Prinzregent Luitpold opened fire on *Warspite* at 172hm, followed at 1917hrs by *Kaiserin* at a range of 110 to 115hm, at 1920hrs by *Friedrich der Große*, at 1922hrs by *König*, at 1924hrs by *Helgoland* and *Oldenburg*, at 1925hrs by *Ostfriesland* and *Thüringen* and at 1933hrs by *Nassau*.

Prinzregent Luitpold reported:

1915. Open fire on a ship of the *King George* class at 172hm with the heavy artillerie.

1917. Signal: 'Battle turn 2 points to port.'

1920. Signal: 'Guidance ahead.' Gradually sheer into the wake of the Flagship.

1930. The enemy line makes a turn.

1932. Signal: 'Battle turn 16 points to starboard.' The fire was ceased, as the enemy was lost from sight. In total 21 salvos were fired at 172 to 160hm: two hits were definitely observed.[9]

And *König*:

1922hrs. An enemy ship at the end of their line (*Iron Duke* or *Malaya* class) strikes an almost full circle to starboard and remains lying stopped. Guns were not traversed. He no longer fires. Heavy Artillerie and Medium Artillerie opens fire on him. Salvos straddle.

1926hrs. The enemy disappears from sight, there on turn on ENE and then onto eastern course.[10]

Friedrich der Große also took *Warspite* as a target, but ceased fire to allow Vizeadmiral Scheer a better overview of the battle.

1920 to 1940 the *Queen Elisabeth* class furthest to the left was shot at along with other ships; range 114–88hm. The target appeared damaged and went in a complete circle, and according to the declaration of various observers also had a list; it maintained only weak independent shots. With turning away it was covered by 4 *Calliope* class cruisers, that with moving away en-echelon obviously manoeuvred for a torpedo shot. At this time our own fire was ceased in view of Fleet Direction.[11]

Of the 20 hits on *Warspite* at this time it is difficult to differentiate between heavy and medium calibre hits, but it is thought there were 9 heavy calibre hits, 4 medium calibre and 7 hits of undetermined calibre. Nor can the times for these hits be certain.

Hit number 10 (we left *Warspite* with nine hits last chapter) was a heavy calibre shell that struck the upper deck embrasure near the forward edge of A barbette, making a 6 feet by 5 feet hole, even though the projectile did not detonate. The shell passed athwartships and caused considerable damage to the sick bay, causing a fire, and passed out the port side. The next hit, 11, was a heavy calibre shell which struck the upper deck in the starboard embrasure and detonated in the boys' mess deck, causing much damage. Hit number 12 was a heavy calibre shell that struck the plating of the forecastle deck adjacent to the aft funnel, however failed to detonate. The shell passed through the boiler room ventilator and made a hole 8 feet by 3 feet in the shelter deck plates. Hit number 13 was a heavy calibre shell that in part penetrated the 9 inch main armoured strake. This shell struck at station 157 to port and made a hole 2ft 6in × 2ft, the top of the hole being in the 6 inch armour and lower part in the 9 to 13 inch (520lb) tapered armour. The shell exploded in the port fresh water tank 12 feet from the point of impact. This allowed sea water to pour into the port wing engine room. The next hit was a heavy calibre projectile that exploded in the aft funnel casing. Splinters penetrated the battery deck and completely collapsed the boiler room down takes. Hit number 15 was a heavy calibre shell that hit the main derrick from the port side and detonated on the starboard side of the forecastle deck inboard of the forecastle deck 6 inch cannon. The 6 inch gun shield was riddled like a sieve, and fragments pierced the aft part of the 6 inch casemate and ignited four cordite charges. All the crew of the aft 6 inch casemate gun were badly burned along with some of the next gun. Hit number 16 was of unidentified calibre and wrecked the warrant officers' galley. Hit 17 was a heavy calibre shell that struck the forward superstructure, about station 93 on the starboard side. The night defence shelter was wrecked. The next hit, 18, was of undetermined calibre and passed through the forward funnel without detonating. Hits 19 and 20 were of unidentified calibre and passed through the aft funnel, causing much splinter damage. The next hit of unidentified calibre struck the starboard 6 inch gun shield and wrecked the mounting. Hit number 22 was of unidentified calibre and struck the main derrick, which then fell across the picket boat. The explosion of this shell wrecked the other ship's boats. The next shell was of medium calibre and passed through the heel of the main mast. Hit number 24 was probably of 30.5cm calibre and struck the starboard aft part of the aft superstructure, and then hit the communications tube of the torpedo control tower. This armoured tube (4 inches in thickness) was struck and a large piece 2 feet 6 inches deep and extending round half the circumference of the tube was broken off. Hit number 25 was a 15cm calibre shell which struck the side of X turret, without causing damage. The next projectile was of heavy calibre and struck the 13 inch thick belt without piercing. The following heavy calibre high–explosive shell burst on the 13 inch main strake of the armoured belt about 8 feet forward of hit 26 and exploded on the armour without piercing. Hit number 28 was a 15cm shell that struck the left-hand 15 inch gun of Y turret, 6 inches short of the muzzle. This gun was put out of action and had to be replaced. The last recorded projectile to hit was a 15cm shell which penetrated the wardroom and passed overboard. The aft superstructure, main stays, searchlights, 15 inch director tower, bridges and compass platform were all damaged by splinters.

At 1926hrs *König* lost sight of *Warspite* whilst *Friedrich der Große* lost sight of her at 1934hrs. *Helgoland* ceased fire at 1935hrs as the enemy had 'vanished in the haze'. The last ship to cease fire on *Warspite* was *Ostfriesland* at 1945hrs, and therefore after the German line had made a battle turn onto the opposite course. *Warspite* made good her escape in smoke and haze after being battered by 29 hits by shellfire and suffering 14 killed, including two civilians, and seventeen wounded. Her speed had been reduced to16 knots and later that evening Rear Admiral Evan-Thomas ordered *Warspite* to retire and proceed to Rosyth for docking. *Warspite* had been knocked out of the battle.

At 1924hrs and 1927hrs Admiral Jellicoe received reports from *Southampton* and *Lion* respectively about the position of the German battle fleet, as the deployment on the eastern wing column continued. Nevertheless, the deployment was being delayed as a speed reduction was necessary to allow Vice Admiral Beatty to press on to the head of the fleet. Behind *Iron Duke* ships had to sheer out of line, and in the tail Divisions speed had to be reduced to 12 knots. Even though Beatty's Squadron was making 26 knots his course was converging with that of *King George V*, leading the fleet, so that the battleship had to give way to port. By 1933hrs Beatty was far enough ahead to allow Jellicoe to order a speed of 17 knots.

At around 1922hrs Rear Admiral Hood's 3 Battle Cruiser Squadron turned through 16 points to starboard onto an easterly course and took station ahead of Vice Admiral Beatty's 1 and 2 BCS. At 1926hrs Beatty's battle cruisers changed course from east to ESE to follow the 3 BCS. Whilst the Germans were firing on *Warspite*, *Defence* and *Warrior* and were preoccupied with the rescue of *Wiesbaden* they failed to recognize the concentration of battle cruisers directly ahead of them, especially as they had no reconnaissance line of either torpedobootes or small cruisers. At 1919hrs *Lion* struck *Lützow* with two 13.5 inch calibre shells. The first hit the forecastle, whilst the second struck the port casemate roof and penetrated before passing forward to detonate just behind turret B. A fire started amongst the damage control material stored there, which created a great deal of smoke. At 1920hrs *Lützow* put the destroyer *Acasta* out of action with two 15cm shells, one of which hit the engine room and burst several steam pipes and caused five casualties and the engine room was evacuated. The steering gear was also shot away.

Princess Royal fired intermittently, whilst the other battle cruisers maintained a destructive fire on their German counterparts. Between 1921hrs and 1927hrs *Tiger* fired seven salvos and *New Zealand* fired eleven salvos, although the effect of their fire could not be observed. Nevertheless, *Tiger* was hit by a 15cm shell and at 1930hrs *Lützow* hit the light cruiser *Falmouth* with a 15cm shell. However arguably it was the fire of the 3 BCS that was most effective and achieved the greatest British success during the entire battle. At 1922hrs Rear Admiral Hood executed an excellent manoeuvre to bring himself approximately two nautical miles ahead of the British battle fleet, whereon he renewed his battle to starboard.

At 1920hrs Vizeadmiral Hipper ordered a turn onto SE as he was being forced away from the encircling and tightening ring of enemy capital ships, of which he could scarcely see anything. The German Panzerkreuzer, with *Lützow* at their head, were clearly visible to the English battle cruisers of the 1 and 3 Battle Cruiser Squadrons and now they covered *Lützow* with a hail of fire that left a lasting impression on those who endured it.

> To the front of the German head, from the NW to the NE, there was suddenly an unbroken line of muzzle flashes of heavy ships, firing salvo after salvo with powerful results and which the German ships could scarcely answer to, as not one British dreadnought could be recognized in the battle smoke. SMS *Lützow* and *König* came under an especially heavy fire. It seemed as though several ships were firing at them at once.[12]

Korvettenkapitän Paschen described it thus:

> The English battle cruisers required our entire attention. They stand to port aft, as we have swung onto an easterly course, 130hm away, for us barely recognizable. And then it began, which made all previous look like a game. Whilst the target of our guns was hidden from me by smoke, I gave the direction to the aft position, when suddenly a hail of hits struck from port aft and port ahead. There was nothing to see other than red flashes, not the shadow of one ship. Our turrets were directed hard aft to port and fired as well as was possible on our old friends, the battle cruisers of Admiral Beatty. From there a shell penetrated the oberdeck abreast the forward funnel, penetrated the casemate and detonated behind the base of turret B, causing a considerable fire forward and throwing both armoured doors out of the casemate on to the forecastle. The detonation occurred directly below the command position (conning tower) however caused this little damage, just as the two nearby lying forward casemates.[13]

Lützow was hit eight times between 1926hrs and 1934hrs, all from *Invincible* and *Inflexible*. The most devastating of these hits were 2~12 inch shells that struck the forward broadside torpedo room and 2~12 inch shells that struck the bow torpedo room. At 1926hrs one shell struck below the armour in the broadside room, and the other struck the lower edge of the 100mm thick forward belt. Both penetrated the broadside room. The two other shells struck at 1929hrs in the bow torpedo room below the water line. The entire forecastle ahead of frame 249 and below the waterline immediately filled with water. Speed was reduced to 15 knots and then 12 knots to reduce pressure on bulkhead 249, but water quickly leaked from compartment XIV into compartment XIII through the un-tight sides of bulkhead

249 and through speaking tubes. At 1927hrs a 12 inch shell struck the upper deck of the forecastle and then at 1928hrs a shell struck the belt armour just below the port IV 15cm casemate gun. The shell did not detonate and was found on the sloping armour. Seaman Fritz Loose wrote:

> A heavy shell – 34 or 38cm – penetrated the outer hull side directly above the waterline and below the fourth 15cm gun being served by me. Fortunately the heavy shell did not explode. Through the rising air pressure the entire serving crew of the gun were hurled away, and the heavy 15cm gun barrel was pushed from the pivot, and the ball race was broken…. Thereon I departed the casemate in order to get a hoist. As I left the adjacent area and closed the bulkhead door to the next compartment a hit struck the area just traversed by me. With my further journey to the spare part store a steward stood before the Offizieres pantry with a full bottle of sparkling wine (Sekt), which I emptied in a moment: as thanks I patted him on the shoulder and ran off. My comrades of the gun crew believed me to be lost with the impact of the shell and were very pleased when I returned uninjured.
>
> The Zimmermannsmeister, a Deckoffizier, who had the task of supervising damage control, appeared in the casemate to ascertain the effect of the reported hit on our cannon. We opened the manhole cover and I climbed down into the coal bunker beneath our gun. From above I had already seen the beam of light emanating from the large hole in the belt armour and the water in the coal bunker. When I stepped down onto the coal I immediately slipped into the water. After I returned to the casemate and made my report to the Deckoffizier I was admired by my comrades, as by slipping into the water I was wet through and was as black as coal in every sense of the word…. The forecastle, the fore part of the ship, was rent apart by several hits and showed holes which a railway locomotive could comfortably have driven through. Several thousand tonnes of water had penetrated and still the ship continued ahead and fired.[14]

At 1930 two further 12 inch shells struck; one on the belt armour above the waterline between the port III and IV casemates, and one on the port side net shelf just beneath the V 15cm cannon.

Korvettenkapitän Paschen related:

> The fateful red flash from port ahead came from the British 3 Battle Cruiser Squadron, which was ahead of the enemy main body, and had steered towards the gun flashes and had arrived within effective gun range unseen. Seemingly at this moment we had already received a fatal wound from them, as it later transpired. Every ship has a weak point and our Achilles heel was the broadside torpedo room, situated before A turret. Here unfortunately, out of considerations for space, the torpedo bulkhead had been omitted;

this incomparable protection against underwater hits, that distinguished the German ships so advantageously against all from abroad. And so two enemy heavy shells successfully penetrated here beneath the armoured belt and their explosive result was so thorough, that the entire forecastle before turret A practically immediately filled. It gave the ship a powerful jerk, and our artillerie direction position did not miss out, as I was thrown powerfully with my head against the armoured wall, whereby my cap was removed because the direction indicator was once again completely under water.[15]

Then suddenly at 1930hrs the mist and haze surrounding 3 Battle Cruiser Squadron dissolved for a short time and the German ships could recognize *Invincible* as the black smoke and powder smoke cleared away from her, although still veiling the other battle cruisers. *Lützow* and *Derfflinger* concentrated fire on this conspicuous ship at a range of 100hm to 88hm. Korvettenkapitän Paschen described what happened next:

Meanwhile we had turned onto a southerly course, and suddenly an English battle cruiser of the *Invincible* type appeared out of the haze clearly and relatively near 4 points to port astern. I cannot fully say, what satisfaction I have felt to finally have this pest available before my eyes, and as quick as lightning the commands were given out. However, already a dark object slides between my periscope and the opponent, the corner of the Admiral's bridge, which limits the angle of vision of my periscope object lens to about 10°. 'Has the aft position measured?' – '*Jawohl*! 100hm!' – 'Direction aft position!' Kapitänleutnant Bode gives brief and clear orders, and to the inexpressible joy of the whole ship, 15 seconds later our guns crash out again, with exception of B turret. I heard everything myself through the headphones; what Bode and the artillerie transmitting station said, and now also saw the opponents again. 'Over! 4 down, salvo! Straddle! Salvo!' As the sound of the fall of shot indicator screeched the columns flickered out of the water around the enemy and again the beautiful and unmistakable dark red flares up. Such a shooting mark, to use a hunting expression, makes us accurate shots, when the enemy has seen us over twice as long. It continued only a few seconds and then the red flames cover the ship as it blows up. It was *Invincible*, – the 'unconquerable' conquered! Beside ourselves *Derfflinger* has also fired on this target. For my highly venerated brother in arms I do not wish to take from his success, but I must say the Kapitänleutnant Bode was the author of this success: the screeching sound and the straddling salvo, the red flames, all together were so unmistakable, and to me seem like they occurred yesterday.[16]

Whilst the I Artillerie Offizier of *Derfflinger*, Korvettenkapitän von Hase, described the events as follows:

Several heavy shells pierced our ship with terrific force and exploded with a tremendous roar, which shook every seam and rivet. The Commander had again frequently to steer the ship out of the line in order to get out of the hail of fire. It was pretty heavy shooting. This went on until 7.29 p.m. At this moment the veil of mist in front of us split across like the curtain at a theatre. Clear and sharply silhouetted against the uncovered part of the horizon we saw a powerful battleship with two funnels between the masts and a third close against the forward tripod mast. She was steering an almost parallel course with ours at top speed. Her guns were trained on us and immediately another salvo crashed out, straddling us completely. 'Range 9,000!' roared Obermatrosen Hänel. '9,000 Salvoes-fire!' I ordered, and with feverish anxiety I waited for our splashes. 'Over. Two hits!' called out Oberleutnant zur See von Stosch. I gave the order: '100 down. Good, Rapid!' and thirty seconds after the first salvo the second left the guns. I observed two short splashes and two hits. Oberleutnant zur See von Stosch called: 'Hits!' Every twenty seconds came the roar of another salvo. At 7.31 p.m. the *Derfflinger* fired her last salvo at this ship, and then for the third time we witnessed the dreadful spectacle that we had already seen in the case of the *Queen Mary* and the *Defence*.

As with the other ships there occurred a rapid succession of heavy explosions, masts collapsed, debris was hurled into the air, a gigantic column of black smoke rose towards the sky, and from the parting sections of the ship, coal dust spurted in all directions. Flames enveloped the ship, fresh explosions followed, and behind this murky shroud our enemy vanished from our sight. I shouted into the telephone: 'Our enemy has blown up!' and above the din of the battle a great cheer thundered through the ship and was transmitted to the fore-control by all the gunnery telephones and flashed from one gun-position to another...(I) shouted to my servant: 'Bravo, Hänel, very well measured!' and then my order rang out: 'Change target to the left. On the second battle cruiser from the right!' The battle continued.[17]

The Gunnery Officer of *Invincible*, Commander Dannreuther, stated that she had been hit several times when she was struck on Q turret and the shell had detonated inside, blowing off the turret roof. A great explosion followed almost immediately as the magazine exploded and the ship broke in two and sank within 10 to 15 seconds. The magazine of A turret also exploded. The two halves of the ship came to rest on the bottom and were conspicuous above the water for some time. The time of the explosion was 19.32hrs. It had taken *Lützow* just two minutes from sighting her opponent to destroying her. One of the six survivors of *Invincible* was her Gunnery Officer, Commander Dannreuther.

Whilst these events were unfolding Vice Admiral Beatty's 1 and 2 BCS finally pulled clear of the leading battleship Squadrons, giving them a clear field of fire and the German head was suddenly taken under a withering fire from the NW to the NE by an unbroken line of muzzle flashes from heavy ships, firing salvo after salvo, which the German ships could scarcely reply to as not one British capital ship could be recognized in the smoke and haze. The concentration of the British cannonade which began at 1917hrs is best shown in the following table:

Time	Ship firing	Range (metres)	Salvos	Target
1917	*Marlborough*	13,000	7	*Kaiser* class
1922–1939	*Revenge*			Battleship and *Wiesbaden*
1924	*Agincourt*	10,000		I AG and *Wiesbaden*
1925	*Hercules*	12,000		*Kaiser* class
1926	*Superb*			*Wiesbaden*
1927	*Thunderer*		3	*Wiesbaden*
1929	*Royal Oak*		4	*Wiesbaden*
1930	*Iron Duke*	12,600	9 (43 shots)	*König*
1930	*Benbow*		1	
1930–1945	*Bellerophon*			*Wiesbaden*
1930	*Colossus*		3	Battleship then *Wiesbaden*
1931	*Conqueror*	12,000	3	*König* class then *Wiesbaden*
1932	*Orion*	11,100	4	Probably *Markgraf*
1932–1945	*Vanguard*		42 shots	*Wiesbaden*
1932	*Collingwood*		8	*Wiesbaden*
1933	*Monarch*		2-3	*Wiesbaden* and *König* class
1933–1945	*St Vincent*		'A few'	*Wiesbaden*
1934	*Temeraire*		5	*Wiesbaden*
1940	*Neptune*	11,000	2	Battleship
1940	*Canada*		2	–

The British cannon lit up the hazy horizon with the flash of gunfire, to which the Germans were unable to reply because of poor visibility. Conditions for the British were at times also poor and many of the battleships had to check their fire, but nevertheless the shellfire of *Iron Duke* was particularly effective and *König* was hit eight times and *Markgraf* once. The war diary of SMS *König* reported:

> 1928hrs. *König* is again in the heaviest enemy fire from the Northeast and eastern directions. Enemy in approximately 290° and 360° and cannot be made out in the hazy air. Only the flash of the guns can be recognized. Several ships have moved their fire onto *König* (close impacts without pause).

> 1931hrs. *Wiesbaden* lays unmanoeuvrable in approximately 300°. An enemy destroyer, that would attack her, is chased away by our medium artillerie fire.

> 1932hrs. Hit with us.

1935hrs. Violent vibration port forward. The ship lays over to port approximately 4½°.

1936hrs. Hit in the forecastle. Splinters and gas cloud come on the bridge. Fire in the foreship.

The movements of our own battle cruisers, that east of us draw south, are followed, and we slowly turn onto course south.

1938hrs. Hit on the top of the conning tower, the shell deflects away, detonates approximately 50m distant from the ship. Squadron Chief slightly wounded.[18]

Skagerrak Battle   19.20hrs to 19.30hrs

As the times for many of the hits on *König* for the period 1932hrs to 1938hrs are unknown they will be taken in sequence from aft to forward, as was German practice. There were four hits on the aft citadel armour between frame 43 and frame 57 of 6 inch calibre which had no noticeable effect other than some damage to the net booms. A heavy calibre shell, from the hit diagram a ricochet, struck near the top of the aft funnel. The upper starboard searchlight was thrown down onto the deck and was wrecked. One of the port BAK (Balloon defence cannon) was damaged by splinters. At 1938hrs a 13.5 inch shell struck the top of the conning tower and was deflected away, detonating 50 metres from the ship. A grove was produced in the roof to a depth of 15mm and a piece of the angle bracket on the edge of the roof was rent off, one piece striking Kontreadmiral Behncke and wounding him.

The next hit in order was a 13.5 inch projectile that struck at frame 93 on the casemate armour, just aft of the port No.1 15cm cannon. A hole 700m by 400mm was made in the 150mm casemate armour. Some fire extinguisher pipes were torn and caused the flooding of the artillery workshop, wood bunker XII and on the armoured deck. At the same time the forward munitions chamber was flooded and the munition in the hoist to munition chamber 14 burned, partly caused as a result of another hit in the port No.1 casemate. The port oil boiler (No.1) was permanently disabled and the starboard and middle oil boilers were temporarily put out of action by smoke and gas danger. There were a total of 9 dead, although it is unclear which died as a result of this hit and which were attributable to the hit at frame 99–100.

The hit to port at frame 96 at 1935hrs was the most dangerous of all the hits. This 13.5 inch shell struck just below the armoured belt, below the waterline, and penetrated the hull, chipping off a semi-circular piece 185mm in radius of armour. The protective bunker and torpedo bulkhead were penetrated and the bottom piece of the shell came to rest in munitions chamber 14. A large piece of torpedo bulkhead was also thrown into this munitions chamber. To port wing passage compartments XI and XII were flooded, along with munitions chambers 12 and 14. To starboard wing passage compartments VI, VII and VIII were counter flooded for a total of 361 tonnes. In munitions chamber 14 some boxes, shells and cartridges were buried under coal. Approximately 15 cartridges burnt. This had been an extremely dangerous and damaging hit and had caused 4 dead.

The next heavy hit forward struck at frame 99–100, in the forward part of the port No.1 casemate. The outer skin was penetrated and in conjunction with the hit at frame 93 there was smoke and gas danger in munitions chambers 12 and 14 so that these were flooded. The munitions in the hoist burned and the shell body was found in the 15cm hoist. As a result of this hit a total of 27 men were killed and one was badly wounded.

A heavy calibre shell struck at frame 113 to port and penetrated the unarmoured hull. The citadel transverse bulkhead of 170mm thickness was pushed aft 1.3 metres and there was other material damage, and a fire resulted which was extinguished.

A further hit forward struck the right face of A turret and glanced off, detonating above the upper deck, which was holed by splinters.

The final hit during this period at 1936hrs struck the upper deck between the capstans and holed the deck. A small fire was caused which was soon extinguished.

As a result of flooding *König* immediately took up a 4½° list to port. Of these hits seven are credited to *Iron Duke*, and one to *Monarch*.

Markgraf was hit at 1935hrs by a 13.5 inch projectile credited to *Orion*. The shell struck the 150mm thick casemate armour of the port No.6 casemate and detonated. Splinters put the port 15cm gun out of action and penetrated athwartships to the starboard No.6 15cm cannon where the munitions hoist was put out of action. Two cartridges of the port gun ignited. Nine men were killed immediately, two men later died; in addition 10 men were badly wounded.

Markgraf was also heavily shaken aft by a near miss at 1933hrs and this might have caused the port propeller shaft to have been bent so that the shaft bearings overheated and the port engine had to be stopped.

Of the other German ships *Derfflinger* was hit three times and *Seydlitz* once during this period. At 1926 a 12 inch shell, probably from *Indomitable*, fell short underwater near frame 25 to port, the detonation of which caused some skin wrinkling and flooding. The other two hits occurred at 1930hrs, the first striking the joint of two armoured plates and shattered on impact, causing some damage behind the armoured plate, the other hitting at frame 61 and shattering against the 260mm armour.

The hit on *Seydlitz* was at 1934hrs and was at frame 42 to port on the belt armour. The armoured plate was not penetrated but was pushed back approximately 30mm and two net booms were damaged.

With so many British battleships firing on *Wiesbaden* it was inevitable she would suffer a great number of hits, and between 1920 and 1945hrs it is likely that some 300 shells were fired at her, from which 10 or 12 hits were claimed. As the Germans had learned on April 25 with firing at *Conquest*, many ships firing at the same target caused difficulties with spotting and accuracy. Nevertheless, at about 1943hrs *Wiesbaden* was able to fire a torpedo towards the British line, even though she had been hit by the 3 BCS and 1 Cruiser Squadron, and had been hit by a torpedo from *Onslow*.

Oberheizer Zenne wrote:

Our ships came somewhat closer, then again got farther away. We had already hoped that we would be rescued. Now there was a small break in the fighting (fire pause). We utilized this to quickly throw any shells and cartridges found on deck overboard, and to rescue our comrades from the water. Our ships of the *König*, *Ostfriesland* and *Nassau* class came closer, then again turned away. A torpedoboot Morsed to us, however, we could give no answer. The enemy was in a semicircle around us, and then moved in the direction of our ships. I have certainly seen 8 ships each with 4 funnels, and several smoke columns. Meanwhile it had become dark. Now we unwounded (approximately 30 men) bandaged our badly wounded, including the I Offizier, who was badly wounded in the head, and laid him in a hammock on the starboard side (the Commander and the remaining Offiziers and Ingenieurs were dead). Then we got dry clothes and something to eat, and two bottles of wine for the wounded. About midnight I went below deck, to see how it was there. Under the forecastle in compartment XVI it was quite unscathed. In compartment XIV and XV the hull side was shot through, with torn up sacks in the holes. The bulkhead to compartment XVI was penetrated and there was some water on deck. The armoured hatch to the munitions chamber was closed. In compartment XIII there was two holes in the hull side. I could only get to compartment XII with effort. The hull side was holed from the deck to above. The water struck through several holes through the armoured deck to the official (Government) hold. The hatch of the torpedo loading arrangement was missing. In the torpedo room was some water, however the torpedoes could still be recognised. The way to compartment XI was blocked. I stopped up the lowest hole in the stoker's bathroom with some sacks and a wedged board. Then I went on the Oberdeck and in the ventilation shaft down into compartment X. Compartment X was not damaged; in the boiler room the water only stood door high. I attempted to extinguish the boiler with the fire hose, but I did not succeed. With the opening of the grate on bulkhead 62 water came from compartment XI. Thereon I made the bulkhead tight. In compartment IX a hit had gone through the bunker, had gone through the air shaft and all was torn. A second hit went through the funnel neck. Also the drying room was full of water to door height. Bulkhead 46 was bent. In compartment VII and VIII there were several hits, several holes in the hull side, in the bunker and air shaft, which were totally destroyed. In the boiler room the water was somewhat over door height. The bunker lid to the chute was closed, coal lay in the zwischendeck. In compartment VI was fire, there I could only look. The clothes lockers lay in a mess and burnt. The wall to the coal bunker on starboard was torn, and there it also burnt. Through the air shaft in compartment X I went again on the Oberdeck, and down into compartment V. There all lay in a mess, also several dead comrades. The door to the engine room was open, however I could not pass, because the water stood too high. Then I succeeded in passing through bulkhead 23. The armoured hatch to the munitions chamber was open, above the Platform deck stood some water. Together with another man we were able to close the armoured hatch and shored it up. Further aft was totally blocked. Then I made a report to the I Offizier. He gave me the order, that if the ship did not sink, I should throw the secret books overboard.

Now I saw the Oberdeck [upper deck]. Of the funnels the first was holed, the second and third were completely shot away. The masts still stood, the flag flew. On the starboard second gun the barrel was split on the mouth and the port second gun slanted because the deck was torn up. In the kitchen all was smashed, likewise the air shaft to the 4 boiler room, and also the first and second boiler rooms, and the engine room, whilst the air shaft to the 3 boiler room was slightly damaged. The motorboat burnt. Both cutters were shot through. The hammock boxes on starboard were all torn up, and there lay several dead comrades. The starboard 3 gun stood level, it was loaded, however, but did not shoot any more. The port 3 gun threatened to fall down, the entire deck was torn up. The Commander's salon was parted in two halves, likewise the cabin of the Navigation Offizier and of the I Offizier. The aft gun could turn no more. The stern was totally rent up, and the ship's propeller shaft (housing) from compartment VI had caught fire. A seaman and I succeeded in extinguishing the fire. The Balloon Defence Cannon were almost undamaged, likewise the hand rudder and the compass, mainly all aft of the mast. The Obermatrose Schuster remained in the aft crow's nest until the last.... About 3 o'clock in the morning SMS *Wiesbaden* lay somewhat more over to starboard. Floats were let down aft. It was quite light. A cruiser and a destroyer each with 4 funnels came in sight, but took no notice of us. The ship lay deeper and deeper. Then we all went aft and down onto the float, the badly wounded had to be left behind. In total quiet *Wiesbaden* suddenly vanished beneath the waves with flying flag.[19]

Aboard the Fleet Flagship, SMS *Friedrich der Große*, Vizeadmiral Scheer was under increasing pressure to do something to relieve the pressure on the sorely pressed head of his line. At the head of the line the I AG had come under very heavy fire and had given way in a staggered formation, en-echelon, onto a SE course, in front of the III Squadron. Vizeadmiral Scheer believed the British line was more to the east than was the case and with the wind WNW to west and going further to the west, so that the dense smoke from his ships swept towards his opponents, the visibility was poor and getting poorer, whilst his own ships were clearly evident against the setting sun. To turn his line onto a southerly course would mean his ships would have to pass through a turning point and would easily be targeted, whilst a southerly course with the enemy in the east would result in a tactical disadvantage. Kapitän zur See von Trotha later wrote:

To oversee the development of the battle Admiral Scheer had stood freely on the open upper bridge. Now, however, the enemies heavy shells began to land around *Friedrich der Große* and a saltwater torrent rained over the ship reminding us to seek the shelter of the conning tower. We arrived in the conning tower. It was a narrow intimate space measuring only a few metres in space, with the front protected by armour almost ½ metre thick. It was only possible to see or use the observation glasses through the vision slits, which went through the armour. One could feel the strain on the nerves that affect men serving in this intimate space, and a sense of power. Not one unnecessary word was spoken, only brief reports and orders. Here is the brain of the ship, and the brain of the entire fleet.

The entire fleet of over 100 ships and torpedobootes was in the hands of this narrow, armoured position. In addition to the Chief of Staff and the necessary Admiralstaboffiziers (Astos)[20] two flag-Leutnants have their place beside Admiral Scheer – for flag, searchlight and wireless signals. They sift through the various reports that arrive from speaking tubes, telephone and other connections and from flag signals and the wireless room. Near them work the Fleet Navigation Offizier and his Obersteuermann[21] unconcerned, like in peacetime manoeuvres, and plot the course of the running battle and the position of the fleet, whilst in another position, after all reports, a sketch of the battle situation is drawn.

The Commander stands at the front, near him the Manoeuvring Offizier, his Signals Offizier and the Battle Helmsman, who holds the heavy, advancing ship tight in the wake of the next ahead, so that the artillerie can be concentrated against the enemy. The engine-telegraph is nearby. On one side the Torpedo Offizier follows the course of the battle, awaiting the moment when he can loose his arm against the enemy. The Artillerie Offizier is enclosed in a separate position, from where he directs the heavy artillerie. The observation positions high in the foremast and in the aft conning tower give reports and counter reports from all sides of the ship. Reports are passed from the speaking tube position. Salvos from the 30.5cm turrets crash out ahead and aft of the conning tower and yellow powder smoke temporarily blocks the view, just as the columns of water from the enemy shells landing short in the water.

Admiral Scheer oversees the situation calmly, no differently to what we were accustomed to on training cruises. It was his custom in such difficult decisive moments to allow each individual to carry out his work and take responsibility. View, thoughts and decisiveness must remain free so a decision could be reached in seconds, and the situation and battle tasks could be overseen and mastered, whilst the powerful mass of large ships, small cruisers and many torpedobootes operated in a storm of fire. The British battle line could not be seen because the smoke, haze and artificial smoke that cover *Wiesbaden*, hindered the view. From a report of Admiral Hipper it was supposed that the head of the enemy was in the east, and from the reports of several torpedobootes it was learned that seemingly we stood opposite the entire English Fleet, a very powerful force. Attack – in a strength similar to the enemy – was the solution.[22]

As the carriage of cameras was forbidden aboard German warships during World War One, photographs of the German ships during the battle are rare. This photograph shows the I AG whilst engaged with the 1 BCS and 5 Battle Squadron. Ahead is *Lützow*, followed by *Derfflinger* and *Seydlitz*. *Derfflinger* has just fired a salvo.

Another rare photograph of the I AG engaging the British forces. *Derfflinger* has just fired, and *Seydlitz* is caught at the instant of firing, the flash from her cannon clearly visible.

German torpedobootes during the battle, whilst a small cruiser can be seen in the middle background, probably *Regensburg*.

German torpedobootes in the lee of the I AG.

The small cruiser *Wiesbaden* before she was disabled.

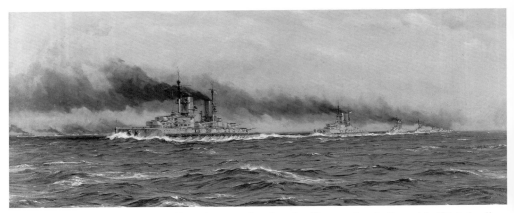

A painting by the marine artist Claus Bergen, showing the German battle line with *König* leading. The aft funnel of the German battleship has been painted red as a recognition device.

Another painting by Claus Bergen, this time showing the Panzerkreuzer *Lützow*, badly down by the bows after suffering multiple hits. The torpedoboot *G39* approaches from aft to transfer Vizeadmiral Hipper to another flagship.

The Panzerkreuzer *Moltke* returning home after the battle.

A view of *Moltke* after the battle. It is evident that she is down by the stern with approximately 1000 tonnes of water in the ship.

A photograph of *von der Tann* after the battle. Turret A is jammed on a bearing of 120° after being struck by a shell.

The small cruiser *Frankfurt* during trials.

A view of damage to the aft
superstructure of *Frankfurt*.

Damage to the aft
superstructure of *Frankfurt* after
the Skagerrak Battle.

The entry hole of a shell which struck the
small cruiser *Frankfurt*.

The small cruiser *Pillau* was hit by a 12 inch shell from the 3 Battle Cruiser Squadron, which destroyed the starboard side of the bridge.

The entrance hole of the 12 inch shell that struck *Pillau*.

A fine study of the small cruiser *Wiesbaden*.

The small cruiser
Elbing, originally
ordered by the Russian
Navy and taken over
for German service.

The Panzerkreuzer
Derfflinger returning to
harbour after the battle.
A hit has sheared off
the III 15cm cannon,
and various other hits
can be seen.

Derfflinger showing
the starboard side.
Interestingly all the
hits on *Derfflinger* were
on the port side or
from astern.

Offizieres enjoying breakfast on the quarterdeck of *Seydlitz* on the morning of 1 June 1916. Paster Fenger has his head bandaged, and behind him sitting on the skylight is Doctor Robert Amelung.

A view of the casemate where Paster Fenger was wounded when a shell detonated inside. He was the sole survivor of the casemate crew.

Hit number 13 on the port side of *Seydlitz* failed to penetrate the thick belt armour.

This heavy hit struck the rear of turret C after the turret had already been knocked out, but nevertheless caused another cartridge fire.

A view of the bridge and conning tower of *Seydlitz* after the battle. A so called 'leak mat' covers the entrance hole of hit number 7.

A hit to the port casemate of *Seydlitz*. All serving crew of the 15cm cannon perished, apart from five wounded and the gun was put out of action. The lower hit did not penetrate the thick belt armour.

Hit number 2 to *Moltke*. Although the armoured plate has not been penetrated the outer skin below the belt armour had been damaged and allowed some flooding in the wing passage.

A view of the rubble left after a heavy shell struck to the rear of the aft conning tower of *von der Tann*.

Hit number 6 on the battleship *Großer Kurfürst* left a calibre sized hole in the casemate armour and killed six men of the serving crew of the II 15cm gun.

This hit on the citadel armour of *Markgraf* failed to penetrate the armour.

Markgraf was struck by a shell that holed the foremast.

The result of a hit on the aft belt of battleship *Markgraf*, which penetrated and caused some flooding.

The interior of the port VI 15cm casemate of *Markgraf*, after being struck by a heavy shell. The gun was put out of action. Nine men were killed immediately and two died later from their wounds.

A view of the hit to the battleship *Helgoland*.

During the night encounters the battleship *Nassau* attempted to ram the British destroyer *Spitfire*. The resulting collision caused damage to the bow of the German ship.

A group of Offizieres on the quarterdeck of the battleship *Rheinland*.

Damage to the bridge of the German battleship *Nassau*, after being struck by a 4 inch shell from a British destroyer during a night encounter.

The battleships *Westfalen* and *Nassau* on the occasion of the opening of the new III Entrance to Wilhelmshaven harbour.

The battleship *Westfalen* in a Norwegian fjord before the war.

Admiral Scheer mit Offizieren seines Stabes auf S. M. S. Friedrich der Große.

Vizeadmiral Scheer, after his promotion to Admiral. He is with his dachshund.

Admiral Scheer and his Staff aboard *Friedrich der Große*. The commander of the battleship, Kapitän zur See Fuchs, seems to have made a joke. To Admiral Scheer's left is Kapitän zur See von Trotha, to his right Kapitän zur See Levetzow.

Admiral Schmidt

Vizeadmiral Franz Hipper, commander of the I Reconnaissance Group, which he led as Commander of Reconnaissance Ships. He is wearing his Pour le Merit, awarded for his performance in the Skagerrak Battle.

Vizeadmiral Ehrhard Schmidt, commander of I Squadron.

Vizeadmiral Hipper and his staff.

Kapitän zur See and Kommodore Ludwig von Reuter, commander of IV Reconnaissance Group, pictured after the war.

The I Leader of Torpedobootes (I FdT), Kapitän zur See and Kommodore Michelsen.

The II Leader of Torpedobootes (II FdT), Kapitän zur See and Kommodore Heinrich.

Commander of the IX
Torpedobootes Flottille,
Korvettenkapitän Goehle.

Three Torpedobootes Flottille commanders (from
left to right): Korvettenkapitän Max Schultz (VI
Flottille), Korvettenkapitän von Koch (VII Flottille),
and Korvettenkapitän Goehle (IX Flottille).

The British light
cruiser *Chester* after
the battle, showing
some of her damage.

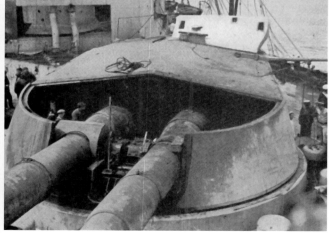

A heavy shell from *Lützow*
struck Q turret of *Lion* and
detonated inside, blowing off
part of the turret roof.

A shell hit on *New Zealand* punched out a neat hole in the armour of X turret barbette.

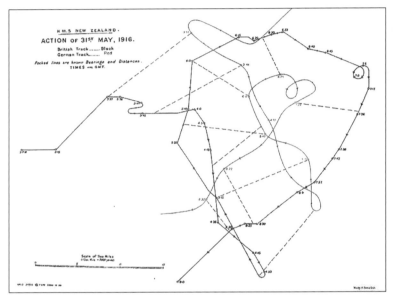

The track chart of *New Zealand* which clearly shows the circle described by Vice Admiral Beatty's 1 Battle Cruiser Squadron, but was removed from other charts.

Below on the left, Obermatrose Bursche holds his cat, Tiger, along with *Derfflinger's* I Offizier, Korvettenkapitän Max Fischer's cat, whilst on the right two cats aboard HMS *Orion* have a 13.5 inch cannon muzzle as their vantage point. Cats have long been the mariner's friend; both as company and to keep vermin such as rats and mice under control.

At 1936hrs Vizeadmiral Scheer gave the order to the line for a 'Battle turn to starboard', and three minutes later for 'Course west'. This would relieve the overwhelming pressure on the head of his line. In the meantime the I FdT, Kommodore Michelsen, aboard *Rostock*, had reached the head of the German line with the III Flottille and the 1 TBHF, after their fruitless attack at 1845hrs. At 1937hrs *Rostock* gave the attack order: 'Run out to the attack', or 'Ran an den Feind!'

The commander of the III Flottille, Korvettenkapitän Hollmann, wrote:

Flottille III 'Z Vor' and blinker message from FdT cruiser: 'run to Port ahead'.

I pulled the Flottille ahead of *Rostock* and ran on the muzzle flashes to port ahead. The ships themselves could not be seen through the powder smoke lying on the water. I gave the signal: 'To shoot turn away to starboard; shoot 3 torpedoes.' Indistinct ship outlines first appeared out of the powder smoke at 65hm. As during the run in the Flottille scarcely received any fire, I intended to go nearer to shoot, so the ships could be better made out and the position of the enemy line and ships (interception angle) could be determined, as the I FdT signalled me by FT: 'To III Flottille: don't attack.' A break off of the attack was possible as it was not under effective fire.

I pull back the Flottille by a turn of the Groups, which gradually sheered into my wake.

The order 'do not attack' was not taken in by all bootes before the turn away. *G88* and *V73* each launched one torpedo at approximately 60 hundred. Result not observed as the ships lay in smoke.

Return to *Rostock* that now stands near the 1 Division of the III Squadron.

V48 (not observed by me, but according to later information) had attacked a damaged destroyer, on the return behind the line. *S54* and *G42* had supported the Group Leader boot in the battle against the enemy destroyer.

During this battle *V48* was damaged by an artillery hit of the destroyer, and was later taken under heavy fire, and did not return to the Flottille.[23]

Whilst running in to the attack torpedoboot *S32* opened fire on the disabled *Shark* and on the return engaged her again, whilst *V48*, Flottille boot of Korvettenkapitän Theodor Riedel and under the command of Kapitänleutnant Friedrich Eckoldt, *S54*, under Kapitänleutnant Karlowa, and *G42*, Kapitänleutnant Bernd von Arnim, also engaged her. At first *Shark* fired from two guns and hit *S32* near the bows, and *V48* amidships, which forced the torpedoboot to stop. *S54* fired two torpedoes at *Shark*, one of which hit abreast the aft funnel and sank her with only six survivors. *G42* attempted to take *V48* in tow, but under the fire of the British battleships secondary, and then heavy artillery the attempt failed, as did one to take off the crew. The *V48* is believed to have fired four torpedoes at the British line.

At 1936hrs Vizeadmiral Scheer signalled 'Battle turn to starboard', whereby each ship turned individually onto the opposite course, after the following ship began their turn, therefore the entire line executing a 180° turn in sequence. This manoeuvre had often been practised but was difficult to carry out, more so when under enemy fire. On this signal Kontreadmiral Mauve began to turn, however, as the II Squadron had fallen far astern during the pursuit and the last ship of the I Squadron, SMS *Westfalen*, Kapitän zur See Redlich, considered them as a separate unit and therefore turned his ship without waiting for the II Squadron to complete their turn. At 1939hrs the signal 'course west' went on the flagship and *Westfalen* became the new fleet guide.

With the battle turn *Warspite* was finally lost as a target and only *Ostfriesland* could fire two salvos after the turn at a range which quickly increased from 125 to 160hm. As the wireless position on *König* had fallen out the FT message for the battle turn was not received and only at 1941hrs when the signal for course west was seen did the ships of the 5 Division turn and increase speed to catch up with the 6 Division. At this point a shaft bearing aboard *Markgraf* began to overheat and the port engine had to be stopped, so that she could only maintain her place in line with difficulty.

With the destruction of *Invincible* and battle turn away to the west another phase of the battle had come to a close. This phase had been no less successful for the Germans than the previous phase. Another two large warships, *Defence* and *Invincible*, had been totally destroyed and the battleship *Warspite* had been knocked out of the battle. Against this *Lützow* had been badly damaged. Vizeadmiral Scheer had not disengaged because of a feeling he was in a critical position. In a letter to the American author, Commander H. Frost, Vizeadmiral Scheer said:

> While the battle is progressing, a leader cannot obtain a really clear picture, especially at long ranges. He acts and feels according to his impressions. In looking at the diagrams that are made subsequently, it would seem as if we must have regarded our situation as critical. In reality this was not the case. We were under the impression of the splendid effectiveness of our gunfire and of the fact that the entire battle line remained most conveniently arranged both while under fire and during the regrouping for the night march.[24]

Chapter 6

Vizeadmiral Scheer Attacks

A fter the German battle turn onto a westerly course from 1936hrs only *Lützow* did not follow as at 1937hrs she had reduced speed and began to withdraw to the SW. Speed was reduced to 15 knots and then to 12 knots, to reduce water pressure on bulkhead 249. The Panzerkreuzer had been badly hit forward and the entire area below the armoured deck ahead of bulkhead 249 had immediately filled with water. However, worse was to follow as the flooding spread. *Lützow*'s Leakage Report explained how the water leaked from compartment XIV to compartment XIII:

> Through the ventilation shafts, that were still not watertight, and through the un-tight sides of bulkhead 249 and in the speaking tubes, water quickly penetrated from compartment XIV to compartment XIII and spread itself there over the forward rooms, the starboard forward engine instrument panel, cool room machinery, starboard drainage pump room and gradually in the diesel dynamo room. On the port side the water penetrated gradually in the forward torpedo compressor room.[1]

However, this situation had been foreseen and reported in *Lützow*'s trials final report. It ran in part:

> With the commissioning of the ship the hull, engines and boilers were found in good condition. The execution of the ship's construction was generally good. Only the ship's structural water tightness and closing of the drainage, flooding and feed water shutters give cause for complaint because of numerous leakages.[2]

Having found these problems during trials, rectification work was undertaken before the Skagerrak Battle, but the extent remains unknown.

The leakage report continued:

> The Meister personnel skilfully propped bulkhead 249. The main drainage means were used for the forward diesel motor room, auxiliary means for the forward switch position. The middle drainage pumps were utilized, because both the connecting linkages for the two forward pumps were unclear through damage.[3]

When Kapitän zur See Harder reported to Vizeadmiral Hipper that the ship could no longer maintain speed, and in combination with the wireless being out of action, the BdA decided to transfer to another ship for use as flagship, at first intending to board his old flagship, *Seydlitz*. At 1945hrs Vizeadmiral Hipper disembarked from *Lützow*. Fähnrich zur See Mardersteig had his battle station in the aft conning tower and described the scene thus:

> Our own torpedobootes come nearer. They are bootes of the 1 Half-Flottille. *Lützow* seems to stop. The noise of battle diminishes. Or is this only a deception? Quickly an individual boot approaches. It is *G39*, Commandant Oberleutnant zur See von Loefen. The flag 'Anna' climbs up the forward mast. This announces the putting alongside manoeuvre. The torpedoboot carefully approaches the port aft side, near the torpedo protection nets, which are hanging down. There appear the people of the BdA Staff, signal personnel and Staff Musician. They go towards the torpedoboot lying alongside. A second group of Offizieres of the BdA Staff, in their midst Admiral Hipper himself. With a bold leap from a quickly bent knee the Admiral jumps across to the torpedoboot. In quick succession the others follow. With the lowering of the flag 'Anna' the boot casts off. Admiral Hipper and his Staff have quit the ship.[4]

The II Wireless Offizier, Leutnant zur See Kienast, wrote:

> With the BdA and his Staff we quit *Lützow*, which had been hit 24 times in a cauldron of heavy shells. Conscientiously the Staff writer even took his battered typewriter across to the torpedoboot! With 'Hail the Forester', Admiral Hipper and the *Lützow*'s Commander parted, just as old hunting companions.[5]

Vizeadmiral Hipper also gave Kapitän zur See Harder permission to sink his ship if the damage became too great. Whilst *G39* took Vizeadmiral Hipper and his Staff aboard the bootes *G40*, *G38*, *V45* and *G37* developed a dense smoke screen by the use of oil in their boilers and artificial smoke.

The leadership of the I AG was taken over by Kapitän zur See Hartog aboard *Derfflinger*. On this ship the wireless could only receive and the signal halyards had been burnt or destroyed. The bridge signalling searchlights were all unserviceable so that Kapitän zur See Hartog had no means to communicate with the other ships of the I AG apart from with flags from the battle signal station adjacent to the casemate.

On the British side the sudden reversal of course to the west by the German line went largely unnoticed and one by one the British battleships ceased fire, and as Commander Frost said: 'Before the line could reach a proper degree of regularity, the great chance to damage the Germans had been lost.'[6] It was not until 1944hrs, four minutes after the last British battleship had ceased fire, that Admiral Jellicoe changed his fleet course to SE, but this was inadequate to hold contact with the Germans. The two remaining battle cruisers of the 3 BCS lost contact with the German ships when they hauled out to port to avoid the wreck of *Invincible*. However, Rear Admiral Napier, with his light cruisers *Falmouth* and *Yarmouth*, had positioned himself to the NE of I AG and soon after 1930hrs he observed the German battle cruisers turn to the west. However, he did not report this until Vice Admiral Beatty enquired of him at 1940hrs: 'What bearing are the enemy battle

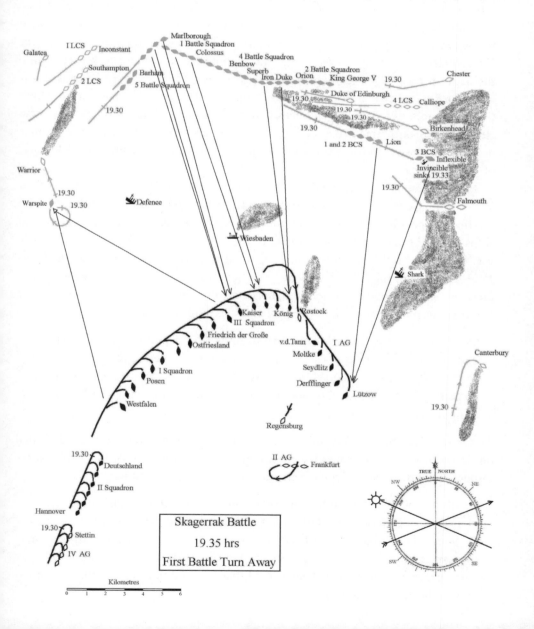

Skagerrak Battle

19.35 hrs

First Battle Turn Away

Kilometres

cruisers?' Rear Admiral Napier replied that he had last seen them at 1920hrs in battle with the 3 BCS and that they had altered to course west, however this time is clearly in error. Meanwhile, *Lion, Princess Royal, Tiger* and *New Zealand* had been forced to cease fire as between 1937hrs and 1940hrs they were obliged to evade torpedoes from the III Flottille.

Beatty believed that the I AG were on the same course as *Lützow*, which he had seen turning onto a SW course, and therefore at 1944hrs he swung onto a SE course and then at 1948hrs onto course SSE. At 1950hrs Vice Admiral Beatty ordered the 3 BCS to take station astern of *New Zealand*, the rear battle cruiser of the 2 BCS. At 1953hrs the 1 and 2 BCSs reduced speed to around 18 knots so that the distance to the battleship squadrons would not increase, and began a turn to course south. Nevertheless, just as *Inflexible* began the manoeuvre to come astern at 1955hrs, the flagship *Lion* began turning in a circle. It is stated that the gyro compass went out of order and that it was easiest to complete a full circle, a manoeuvre which took seven minutes. At 2001hrs *Lion* stood in the same position as when the course alteration to south was ordered. For reasons of his own Beatty had this circular manoeuvre erased from the track charts of the Jutland Dispatches, except for that of *New Zealand*.

The tactical advantage held by the British around 1935hrs was lost when Vizeadmiral Scheer turned away to the west. Admiral Jellicoe would not follow the German ships. He believed that all German ships, including cruisers and capital ships, carried mines on board and that a turn away was employed to facilitate their use. He also feared being lured into a U-Boat trap. In his book *The Grand Fleet, 1914–1916*, Admiral Jellicoe went to great lengths expounding the virtues of the German capital ships. After noting that German projectiles were better performed and that German ships were better protected he went on to say:

> On the other hand, British capital ships mined or torpedoed rarely survived. The recorded instances of escape are the *Inflexible* (mined in the Dardanelles) and *Marlborough* (torpedoed at Jutland), and in the latter case, although the torpedo struck at about the most favourable spot for the ship, she had some difficulty in reaching port.[7]

As early as October 1914 Admiral Jellicoe sent a memorandum to the Admiralty outlining new tactics dictated by the use of new weapons. His Grand Fleet Battle Orders made the tactical doctrine standing orders which ran in part:

> Until the enemy is beaten by gunfire it is not my intention to risk attack from torpedoes... generally speaking it is to be understood that my intention is to keep outside torpedo range of the enemy's battle line.... If I have any reason to suspect that the turn away is made for the purpose of drawing us over submarines or mines it may be expected that I should not follow a turn of this nature shortly after deployment.

The then First Sea Lord, Fisher, was in full agreement. Indeed the Grand Fleet Battle Orders as written by Admiral Jellicoe seemed to fly in the face of the best traditions of the Royal Navy. Previous naval doctrine had been to pursue an enemy then flying, and it was fortunate the Articles of War had been amended since when on 14 March 1757 Admiral John Byng had been executed on the quarterdeck of *Monarch* because he did not 'do their utmost against the enemy, either in battle or pursuit'. It would be difficult for Jellicoe, or any commander, to defeat an enemy without engaging him closely.

Admiral Jellicoe now found himself in a situation where the enemy had turned onto the opposite course and he believed the trap he feared most had been sprung. Already there had been a number of U-Boat reports during the battle, although no U-Boats were actually present. The best protection against submarines and mines was destroyers, but these were engaged in steaming to the head of the British line. In the conditions of poor visibility Jellicoe was unsure of what further course of action he should take. He believed the High Sea Fleet was taking course for the German Bight and his only resolve was to quickly lay course across the probable German line of retreat and attempt to renew contact. Therefore, as mentioned, he altered course to SE at 1944hrs.

At around 1945hrs *Marlborough* altered course to avoid a torpedo, but at 1954hrs a heavy explosion occurred beneath the bridge and the ship took up a 7° list to starboard. A torpedo had struck *Marlborough* at stations 86–88, about 20 feet below the waterline. A hole 20 × 26 feet was blown in the hull side and the wing bulkhead was penetrated and blown inwards from the middle deck to the inner bottom. The inner coal bunker bulkhead was likewise damaged. The hydraulic machinery room, electrical stores, dynamo room, coal bunkers and wing compartments, transverse coal bunker, all double bottom spaces between stations 66 and 111 and the forward boiler room (A) were flooded, which gave the ship a list to starboard of 7°, this being subsequently reduced by trimming to 2¾°, there eventually being 1000 tonnes of water in the ship. The six boilers of the forward stokehold were put out of action but *Marlborough* could still make 17 knots and hold her place in the line. Two men in the No.1 dynamo room lost their lives. *Marlborough* reported avoiding three more torpedoes.

Marlborough also suffered damage to the right 13.5 inch gun of A turret around this time. After firing five shots the inner tube was cracked all the way around and a large piece of jacket was broken off. Although thought by some to be the result of a shell hit, this damage was attributed to the premature explosion of a shell.

At the same time officers aboard *Revenge*, in A and Y shell rooms, the director tower and spotting tower all felt a shock as if the ship had struck something. A large oil patch and portions of wreckage came to the surface and it is probable that she was struck by a torpedo which failed to detonate and broke up. It is thought that these torpedoes came from *Wiesbaden* and *V48*.

Vizeadmiral Scheer had successfully broken off contact with the Grand Fleet, but he thought it too soon to begin a retirement to the German Bight. Breaking off contact with the Grand Fleet meant losing the initiative, and so far Vizeadmiral Scheer had maintained independent initiative and had held the numerically superior Grand Fleet at bay. If the British could be held off until nightfall then Scheer could retain freedom of action, and therefore he decided on renewing battle with the British and striking a blow against the middle of the British line. His reasons for this were much simpler than suggested by many writers. He wanted to maintain the initiative he had held up until now; he wanted to attempt to save the badly damaged *Wiesbaden*, or at least her crew; he wanted to avoid the appearance of a retreat, and finally he wanted to disrupt the enemy plans for the remaining hours of daylight.

Vizeadmiral Scheer wrote:

> It was still too early for a nocturnal move. If the enemy followed us, our action in retaining the direction taken after turning the line would partake of the nature of a retreat, and in the event of any damage to our ships in the rear, the Fleet would be compelled to sacrifice them or else to decide on a line of action enforced by enemy pressure, and not adopted voluntarily, and would therefore be detrimental to us from the very outset. Still less was it feasible to strive at detaching oneself from the enemy, leaving it to him to decide when he would elect to meet us the next morning. There was but one way of averting this – to force the enemy into a second battle by another determined advance, and bring the torpedobootes to the attack. The success of the turning of the line while fighting encouraged me to make the attempt, and decided me to make still further use of the facility of movement. The manoeuvre would be bound to surprise the enemy, to upset his plans for the rest of the day, and if the blow fell heavily it would facilitate the breaking loose for the night. The fight of the *Wiesbaden* also helped to strengthen my resolve to make an effort to render assistance to her and at least save the crew.[8]

Der Krieg zur See elaborated:

> The decision was responding to the intuition of the moment and so daring, so surprising and contrary to established practice was this tactic that only success could justify it. The English would doubt Scheer's intuition though. They believed the appearance of the 3 BCS to the east caused the German leader to think the British line was more to the east than it was, covered by the dark horizon and that Admiral Scheer was attempting to secure a free passage to Horns Reef. They also thought Scheer was perhaps trying to cut off what he thought was a separate unit in the 5 Battle Squadron, positioned to the north.
>
> This assumption is wrong. Admiral Scheer's plans and maps show he was correct in his assessment of the position. In the uncertain situation the German leader showed great resolve.

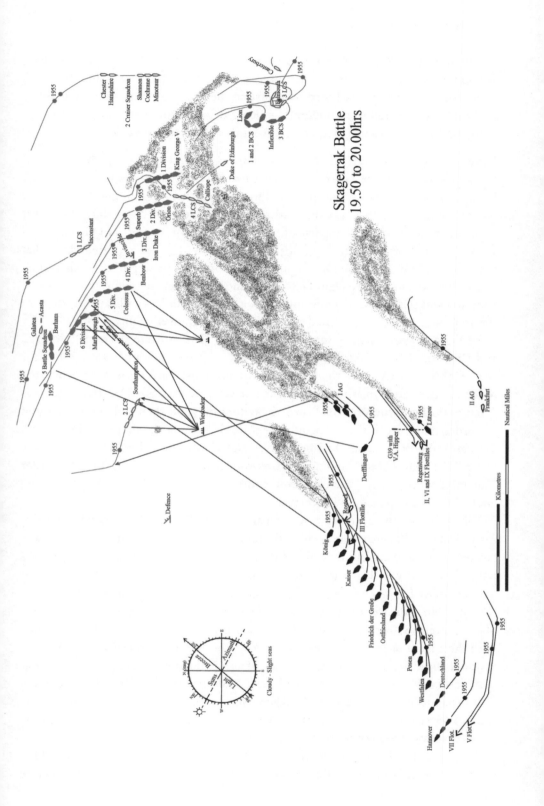

Skagerrak Battle
19.50 to 20.00hrs

Soon after 1950hrs Admiral Scheer turned his battleship Divisions two points to starboard, to bring them nearer the enemy. At 1955hrs the signal to make a battle turn to starboard was hoist on the flagship. At the same time the Fleet Chief ordered Kommodore Michelsen to send some torpedobootes from the III Flottille to assist *Wiesbaden* during this pause in the battle.[9]

Many critics of Admiral Scheer deride and berate him for giving the saving of *Wiesbaden* as one of the factors in making his decision. However, Commander H. Frost later commented on the spirit that was behind this last thought: 'Despite the terrible propaganda that was directed against the German Navy during the war by its enemies, there was a spirit of loyal comradeship among its Offizieres and sailors that is worthy of the highest praise. Despite the often repeated claim that the German Offizieres, ashore and at sea, were only too willing to drive their men into useless slaughter, the plain facts of Jutland show a remarkable spirit of loyalty, cohesion and self sacrifice. Time and time again commanders and captains came to the assistance of their threatened comrades with magnificent courage.'[10]

At 1955hrs *Friedrich der Große* made the signal 'Battle turn to starboard'. At 1952 and 1954 the II FdT, Kommodore Heinrich, on his own initiative, gave orders for the VI TBF and IX TBF to attack. The orders must have been given when the order for the battle turn was hoist, but not yet executed. At 1952 the order was given optically to the VI TBF, 'Torpedoboote Ran!', and then at 1954hrs followed the order to the IX TBF, 'Torpedoboote Ran!' It was not the first occasion during the battle the 'Ran' signal had been given. At 1726hrs the II FdT had given the order 'IX Flottille Ran!', and at 1937hrs *Rostock* had given the III TBF the order 'Auflaufen zum Angriff' (Ran an den Feind!) or 'Run out to the attack' ('Attack the enemy'). Some explanation is necessary.

When the the Imperial Navy was expanded shortly after its formation in 1871, many Armee Offizieres were seconded to the Navy, and they at first brought many Armee terms and traditions. One of these terms was 'Ran!' which simply means 'attack', or as it was 'Have at them!' In the Imperial Navy signal book, a copy that may be viewed at the British Public Record Office, beside the signal 'R' is noted 'Bring about a decision with all means. Have at them, ram.' Whilst in the 1870s, 80s and even 1890s the prospect of ramming the enemy might have been feasible, with the advent of long-range heavy artillery this option disappeared, and by 1916 it would never be contemplated. The idea of a torpedoboot ramming a large warship is ludicrous. However, the signal book remained unamended. The following signal 'T', brought an even stranger anachronism, 'Auf der feindliche *Tete* (feindliche Spitze) operieren,' that is, operate on the enemy head, but why on earth would the signal book use the French word *Tete*, for head?

The signal for the torpedobootes to attack was the forked red 'Z' pennant, which went on the mast of the II FdT flagship, *Regensburg*. The fact that Kommodore

Heinrich was able to act on his own initiative speaks volumes for the training of the High Sea Fleet and it was a bold and intelligent decision made at just the right time, as we shall see later. The II TBF were not at first able to join this attack as they lagged behind, a result of their being delayed when Kontreadmiral Boedicker ordered the Flottille to give way to the II AG at 1927hrs.

Kommodore Heinrich wrote:

1937hrs. After this fight I intend to again hold onto the Panzerkreuzer. The II Flottille thereby receives the signal Z Zero. (Follow the Leader). The Leader of the II AG forces the II Flottille away to the SW by the signal 'Give Way.'

1935hrs. Under the guidance of *Derfflinger* the I AG turns onto a northerly course for the third time. *Lützow* had fallen out, unmanoeuvrable. Four bootes were dispatched to him for his protection.

Regensburg followed the I AG with AK. The II Flottille was so far to the rear because of the 'Give Way' order of the II AG that it took a long time for them to catch up.

The VI and IX Flottilles, which were not so far to the south as *Regensburg* and the II Flottille through the battle with the light forces, closed near *Regensburg*.

Of the enemy nothing was to be seen, except a large 4 funnelled cruiser in the NNW, which vanished in a great torpedo explosion.

The heavy impacts came from three sides.

The battle course of the I AG was approximately east, and the Panzerkreuzer lay in a heavy, effective fire. The Flottilles and with them *Regensburg*, were to the east and were fired on by heavy artillery for a long time. Our head was seized fast.

I had the conviction that now was the crucial moment for the fate of our Panzerkreuzer and I determined on a ruthless mass attack by the Flottilles.

1952hrs. The VI Flottille and IX Flottille receive the attack order.[11]

Nevertheless, at 1955hrs the I FdT, Kommodore Michelsen, on orders from Vizeadmiral Scheer, was diluting his torpedoboote forces. At 1955hrs he ordered boats from the 1 and 12 TBHF to go to the assistance of *Lützow*, even though the 12 HF were part of Kommodore Heinrich's command. A short time later, at 2000hrs, he ordered the III Flottille to rescue the crew of *Wiesbaden*. The I FdT and II FdT held equal authority, but nevertheless *G37* and *V45* of the 12 HF conformed to Michelsen's order, even though they had just been ordered to attack, and along with *G38* and *G40* of the 1 HF went to *Lützow* and laid a smoke screen to cover the badly damaged Panzerkreuzer. The *G39*, also of the 1 HF had embarked Vizeadmiral Hipper and his Staff to transfer him to another ship previously. However, the mission by the III Flottille did not meet success, as Flottille Chief Korvettenkapitän Hollmann reported:

Flag signal on *Rostock* to III Flottille: 'III Flottille go to recover crew of *Wiesbaden*, direction NE.'

I did not think it right that the Flottille Chief should take himself out of the battle for such an individual task, therefore immediately after receiving the order I gave the blinker signal order to the Group Leader standing behind me on *V71*[12]: 'With your 3 bootes go to *Wiesbaden* and rescue the crew, direction NE.' However, then I run in the direction of *Wiesbaden* with the Flottille boot before the blinker signal was taken in by *V71*, as the I FdT had made the signal: 'III Flottille: faster.'

As I passed between the en-echelon first and second Divisions of the III Squadron with course on *Wiesbaden*, our own line opened fire again towards the battle cruisers lying to the north. *Wiesbaden* lay in heavy enemy fire, salvos of heavy enemy fire lay ahead of my bootes running towards *Wiesbaden*. I held further conduct of this special task as unreasonable, synonymous with the loss of still undamaged bootes with a still strong torpedo armament without a chance for success; apart from the fact that the continual running of the bootes between the lines would disrupt their fire. Therefore I turned back through the same gap in the line and returned to *Rostock* and reported to the I FdT by blinker signal the grounds for not carrying out this order.[13]

Nevertheless, despite being under a heavy fire two of the German torpedobootes launched torpedoes against the British battleline. *V73* fired one torpedo, and *G88* fired three torpedoes against the second and third groups of enemy capital ships, at a range of 6000m, which they held to be battle cruisers. Their targets were in fact *Colossus* and *Marlborough*'s Divisions.

With the turn to starboard in the gap of the III Squadron *V73* fired one, and *G88* fired three torpedoes against the middle of the enemy battle cruisers positioned to the north. At the time that the torpedoes would reach the enemy line *G88* observed two torpedo detonations briefly after one another on the western two enemy battle cruisers.[14]

Colossus, *Neptune*, *Agincourt* and *Barham* all took evasive action to avoid these torpedoes.

At 1955hrs Vizeadmiral Scheer had signalled for a battle turn to starboard, back onto an easterly course towards the middle of the British battleline. From the maps in Scheer's book it is apparent that he was under no delusions as to where exactly the British line lay, and if anything he had them more to the SE than they actually were. Perhaps a better course would have been to the south, or SSE to parallel the British course and fight on a course that would have taken him towards the German Bight. This would have allowed him to disengage at any time with a turn back to the west. However, such a course would have meant abandoning *Wiesbaden*. Admiral Scheer wrote:

The battle that developed after the second change of course and led to the intended result very soon brought a full resumption of the firing at the van which, as was inevitable, became the same running fight as the previous one, in order to bring the whole of the guns into action. This time, however, in spite of 'crossing the T', the acknowledged purpose was to deal a blow at the centre of the enemy line. The fire directed on our line by the enemy concentrated chiefly on the battle cruisers and the Fifth Division. The ships suffered all the more as they could see but little of the enemy beyond the flash of fire at each round, while they themselves apparently offered a good target for the enemy guns. The behaviour of the battle cruisers is specially deserving of the highest praise; crippled in the use of their guns by their numerous casualties, some of them badly damaged, obeying the given signal, 'At the enemy', they dashed recklessly to the attack.[15]

As the Germans were carrying out the battle turn to starboard the British 2 Light Cruiser Squadron came in sight in the NNE and at 2005hrs *Derfflinger* and *Markgraf* opened fire on Commodore Goodenough's cruisers, followed quickly by *König*, *Großer Kurfürst*, *Kaiser* and *Prinzregent Luitpold*. The 2 LCS quickly turned away to the north. Commodore Goodenough reported that the German Fleet was in sight SSW of *Southampton*, and steering ESE. At 2005hrs the Grand Fleet divisions turned from course south to SW by south, in an attempt to re-establish contact with the German ships. At this moment the leading ship, *King George V*, and also *Duke of Edinburgh*, reported a U-Boat to port ahead, the fourth false sighting for the day. Admiral Jellicoe therefore swung back onto course south at 2009hrs, but all these manoeuvres brought the British line somewhat into disarray with increases and reductions in speed, and the divisions overlapped. *Marlborough*'s Division were still firing on *Wiesbaden* when suddenly the last ships of *Colossus*' division sighted one, then two, three and four German Panzerkreuzer (battle cruisers) emerging from the smoke and haze with their accompanying torpedobootes.

However, the German line was having disruptions of its own. Korvettenkapitän von Hase wrote:

While we were steering west the Commander came on to the bridge and reported to the Captain: 'The ship must stop at once. The after torpedo-net has been shot away and is hanging over the port screw. It must be cleared.' The Captain gave the order: 'All engines stop!'

I surveyed the horizon through the periscope. There was nothing of the enemy to be seen at this moment. The *Seydlitz*, *Moltke* and *von der Tann* were not in very close touch with us, but they now came up quickly and took their prescribed stations in the line. It was a very serious matter that we should have to stop like this in the immediate neighbourhood of the enemy, but if the torpedo-net were to foul the screw all would be up with us. How many times we had cursed in the ship at not having rid ourselves of these heavy steel torpedo-nets, weighing several hundred tons. As we hardly ever anchored at sea they were useless and, in any case, they only protected part of the ship against torpedo fire. On the other hand, they were a serious source of danger, as they reduced the ship's speed considerably and were bound sooner or later to foul the screws, which meant the loss of the ship. For these reasons the English had scrapped their torpedo-nets shortly before the war but we did not do so until immediately after the battle of Skagerrak, as a result of our present experience.

The boatswain and the turret-crews of the 'Dora' and 'Caesar' turrets, under Oberleutnant zur See Boltenstern, worked like furies to lift the net, make it fast with chains and cut with axes the wire-hawsers and chains that were hanging loose. It was only a few minutes before the report came: 'Engines can be started.' We got underway at once.[16]

Nevertheless, Korvettenkapitän von Hase was mistaken in his recollections as the war diary of *Derfflinger* records this event as occurring sometime after 2005hrs. Kapitän zur See Hartog wrote in his KTB:

2005hrs. *Derfflinger* had already suffered under the enemy fire so that the FT could only receive.

It was not possible for me to signal my arrangements: 'Follow the Leader', 'Fire distribution from the right,' to the other Panzerkreuzers.

I went without signal in port line of bearing with the Panzerkreuzers onto a northerly course to starboard ahead of the head of the main body towards the enemy. At this moment we had to stop for two minutes to clear the nets, that could foul the screws.[17]

Because *Derfflinger*, at the head of the entire German battleline, had stopped for two minutes to clear her anti-torpedo nets the ships of III Squadron quickly approached and began to bunch up, some having to stop their engines and even go astern. *Markgraf* reported:

This situation worsened further with the following course alteration to starboard, as the ships ahead reduced speed because of the I AG passing in front of them and thereby caused a bunching up of the entire line. The ships lay for a brief time almost without speed, tightly bunched, and offered an excellent target for the enemy fire, without ourselves being able to fire.[18]

As the German capital ships emerged from the smoke and haze the Grand Fleet battleships were once again able to open a deadly and destructive fire on them, best characterized by the following table.

Time	Ship	Range	Target
1956	*St Vincent*	9100m	Torpedobootes
2004		8700m	Battleship
2004	*Agincourt*	10,000m	*Wiesbaden*
2006			*Derfflinger* class
2004	*Neptune*	9300m	*Derfflinger* class
2005	*Revenge*	10,000m	
2005	*Colossus*	8200m	Torpedobootes
2012			Battleship
2010	*Ajax*	17,400m	1 salvo
2010	*Valiant*		–
2012	*Marlborough*	9600m	*Wiesbaden, König* class
2012	*Hercules*	8200m	
2013	*Iron Duke*	14,000m	
2014	*Monarch*	16,500m	*König* class
2015	*Royal Oak*	12,800m	*Derfflinger*
2015	*Orion*	17,400m	*Derfflinger* class
2016	*Centurion*	16,000m	*Kaiser* or *König* class
2017	*King George V*	11,700m	*Derfflinger*
2017	*Temeraire*	11,000m	
2017	*Bellerophon*	10,000m	
2017	*Benbow*	–	*Derfflinger*
2020	*Canada*	–	
2020	*Superb*	10,000m	
2020	*Collingwood*	7300m	
2020	*Vanguard*		Torpedobootes
2020	*Malaya*	9600m	

During this period, at 2017hrs, the 1, 2 and 3 Battle Cruiser Squadrons also opened fire, but it was not so effective. HMS *Barham* was also firing and is credited with some hits on the German battleships.

As this firing was beginning Admiral Jellicoe executed a turn three points towards the enemy at 2005hrs, onto course SW by S. This placed the fleet in a complex formation consisting of six parallel columns disposed in a 3–point line of bearing. Whilst Jellicoe was correctly disposed for the expected contact and his right flank encountered the Germans at close range, the left flank was virtually out of the fight. Now a finish fight would surely occur as the Germans were headed directly into the centre of the Grand Fleet at incredibly close ranges and were severely outnumbered. They were in the most unfavourable and critical situation possible.

The German ships soon began to suffer and between 2000 and 2030hrs a total of 38 hits could be counted on the German capital ships, although 55 per cent of these were made at the point blank range of 71 to 90hm, and the remainder at less than 130hm. Even though *Lützow* had turned away to the SW and had been screened by torpedobootes with a protective smoke screen, by 2007hrs he had become a clear target for *Orion* and perhaps also *Monarch*. At 2007hrs a shell struck the port casemate and put the port combat signal station out of action, killing the signal personnel. At 2015hrs a shell struck the right barrel of A turret and detonated just outside the gunport, disabling the gun and showering splinters into the turret. Likewise at 2015hrs a heavy shell penetrated the deck between C and D turrets and destroyed the aft combat dressing station. In addition the electrical cable to D turret was destroyed, leaving D turret on hand training.

> And then the dance begins again. Red flashes to port, out of the haze. 'To the guns!' With this sentence I was again in the gunnery position. 'Direction indicator!' 100hm, on that muzzle flashes, salvo! – No shots fall. When they again flash, again: 'Salvo!' – No shots. It is impossible for the gun leaders to take sight. Would that we had the 'director'! Two or three hits vibrate the ship again aft. One of these detonates on the zwischendeck between turrets C and D, and by this the aft dressing station suffers heavy casualties among the wounded, that Doctors and medical personnel are serving. At the same time this hit strikes a part the electric power cable for turret D, that here for a short stretch is routed above the main armoured deck. The enemy hits found such places with fatal certainty. Turret D was then totally on hand training, which for a 30.5cm turret amounts to practically a total loss. Also the main armoured deck is ruptured by this hit – the only case –, in which the powder magazine lying directly beneath was disrupted.[19]

This hit also badly wounded Marine Stabsärzte Florus Gelhaar. An orderly wrote:

> The Stabsärzte (Staff Physician), to my surprise, was still alive, however his head was badly wounded. He succumbed to this wound some days later in the Wilhelmshaven Naval Hospital.[20] From this time, it was said throughout the ship, as he could not particularly stand well, he said: 'The wounded should be brought to the ship's infirmary, so the Stabsärzte can concern himself with them.'
>
> I was amazed to hear that he was still alive. At the same time I say he was in a bad way, and only his extraordinary will to perform his military and professional duty, and his feelings of human sympathy, kept him going.[21]

At 2016hrs a shell struck near B barbette, causing some flooding and then one minute later, at 2017hrs, a projectile struck the starboard side of B turret, punching out a piece of armour and disabling a gun.

> The water is churned up by the impacts of the salvos. Millions of dead fish float with white bellies up, resplendent on the water. *Lützow* is continually hit now. A shell strikes the second gun turret. The air pressure tears the cap from my head. The turret stands at most 10 metres distant from me. Smoke comes from inside. Not long after the turret hatch opened. One, two people jumped

out, as black as if negroes. They bring two others and lay them on deck. Are they dead or wounded? One is completely charred, his clothes burned from his body. Here the turret Offizier, Kapitänleutnant Fischer, was also carried from the turret. He is also dead. Others are unconscious or else dead, they have no wounds or burns. They are completely naked. The air pressure of the detonation must have torn the clothes from their bodies.

The commander stands steadfastly on the bridge, despite the impacts of the projectiles. In complete calm he gives orders for the engines and rudder. All the frequently ordered course alterations were faultlessly repeated and the commander handled himself as if at an exercise, only with greater calm than at battle practice and no cigarettes disturbed his concentration. As if through a miracle we were not wounded, although the deck and bridge were covered in splinters and the chart house looked like a sieve.[22]

Finally between 2015 and 2030hrs a heavy shell struck the upper main mast causing the topmast to fall on deck. From inside the aft conning tower Fähnrich zur See Mardersteig reported:

All hell is loose. Bursting shells, howling splinters, steel on steel, humming transverse bulkheads, impacts and detonations without end. The whole hull trembled and vibrated. Do we also shoot? Nobody can answer this question. Hundreds of grey and white fish bodies drift close past the ship. Impact on impact has brought them from the depths of the North Sea to the surface. Fires flicker. A deafening impact strikes directly beside the aft conning tower. Leutnant Sch.[23] calls 'The funnel has fallen!' However, it was only the upper half of the mast which fell down from a great height. 'Smoke and gas danger in the aft position!' A poisonous yellow–green gas pours from a speaking tube. Quickly a sailor takes off his jacket and blocks the threatening speaking tube. Near misses vibrate the aft ship with torrents of water. Water drops hang from the vision slits of the aft armoured position. Then a tremendous sizzling and clatter of splinters on the conning tower itself.[24]

Lützow could count himself as unlucky during this period.

Also unlucky at this time was brother in arms *Derfflinger*, which was hit a total of 14 times during this period. Being hit so many times at short range it was no wonder the British sailors nicknamed *Derfflinger* 'The Iron Dog.' At 2014hrs a 15 inch shell from *Revenge* struck the roof of D turret, penetrated the 110mm thick armour and detonated on the right gun cartridge hoist, igniting approximately 1000kg of powder and putting the turret out of action. Seventy-five men died. Between 2016 and 2017hrs *Derfflinger* was struck another four times by *Revenge*. One projectile struck the barbette of C turret, penetrated the 260mm armour and detonated above the turntable between the two cannon. Once again propellant charges burned and the turret was put out of action. A total of 68 men lost their lives. Zimmermannsgast (carpenter) Schwendler related the grisly scene:

> We go over the deck and work our way to the aft turret, which has a 38cm shell hit between the barrels. There we received the penetrating smell of burned corpses from the fire. Also – I must say – I had an uncanny feeling, as we looked inside through the hole made by the hit. It was altogether frightening. What a terrible view was offered to us. Our dear comrades were crushed under the iron rubble, mutilated and burned black as to the indiscernibly charred.
>
> An inexpressibly painfully sad conviction seized me. We must dry our eyes. My friend continues to pull me. With a fearful view we looked at each other; we continued. The last turret had a hit on the roof. We climbed high. You had to lie down flat to be able to see in. Unwillingly I held my breath, so as not to be too frightened by the grisly sight. Here there was also great destruction. Directly below the opening lay a familiar seaman in still unburned clothes, only his face sagged. He still held his telephone receiver to his head with his hand. To his right behind stood a dead person, pushed somewhat back into the iron rubble, with his clothing and body completely burned. His right hand was raised with an outstretched index finger, just as a supervisor. Here and there a foot, an arm or a head stuck out from the rubble. It was an indescribably terrible sight. The wretched smell soon forced our rapid withdrawal.[25]

There were two hits on the quarter deck, one on the outer skin at frame 22 and one at frame 27. The latter caused a 5 metre diameter hole in the battery deck and caused great devastation. The last hit from *Revenge* at this time penetrated the forward funnel about 1 metre from the upper edge. Then at 2016hrs a shell made a glancing blow against the rear of A turret barbette, holing the batterie deck. At the same time a 12 inch projectile struck the barrel of the port III 15cm cannon and then detonated on the gun shield. The gun barrel was broken off but the 80mm gun shield was not penetrated. The next shell hit at this time was a heavy calibre shell which struck the belt below the port VI 15cm gun. The shell struck the joint of two plates and shattered without penetrating. A hole 1150mm by 450mm was made and a piece of armour was broken off and thrown inside. The next hit struck on the belt between C and D turrets, but did not penetrate. The final hit at 2016hrs went through a skylight on the quarter deck.

At 2020hrs a heavy shell penetrated *Derfflinger*'s superstructure and detonated in the infirmary, making a large hole in the superstructure and decks. Sometime after 2020hrs *Royal Oak* struck *Derfflinger* with two 15 inch shells, both through the aft funnel. The final hit of this period was a 12 inch projectile fired by *Bellerophon* which struck the forward conning tower. Korvettenkapitän von Hase described the impact of this hit:

So far we in the armoured tower had fared very well … my train of thought was sharply interrupted. Suddenly, we seemed to hear the crack of doom. A terrific roar, a tremendous explosion and then darkness, in which we felt a colossal blow. The whole conning tower seemed to be hurled into the air as though by the hands of some portentous giant, and then to flutter trembling into its former position. A heavy shell had struck the fore-control about 50 cm. in front of me. The shell exploded, but failed to pierce the thick armour, which it had struck at an unfavourable angle, though huge pieces had been torn out. Poisonous greenish–yellow gases poured through the apertures into our conning tower.[26]

Between 2000 and 2030hrs next in line *Seydlitz* was struck by heavy shellfire a total of six times.

At some stage between 2000 and 2020hrs a heavy projectile fired by *Hercules* fell short and exploded in the vicinity of the hull side causing some leakage and filling two wing passage compartments. Between 2014 and 2020hrs a shell, apparently fired by *New Zealand*, struck the port hull side citadel armour at frame 91 without penetrating. At the same time a shell from *Hercules* struck the aft upper searchlight platform, then flew overboard and detonated. The starboard upper searchlight was destroyed. Between 2014 and 2020hrs a shell impacted short and then struck the outer skin at frame 118, penetrating and detonating thereafter. The dressing station was destroyed and splinters showered the upper deck and conning tower. This hit allowed flooding later on. At 2027hrs a 15 inch shell struck the right barrel of E turret, putting that gun out of action. Today this cannon can be seen outside the Naval Museum at Wilhelmshaven. Finally, at 2030hrs a 12 inch projectile, apparently from *St Vincent*, struck the aft wall of burnt out C turret. A piece of armour and splinters entered the turret and ignited charges on the loading trays, causing another fire.

During this battle phase, at 2019hrs, *von der Tann* was struck from aft by a 15 inch shell thought to have been fired by *Revenge*, which hit at the rear of the aft conning tower. Although the tower was not penetrated splinters entered the vision slits and four men lost their lives.

The German battleships also suffered during this short period. At 2018hrs *König* was hit by a 13.5 inch shell reportedly from *Iron Duke*, which struck just below the VII 15cm casemate, passing through the rolled up torpedo nets and upper edge of the citadel armour, exploding in the Unteroffiziere room in compartment VI near frame 47. Three men were killed.

It was during this phase of the battle that *Großer Kurfürst* suffered most, being hit seven times with four of these hits occurring within two minutes. From bow to stern these hits were as follows: A 13.5 inch shell detonated on striking the armoured plate at frame 125, the punched out pieces of armoured plate penetrated the side splinter bulkhead and remained lying in the rope store. There was some flooding to the depth of 1 metre. The next shell to hit was a ricochet which struck near the first hit at frame 127. The effects of this hit could not be differentiated from those of the first hit. Damage to the hull below the armour meant that all the rooms below the armoured deck from frame 119 to 133 eventually flooded, with a total of 800 tonnes of water in the ship.

A further hit of 15 inch calibre struck the upper deck at frame 110 and detonated, fragments striking A turret barbette. A hole was blown in the upper deck and two men were killed. Another 15 inch shell struck the citadel armour at frame 100 and detonated on impact. A piece of 200mm thick armour was punched out and remained laying on the Zwischendeck. The outer bunker from frame 98 to 103 flooded and a total of 12 men that were in the midship battle dressing station were wounded.

A 15 inch shell struck the 170mm thick casemate armour between the II and III port 15cm casemates. A 650mm circular hole was made in the armour but the shell detonated on impact. The barrel of the II casemate gun was damaged by splinters but remained serviceable. In casemate II 10 men were killed but 3 men could save themselves. In casemate III 4 men were wounded and two men were badly wounded. A further 15 inch shell struck the main belt armour at frame 79, just abaft the fore funnel, near the waterline. The armoured plate was pushed in and some wing passage cells were flooded. Another short shot burst in the water aft of E turret and caused some splinter damage to the hull.

Initially *Großer Kurfürst* took on a list of 4° but this was reduced to 1° by counter flooding.

At 2014hrs *Markgraf* was struck by a 12 inch shell thought to have come from *Agincourt*. The shell struck at frame 105, between A and B turrets, 2.2m above the waterline and exploded on impact without penetrating. A splinter from this shell hit the foremast observation position and badly wounded an Offizier and a seaman.

Kronprinz was not hit, but remained under heavy fire. The I Artillerie Offizier Korvettenkapitän Viktor Habedanck wrote:

> From 7.38hrs we had a hard trial, as to starboard ahead we had the entire, invisible English Fleet, which had drawn itself around our head in a southeast direction, and we received a heavy fire. Only 4 or 5 muzzle flashes from individual ships could be made out. The English could see us sufficiently well on the bright western horizon, as if caught in the dawn, whilst he was hidden from our view against the dark eastern horizon in the haze and powder smoke. We could not return the fire.[27]

Aboard *Kaiser* there was one hit. At 2026hrs a 12 inch shell struck on the batterie deck just aft of the VII 15cm casemate and penetrated the artillerie workshop hammock store. The shell did not detonate, but the filling burned and caused a fire amongst the hammocks, which was quickly extinguished. A short shot to starboard caused damage to the outer hull, spars and booms of the torpedo nets and an accommodation room.

Navigation Offizier Korvettenkapitän Studt, wrote:

Upon returning to the west we met our *Wiesbaden*, which had been shot into a wreck, a moment that touched the heart. A heavy hit in the engine plant had forced them to a stop, and now they lay still between the battling lines, an easy target for the English artillery which had firmly bitten her, and water was already up to the upper deck and the hands could no longer serve the cannon. And we wondered: will the Fleet Chief leave the ship to its fate?

Then came a new signal already through the line: 'Battle turn to starboard for line ahead in opposite direction.' No, we would not leave our comrades to be overtaken by death, the Fleet Chief would once more come to their support. However, it was already too late, the fearful English shells had made her a wreck.

The Fleet Chief would make a renewed advance against the enemy and even if he could save *Wiesbaden* there was a higher purpose. The hour was 8. It was still too early for the rearmarch, the enemy still too little shaken. Therefore he determined to make one last powerful blow against the enemy. And he reached his intention fully and totally. The massive blow was unexpected by the English. Once again we threw our magnificent Panzerkreuzers, which had in part received heavy damage, with utmost strength against the enemy line, and brought the torpedoboot Flottilles to the enemy. A hail of shells of all calibres showered them as they pressed home the attack to within 60 hectometres. However, the blow was seated. As the next Flottille went to the attack and as they came from the haze of the eastern horizon, they found that already there was nothing to see of the enemy. Obviously he had turned away, and was now gone. Our Fleet Chief now has freedom of action again.

Again a turn was made and the Fleet went with firstly a western, then a southern course, from the battle area towards Horns Reef. There we would meet the enemy if he still wanted to fight.[28]

At 2015hrs *Helgoland* was hit by a heavy calibre shell on the belt armour, ahead of the citadel, at frame 105 just above the waterline. The armour here was 150mm thick and the shell broke up without detonating, however made a hole 1.37m by ½m in the armour. A large piece of shell was found on the deck and the shell calibre was determined as 34.3cm, or 13.5 inch, according to *Helgoland*'s war diary. When the shell broke up a green gas cloud was seen outside the ship. Approximately 80 tonnes of water flooded into the ship.

On the British side only *Colossus* was hit. At 2016hrs she was hit just abaft the forward funnel by a shell which exploded and caused a fire in the port gun decks and

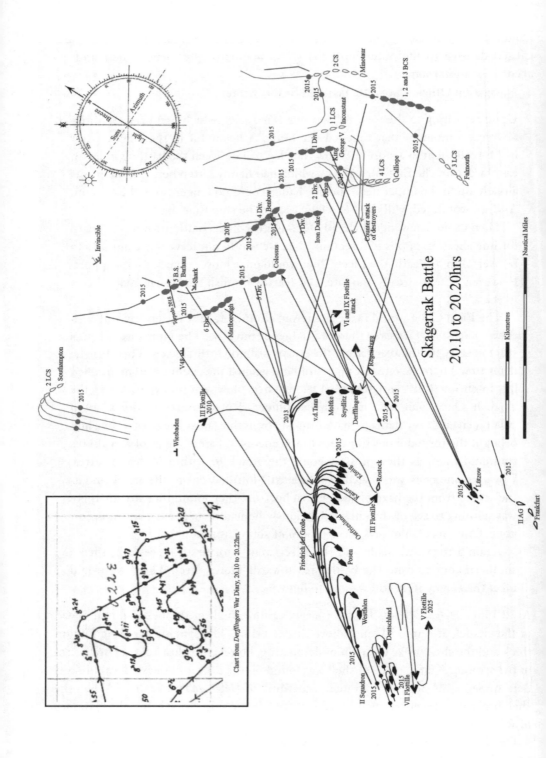

Skagerrak Battle
20.10 to 20.20hrs

Chart from *Derfflinger's* War Diary, 20.10 to 20.22hrs.

signal deck. Some 4 inch gun charges had been ignited by splinters but the fire was soon extinguished. The other shell struck the sounding platform on the port signal deck but passed overboard without detonating. Both shells are thought to have come from *Seydlitz*. Then one minute later, at 2017hrs, a shot impacted just short of A turret and splinters penetrated the fore funnel and other unarmoured parts of the ship in about twenty places. The starboard No.1 searchlight was wrecked and several men were wounded, some badly. At 2018hrs another short shot sent more splinters flying into the forecastle.

The German line was quickly approaching that of the British, but even though they themselves were under an increasingly heavy fire nothing could be seen of the British ships but the continuous flickering of muzzle flashes. To make matters worse the German line had become bunched. At 2013hrs Vizeadmiral Scheer gave the order '9R' to the I AG, and at the same time the signal: 'Große Kreuzer Gefechtswendung rein in dem Feind! Ran!', that is 'Battle cruisers battle turn to the enemy! Have at them!'

Korvettenkapitän von Hase wrote the following in his book *Kiel and Jutland*:

THE FOURTH PHASE OF THE SKAGERRAK BATTLE (8.05 P.M. TO 8.37 P.M.). THE DEATH RIDE OF THE BATTLE CRUISERS. ADMIRAL SCHEER EXTRICATES THE FLEET FROM THE ENEMY ENVELOPMENT. DESTROYER ATTACKS. THE ENEMY SHAKEN OFF.

Meanwhile the Commander-in-Chief had realized the danger to which our fleet was exposed. The van of our fleet was shut in by the semicircle of the enemy. We were in a regular death-trap. There was only one way of escape from this unfavourable tactical situation; to turn the line about and withdraw on the opposite course. Above all we must get out of this dangerous enemy envelopment. But this manoeuvre had to be carried out unnoticed and unhindered. The battle cruisers and the torpedoboats had to cover the movements of the fleet.

At about 8.12 p.m. the Commander-in-Chief gave the fleet the signal to turn about on the opposite course and almost at the same time sent by wireless to the battle cruisers and destroyers the historic order: 'Close the enemy.' The signal man on our bridge read the message aloud, adding the words, which stood against it in the signal book: 'And ram! The ships will fight to the death.' Without moving an eyelid the Captain gave the order: 'Full speed ahead. Course S.E.' Followed by the *Seydlitz*, *Moltke* and *von der Tann*, we altered course south at 8.15 p.m. and headed straight for the enemy's van. The *Derfflinger*, as leading ship, now came under a particularly deadly fire. Several ships were engaging us at the same time. I selected a target and fired as rapidly as possible.[29]

Korvettenkapitän von Hase was an Anglophile, and this is illustrated by the title of his book, *Zwei Weiße Volkes*, or Two White People, and when it was translated into English the book received the revised title *Kiel and Jutland*. Like many post-war Germans he wished to placate the British public. With his term 'Death Ride of the Battle Cruisers' he sought to highlight the role of his ship, and his mention of ramming the enemy, five nautical miles distant, is pure fantasy. His writing contains the contradiction 'we altered course south at 8.15 p.m. and headed straight for the enemy's van.' According to the track chart of *Derfflinger* the Panzerkreuzer began altering course to the south at 2013hrs, therefore before the order to 'Ran!' was taken in and at 2015hrs *Derfflinger* was already on course south. The British van bore to the east. Therefore at this point *Derfflinger* had already paralleled the course of the British line, and maintained this parallel course for the next five minutes. Many of the artillery hits at this time came from abaft. Of the fact that the German line was in a precarious position there is no doubt, but Korvettenkapitän von Hase's account is inaccurate and has more to do with giving his book colour than with actual events.

The account of Korvettenkapitän von Hase did not escape the criticism of Vizeadmiral Scheer. When the German battle line began to bunch up Vizeadmiral Scheer seems to have become impatient, the Panzerkreuzer were blocking the way and were causing the line to become compressed, and he therefore gave them the order to have at the enemy, or in other words, attack! The Landesmuseum Hannover has in its collection some letters written by Admiral Scheer to Vizeadmiral Carl Hollweg, which have only recently come to light. On 19 May 1919 Admiral Scheer wrote to Vizeadmiral Hollweg:

> When we made the discovery that the English main force faced us, our head was already on course NE, quadrantally. A turn further to the east was inevitably carried out, the turn ahead appeared questionable.
>
> Initially it only seemed possible, because the line was stretched out, to turnabout onto the opposite course. The artificial smoke and our smoke drifted towards the enemy, as well as to the east. This caused a temporary ceasing of fire. Our westerly course brought the obvious question: What now? To continue to turn to the south would give our behaviour the character of a retreat, with its tactical disadvantages. In this disposition suddenly our Große Kreuzers, which according to our observation had been withdrawn, appeared to break free of the two enemy lines with a southerly course, with a tangle of torpedobootes. This view was reinforced by the impression that they sought to move out of the enemy's fire, therefore: retreat. This led me to signal the Große Kreuzers and torpedobootes: Ran an den Feind! (Attack the enemy!) And since almost simultaneously – I do not have the actual time to hand – the damaged *Wiesbaden* emerged north of our line about 2–3000m distant, because the smoke that had concealed her was removed to the east, I was encouraged by this sight in a <u>sense</u>, I underline this word, we have to advance to her and

turn the line around. I was satisfied that the first turn about had succeeded so excellently that we could confidently repeat this movement. We had practised this often, but had doubted its practical applicability. Also, despite the heavy fire laid on our head there had been no distress calls, and this allayed the fear that the ships were no longer capable of attack.

This battle turn would support the actions of the cruisers and torpedobootes so that the enemy line would have to dodge and would be torn in the middle....

As to the outflanking manoeuvre, this offered us little chance of success. The direction of the lines of the two opponents was approximately as follows: we now operated from the middle to the end enemy ships, so there was the prospect of our envelopment, because of the gap to the NW.

From the previous combat pictures[30] I had no experience in this situation, and remember nothing like this. Then there was the greater speed of the English. What to do with our II Squadron? It was not impossible that they could have suffered greatly if they had been in an artillery battle with the English capital ships....

His *Queen Elizabeth* Squadron, which stood behind and attempted to join to the rear of the English line, was inspired by this. If they had also made a turn with our first battle turn, then our line would have been under pressure ahead and behind, and a repeat advance against the English line would have been impossible. So the Englishmen showed <u>no tendency for tactical handling, only an artillery action in the current battle at long range. This is no great art</u>. The restraint that he showed in his strategy also dominated <u>his tactical approach</u>. Through <u>our shock [advance] however, that was actually against the rules of tactics, we took him</u> to the next morning with a possibility of rejoining battle. An early morning resumption of the battle against the greatly numerically superior enemy would perhaps be poor for us, where we had consumed a considerable amount of munition, how much I did not exactly know.

Our tactical aspiration was always to put the enemy as close as possible to our [main] body, to the advantage of the torpedobootes. This had been done, although the situation was not favourable for them.[31]

As this is a private correspondence Admiral Scheer has been very frank and honest. He says his order 'Ran!' was to urge the battle cruisers to reengage the British forces more closely, not to facilitate the battle turn of the fleet. In another letter dated 15 January 1920 he singles out Korvettenkapitän von Hase for insightful criticism:

I have endeavoured, moreover, to meet the Tirpitz Fleet policy. I had no occasion to highlight their weaknesses, because I know how difficult it was to achieve what we got. Also, we should avoid everything that happened on the land. If I have given up all hope to restore German sea power for future generations then I also hope the English will have a low percentage of world domination. Therefore, it is not useful to further promote English prestige in history, when our democracy already does. In this respect the book of Korvettenkapitän von Hase 'Two White People' stands out. He has certainly played up his battle experiences. But he has missed the 'point'. He portrays the dispatch forward of our Cruisers (signal: Ran an den Feind) as if this was to facilitate our detachment from the grip of the British embrace. The timing sequence of the signals provides quite a different intention: first the second battle turn of the battleships (onto an easterly course), then the order to the cruisers to also attack the enemy (Ran an den Feind). His behaviour has in fact created the impression with me that they seemed to be glad to be able to withdraw from the battle on a southerly course with high speed.

The idea of a chance encounter of the two Fleets, which was even unpleasant for us, and which we could only withdraw from disaster with much luck and a little skill, is deliberately disseminated to our disadvantage and is believed. At sea there are only battles of challenge and encounter. We had challenged, and with Fleet operations sought a meeting with the enemy.[32]

In a letter to the American author Commander H. Frost, Admiral Scheer wrote in a similar vein and tone:

While the battle is progressing, a leader cannot obtain a really clear picture, especially at long ranges. He acts and feels according to his impressions. In looking at the diagrams that are made subsequently, it would seem as if we must have regarded our position as critical. In reality this was not the case. We were under the impression of the splendid effectiveness of our gunfire and of the fact that the entire battle line remained conveniently arranged both while under fire and during the regrouping for the night march.[33]

So from a German perspective there was no 'Death Ride', no headlong charge of the light brigade by the I AG into the maw of the enemy line, but instead there was in fact a considered turn to the south to engage an enemy that was for the most part invisible. Admiral Scheer was perfectly correct to admonish Korvettenkapitän von Hase for embellishing what could have been an excellent account of the battle, but was hamstrung with inaccuracies and fanciful exaggerations.

Just one minute after issuing the signal 9R, 'Panzerkreuzer Ran!', Vizeadmiral Scheer, gave the order 9T, 'Auf der feindliche *Tete* (feindliche Spitze) operieren', that is operate on the enemy head. The commander of SMS *Derfflinger*, Kapitän zur See Hartog, had begun a turn onto a southerly course at 2013hrs, as seen on *Derfflinger*'s track chart, and the war diary records the order 9T as being received at 2017hrs, by which time *Derfflinger* was well and truly on course south, therefore no action was required by Hartog. At 2020hrs *Derfflinger* changed course to the westward and was on this course by 2022hrs.

At 2018hrs, therefore five minutes after his order to the I AG to 'Have at them!' (Ran!), Vizeadmiral Scheer gave the order to the Fleet: 'Battle turn to starboard', whereon once again, for the third time that evening, the German battle line made a 16-point turn onto the opposite course. Because the III Squadron had been compressed behind the I AG, this time the turn was not as easy technically. The last ship of III Squadron, *Kaiserin*, quickly approached the next ahead, *Prinzregent Luitpold*, as the III Squadron bunched up. Even though *Kaiserin* slowed it was necessary to sheer out to starboard, and to resume a place behind *Prinzregent Luitpold* on the opposite course. *Kaiserin*'s war diary related:

2015hrs. With the execution of the signal 9R and 9T there occurred with the head of the Main Body a strong compression, as the fast Panzerkreuzer stood in the fire lee of our own line and the lead ship *König* had to allow the cruisers to pass, and had to turn away to starboard.

Hereby the ships of the III Squadron were pushed closely together and to avoid collision several ships had to sheer out to starboard. *Kaiserin* was forced, despite the reduction to 'kleine fahrt',[34] to sheer out to starboard and came in the lee of *Prinzregent Luitpold*, in the wake of *Kaiser*. This compression of so many ships in strong enemy fire was very unfavourable. In this short time the enemy obtained most of their hits. Through a turn on the signal 'Pennant Green' this was redressed. *Friedrich der Große* thereby turned to port, obviously due to lack of space. As *Kaiserin* increased the distance from *Ostfriesland* by a speed reduction to allow space for *Friedrich der Große*, *Prinzregent Luitpold* came quickly up to starboard with high speed, and *Kaiserin* allowed herself to lag behind *Prinzregent Luitpold*, to reform the battle line as quickly as possible. This position was held until the close of the operation.[35]

Kaiser fared well, but *Kronprinz*, the next ahead, was hampered by *Markgraf*, the next ahead of her. Kapitän zur See Seiferling reported:

About 7.45pm the port engine fell out because of a hot bearing causing vibration in the ship.

From the very unfavourable situation previously described, the Division was ordered to make a battle turn to starboard. With this battle turn *Markgraf* turned ahead of the next astern, to avoid the point on which the enemy salvos were particularly concentrated. Also position en-echelon was taken to avoid the unfavourable line of bearing *König-Kronprinz*, which lay under continuous fire, and taking into consideration the failure of the port engine and reduced speed, and possible new course alterations, much sea room would be required to hold the ship in the Unit. Hereby for the immediate future my attention was taken up, as any falling behind by the ship would be paid for with its destruction.

Gradually *Markgraf* came nearer to the line to starboard and sheered in behind *Kaiser*, in consideration that with the lower cruising speed of the 6 Division it would be easier for the ship to hold its position.[36]

To hasten the turn Vizeadmiral Schmidt turned his I Squadron without waiting for the order to execute the manoeuvre, as he correctly decided that the situation was critical. Therefore the battle turn was not a ripple movement, but more of a simultaneous turn, in order to make room for the ships ahead, which as mentioned, were bunched up. Recognizing the lack of sea room Vizeadmiral Scheer directed Kapitän zur See Fuchs, commander of *Friedrich der Große*, to turn to port instead of to starboard. The official history said:

It was owing to the distinguished tactical training and seamanship of the Admirals and Commanders that during the extraordinarily dangerous minutes the ships of the 5 and 6 Divisions and Fleet flagship manoeuvred at low speed in confined waters, but no collisions occurred nor was the turn of *Friedrich der Große* to port misunderstood.[37]

SMS *König* was still 400m downwind and being straddled by enemy salvos as she laid a smokescreen between the German and British lines. However, the 5 Division still lay under a pernicious fire for some time after the battle turn, apparently from the British battle cruisers. At 2028hrs, three minutes after firing her last salvo, *Kaiser* also began laying a smoke screen.

After signalling for the battle turn at 2018hrs at 2022hrs Vizeadmiral Scheer ordered 'course west' and then at 2027hrs ordered course SW and a speed of 17 knots. Squadrons II and I formed column and took up the new course, however, Squadron III continued on course west in a broad line of bearing formation in the sequence of: *Prinzregent Luitpold*, *Kaiserin*, *Kaiser*, *Markgraf*, *Kronprinz*, *Großer Kurfürst*, and *König*. Squadron III was now some distance from fleet flagship, *Friedrich der Große*.

At this critical time Admiral Jellicoe was busy trying to organize his Battle Squadrons into a cohesive battle line, as they stood in line of bearing by overlapping Divisions. At 2012hrs he ordered the 1 Battle Squadron to take station astern of the 4 Battle Squadron. At 2016hrs he ordered the 2 Battle Squadron to take station ahead of the 4 Battle Squadron. At 2018hrs Admiral Jellicoe ordered Vice Admiral Jerram, commander of the 2 Battle Squadron, to increase to utmost speed, whilst he himself reduced the speed of the battle line to 15 knots at 2020hrs, to allow Jerram to get ahead. At this time the British artillery fire had reached its zenith, with Vice Admiral Beatty's battle cruisers joining in, and the visibility had become very favourable for the 2 Battle Squadron on the eastern end of the line of bearing.

We have seen that at 1952hrs and 1954hrs Kommodore Heinrich, the II FdT, had given the orders to the VI Flottille and IX Flottille, optically, 'Torpedoboote Ran!'

This he had done of his own volition and he deserves the utmost praise. At this time *Regensburg*, his flagship and the Flottilles stood to the south of the I AG, not far from the badly damaged *Lützow*. It was not until 2021hrs that Vizeadmiral Scheer reiterated this order with the signal 'Torpedobootes to the attack!' Two minutes later, at 2023hrs the I FdT, Kommodore Michelsen, gave his own order, addressed to all Flottilles, 'Run out to the attack (Ran an den Feind!)' Therefore it remained for the Flottilles of the reconnaissance forces to make the first and most important attacks on the British line. However, as we have seen, the II Flottille, which mostly still had all their torpedoes, had been diverted with firstly their blow in the air against *Shark*'s division, and then by Kontreadmiral Boedicker's order to give way, and at first they were unable to participate in the attack. Unfortunately three bootes of the VI Flottille remained with them. Therefore only the 11th Half Flottille of VI Flottille and IX Flottille were immediately available.

Of the original strength of nine boats the VI Flottille could muster only four boats, as *V45* and *G37* had been allocated to escort *Lützow*, and *V69*, *V46* and *S50* were with the II Flottille. Therefore only *G41*, the Flottilleboot of Korvettenkapitän Max Schultz, and *V44*, *G87* and *G86* could advance against the enemy. These boats had been involved in the two previous attacks against the British and had expended some of their torpedoes. Of the IX Flottille, *V27* and *V29* had been lost, so that now there remained nine boats, *V28*, the Flottilleboot of Korvettenkapitän Goehle, and *V26*, *S36*, *S51*, *S52*, *V30*, *S34*, *S33* and *S35*. These boats had also fired some of their torpedoes in previous attacks.

The only other Flottille that was in a position near enough to attack was the III Flottille, under Korvettenkapitän Hollmann. Their abortive mission to rescue the survivors of *Wiesbaden* meant they had lost *V48*, stranded between the lines, and *G42* had not yet rejoined the Flottille since their advance. Therefore there remained *S53*, *V71*, *V73*, *G88* and *S54*, and these boats had been involved in heavy fighting and had already fired some of their torpedoes.

The flagship of the II FdT accompanied the VI and IX Flottilles until they were abeam *Derfflinger*, which by this time was steering south, and then turned back whilst under a heavy fire to fetch up the II Flottille. The 11th Half Flottille of the VI Flottille, under the command of Korvettenkapitän Max Schultz, led the attack from *G41*. Almost immediately the boats came under the concentrated fire of the British line, with *Royal Oak* opening fire on them at 2016hrs, *Agincourt* at 2018hrs, *Marlborough* at 2019hrs and *Temeraire* at 2020hrs, whilst at the same time *Vanguard* opened fire with her main armament of 12 inch cannon.

The German boats approached to a range of 70hm and then *G41* was struck by a medium calibre shell in the forecastle. Two Offizieres and two men on the bridge were wounded by splinters. Shortly afterwards at about 2025hrs, a heavy shell, probably from *Vanguard*, exploded on the water just ahead of G86. Shell fragments wounded the commander, Kapitänleutnant Grimm, and nine men, penetrated the wireless room, command bridge and wheelhouse. A torpedo head in a forward tube was damaged and the forward oil bunker leaked. As more British ships joined in firing on the Torpedobootes Korvettenkapitän Schultz turned and fired his torpedoes. With his last strength the badly wounded Torpedo Offizier of *G41*, Oberleutnant zur See Wagner, personally fired two torpedoes, whilst the other three boats of the 11 HF each fired three torpedoes.

Korvettenkapitän Schultz wrote:

The I AG receives a very lively fire from the assembled enemy line, therefore the new Unit coming from the east must have turned – which the Panzerkreuzers could not be expected to last long against. The II FdT gives first the IX and then the VI Flottille the order 'Z Vor'.[38]

With AK[39] course was taken ESE on the enemy line, which gradually had got around the head of our own Main Body and especially the Panzerkreuzer. We approached these to 70hm under a violent fire from heavy and medium artillery of the enemy. As the salvos covered the boot *G41* received the first hit of medium calibre on the forecastle, which threw splinters on the bridge badly wounding two Offizieres and 2 men, and lightly wounding one man. The boot turned away to shoot the torpedoes before the eventual destruction of the boot was assured.

A total of 11 torpedoes were fired.

Owing to the deliberate development of smoke after the turn away the result of the torpedoes was not observed, nevertheless, the fact that the enemy broke off the battle as a result of the attack by the VI and IX Flottilles proves it was effective, and the I AG was helped out of a critical situation....

With a western course a connection with our own line was sought and a report was given to the II FdT, that *G41* had no more torpedoes, and the 11 Half Flottille had only one available each. As *G41* had fired all the torpedoes she would remain with the Main Body for the march home, to act as destroyer defence and to assist sinking ships.[40]

Each of the four boats returned safely to the German line under the cover of smoke and haze, although *G86* had her speed reduced to 25 knots, and *G41* also had her speed greatly reduced. For a certain time this smoke veiled the attack of the IX Flottille, a little further to the north. However, after passing through the smoke the British ships redirected their deadly fire onto this Flottille. As the range closed to 70hm the Flottilleboot, *V28*, maintained a hit in the forecastle and Korvettenkapitän Goehle decided it was time to launch his torpedoes before his boats were put out of action. The Official History reported:

Despite the destructive fire all bootes reached a firing position. *V28* turned away but launched one torpedo, whilst a second remained stuck fast in its tube.

Likewise *S51* and *S36*, Kapitänleutnant's Dette and Franz Fischer, could loose but one torpedo each. *V26*, the Leaderboot of the 17th Half Flottille, under Kapitänleutnant Ehrhardt, fired two torpedoes, a third had to be held back as after the first two the target was obscured by a thick black cloud and then *S52* fouled the range. The shell splashes of incoming salvos made the view towards the enemy difficult. After launching torpedoes at 60 to 70hm the torpedobootes withdrew through smoke and artificial smoke, being pursued by enemy cruisers and destroyers. Despite the smoke, *S35*, Kapitänleutnant Ihn, which besides his own crew also carried some of the survivors of the previously sunken *V29*, including commander Kapitänleutnant Erich Steinbrinck, was hit amidships by a heavy shell, broke in two and sank. About 2030hrs S51, Kapitänleutnant Dette, was hit in a boiler and the forward rudder engine fell out. The Flottilleboot, *V28*, could only make 17 to 19 knots because of a large leak in the forecastle. Therefore Korvettenkapitän Goehle gave command of the Flottille over to Kapitänleutnant Ihn, the Commander of the 17th Half Flottille. Later on Korvettenkapitän Werner Tilleßen, commander of the 18th HF, took command and the boats gathered with *Rostock*, whilst *V28* and *S51* followed at reduced speed. The targets had been en–echelon and observation of hits through the smoke and water spouts was made impossible.[41]

Nachlaß Kapitänleutnant Hambruch of V28 stated:

As we penetrated the smoke and haze a fantastic sight was offered to us: before us stood in bright light in a wide curve from north to south–east 24 English battleships, and we gave the corresponding report that the entire English fleet had been sighted, as previously only individual ships and a single unit had partly come in sight. Fire of all calibres of this powerful fleet tried to stop our attack, a barrage in which every wretch sat, but nevertheless we had to advance into effective range to make sure our attack was successful. Measuring the range in the violently moving boot was not possible, as I was asked by the Flottille Chief whether we could now shoot, and as I was under the impression of the impacting shells, I could only answer: Herr Kapitän, if we do not shoot now we will not get rid of these torpedoes. Thereon we turned to shoot the torpedoes and under a black smoke cloud and haze returned to our cruiser. A salvo of 15cm shells struck us in the forecastle, tearing a barn door sized hole. To relieve the strain on the forecastle the forward boiler was blown off and the boiler room was propped up, but we could still run at medium speed and during the retirement we connected to the I Squadron. The torpedo attack had the result that the enemy divisions turned 4 points away, his tactical cohesion lost, whilst our fleet made a 16 point turn for the third time and took course on Horns Reef.

Immediately after the attack by the IX Flottille the III Flottille put in an attack, and although the German battleline had already turned away the III Flottille broke through the line between the second and third ships of the III Squadron. Flottille commander, Korvettenkapitän Hollmann, continued:

> 2023hrs: Z Vor. The Flottille runs on opposite course on the eastern wing of the 1 Division of the III Squadron, which is almost en-echelon, through a gap between the 2 and 3 ships against the enemy. The bootes of the VI and IX Flottilles, returning from the attack, lay a black smoke cloud between ours and the enemy line. I run north of the smoke cloud, then SE towards the supposed enemy, however once on the other side of the smoke veil do not sight any enemy heavy ships, only enemy destroyers and behind them light cruisers to the south. Therefore I swing on a southerly course, then on westerly course to again close on our Main Body, and reply to the fire of the south positioned enemy destroyers at approximately 60hm, which mainly fired at an apparently unmanoeuvrable German boot at short range. In part hits on enemy destroyers were observed.
>
> 2058hrs: Again on the western end of the elongated smoke cloud I push through this ahead to north, as when I had started the planned attack towards the east, in the north a heavily damaged motionless cruiser was seen, whose hull resembled *Wiesbaden*, with the funnels partly destroyed. However, the small cruiser could no longer be seen. Thereon course was taken to the tail of our own Main Body.[42]

The III Flottille had a brief fire fight with some boats of the 12 Destroyer Flotilla at a range of about 60hm. *G88* fired a torpedo at this range, on a destroyer that had been mistaken for a cruiser, whilst *S54* fired a torpedo at 90 to 95hm against the British line.

The mission of the VI and IX Flottilles around 2020hrs could serve as a model example of a daylight attack. It was made at the correct tactical moment, to relieve the head of the German line, from a favourable position against a worthwhile target, the main force of the enemy. It was made at the best point in time, with the approach of dusk, and both Flottille leaders pressed home their attacks to within 6000m, despite the heaviest counter fire.

We have seen that the Grand Fleet battleships were conducting an effective fire on the German capital ships, which reached its peak at around 2020hrs. From that moment onwards the volume and effectiveness declined steeply. There were several reasons for this. The German battle line had turned away, and the I AG had likewise turned away, onto a southerly course, and then followed the battle squadrons to the west. Then, smoke from *König*'s smoke screen and the approaching torpedobootes was being blown ahead of the south-westerly breeze, therefore fouling the range.

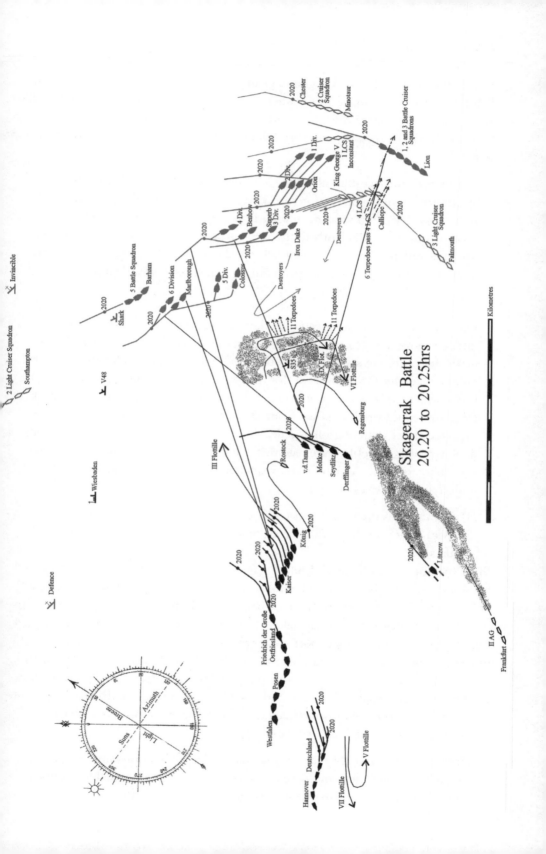

Skagerrak Battle
20.20 to 20.25hrs

Finally the Grand Fleet had begun to change target to the German torpedobootes. What was Admiral Jellicoe to do when he saw the four boats of the VI Flottille advancing to the attack? And they were soon followed by the nine boats of the IX Flottille. It will be remembered that Admiral Jellicoe's Grand Fleet Battle Orders stated:

> The torpedo menace must always be born in mind.... Until the enemy is beaten by gunfire it is not my intention to risk attack from his torpedoes, although it is always possible that if we were inferior in strength on meeting it might become necessary to close sufficiently to attack by torpedo. Such a movement, however, would be ordered by me, and generally speaking it is to be understood that my intention is to keep outside torpedo range of the enemy's battle line.

And further:

> Exercises at sea and exercises on the tactical board show that one of the most difficult movements to counter on the part of the enemy is a 'turn away' of his battle line, either in succession or otherwise. The effect of such a turn (which may be made for the purpose of drawing our Fleet over mines or submarines) is obviously to place us in a position of decided disadvantage as regards attack from torpedoes fired whether from ships or from destroyers.... It may be expected that I shall not follow a decided turn of this nature shortly after the deployment as I should anticipate that it is made for the purpose of taking us over submarines. ... Action on approximately similar courses will be one of the underlying objectives of my tactics:
>
> (1) Because it is the form of action likely to give the most decisive results.
> (2) Because it is probable that the Germans will make use of mines if they can do so.[43]

With the approach of the VI Flottille (four boats) Admiral Jellicoe thought that his worst fears had been realized, a torpedo attack by enemy forces. At 2021hrs he ordered Vice Admiral Jerram and his 2 Battle Squadron to turn away four points to port, that is 46 degrees. A minute later he ordered all battle squadrons and attached cruisers to turn two points to port, away from the enemy. In view of the previously ordered signals there was some confusion aboard the British ships. At 2025hrs Jellicoe ordered a further turn of two points away from the enemy. Nevertheless, despite his somewhat confusing and conflicting signals the British Division commanders successfully manoeuvred their Divisions back into a cohesive line.

The Official German History related:

> The British only have the unusually favourable light conditions and the smooth seas to thank that they could recognise the tracks of compressed air bubbles of the torpedoes in time to take evasive manoeuvres on the threatened ships.[44]

The 11 torpedoes fired by the 11th Half Flottille between 2022 to 2024hrs were directed towards the head of the British line, however at the same time the 2 Battle Squadron turned away 4 points and this would have taken the ships beyond the range of the German torpedoes. Of these torpedoes eight were sighted by British ships. About 2030hrs six of the torpedoes passed through the 4 Light Cruiser Squadron, or ahead of the 2 Battle Squadron. One passed about 200m ahead of *Iron Duke*, whilst *Inflexible* sighted one passing about 100m astern.

The IX Flottille fired about the same amount of torpedoes as the VI Flottille, towards the rear of the battle line. About nine tracks were sighted by the 6 Division, whilst the 5 Division sighted three, and these were avoided by the 1 Battle Squadron between 2033 and 2037hrs. At 2025hrs *Colossus* turned to port to avoid a torpedo reported as running erratically. *Collingwood* sighted another heading directly towards her and she turned so that the torpedo was seen to pass barely 10m astern. A second torpedo track passed less than 10m ahead.

Marlborough sighted two torpedoes on the starboard bow at 2033hrs and turned away to port, and then back to starboard, so that one track passed close ahead and one passed astern. A third torpedo on the starboard beam could not be avoided but was running too deep and passed beneath the ship at the level of Y turret.

At 2035hrs *Revenge* turned to port to avoid two torpedoes, one of which passed less than 10m astern.

After turning to port *Hercules* sighted a torpedo 730m to starboard and she continued to turn away, so that the torpedo track passed 35m ahead, whilst a second torpedo passed quite close astern.

Agincourt avoided one torpedo which passed 90m ahead, whilst at the same time another passed 45m ahead. A third torpedo, which was running slowly, passed close astern. Another four torpedoes are reported to have passed through the 5 Battle Squadron. Of the total of 22 torpedoes, fired by 13 torpedobootes, approximately 19 had passed through the British line.[45]

Of the other Flottilles, the II Flottille had its orders cancelled before they could attack, and the VII Flottille remained near the II Squadron due to a misinterpretation of orders. Korvettenkapitän Koch wrote:

> About 8.30pm on the flag and FT signal: 'To all Flottilles 'Torpedoboote to the attack', the Flottille quit their position with the II Squadron and set off to the attack in the north. With the unclear situation a success seemed questionable, the danger of the missed blow being very much a possibility. It would have been haphazard to advance without having the necessary information about the enemy line. From *Frankfurt*, which was mistakenly taken for *Regensburg*, the searchlight signal 'S' was taken in ('S', assemble in the shooting direction) and was perceived as direction to the Flottille.

The Flottille turned to the south again to 'assemble'. Shortly afterwards from the northerly positioned *Rostock* a signal was read: 'V Flottille to *Rostock*', and from this it was determined that the V Flottille went to the attack, and the VII Flottille should position ahead in the eventual new battle direction (S–SW). Accordingly the Flottille went at high speed in a southerly direction.[46]

The V Flottille ran out to the attack at 2038hrs, on receiving orders from *Rostock*, and advanced through the thick smoke. Once clear of the smoke only British destroyers and light cruisers could be sighted so that at 2050hrs the attack was abandoned. A fire fight with these units developed and it was noted that from the shell impacts that the enemy partly fired with 6 inch cannon. The V Flottille received orders to proceed south and took up a SW course, so that soon the British were lost to view. The V Flottille had encountered the British 12 Destroyer Flotilla.

Meanwhile, the 12 Flotilla Leader, *Faulknor*, had opened fire on the disabled German torpedoboot *V48*, which was proceeding in a southerly direction at slow speed. The British 2 LCS and *Valiant* also had this hapless torpedoboot under fire, *Valiant* with her secondary battery. Then the destroyers *Obedient*, *Mindful*, *Marvel* and *Onslaught* attacked *V48*, so that she capsized to port and sank. There was only one survivor who was picked up by a neutral steamer eight hours later.

From a German perspective this phase of the battle had not been as successful materially as the previous phases. However, Vizeadmiral Scheer had displayed a certain tactical prowess that Admiral Jellicoe had been unable to match. Despite his vast numerical inferiority Vizeadmiral Scheer had so far kept Admiral Jellicoe guessing and had maintained the initiative, and to a great degree had determined the actual course of the battle. He correctly sensed that he must maintain that initiative and keep the British at arm's length until nightfall. As Frost put it:

> In our opinion, Scheer's very simplicity has deceived his critics. He was a fighting Admiral, no hot headed, impetuous Nelson, but an icy, calm U.S. Grant. He believed, contrary to Jellicoe, that caution is often the most dangerous attitude. Boldness and surprise seemed to him a safer course than to run away. He was willing, contrary to Jellicoe, to leave something to chance.[47]

Whilst Jellicoe had fought in accordance with his Grand Fleet Battle Orders, and felt bound by them, Vizeadmiral Scheer had no such rigid set of orders and was able to act on his intuition and according to the moment. He had therefore kept control of the battle and was well placed as night approached. At this latitude sunset was around 2105hrs, Middle European Time (MEZ), and this was followed by around 25 minutes of twilight.

Chapter 7

The Evening and Final Fleet Contacts

As the VI and IX Flottilles returned to Kommodore Heinrich, II FdT, aboard *Regensburg*, it transpired that the leader boats of the two Flottilles, *V28* and *G41*, and also *S52*, had fired all their torpedoes, whilst the boats of the 11th, 17th and 18th Half Flottilles had only one remaining each. Additionally, *V28* and *S51* had had their speeds reduced to 17 and 21 knots respectively, due to damage. Therefore the group *V28*, *S51* and *S52* assembled near the I Squadron, under the command of Korvettenkapitän Goehle. The remaining boats of the IX Flottille, *V30*, *S34*, *S33*, *V26* and *S36*, together with *G42* of the III Flottille, under Korvettenkapitän Tilleßen, went to join the I FdT aboard *Rostock*, and the VII Flottille. Kommodore Heinrich wanted boats with two or more torpedoes remaining for the night attack, but also retained the 11th HF and three boats of the 12th HF, *V69*, *S50* and *V46*. The bootes *G37* and *V45* remained with *Lützow* as escort.

As Kommodore Heinrich passed *Lützow* about 2102hrs he received information that approximately six British battle cruisers were to port of *Lützow*, bearing SSE. This was based on *Lützow*'s observation of 2049hrs. The II FdT passed this information to the II Flottille, but nevertheless in his attack order at 2108hrs he directed the II Flottille to the sector E to NE. The three boats of the 12 HF went to the sector ESE to SE. However, Kommodore Heinrich quickly amended his order to the II Flottille and at 2110hrs moved their sector to ENE to ESE. At the same time as the boats were detached, at 2115hrs, an order arrived from Vizeadmiral Scheer giving direction of the torpedobootes to the I FdT for the night. However, at 2130hrs Kommodore Heinrich reported his orders for the II Flottille and 12 HF to Vizeadmiral Scheer and the I FdT, Kommodore Michelsen, so that the latter acknowledged that the Flottilles under the II FdT were to act independently.

At 2045hrs Vizeadmiral Scheer ordered the Fleet to take course south, and reiterated this order at 2052hrs. At this time the III Squadron were still strung out to port aft, in en–echelon formation but were endeavouring to join astern of the Fleet flagship.

To the British the movements of the High Sea Fleet after the last collision were a complete mystery. The German ships had suddenly disappeared from sight from *Iron Duke* but this could have been because of the dense smoke from funnels and cordite. All the shooting, from both heavy and medium calibre guns, was now directed against the approaching German torpedobootes, a fact not immediately recognized by Admiral Jellicoe. It seemed to Jellicoe that the end of his line was still violently engaged with the German capital ships and that temporarily he could not see, but would soon again be in visual contact. The British leader believed that the German line had altered course by no more than eight points (about 90°), and therefore had not observed the third battle turn away. Therefore he altered course 5 points to starboard onto course S by W at 2035hrs. He fully expected the Germans to reappear at any time, but in this he was very much mistaken. Like it or not Vizeadmiral Scheer's third and final battle turn away had cost the British any chance of a successful result during the day battle. Sunset was around 2105hrs at this time of the year, and after that there would be approximately 25 to 30 minutes of evening twilight. Therefore there remained time to regain contact with the High Sea Fleet and continue the battle. 'Following the extraordinary restraint that he had shown so far in the battle, it is doubtful that the British Leader's will for this purpose seriously existed.'[1] So commented the official German history on the chance of further battle.

Nevertheless, at 2040hrs Vice Admiral Beatty reported by wireless: 'Enemy bears from me NW by W, distant 10 to 11 miles. My position Lat. 56°56′N., Long. 6°16′E. Course SW. Speed 18 knots.' A short time later he made his well known signal: 'Urgent. Submit van of battleships follow battle cruisers. We can then cut off the whole of the enemy's battle fleet.' This message is reported to have been received in *Iron Duke* at 2054hrs. At 2042hrs Jellicoe had ordered the 4 Battle Squadron onto course SW, and shortly after that advised that the Admiral, him, was resuming responsibility as Fleet guide. At 2100hrs Admiral Jellicoe ordered his Divisions to change course to the west at 17 knots, the maximum speed obtainable by the crippled *Marlborough*. At the same time Vice Admiral Beatty ordered the 3 LCS to 'Sweep to the westward and locate the head of the enemy's line before dark.' Then at 2114hrs Admiral Jellicoe ordered the 2 Battle Squadron to follow the battle cruisers, before at 2121 ordering course WSW, and seven minutes later course SW. It seemed as if the two fleets would again be in battle contact.

At 2045hrs Vice Admiral Beatty lost contact with the German capital ships so at about 2100hrs he swung his 1, 2 and 3 BCS to the WSW, at the same time ordering the light cruisers to reconnoitre to the west, as related above. This disposition soon bore fruit as at 2109 *Falmouth*, flagship of the 3 LCS, reported by flag signal to Vice Admiral Beatty, 'Ships bearing N by W.' A minute later Beatty signalled his battle cruisers to open fire, however, no enemy targets could be discerned. Therefore, at 2117hrs, Beatty turned his battle cruisers onto course west. At the same instant Rear Admiral Napier, aboard *Falmouth*, made out the five small cruisers of the IV Reconnaissance Group steering across his squadrons line abreast at right angles. Flagship *Falmouth* opened fire at a range of 88hm. The IV Reconnaissance Group were under the command of Kommodore Ludwig von Reuter and he wrote in *Stettin*'s war diary:

2117 to 2125hrs. With running ahead on a southern course 4–5 enemy cruisers, seemingly armoured cruisers of the *Hampshire* class, came in sight to port abeam, with others in sight with course SSW, range at the beginning 60–70hm, then over 100hm. The IV AG turned onto a parallel course and opened fire at 70hm range. Lighting conditions unfavourable. The enemy was scarcely recognisable against the dark horizon, whilst our own ships were clearly held against the bright western horizon. The battle was conducted on converging courses. As the enemy reached the head of the IV AG through his superior speed he slowly turned away. The range increased to 106hm. Our own fall of shot could no longer be observed, whilst the fire of the enemy was still effective. I therefore determined to draw the pursuing enemy onto the II Squadron, which was behind me, by a turn away. The enemy did not follow and vanished quickly into the dark.[2]

Whilst *Stettin* and *München* opened a prolonged fire on the British cruisers *Hamburg* could only fire one salvo and *Stuttgart* could only make out one vessel, which was already under fire. The British ships remained unhit. On the German side the small cruiser *München* was hit twice. The first 6 inch shell struck the port aft cutter and detonated inside. All the superstructure and aft No.3 searchlight platform were shot through like a sieve by splinters. The hand rudder wheel was damaged and four men were killed, whilst four others were wounded, one seriously. The second 6 inch shell struck the aft funnel and detonated inside, holing the funnel and mantel. The resulting blast pressure tore or bent various sheet metal panels in boiler rooms I and II and the air over pressure fell to zero, making it difficult to maintain steam pressure. Temporary repairs soon rectified this problem, whilst two men were wounded.

The II AG was travelling on the port quarter of the IV AG and likewise sighted the British cruisers. Kontreadmiral Boedicker's reaction was, however, the opposite of Kommodore von Reuter's. Whereas von Reuter had turned towards the British cruisers, Boedicker turned away, saying he did not want to mask the fire of the II Squadron. '2 light cruisers, seemingly of the Town class, in 162γ (gamma) middle in sight. Report made (FT 2219). Turn to starboard to be able to shoot independently and to make the field of fire free. Immediately battle cruisers were sighted. FT 2219: 008ε (epsilon) enemy battle cruisers steer SW. F d II AG.'[3] *Pillau* reported that the British battle cruisers also opened fire briefly on the II AG.

Enemy battle cruisers, light cruisers and destroyers in sight ahead. Turn away to starboard, with general course SW. Enemy battle cruisers shot at the II AG. Impacts lie poorly. After several salvos the enemy fire ceases.[4]

Whilst this action was taking place at the head of the German line another action was taking place further to the north. At 2105hrs the light cruiser *Castor*, flagship of the 11 Destroyer Flotilla, sighted smoke to the WNW and together with the destroyers turned to investigate. The light cruisers of the 4 LCS, *Calliope*, *Constance* and *Comus*, followed in support. At 2115hrs *Castor* could make out the twelve torpedobootes of the V Torpedoboote Flottille on a south-westerly course, towards the position of the British battle cruisers. The British light forces advanced towards the V Flottille and opened fire at 2118hrs, chasing the German bootes away to the NW where they sought the protection of *Rostock*. *G11* of the V Flottille reported:

> 2115hrs. Light enemy forces come in sight in ESE. It was obviously the same as the Flottille had pushed upon with their attack and who were now attempting to make contact with the port side of our Main Body.
>
> 2125hrs. Our own Main Body comes in sight to starboard ahead. A report about the enemy forces was made to *Rostock*, which was with the Main Body. The Main Body took the enemy under fire, and therefore [we] break through our own line to the starboard side, behind *Rostock*.[5]

At 2126hrs the pursuing British light cruisers suddenly came across German battleships at a range of 73hm, and believed they were of the *Pommern* class. Aboard the German battleships *Prinzregent Luitpold*, *Kaiser* and *Markgraf*, three cruisers with three funnels and a destroyer could be recognized to port aft, and fire was opened on them at 58 to 64hm. *Calliope* launched a torpedo on the Germans at 2130hrs at a range of 59hm, which, however, missed. *Prinzregent* fired one heavy salvo, *Kaiser* two, whilst *Markgraf* fired with her medium calibre cannon as the British ships withdrew into the gathering darkness. The German fire ceased at 2135hrs but, nevertheless, *Calliope* was hit five times by 15cm shells. Of these one struck the breech of the port aft 4 inch gun, wrecking the gun and mounting. A second exploded near the No.2 starboard 4 inch gun beneath the bridge, putting the gun out of action. A third hit pierced the upper deck and detonated in the aft dressing station. A total of ten men were killed and 23 were wounded.

The battle between the cruisers was followed by a clash of the heavy forces. At 2118hrs *Princess Royal* sighted the I AG and soon after *Tiger* sighted the battleships of the II Squadron. Although *Lion* had three guns out of action, *Princess Royal* two, *Inflexible* one gun out and *Tiger* had a list that allowed large amounts of water to enter the ship when she turned,[6] Vice Admiral Beatty did not hesitate to turn towards the sounds of the gunfire and was rewarded with the sighting of the German capital ships. As the British battle cruisers were concealed against the darker eastern horizon they were able to fully surprise the Germans, and once again a British force had arrived within range of the Germans undetected. Vice Admiral Beatty allowed his ships to swing away to port and at 2120hrs *Inflexible*, *Princess Royal*, *Tiger* and *New Zealand* opened fire at a range of 75 to 119hm, and at 2123hrs *Lion* and *Indomitable* joined in.

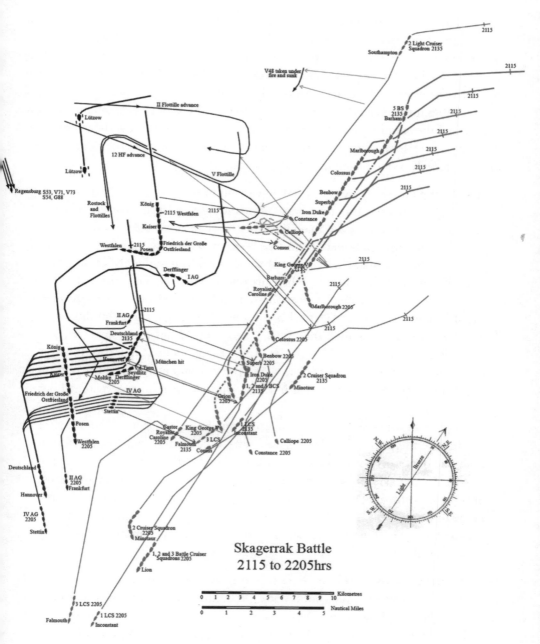

Skagerrak Battle
2115 to 2205hrs

Vizeadmiral Hipper had only just briefly before stopped *Moltke* so he could board her to resume his command of the I AG when suddenly the dark SE horizon lit up with gun flashes and a violent fire once again fell upon the German battle cruisers. Vizeadmiral Hipper was therefore unable to board *Moltke* until 2157hrs. Although their opponents were almost invisible *Derfflinger*, *Seydlitz*, *Moltke* and *von der Tann* replied to the British fire using what cannon they had available. Targeting the enemy was difficult as was the observation of the fall of shot, and therefore the fire was frequently interrupted. It appeared as though *Lion* and *Princess Royal* were firing on *Derfflinger*. *Tiger* apparently took the small cruiser *Pillau* under fire, whilst *New Zealand* and *Indomitable* took *Seydlitz* as target, and soon the German ships began to suffer. Aboard *Derfflinger* a heavy calibre shell struck from port at frame 237 on the 260mm thick armour of A turret barbette. The shot struck a glancing blow and passed down onto the deck on the starboard side, and then overboard where it detonated. A violent concussion was felt inside A turret and some men were thrown off their feet. Korvettenkapitän von Hase wrote:

> About 10 p.m. we sighted our first Squadron bearing on a southerly course. Our captain, who at this time was commanding the battle cruisers, led our squadron on the head of our main fleet, where we were to take station. The rest of the battle cruisers followed the *Derfflinger* without any signal. As we were carrying out this manoeuvre we and the I Squadron suddenly came under heavy fire from the south-east. It had already grown dusk. The mist had rather increased than diminished. 'Clear for Action!' sounded once more through the ship, and a few seconds later I had trained the 'Anna' turret on the target and fired. In the thick mist the 'Bertha' turret could not find the target, so I had to fire as well as I could with the 'Anna' turret alone. Then this, too, was interrupted. A heavy shell struck the 'Anna' turret and bent one of the rails on which the turret revolves, so that it stuck. Our last weapon was snatched out of our hands!
>
> Then Stuckmeister Weber, with great quickness of decision, ran out of the turret and, with the help of some petty officers and gun hands, cleared away the bent rails with axes and crowbars and put the turret in action again, so that it was again possible to fire an occasional shot. I had to shoot almost entirely by estimated range, for only rarely was the Bg. man able to get the range of a gun-flash. I fired at ranges of 8,000, 6,000, 1,000, and so on. It was impossible to observe the splashes. The situation had once more become very uncomfortable.[7]

Nevertheless it seems von Hase's work has suffered in translation, as it was not a rail on which the turret revolved, but a water excluding channel that was rent off and temporarily jammed the turret.

SMS *Seydlitz* was struck five times. At about 2124hrs the No.4 port casemate was hit and put out of action. The next hit at 2128hrs struck the roof of D turret and ricocheted off before detonating. At 2130hrs a hit struck the port, forward Admiral's bridge and exploded approximately 1 metre from the conning tower and 1½ metres above the command bridge. Splinters went mainly through the starboard command bridge and outer side of the superstructure. Some went through the vision slits of the conning tower.

The artillery position of the conning tower was badly shaken but there was little damage. Five men were killed and five were wounded, including the Navigation Offizier inside the conning tower. The other two hits at 2130hrs struck the 300mm belt armour. One hit to port at frame 79 approximately 1.9m above the CWL, on the lower edge of the citadel armour where it joined with the belt armour. The upper plate had a semicircular piece broken off, whereas the lower plate had a semicircular dent. The shell probably broke up or detonated outside the armour as no shell fragments were found inside the shot hole. There was little damage to the inner bunker. The other shell came in a port aft direction and struck the belt near frame 58 to port on the aft edge of the plate, and penetrated. The hole was 0.4 × 0.6m in size and parts of the adjoining plate were broken off. Pieces of armour and shell were thrown into the outer bunker, but to a large extent the armour kept out shell fragments. The first and third hits at this time are thought to have come from *Princess Royal*, the other three from *New Zealand*.

Korvettenkapitän Foerster described the carnage:

On the starboard command bridge I had had a sadder but touching moment: buried under his dead signal maats and gasts lay the Adjutant, Leutnant zur See Witting, his battle signal notebook and secret signal book key wedged tightly under his arm. During the entire battle he and his men had stood on the open bridge next to the command position, so he could more readily see the signals from the flagship and relay them correctly. The last enemy shell had detonated in the vicinity of this group and had done horrible work to the poor men. They were all killed, except for Witting, and were horribly mutilated. As I went to help Witting in his lamentable situation, as he was placed on a transport hammock – he still held his book, although both hands were shredded and a leg severed – he said to me; 'The others first!' In his helpless situation and despite infuriating aches, he wanted not for himself, but help for the others, his signal personnel. He didn't suspect his life was the only one saved from sure death.

I turned away, to save my nerves, as the dance was not yet over. We directed our course south for a none too long night march, and we estimated that we would encounter the enemy at dawn off Horns Reef, for a renewed battle. I went to my command position to make general arrangements for the night readiness, when Obermatrosen Lange came to me and with a most serious look in the world asked: 'May I bandage Herr Kapitän?' I said: 'Very gladly, but where?' Thereon he remarked: 'Herr Kapitän has a large hole in his head.' He held a small mirror for me, and to my surprise saw a cut from above to below on the left side of my face. With pleasure I underwent treatment from Lange, who now dabbed fresh water and washed my sore. He wiped and wiped away at the sore so that all that remained was a 3cm long cut over my left eye, that for six hours had bled unrestrained and dried. He wiped away the dried blood and applied a bandage, which until now I had no time to do. The fresh bandage was beautiful and then I drank water from his drinking cup and ate a piece of bread, and under the circumstance he was particularly proud of his work.[8]

At 2127hrs *Derfflinger* turned away to starboard, followed at 2131hrs by *Seydlitz* and the other ships of the I AG. *Moltke* and *von der Tann* had remained undamaged during this fire fight. The I AG was now following in the wake of the II AG towards the west, and would pass between the II and I Squadrons.

Vizeadmiral Schmidt, commander of the I Squadron, held his course and speed as he was unable to see where the shells landing about the I and II AG ahead of him were coming from. As the I AG closed with them *Westfalen* and *Nassau*, the two leading ships of the I Squadron, were showered with splinters from the incoming enemy salvos. As the I AG moved across the bows of *Westfalen* she was forced to reduce speed and then alter course 5 points to starboard. The first of the I Squadron to open fire was *Posen*, who fired at the British battle cruisers from 2128hrs to 2135hrs. During this period *Lion* was hit once by a 15cm shell from the I AG, which holed a steam pinnacle and detonated in the upper part of an engine room intake, causing some damage and causing a small fire. *Princess Royal* was struck by a 28cm shell from *Posen* at 2132hrs. This projectile struck the starboard strut of the foremast and almost severed it, before passing through the fore funnel and then almost severing the port strut. The shell failed to detonate.

Whilst the I AG, II AG and I Squadron had all been forced to give way because of lack of visibility the II Squadron, under Kontreadmiral Mauve, held their course to close with the enemy. Whilst *Princess Royal* had fired a torpedo at the II Squadron at 2132hrs, this had been without result, but at the same time the British battle cruisers opened fire on their new opponents. Now the 2 Admiral of the II Squadron, Kontreadmiral Freiherr von Dalwigk, swung his flagship, *Hannover*, to starboard onto course SW to bring all his guns to bear. Because of smoke and the poor visibility conditions *Pommern* and *Schleswig-Holstein* were generally unable to reply, whilst of the other pre-dreadnought battleships *Deutschland* fired one, *Hessen* fired five, *Hannover* eight and *Schlesien* nine shells of heavy calibre.

The British battle cruisers soon ranged in on the old battleships of the II Squadron. The war diary of *Hannover* recalled the cannonade:

2108hrs. The cruisers of the IV AG which stood ahead of the II Squadron received fire from port, apparently from heavy artillery. They gradually swung from south, through SW and then to the west. At the head of the II Squadron *Hannover* maintained course with 15 knots.

2120hrs to 2148hrs. The unit found to port of the II Squadron (lead ship 1 point aft of *Hannover*) were apparently the same ships that had opened fire before.

This opponent could not be seen at dusk because of the hazy background. Only once did the hull of a large ship appear from 340° for some seconds. Only the muzzle flash could be recognised in a firing line from approximately 330° to 350°. Therefore, however, we could not fire.

The torpedoes were loaded.

In order to see this opponent and bring the entire artillerie to bear, *Hannover* went onto course SW. The before mentioned units that stood to port now retired with a westerly course behind the II Squadron. At that moment the previously invisible enemy let go of their previous targets and took the II Squadron under fire. Already with the third salvo from the heavy guns *Hannover* was straddled aft with two short shots (-20, -10m) and one wide shot (+60m). The next salvo straddled the bow. Fragments struck the hull side fore and aft, above and below the waterline. The detonations of the shells and the striking of splinters were felt inside the ship. One of the splinters found on deck weighed 2½ kg. The calibre of this fragment (34cm) was determined by measurement of the radius of the curvature. The material of the projectile, judging by the appearance of the fractured surfaces, was tempered steel. The wall thickness of the shell is so thick – already on the splinter 7.5cm thick – that I conclude it to be an armoured piercing shell. Further, the shells detonated with impacting on the water. Up until 1912, the last British armoured piercing shells I have knowledge of, had no fuse and were filled with black powder. If my assumption is confirmed and the fragments result from an armoured piercing shell, then it follows that the English now have semi-armour piercing shells for their 34.3cm guns.

The ships behind *Hannover* went en-echelon, apparently to make room for the aforementioned units, onto a westerly course. *Hannover* followed. The enemy ceased fire very soon afterwards. After a brief time *Hannover* turned onto course SW, and after that back onto a southerly course.

The torpedoes were unloaded.[9]

At 2135hrs a shell seemingly fired by *New Zealand* struck *Schleswig-Holstein*. The 12 inch calibre shell passed through an air shaft and detonated against the aft armoured wall of the port aft upper deck 17cm gun casemate. Most of the explosive effect of the high explosive shell was in front of the 120mm thick armour but a piece of armour was blown in and disabled the gun. Two cartridges burned and three men were killed and nine were wounded.

There was a hit on *Pommern*, probably from *Indomitable*, but details are lacking.

Meanwhile, at 2134hrs, a fragment from a short shell struck the forward crow's nest of *Schlesien*, and killed an order transmitter and wounded the Observation Offizier. The ship was showered with splinters.

Seekadett Günther Schütz, serving aboard *Hessen*, was apparently unimpressed by the proceedings and later he wrote:

It was somewhat hazy, so that the opponents could approach one another. Now we hoped to be able to seriously engage the enemy. However, unfortunately the weather was so unfavourable that we could not shoot on the enemy, despite the close range, which could not have been more than 8000m. Indeed we saw nothing, only the flash before their gun barrels indicated their position.... So, we served merely as a target, because our Panzerkreuzer, which the English had hard pressed and had badly damaged during the hours long battle, and our small cruisers and Torpedoboot Flottilles had moved back behind the II Squadron. Apart from some minor damage to some ships the II Squadron escaped this dangerous situation almost unscathed.[10]

As Kontreadmiral Mauve observed the result of the enemy fire on his line he resolved to disengage from the stronger adversary and therefore allowed his squadron to turn 8 points to starboard, to draw the British towards the German Main Body. Vice Admiral Beatty did not follow this movement and maintained course SW, to pass ahead of the German fleet. Soon the British ships ceased fire as they could no longer distinguish a clear target.

Scarcely had the firing at the van ceased than further firing broke out in the rear of the German line. At 2130hrs the II Torpedoboot Flottille and 1 Half Flottille began their missions against the British main body in the sectors ENE to SE, as related previously. However, before dark they came into contact with enemy forces. At 2130hrs the British 2 LCS, at the end of the British line, sighted a German torpedoboot, apparently *V48*, and *Southampton* and *Dublin* took her under fire and hit her amidships, whilst then destroyers of the 12 Flotilla finally destroyed the unfortunate boot. Thereon the light cruisers observed more German torpedobootes to the NW, closing on the British line from the rear and which were believed to be attacking the 5 Battle Squadron. At about 2150hrs the II TBF avoided the four light cruisers of the 2 LCS by turning away to the west, and at 2152hrs the three torpedobootes of the 12 HF were taken under a violent fire by the 2 LCS. The fire lasted 20 minutes at ranges of 30 to 50hm. The bootes turned away to the west and NW and *S50* received a hit by a 6 inch shell. Although the shell did not detonate, the main steam pipe was badly damaged and one boiler was put out of action, the forward rudder engine and electric lights failed and the torpedoboot's speed was reduced to 25 knots, forcing her to return to the Main Body. It was not until 2210hrs that the two bootes of the 12 HF could resume their previous course and only at 2240hrs could the II TBF likewise resume the search for the British Main Body.

Meanwhile, there had been another action at the head of the German line. The 2 Division of the 4 LCS, *Caroline* and *Royalist*, had not participated in the advance of the light cruisers against the German V Flottille and were travelling independently about 1 nautical mile ahead of *King George V*'s Division, and were soon to be joined by *Castor* and the 11 Destroyer Flotilla. At 2145hrs three German battleships were sighted in the NW, gradually closing on the British battle line. At 2155 the cruiser *Caroline*, under the command of Captain Crooke, reported these battleships to Vice Admiral Jerram on *King George V*, and at the same time dispatched *Caroline* and *Royalist* to carry out a torpedo attack. However, Jerram was of the view the reported ships were British battle cruisers that he had previously lost from view. Aboard *Caroline* Captain Crooke was sure that the sighted vessels were German and resolved to carry out a torpedo attack on his own responsibility. He was of course dealing with the German I Squadron, which had returned to course south at 2145hrs. Aboard *Westfalen* the Germans had recognized several vessels to port ahead but in the twilight it could not be determined if they were friend or foe, and the position of the IV AG was not known with certainty at that time. A searchlight challenge was given but was not answered and soon seven destroyers could be seen in company with a cruiser, so that at 2208hrs *Westfalen* and *Nassau* opened fire at a range of 74hm on the leading cruiser and the destroyers directly behind her, and at the same time swung 6 points to starboard onto a WSW course, to make way for any torpedoes which may have been fired in their direction. However, only *Caroline* and *Royalist* had fired one torpedo each at a range of 73hm. Then both ships turned away after the fifth salvo of *Westfalen*, whilst *Comus* continued for the head of the line before turning away and vanishing in a thick smoke screen.

> From *Westfalen*, that from 2212pm went on course south, several vessels were observed to port, somewhat ahead. As the position of the IV AG was not known with certainty the recognition signal was made with searchlight, which was not answered. Now seven destroyers, apparently on a parallel course and with a Flotilla Escort cruiser at the head were recognised. Probably a guide. *Westfalen* turned onto WSW course, 17 knots and in the twilight opened fire on the escort cruiser. Direction 260°. Range 74–72hm. Continuation: 2 minutes 24 seconds. After the 5th salvo, that lay well, the enemy ran away from the fire at high speed.
>
> Munitions usage: 7–28cm Psgr.
>
> During this battle phase *Westfalen* had no losses or damage.
>
> Course was further taken south, speed 15 knots.[11]

Nassau sighted two torpedo tracks and despite immediate avoiding manoeuvres one torpedo passed close to the bow and the other torpedo track seemingly passed under A turret. *Rheinland* and *Posen* did not sight the attacking enemy forces. The British cruisers remained unhit and escaped the German gunfire by passing through their own line, whilst the destroyers behind *Caroline*, of the 11Flotilla, did not utilize the favourable opportunity to mount a torpedo attack.

With the coming of darkness a number of contact reports began arriving on the British flagship, *Iron Duke*, and also a number of events could be observed. Despite this it appeared Admiral Jellicoe took some time to grasp the situation. At 2121hrs gunfire could be heard 2 to 3 nautical miles ahead of the 1 Division, the 4 LCS was apparently in contact with the enemy, with *Calliope* seemingly under heavy fire. Vice Admiral Jerram turned 2 points away from the enemy onto a WSW course, parallel to the enemy. There were also gun flashes from Vice Admiral Beatty's battle cruisers. At 2125hrs Admiral Jellicoe turned his fleet to the west by Divisions in an attempt to bring the enemy closer. This move quickly brought results as from A turret of *Iron Duke* the faint outlines of up to nine German capital ships could be discerned. Nevertheless, there was no engagement as at 2128hrs Admiral Jellicoe ordered his ships onto course SW, and to form line ahead. Therefore the German ships were lost from view. This was a missed opportunity as a determined blow could have been dealt whilst remaining invisible to the German side, as they had not detected the British columns.

The *Comus*, of the 4 LCS, was seen to be in action and at 2138hrs Jellicoe inquired of her: 'What are you firing at?' to which the reply was: 'The enemy's battle fleet, bearing west.' At this time the position of the British battle cruisers was not known with certainty and the thunder of cannon fire from their direction had suddenly become silent. At 2145hrs Vice Admiral Jerram reported they were no longer in sight and it was unclear to Jellicoe whether he was dealing with Beatty's or German forces, so therefore at 2146hrs he requested Beatty as to the bearing of the enemy. In the same instant *Falmouth* reported the enemy was bearing north, with a WSW course. *Falmouth* then gave her own position, but this was in error by five miles to the north, and if true would have meant Beatty's battle cruisers should have been starboard abeam of the Fleet. At 2155hrs Beatty questioned *Minotaur* as to the location of Vice Admiral Jerram's 2 Battle Squadron, however *Minotaur* replied that they were last seen at 2110hrs. Because *Lion*'s wireless aerials had been shot away there was some delay in answering Jellicoe's question of 2146hrs. Only at 2159hrs was a reply received: 'Enemy battle cruisers and old battleships bearing north 34° west of me, range 10 to 11 miles, steering SW. My position: 56°40′ N, 5°50′ E, course SW, speed 17 knots.'

By 2205hrs this report was in Admiral Jellicoe's hands and the situation was somewhat clearer. At 2157hrs Commodore Goodenough, commander of the 2 LCS at the rear of the line, reported he was in action with German torpedobootes, and 13 minutes later said that these had been driven off to the westward. As Jellicoe had been able to observe this gunfire Goodenough's wireless message cleared up the situation. At the same time gunfire flashes appeared ahead as the German I Squadron drove off the cruisers *Caroline* and *Royalist*.

From all these reports and observations it was clear that the German Fleet was close at hand. *Falmouth* had engaged German small cruisers of the vanguard and Beatty had exchanged fire with the German Main Body. *Caroline* and *Royalist* had made a torpedo attack on the leading German battleships, whilst the latter had taken *Calliope* under fire. To the rear *Southampton* and the 2 LCS had broken the attack of some German torpedobootes. Nevertheless, Admiral Jellicoe remained uncertain about the exact location of the German Main Body as they had not been sighted from the British Fleet since 2059hrs; the observation of nine capital ships from *Iron Duke*'s A turret at 2125hrs had been the individual sighting by a single turret commander. By 2200hrs it was known that the German line was nearby and by holding his course Jellicoe expected to renew contact at any time. Even if he would not commit his Battle Squadrons to a renewed engagement Jellicoe's best chance for success was send his so far uncommitted destroyers to a torpedo attack against the Germans. The sun had set scarcely an hour before and twilight was finished, so now action would call for a night battle. Would Jellicoe be as bold and resolute as Rear Admiral Nelson had been at Aboukir Bay, when the British had fought and defeated a French Fleet in a dramatic night battle? The answer was a resounding no, and at 2201hrs, with the leading battleships of each fleet, *Westfalen* and *King George V*, just 6 nautical miles apart, Jellicoe ordered his battle fleet onto course south, and only Beatty maintained his hitherto course until 2230hrs, when he likewise turned south.

Both British commanders, Vice Admiral Beatty, and Admiral Jellicoe, wished to avoid further battle until the next morning, when the situation would be much clearer. Admiral Jellicoe gave the following reasons for his actions:

> The British Fleet stood between the enemy and his base. Every side was covered by a considerable number of destroyers, in this relation a considerable superiority available as all available were taken to sea when a fleet meeting seemed imminent. Therefore a night battle between heavy ships, with so many destroyers and torpedoboats present would largely be a matter of chance, it being impossible to distinguish between our own and enemy ships, only disaster could result. I also had an advantage of position as the resumption of battle would be on an easterly or westerly course, and I therefore decided to steer south, to be in a clear position to renew the battle.[12]

Admiral Jellicoe set out some reasons for his reluctance to continue the battle:

> It is sufficient to mention the principal arguments against it.
>
> In the first place, such a course must have inevitably led to our battle fleet being the object of attack by a very large destroyer force throughout the night. No senior officer would willingly court such an attack, even if our battleships were equipped with the best searchlights and the best arrangements for the control of the searchlights and the gunfire at night.
>
> It was, however, known to me that neither our searchlights nor their control arrangements were at this time of the best type. The fitting of director firing gear for the secondary armament of our battleships (a very important factor for firing at night) had also only just been begun, although repeatedly applied for. The delay was due to manufacturing and labour difficulties. Without these

adjuncts I knew well that the maximum effect of our fire at night could not be obtained, and that we could place no dependence on beating off destroyer attacks by gunfire. Therefore, if destroyers got into touch with the heavy ships, we were bound to suffer serious losses with no corresponding advantage. Our own destroyers were no effective antidote at night, since, if they were disposed with this sole object in view, they would certainly be taken for enemy destroyers and be fired on by our own ships.

But putting aside the question of attack by destroyers, the result of night actions between heavy ships must always be very largely a matter of *chance*, as there is little opportunity for skill on either side. Such an action must be fought at very close range, the decision depending on the course of events in the first few minutes. It is, therefore, an undesirable procedure on these general grounds. The greater efficiency of the German searchlights at the time of the Jutland action, and the greater number of torpedo tubes fitted in enemy ships, combined with is superiority in destroyers, would, I knew, give the Germans the opportunity of scoring heavily at the commencement of such an action.[13]

Admiral Jellicoe was fond of saying he could leave nothing to chance. Perhaps he had not heard of a 'calculated risk', and when you consider his enormous superiority in every respect the chances must surely have been in his favour. However, Jellicoe's continual thought was of what the Germans could do to him, not what he could inflict on them. There are plenty of examples in naval history of admirals taking a risk to achieve a great victory, for risk is the very essence of victory. At the Battle of Copenhagen on 2 April 1801 Vice Admiral Nelson deliberately disobeyed an order to retreat, saying to his Flag Captain: 'You know, Foley, I only have one eye – I have the right to be blind sometimes,' and then, holding his telescope to his blind eye he said: 'I really do not see the signal.' By disobeying a direct order and continuing his attack Vice Admiral Nelson achieved a great victory. At the battle of Mobile Bay on 5 August 1864 the Union monitor USS *Tecumseh* sank after striking a mine, then known as torpedoes. When Union commander, Rear Admiral Farragut, heard this he shouted: 'Damn the torpedoes ... four bells ... go ahead ... full speed.' By taking somewhat of a risk Farragut achieved a great victory.

American author Commander H. Frost summed up:

A bold commander would have endeavoured to annihilate the High Sea Fleet. That is undoubtedly what Paul Jones, Perry, and Farragut would have done. It is what Nelson did at Aboukir Bay. A cautious commander would have put off the fateful decision, just as Jellicoe did. All that could condone Jellicoe's decision not to fight at night was his positively stated intention to engage the next morning. Unfortunately, it will be shown that when morning came he had found another plausible reason why he could not fight. In fact, our analysis of the conditions existing throughout and after the battle, discloses that Jellicoe had excellent opportunities to take action that would have resulted in a decisive success at 6.55, 7.30, 8.15, 9.40, 10pm, and 3am. In every one of the situations, he found a different set of reasons why it was better to refuse the present opportunity thrust into his hands in order to wait for a better one. Thus, one after the other, he refused six highly favorable opportunities to fight to a decision. He had the fatal defect of not being able to leave something to chance. He who will not risk cannot win![14]

The Official German History wrote the following about Admiral Jellicoe's decision for the night:

The report of German losses on the evening of the battle was nevertheless incomplete, so that Jellicoe had to rely on his own observation primarily. As far as he was concerned there had been extensive contact between the two battle fleets during which the German ships had been repeatedly hit and finally had been able to answer the gunfire only weakly. Although the reason for this had been the poor observation conditions for the German side, Jellicoe believed the shooting skill of his line had overwhelmed the Germans. He had not heard of the loss of *Queen Mary* or *Indefatigable*. The two battle turns away seemed to indicate success in that every meeting with the Grand Fleet forced the Germans to turn away as quickly as possible. The three German torpedoboot attacks between 8.10 and 9.15pm convinced him that the German torpedo was their main weapon, however he considerably overestimated their role. With his experience in the day battle the English Fleet commander should have fallen upon the Germans with his whole superiority, but no thought could have been further from his mind. Further battle must have provided him a full yield but with dusk he consciously avoided further action, despite the alleged superiority of British arms, shooting skill and tactics. The day battle was therefore at an end, without the British Fleet obtaining the huge successes promised by renewed battle and firm resolve.[15]

Chapter 8

The Night and Battle of the Destroyers

When the Grand Fleet and Battle Cruiser Fleet went onto course south at 2201hrs and 2230hrs respectively, the day battle was over. With this conscious evasion of further battle Admiral Jellicoe and Vice Admiral Beatty had given Vizeadmiral Scheer a free passage to Horns Reef, a course he was determined to follow regardless. Whilst Admiral Jellicoe wished to avoid a night battle at any cost, the Germans saw in such the best possibility for the intended breakthrough to Horns Reef. If they did not force their way through there was a strong possibility of being cut off and being attacked in the rear by new forces from the north, west or south. It was essential for the Germans to make Horns Reef and the repeated turning away of the head of the line up until 2120hrs was very unfavourable. The turning away of the German head at 2208hrs because of the threat of torpedo attack from the British cruisers *Caroline* and *Royalist* brought another terse wireless message from Vizeadmiral Scheer at 2210hrs: 'Main Body course SSE ¼ E. Hold course! Speed 16 knots.' At about 2215hrs *König*, the last ship in line, lost sight of *Lützow*, who could no longer keep up. At first *Lützow* could run at 13 knots but this later had to be reduced to 7 knots to reduce water pressure on the forward bulkheads. As Vizeadmiral Scheer expected to meet the Grand Fleet off Horns Reef the following morning it was imperative to maintain speed and arrive there first.

The turning away by the head also had another detrimental effect, as *Rostock* and the V and VII Flottilles were considerably delayed, making contact with the enemy more difficult. By 2110hrs Kommodore Heinrich had allocated the II Flottille and 12 HF their sectors to search for the enemy. At 2202hrs the I FdT, Kommodore Michelsen, gave instructions for the other Torpedoboote Flottilles. In summary: ENE to ESE– Flottille II (10 bootes); ESE to SE– 12 HF (2 bootes); SE to S by E–VII Flottille (9 bootes); S by E to SSW– V Flottille (11 bootes) and SSW to SW– IX Flottille or 18 HF (5 bootes). The torpedobootes were dispatched on the assumption the British were under the Jutland coast and would

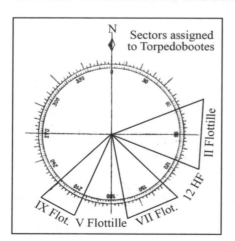

renew battle off Horns Reef on the following morning. The mission of the Flottilles was to attack the enemy during the night and then return to the Fleet for battle the following day. Kommodore Michelsen estimated the British further to the north than they actually were.

Many of the German torpedobootes were partially coal fired[1] and because of the demands placed on them during the day these fires were badly clinkered, and the bootes steaming for the head of the German line, of the V and VII Flottilles, could only make 18 knots in some cases and generally no more than 21 knots. At 15 knots speed they were conspicuous by the sparks coming from their funnels and much smoke. Korvettenkapitän von Koch was Flottille Leader of the VII Flottille and wrote in his war diary:

> On the orders of the Fleet Chief to I FdT: 'Assemble torpedobootes for the night effort' the VII Flottille was detached from the I FdT about 11hrs and was assigned the sector SE to S by E as its area to advance into, from the estimated instantaneous position of SMS *Rostock* – square 165 γ. (Gamma) (The estimated ships position of the Flottille itself stood 25nm further NNE). The Flottille broke through the end ships of our own line, which still steered a southerly course, and assembled first on course SSE ¼ E for the night advance. It was intended for the Group *S24* (*S16*, *S18*) to go on this course, the Group *S15* (*S17*, *S20*) on course S by E ½ E, the Group *S19* (*S23*, *V189*) on course SE ½ S, and to advance at a speed of 17 knots.
>
> To starboard of the VII Flottille is, in the adjoining sector, the V Flottille, to port the 12 HF, then II Flottille.[2]

The I FdT, Kommodore Michelsen, wrote about the dispatch of his Flottilles and also the importance of having the bootes return to the fleet by dawn:

> Towards 9.30pm an FT order from the High Sea Chief arrived with me to manage the <u>collected</u> torpedobootes for the night. Since I assumed that the II FdT had in the meantime already given orders for the night to the torpedobootes with him and they may have already been dispatched, and because I did not know the combat readiness of these Flottilles (especially their number of torpedoes) I thought it wrong to thwart the orders of the II FdT, and thereby lose valuable time during the short night. At the same time came the FT message from the II FdT that the II Flottille had been dispatched from Square 007 epsilon 4 in the sector ENE to ESE and the 18 Half Flottille in the sector ESE to SE. Meanwhile the VII, V Flottilles and 18 Half Flottille had closed on *Rostock*. About 10pm from Square 165 gamma 4 (as later turned out the position was approximately 30nm further north) I detached the VII Flottille to advance in the sector SE to S by E (the area subsequently assigned by the II FdT to the 12 Half Flottille) and the V Flottille in the sector S by E

to SSW. In addition at about 11.30pm I gave all Flottilles the FT order: at 3am assemble with our Main Body at Horns Reef just as the route around Skagen. For these arrangements it was decisive that:

1. It was chanceless for torpedobootes attacking an enemy at night to withdraw, as the old bootes of the V and VII Flottilles had been running at high speed for the past few hours and the coal fires were not prepared for smokeless travel, so that above 15 knots speed smoke and sparks resulted and would give the bootes away early.

2. There was the possibility that with the breaking off of battle the enemy stood in the east under the Jutland coast and would run south so at dawn would renew battle off Horns Reef. In this case the advance of the Flottilles in the arranged direction would cause heavy damage to the enemy during the night. There appeared a prospect the enemy would follow and this assumption was of paramount importance.

3. I thought it was necessary to assemble with the Main Body at dawn in the event of a new battle (it must be expected that the enemy would receive reinforcements from the English coast) and the bootes must be in position, and also to avoid the torpedobootes falling victim to enemy light forces at dawn. That the bootes found nothing is therefore due to the fact that the enemy only followed with light forces, with the exception of a few large ships. Perhaps the uncertainty of our position also played a part, and wide stretches remained unsearched, and this should have been avoided. That the enemy did not follow in greater strength, and just as I heard went to Jammer Bay, is very unfortunate in regard to the Flottilles, but I do not accept it.[3]

The V Flottille, under the command of Korvettenkapitän Heinecke, suffered various delays and could only begin their advance as a unit at midnight. Unfortunately neither torpedobootes nor small cruisers had been in contact with the British main body before darkness fell, which was essential for a successful attack. As he mentions in his orders the Flottilles were to rendezvous with the Main Body at Horns Reef at 0300hrs, with the exception the II Flottille, which was to take route home via the Skagen. This was doubtless a mistake as the bootes of the II Flottille were the largest and most combat capable in the fleet, and mostly retained the majority of their torpedoes.

After the V and VII Flottilles had been dispatched Kommodore Michelsen had only the five bootes of the IX and III Flottilles at his disposal and he attached his flagship, *Rostock*, to the IV AG. The II FdT, Kommodore Heinrich, took his flagship, *Regensburg* and the six bootes of the III Flottille, behind *Derfflinger* and then *von der Tann*, as last in line. At about 2327hrs he found *S50* of the 12 HF. Korvettenkapitän Hollmann, the Chief of the III Flottille wanted to also take his boats in a night attack, but Kommodore Heinrich held them back as a reserve for unforeseen circumstances.

As the Flottilles were being given orders and being detached, the II Squadron was still positioned at the head of the German line, and Vizeadmiral Scheer believed this an inappropriate place for these ships because of their low resistance to torpedoes. Therefore at 2210hrs, included in his order: 'Main Body course SSE ¼ E. Hold course! Speed 16 knots,' he had added: 'II Squadron at the end.' At 2220hrs *Westfalen* turned to starboard onto SW by S, to take the I and III Squadrons clear of the II Squadron, which again delayed the passage to Horns Reef. Vizeadmiral Schmidt, the Chief of I Squadron, was engaged in signalling *Westfalen* to steer back onto course SSE when he received Vizeadmiral Scheer's signal of 2229hrs for the night cruising formation: 'II Squadron behind III Squadron. Große Kreuzer (Battle Cruisers) to the rear. II AG ahead, IV AG to starboard.'

At this time the II AG was still engaged in steaming for the head of the line and was to port abeam the I and II Squadrons, whilst the IV AG were to starboard of these, because of the II Squadron's repositioning. The II Squadron had still not begun to carry out their orders to proceed to the rear of the line when at 2220hrs the leading ship, *Hannover*, sighted a smoke cloud from four large ships dead ahead and also for a moment a clear top lantern,[4] and reported by wireless: 'Enemy in sight ahead. Four ships, 166 gamma. 2 Admiral of the II Squadron.' What they were seeing was the armoured cruisers of the 2 Cruiser Squadron about to join with Vice Admiral Beatty.

Kontreadmiral Freiherr von Dalwigk ordered the IV AG by blinker signal to close on the light. At the same time Kommodore Michelsen directed the 18 HF to attack the reported enemy forces and search the sector SSW to SW. However, nothing came of this.

Soon after Kontreadmiral Mauve received orders for his II Squadron to take station astern, however he paused whilst the situation ahead was cleared up. As no further contact reports were received he carried out a battle turn at about 2250hrs, onto the opposite course and at 2310hrs swung in behind *König*, the last ship of the III Squadron. To carry out this change in night cruising formation in darkness and so near the enemy was really quite dangerous.

It was only between 2157hrs and 2205hrs that Vizeadmiral Hipper and his Staff had finally succeeded in boarding the Panzerkreuzer *Moltke* from *G39*, and hoist his flag. Apparently the order to take station at the rear of the line had not been received aboard *Moltke* and no sooner had Vizeadmiral Hipper boarded his new flagship than he gave orders to proceed to the head of the line at 20 knots. Nevertheless, only *Moltke* and *Seydlitz* could carry out this order. Because of battle damage to *Derfflinger* and clinkering of *von der Tann*'s boiler fires these two Panzerkreuzer could make only 18 knots speed and the distance between *Moltke* and *Seydlitz* on one hand, and *Derfflinger* and *von der Tann* on the other, quickly increased. When the two latter ships were abeam the Fleet flagship they received orders to join the end of the line, behind the II Squadron. Soon after 2300hrs the difficult transformation into night cruising formation had been achieved.

As the High Sea Fleet was assuming its night cruising formation Admiral Jellicoe was making his own arrangements. We have seen how his thoughts were dominated by avoiding action with the enemy. At 2217hrs Admiral Jellicoe gave the signal: 'Assume 2 organisation. Form Divisions in line ahead columns disposed abeam to port. Columns one mile apart.' With this order the six divisions of the day battle were formed into three squadron columns, with the 5 Battle Squadron forming a fourth column on the eastern wing. Therefore the six columns were reduced to three fairly close columns that would make the task of the torpedobootes even more difficult, whilst making it easier to avoid battle and maintain contact between elements of the main body of the fleet. However, if a wing division came into contact with battleships or were attacked by torpedobootes and turned away from torpedoes onto the other columns, then a dreadful confusion would result. In contrast to the Germans, the British Fleet Chief would not employ a single destroyer offensively, and instead at 2227hrs Jellicoe ordered them to take station 5 nautical miles astern of the battle fleet. He was afraid his destroyers would mistake him for the German fleet and in the confusion he would fall victim to his own destroyers.

There were three routes back to Wilhelmshaven available to Vizeadmiral Scheer, apart from the route via the Skagerrak and Kleinen Belt, which was substantially longer. Firstly there was the route via Horns Reef and Amrum Bank, secondly the route between the British and German minefields to the west of Helgoland, and thirdly the route off the Frisian coast off the Ems to the Jade. These routes were all well known to the British Admiralty and Admiral Jellicoe. It was unlikely that the High Sea Fleet would go via the Ems as this route was considerably longer than the other two. The location of the High Sea Fleet at 2200hrs was 175nm via Helgoland and 142nm via the Horns Reef route. Despite this Admiral Jellicoe steered his forces to a point where he could cut off the Ems and Helgoland routes. To block the Horns Reef route he had submarines off Vyl light vessel but at 2232hrs he dispatched the destroyer minelayer *Abdiel* to proceed at high speed and reinforce the submarines with a mine barrier south of their position.

Nevertheless, Vizeadmiral Scheer had given the British advance warning of his intentions for the following day. At 2206hrs he sent a request to the Naval Airship Department that 'Early reconnaissance near Horns Reef urgently required.' As early as 2310hrs this request was in the possession of the British Admiralty, after being intercepted and decrypted by British Naval Intelligence. However, here the 'intelligence' ceases and the spin begins. British sources argue that this priceless piece of information was not passed to Admiral Jellicoe, for various reasons, varying from Operations Chief Oliver having a well earned sleep, to that the 2258hrs message to Jellicoe: 'At 9pm [10pm] rear ship of enemy battle fleet in Lat. 56°33'N,

Long. 5°30'E, on southerly course,' was sufficient indication of the route home that Vizeadmiral Scheer intended to take. Admiral Jellicoe received this message at 2323hrs but was convinced that the position given was wrong, and taken together with the noon message that the High Sea Fleet was still in the Jade River it ruined any belief Jellicoe had that the information being passed by Operations Department head Oliver was reliable. So, the ruse formulated by the group of junior Wireless Offizieres of the High Sea Fleet was still having an effect out of all proportion to its modest application.[5] Admiral Jellicoe had lost faith in his intelligence. Nevertheless, there was still hope as at 2341hrs the British Admiralty sent a message to Admiral Jellicoe quoted in the Jutland Dispatches as saying: 'At 10.41pm [2341hrs MEZ] the Admiralty informed the Commander in Chief that the enemy was believed to be returning to its base as its course was SSE ¼ E and speed 16 knots.'[6] About this communication Patrick Beesly wrote:

> This signal was sent to Jellicoe at 10.41pm, and should have provided him with an unmistakable indication that Scheer was intending to use the Horns Reef swept channel. Jellicoe either chose to draw a different conclusion or, more probably, ignored it altogether because he had come to the conclusion that the information provided by the Admiralty was totally unreliable and misleading. Whatever his motives, he did not make the necessary alteration of course or alert his rear screen to the probability that a collision with the German Fleet was imminent.[7]

Admiral Jellicoe blamed others for his failure.

> These errors were absolutely fatal, as the information if passed to me would have clearly shown me that Scheer was making for Horn Reef. The information which was so conclusive would have led me to alter course during the night for the Horn Reef, instead of waiting till daylight to close the Horn Reef if no information respecting enemy movements towards one of the other channels to his base had reached me by daylight, as was my intention.[8]

Marder went on to say that not passing on these signals was criminal neglect on the part of the Operations Division. Nevertheless, at no stage did Jellicoe ever take course on Horns Reef, despite what he said.

As the two opposing forces began their night march the Germans were positioned slightly behind the southerly steering British. At 2330hrs the German lead ship, *Westfalen*, was only 6nm to port aft Vice Admiral Beatty's battle cruisers and the same distance to starboard abeam the western wing column of the Grand Fleet. The two fleets were on a converging course, and a further clash was inevitable.

Because of the repeated course alterations of the German Squadrons with assuming their night cruising formation neither *Moltke* or *Seydlitz* of the I AG, nor *Frankfurt* or *Pillau* of the II AG had succeeded in gaining the head of the Fleet as they had intended, but were still off to the port side. The IV AG were positioned to the port side of the battleships, although the Leader of the IV AG, Kommodore von Reuter, assumed himself to be SW, or to starboard of his line. Kommodore von Reuter wrote:

> In accordance with an FT from the Fleet, after passing the II Squadron which was turning to port, I took the Fleet speed and course. I took it that our own Main Body stood to port and therefore north east of the IV AG. The already arriving darkness did not allow me, taking into account the military situation, to explore the exact position of the Main Body by steaming nearer. Until the morning, when the Main Body was sighted to starboard, I remained with this assumption.[9]

The small cruiser *Elbing* could not keep up with the II AG because of condenser damage. 'As towards 2120hrs the II AG steered south, the port engine failed due to a leaking condenser. Report to the F.d.II.AG.: "Ship can only run at 20 knots". The F.d.II.AG. orders: "Join to IV AG."'[10] Further east, but more to aft, was the VII Flottille. At about 2230hrs the 14 HF was running out behind the III Squadron when one of these battleships mistook them for British destroyers and fired a salvo at 18hm, which impacted 50m behind the stern of *S23*. With that the Flottille Leader, Korvettenkapitän Koch, turned onto course SE to run clear of his own Main Body. Now the German cruisers and torpedobootes were abeam their own Main Body, closing with British light forces.

As the British destroyers were manoeuvring to take up their night cruising formation, as ordered by Admiral Jellicoe, the VII Flottille arrived at a speed of 17 knots. At 2250hrs the Leaderboot, *S24*, sighted a series of destroyers ahead. With the range quickly reducing to 400 to 500 metres these boats were still taken for the II Flottille but when *S24* showed the recognition signal it went unanswered so at 2258hrs *S24*, *S16*, *S18* and *S15* each launched one torpedo. The Germans were dealing with the Flotilla Leader *Tipperary* and the 1st Division of the 4 Flotilla.[11] The torpedo shot of *S24* continually broke the surface and could possibly have warned the British of the attack, and no torpedoes hit. Of the British boats only *Garland* opened fire about 2302hrs and soon after a torpedo ran close to her stern. The German bootes turned away as Korvettenkapitän Koch believed his main role was to find British capital ships. The British destroyers did not follow and contact was broken off.

At the same time there was contact further to the south as the two cruisers of the II AG pushed onto the 11 Destroyer Flotilla, led by Commodore Hawksley aboard the light cruiser *Castor*. Kontreadmiral Boedicker believed he had five enemy cruisers in sight and reported as much by wireless. *Frankfurt* and *Pillau* launched one torpedo each at 1000 metres range before turning way to the west, so as not to draw the enemy onto their own Main Body. The British did not follow.

Behind the II AG came the IV AG and at 2305hrs *Castor* sighted three cruisers to starboard, seemingly under the direction of an armoured cruiser. As reported by *Castor* one of the German ships gave the British recognition signal, or at least part thereof, then the Germans illuminated searchlights and opened a rapid fire at a range of 10hm. *Castor* immediately replied at 2315hrs and fired on *Hamburg* and *Elbing*, to the rear of the German IV AG line. This time the participants were willing, to their credit, and there was damage on both sides. The battle lasted five minutes. SMS *Hamburg* was hit three times: one direct hit passed through the aft funnel, without detonating; another hit struck in the port side bunker in Compartment IV, 1 metre above the waterline; the final hit struck an engine room ventilator and skylight to port. To port three gun crew were wounded, two badly. The large wireless antenna was ripped, an artillery speaking tube to port and a telephone cable were damaged. In the port bunker three stokers were badly wounded, and of them two later died.

HMS *Castor* was straddled with the first salvo and was hit a total of ten times. A large hole was made on the starboard side beneath the No.2 starboard 4 inch gun. The shell detonated in the heads and splinters were thrown all about. Two men were killed in the heads, likewise three men of an ammunition supply party. One shell passed through the upper mess deck, just above the waterline, and passed out the port side without exploding. Three shells struck the fore bridge, doing extensive damage and cutting all electrical circuits. These shells killed five men on the bridge. One shell detonated on the forecastle, killing two men. Several shells struck the hull side armour, with splinters causing damage to the aft 4 inch cannon, funnels, aft control, casings and boats. One shell struck the motor boat, setting her on fire, which clearly illuminated the cruiser and made her a better target. In all, 12 men were killed and 23 were wounded, and only the armoured belt saved her from further damage. The destroyer *Marne* was also hit by a 10.5cm projectile, which however, caused little damage. Both sides turned away, and as the British did *Castor*, *Magic* and *Marne* each fired a torpedo. One torpedo passed under *Elbing*.

At 23.20hrs to port abeam several enemy vessels were made out running on a southerly course. *Elbing* lit up [searchlights] and fired, the IV AG fell in. The enemy received several hits and turned away. Briefly after, the track of a torpedo was seen, which came from port aft towards the ship. The attempt to avoid it with port rudder was without success. The torpedo ran under the ship from aft to forward without detonating.[12]

The other destroyers did not open fire as they were either blinded by *Castor*'s fire, or else believed the opponents were their own ships, which were fired on by mistake.

Whilst this action was underway, on the other side of the IV AG the Panzerkreuzer *Moltke* and *Seydlitz* were pushing towards the head of the line and were 1000m to port abeam the head of I Squadron. At 2335hrs they passed directly ahead of

Stettin, flagship of the IV AG. To avoid a collision *München*, *Frauenlob* and *Stuttgart* steered away to port and immediately four cruisers of the Town class came in sight 30hm to port aft. It was the 2 Light Cruiser Squadron, on a converging course. The German ships showed the British recognition signal, but this time the reply was deadly. The second ship in line, *Dublin*, opened fire at the very short range of just 700m and at the same time the German ships illuminated their searchlights and opened fire. In a battle of unprecedented violence *Stettin* and *München* fired on *Southampton*, whilst *Frauenlob* and *Stuttgart* concentrated on *Dublin*. Because only the two leading British ships, *Southampton* and *Dublin*, illuminated their searchlights, *Nottingham* and *Birmingham* remained unfired upon and could rain their salvos down upon the German cruisers. The Germans already suffered from a disadvantage in that they were inferior in combat strength, being outgunned with their 10.5cm cannon facing British 6 inch (15cm) guns, whilst the British light cruisers carried a 2 inch thick belt armour, whereas the German small cruisers had no belt armour. Nevertheless, after the first salvos the two leading British cruisers were set afire in several places. *Stettin* turned to fire a torpedo but was hit twice. One shell hit the aft sponson gun shield, which was deeply indented, putting the gun out of action. The second struck the hull side just behind the port No.2 gun and detonated inboard. *München* was hit once through the second funnel, whilst two short shells caused splinter damage. Nevertheless, *München* managed to fire a torpedo. On *Hamburg* a shell struck the fore funnel and showered the bridge area with splinters, killing ten men. The Commander, Fregattenkapitän Gaudecker, the Navigation Offizier, one man on the signal deck and command bridge and one of the forward gun crew were wounded. *Elbing* was hit once by a shell in the wireless room, where four men were killed and 14 were wounded. Suddenly there was a tremendous explosion that drowned all else out. At the beginning of the action *Southampton* had launched a torpedo aimed at the German searchlights, which were the only thing visible according to her torpedo officer, which now struck *Frauenlob* in the port auxiliary machinery room.

Obermaschinist Max Müller wrote:

Towards 11[40] the engines made revolutions for 15 knots when a violent explosion occurred in the aft ship, in the auxiliary engine room, (a crash and a cracking) which due to my recollections of S.M.S. *Danzig*[13] could only come from a torpedo hit. At the same moment the engines stopped, probably as a result of bending the propeller shafts, the lights extinguished and through the bulkhead to the port auxiliary engine room a violent rushing of penetrating water could be heard. This rushing could be heard through the speaking tube in the starboard engine room.[14]

Another survivor, Fähnrich Stolzmann, wrote:

It was shortly before 23.30am … suddenly a searchlight illuminated.

One of our Group had seen a silhouette and lit it up. At scarcely 1000 metres distance we could see the well known form of an *Arethusa* type clearly illuminated. Those who had discovered him already had him under a violent fire.

The other ships of our Group shone their searchlights into the night. A new opponent of the *Arethusa* class was seen in the darkness.

In the searchlight's beam their dark shapes appeared ghostly.

Each of our ships immediately took the enemy under fire. It was difficult for *Frauenlob*. Instead of the single superior enemy opponent of August 28th 1914,

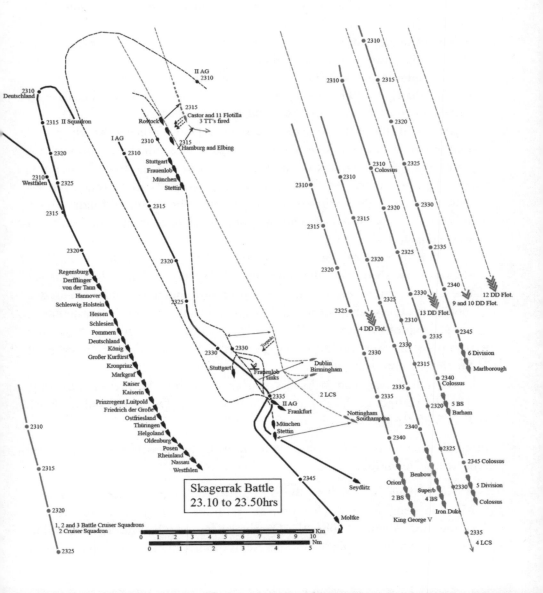

Skagerrak Battle
23.10 to 23.50hrs

there were now three enemies. One of these was taken under rapid fire by us, before he could get our range.

'Salvo, fire!' … the loud commands of our Artillerie Offizier resounded over the entire ship. How beautiful and reassuring those sounds were!

However, after only a few minutes we had two new opponents. Naturally we could not fire on them. Destructive salvos struck our aft deck with a tremendous crash. The enemy was only 1000 metres distant, and scarcely a shell could get past … there were continuous crashes on our ship … fire a salvo, and receive three back, and so it went for some minutes….

'Fire in the aft ship!'

So went the yelling through our ship. Manoeuvring we attempted to extinguish the flames….

Then the ship lifted, as if from a powerful impact … a vibration went through the entire hull … the lights went out, the searchlights extinguished … the engines stood still. That was a torpedo hit!

Immediately the ship took up a list to port. I went aft. From the stairways and openings of the aft ship smoke and steam climbed up …

Meanwhile the port engine room leaked like a sieve. Thick water jets poured into the room … in the water they attempted to locate the leak … in vain, the water was rising too quickly! 'Attempt to hold the engine room by draining with pumps!' instructed Oberingenieur Hahn, our Leading Ingenieur. All hands moved … Nevertheless, it was too late! The Auxiliary Engine room, which the deadly torpedo had hit, was already full of water. All the generators were submerged.

I came to the aft bridge. *Frauenlob* already lay heavily over to the side. The sea already washed about the approximately seven metre high deck. One felt that from second to second the ship lay over more and more, and the capsizing motion became ever quicker …. The aft ship was a place of devastation. A savage heap of rubble; shot-down searchlight positions, ventilator heads and iron parts that were no longer recognizable…. The fast capsizing moment of the ship became even faster.

From the funnels comes the hiss of air escaping from the interior of the ship. The last vestiges of the ship disappear in the deep. Our lively, valiant, brave *Frauenlob*. People are swimming all around.[15]

From the engine room of *Frauenlob* a survivor, Obermaschinistenmaat Siegrist, reported the following:

About 11 o'clock I went to the starboard main engine room and replaced Maschinisten Johnke who had time off. With the replacement there were 120 revolutions. About 23.20hrs the Oberingenieur, who had been present until then, quit the engine room and went to his cabin. Overall all was quiet. About

23.30hrs he again came in and said: 'The battle will begin immediately!' Then I heard the call from above: 'To the guns!' At the same time our first port salvo fell. Several commands came from the bridge for the engines, e.g. '130 to 140 revolutions!' About 23.39hrs came the last command from the bridge, and a few minutes later there followed a violent detonation, both engines suddenly stood still and no longer allowed movement. The lights went out. The Oberingenieur questioned me what happened in the port engine room. On questioning the port engine room I received no answer, and through the speaking tube could hear water in the port engine room. The Oberingenieur gave the order to drain the port engine room with the middle circulation pumps. I opened the slide-gate valve and suction valve of the circulation pump. Therewith [while I was] occupied with that came the order from above, that the ship could not be held, and all men should quit the engine room: also the Oberingenieur gave the order, to fully stop the engines, and that done we abandoned the engine room. As I came on the Oberdeck, we received a violent fire for a few minutes from close range, the ship lay more and more to port, so that the water already came through the engine room skylight into the port engine room. There I met the Leader of the Leak Service (Obermaschinisten Birmelin) and I asked, whether we could hold the ship with counter flooding. He said we already had too much water in the ship and any attempt was chanceless. Then apparently the ship received several hits in the Zwischendeck, so that the cabins of the Minen personnel (port compartment V) filled. The port 4 gun (Bootsmannmaat Schmidt) still fired. I saw that the hull side below the gun had a large tear (rent), and the ship sank deeper, and at this moment the Commander brought out three cheers for the His Majesty the Kaiser. Then I sprang overboard and attempted to rescue myself. The Oberingenieur went in his cabin, and I saw him no more. All the Offizieres were on the bridge.

Several times I was dragged back by the whirlpool of the sinking ship and with great effort I came free of the ship. At some distance drifted a float. After I swam and reached it, I discovered that it was overloaded. It was called to me that further away a free float drifted. I swam over to it and swung myself up. Not far away floated Obermaschinist Müller. I took him on my float and we drifted on the sea. There was nothing more to see of S.M.S. *Frauenlob*. Towards 1 at night we saw a destroyer, which however, proceeded. The night was cold and the sea rose. Often we were thrown out of the float. The next morning we discovered several smoke clouds on the horizon, one of which later turned out to be a Dutch trawler. After the trawler cruised past several times, it headed directly towards us, and we discovered it was the trawler *Thames*. The Captain called to us, we were saved. The treatment aboard was good. (in original signed) L. Siegrist.[16]

The Commander of *Frauenlob*, Fregattenkapitän Hoffmann, and 323 others perished with the sinking and there were only eight survivors.

It was only with difficulty that *Stuttgart*, Fregattenkapitän Hagedorn, succeeded in sheering away to starboard to avoid the sinking *Frauenlob*. With that *Stuttgart* lost contact with the IV AG and took station on the I Squadron, as they came in sight to starboard. *Hamburg* also turned away to make room for *Moltke*, which passed across her bow midway through the battle. *Elbing* and *Rostock* followed *Hamburg* and then tried to rejoin *Stettin* and *München*. *Seydlitz* lost sight of *Moltke*, being unable to keep up with the high speed of the latter, 22 knots, and from a position 10nm to east ahead of the German line steered independently to Horns Reef.

Likewise, the British 2 LCS turned away. *Southampton* had been badly damaged and hit up to 15 times. There were many hits on the hull plating, some of which penetrated and all four funnels were perforated. Only one 6 inch and one 3 inch cannon were damaged but three other starboard guns were put out of action because of losses to their crews. There were three cordite fires and both aft searchlights were wrecked, along with the one forward one. There were 35 dead and 41 wounded crew. *Dublin* was hit by 5–15cm shells from *Elbing* and 8–10.5cm shells from the other small cruisers. Seven hits were on the hull side, whilst the chart house was wrecked as were other light structures. Despite this there were only three dead, however one of them was the navigator. A total of 24 men were wounded. As all charts were destroyed when the chart house was hit, and as the navigation office was dead, *Dublin* became separated from the 2 LCS and could only rejoin them after daybreak.

At the beginning of this battle *Seydlitz* and *Moltke* were between the IV AG and the German Main Body, but at the conclusion of the action they were positioned to the south of the IV AG, with one ahead to port and one ahead to starboard. The IV AG were still firing and Kapitän zur See von Karpf, commander of *Moltke*, was considering whether to join in when suddenly four large enemy warships appeared to port. These were the last four ships of the 2 Battle Squadron, the starboard wing column of the British fleet. *Moltke* turned away in an attempt to close with her own Main Body, but nevertheless she had been sighted from *Thunderer* and is reported to have shown her coloured recognition lights, three red and three green lights on the main mast. The Captain of *Thunderer*, Captain Fergusson, decided not to fire 'unless obvious attack was intended'. He did not wish to reveal the location of the battle fleet. *Moltke* resumed her hitherto course on the orders of Vizeadmiral Hipper, but again ran into the same four British ships at 2355hrs and again at 0020hrs on 1 June. The encounters were so sudden that *Moltke* was unable to utilize her torpedo arm without prolonging contact with the four battleships. *Moltke* went onto a southerly course and finally regained contact with the German Main Body at 0230hrs.

Likewise, *Seydlitz*, Kapitän zur See Egidy, found her passage east barred by the Grand Fleet. At 0045hrs Seydlitz sighted three large enemy warships to port at a range of 1500 metres, on a southerly course.

Seydlitz's war diary reported:

0045. The tar–oil supplemental firing no longer works.

0030. Lively battle aft, right. Revolutions temporarily fall to 19 knots. Increase later to 20 knots. (speed through the water was 2 knots lower).

0040–0045. Temporarily reduce to 7 knots, course SW, for extinguishing a fire on the forecastle. Then again to course SE. To port abeam approximately 1500m distant 3 *Malaya*s on course south. English recognition signal shown and turn away to the north. Enemy disappears from sight in our own smoke. FT signal from Z Station to *Friedrich der Große* and *Moltke*: 4 enemy Battle Cruisers Grid 093 alpha, steering SSE.

0045. It was irreproachably seen from several observation positions on *Seydlitz* that the ships were 3 battleships of the *Malaya* class.[17]

No explanation was given as to why the wireless report mentioned '4 enemy Battle Cruisers'.

The *Seydlitz* I Artillerie Offizier Richard Foerster wrote along similar lines:

Under the forecastle there was a fire. One of the last hits had penetrated the sail locker, where there were stowed large provisions of hammocks, covers, sail cloth etceteras. These now burned with a bright light and the men untiringly fought the flames with fire extinguishers and pails, without being able to finally suffocate the flames. Over and over the flames climbed high from the forecastle. Surrounded by the enemy, on a dark night, this light beacon was most disagreeable.

So we drove through the dark night with this blazing torch. Then during this crucial moment the aft command position reported: 'Darkened vessels approach from port aft.' With their superior speed they were soon abeam of us and to our grim surprise we recognized them as English dreadnoughts. Against the already dawning morning we clearly saw their type silhouette. Therewith we quickly turned away to starboard. Had the English seen us? I could almost not believe it, but conditions on their side were particularly unfavourable. We stood against the darkened western heavens; the wind blew our funnel smoke directly at them and this worked in our favour, and finally the English had no training in night vision.[18]

Seydlitz's combat report read:

At about 00⁴⁵ whilst on course for Horns Reef (SE) 3 large ships of the *Malaya* class were sighted to port abeam at a range of approximately 1500m, with course south. *Seydlitz* turned away onto course north and for confusion of the English utilized the English recognition signal (P.L.). Coincidentally at the same time a light lantern burnt in the main top, seemingly through induction from the FT antenna. In the protection of our own smoke the enemy ships were shaken off. The position and course of the enemy ships was reported through wireless. At about 1[03] a torpedo boat attack was observed in the direction the *Malaya*s had gone. About 1[23] a further battle was seen in the same direction at a great distance.

The rest of the night passed quietly. In the morning, after passing Horns Reef *Seydlitz* was again in contact with her own forces.[19]

None of the ships of the 5 Battle Squadron reported seeing *Seydlitz*, however shortly after 0100hrs the light cruiser *Fearless*, on station astern of the British 6 Division, sighted a capital ship passing down the starboard side on a northerly course. As she had not been taken under fire by the battleships ahead no action was taken. The commander of the 6 Division, Vice Admiral Burney, reported that smoke was seen ahead and a large ship was challenged by *Revenge*, which answered incorrectly. Aboard *Revenge* they thought they were dealing with a torpedoboot and ordered the 6 inch battery to open fire, however, the ship had disappeared before this fire could be opened.

The British had again missed the chance of destroying a German capital ship. As Frost wrote:

Again, the British had lost a priceless opportunity. It is true that Burney can give some good reasons for failing to open fire. It would be unwise to expose the position of his Division to the enemy, as it was separated from the battle fleet. Also, *Marlborough* was damaged, but here was the practical certainty of sinking a German capital ship, which also was separated from her battle line and probably also was disabled. Jellicoe's defensive attitude had certainly penetrated throughout his entire fleet. Never was a fleet better indoctrinated with the ideas of its commander in chief.[20]

Because *Moltke* had her wireless station put out of action during the day, it was only at 0227hrs that a contact report could be relayed through escorting torpedoboot *G39* about the three encounters with heavy forces. Up until midnight Vizeadmiral Scheer only had reports about the clashes of light forces. None of the Flottilles had reached the enemy battle fleet, just light cruisers and destroyers. Vizeadmiral Scheer could not be sure he was dealing with the enemy rearguard and it seemed more probable the British flotillas had been directed to attack the German Main Body, with their light cruisers in support. The High Sea Fleet had been well trained to ward off destroyer attacks, and their skill would be put to the test during the very short night. Nevertheless, Vizeadmiral Scheer was more concerned with gaining the Horns Reef by dawn, as he fully expected to resume battle with the Grand Fleet there with sunrise. The order at 2210hrs: 'Main Body course SSE ¼ E. Hold course! Speed 16 knots,' showed Vizeadmiral Scheer's determination to gain Horns Reef and shrug off any destroyer attacks. Therefore, soon after midnight the High Sea Fleet stood on the position where briefly before the Grand Fleet had stood. At this time the cruisers *Rostock*, *Stuttgart*, *Elbing* and *Hamburg* had not succeeded in taking their allotted station but were forward abeam the I Squadron forming a kind of side cover protection for the German line, and the cruisers were in a position where contact with the enemy was probable.

On the British side the 4 Destroyer Flotilla, with the leader *Tipperary*, under the command of Captain Wintour, were closing with the German Main Body. About 7 nautical miles east of these was the light cruiser *Champion*, under Captain Farie, with seven destroyers of the 13 Flotilla and two destroyers of the 10 Flotilla.[21] To port nearby *Champion* and her Flotilla were four destroyers of the Harwich 9 Flotilla and another destroyer from the 10 Flotilla.[22] Still further to the rear and NE was *Faulkner* and the 12 Flotilla,[23] under Captain Stirling, and near them was the 6 Battleship Division, which owing to the damage to *Marlborough* could not maintain the fleet speed and had gradually fallen behind.

This was the situation as towards 0030hrs Captain Wintour and the leading boats of the 4 Flotilla sighted the shadowy outlines of a line of large warships to starboard, apparently travelling on a south-easterly course, with the destroyers overtaking them. It was impossible to say if they were friend or foe, so the Flotilla remained on its course for another minute or so, but swung their torpedo tubes out to starboard. All remained quiet as the two lines of ships converged and as the range decreased to 1000 metres Captain Wintour aboard *Tipperary* showed the recognition signal. The answer came as a torrent of incoming shells. The very first salvo damaged *Tipperary*'s forecastle, sweeping away her bow gun and setting the forecastle afire, and destroying her fore bridge. Then the main steampipe was damaged, shrouding the boat in steam. *Tipperary* was continually hit forward and came to a stop. Nearly all the personnel amidships were killed or wounded and the boxes of ammunition forward were exploding one after another. The battleship *Westfalen* had opened fire and the following *Nassau*, *Rostock*, *Elbing* and *Hamburg*, together with torpedoboot *S32*, all joined in firing on hapless *Tipperary*. The battleship *Rheinland* opened fire on the British armoured cruiser *Black Prince*, which was to port of the 4 Flotilla.

'Fire opened on an enemy cruiser with 4 funnels and 2 masts with the medium artillerie. Range 22–26hm. The cruiser was shot at by other ships at the same time.'[24]

The War Diary of *Westfalen* recorded:

In 014ε (Epsilon) middle, IV, in direction 300° approximately 18hm away a vessel comes in sight, a destroyer or cruiser. *Westfalen* opens fire. In the searchlight beam a large English ensign was recognised in the foretop, in addition to the bow and stern guns 2 or 3 broadside guns, completely behind armoured shields (the form of the shields was like our B.A.K.s). On the bow was painted the number 60.[25] The ship's hull was painted grey. Apparently a Flotilla Leader cruiser. He fired two torpedoes from upper deck tubes, which were avoided by a turn away and we opened artillery fire (high explosive shells) …The first salvo of *Westfalen* struck the cruisers forecastle gun and command bridge, and the next salvo sank the ship. The light cruiser fired with its stern gun until the last moment, which was finally served by only one man. Duration of the shooting 5 minutes. Range 18hm to 14hm. Munitions usage: 92–15cm Spgr. 45–8.8cm Spgr.[26]

Tipperary sank at about 0300hrs and suffered 185 dead, whilst eight men were taken prisoner by the Germans.

The following boat, *Spitfire*, was hit on the torpedo davit, and the following destroyers, *Sparrowhawk*, *Garland*, *Contest* and *Broke* were also taken under fire and all turned away to port, loosing torpedoes at a range of 900 metres. The destroyers following *Broke*, the *Achates*, *Ambuscade*, *Fortune*, *Porpoise* and *Unity*, failed to fire their torpedoes apart from *Ambuscade*.

Between 0030 and 0036hrs *Westfalen*, *Nassau* and *Rheinland* were struck by shells around their forward funnels and searchlight groups. *Westfalen* was hit in the forward funnel and the No.2 searchlight was completely destroyed. Splinters damaged the No.3 searchlight but it remained serviceable and the cable to the No.1 searchlight was also damaged. The fore funnel was torn open for several square metres and there was much splinter damage. Two men were killed, 1 was badly wounded and 7 were lightly wounded, including the commander, Kapitän zur See Redlich. *Nassau* was struck by two 4 inch shells. The first struck the port side support of the forward searchlight stand. Searchlights 2, 3 and 4 were all damaged and there was splinter damage to the upper and lower bridges and upper, forward funnel. One Offizier and 9 men were killed and 14 were wounded. The second shell was also 4 inch calibre and hit the aft searchlight bridge superstructure and damaged the number 5 and 6 searchlights. One man was wounded.

As reported in *Rheinland*'s war diary she was hit at 0036hrs by a 6 inch shell, which bears out the idea that she was in fact engaged with *Black Prince*. The projectile struck the port side at frame 86/87 just above the 100mm thick citadel armour and detonated against the armoured transverse bulkhead at frame 86. The explosion destroyed a bootsmann cabin and splinters damaged the forward funnel to port and the No.3 and No.4 searchlights.

For their part the German small cruisers were in a difficult situation, placed between their battleships and the opposing destroyers. When they recognized torpedoes being fired from the British destroyers they found their escape blocked by the line of battleships. *Rostock* succeeded in passing between *Nassau* and *Rheinland* as the latter gave way, but *Elbing* was squeezed by *Stuttgart* and was forced to pass ahead of *Posen*. Because of the lively battle the Commander of *Posen*, Kapitän zur See Lange, only belatedly realized that his ship and the small cruiser would unavoidably collide.

> There *Stuttgart* turned back to port very late, and *Elbing* was forced to break through [the line] ahead of *Posen*. From *Elbing* the situation did not appear dangerous. It was taken that *Posen* could well see the illuminated *Elbing* and correspondingly would give air to starboard. As the collision appeared inevitable, it was attempted, to avoid the stern with hard starboard rudder. As then it became known that *Posen* herself had laid hard starboard rudder, the rudder was taken off. The collision resulted to starboard aft and was relatively weak.[27]

At first the ship took on a list of 18°, but this could be righted by counter flooding. The starboard engine room filled with water, and after that also the port engine room. Because of this the steam condensed in the pipes to the rudder and generators, and the rudder and lighting failed. At first the port battery could still be used, however a report could only be conveyed by Morse signal as the wireless room had previously been destroyed. The cruiser lay unmanoeuvrable to starboard aft of the German line and incapable of further action. About 0200hrs the torpedoboot *S53* took off 477 men, leaving only a skeleton crew aboard to attempt to save the ship. This proved impossible and when towards 0300hrs British destroyers and a cruiser were sighted Fregattenkapitän Madlung ordered explosive charges detonated to scuttle the ship, which sank by the bow. The Germans took to a cutter whilst the British cruiser fired a few shells into the sinking cruiser. The cutter drifted away and thereby soon found the exhausted doctor of *Tipperary* and hauled him aboard, and then found about 100 survivors from this destroyer drifting in the water. Fregattenkapitän Madlung did not hesitate to light a flare to try and attract the attention of the British ships. Five hours later the Germans were rescued by a Dutch trawler.

Kapitän zur See Lange of *Posen* wrote in his war diary:

> The small cruisers fired to port for a short time, the aft most cruiser stands at short range to port abeam of SMS *Posen*. We make the E.S. [recognition signal] which was not answered. The cruiser was recognised as SMS *Elbing*. Suddenly SMS *Elbing* quickly came nearer, apparently not recognising SMS *Posen*. Then it was realised that *Elbing* would breakthrough near *Posen*. To reduce the effect of the unavoidable collision I turned hard to starboard, allowed stop and then astern. SMS *Elbing* was rammed at a very acute angle. *Posen* remained undamaged. SMS *Elbing* was lost from sight to starboard. What kind of damage he had could not be known from here. Turn back onto the ordered course.[28]

After contact between the German line and the 4 Flotilla was broken both groups resumed their hitherto courses and the result was an inevitable second collision, literally, between the two opposing forces. *Nassau* sighted a destroyer 400m ahead, it was *Spitfire*, and altered course to ram her. *Spitfire* attempted to evade the collision with rudder hard to starboard, but the two ships crashed together, port bow to port bow, so that *Nassau* heeled over 5° to 10° to starboard. With the guns of turret A at maximum depression the 28cm shells that were fired only passed through the bridge and middle funnel of the destroyer without detonating, but the muzzle pressure was enough to rent away the searchlight deck, bridge, mast and forward funnel. The ram bow penetrated the destroyer for 20 metres to the second watertight bulkhead and started fires. A total of six men were killed and three were badly wounded. However, *Spitfire* survived and made it home using her three serviceable boilers.

Nassau was also damaged in the encounter, as related in her war diary:

About 1.31am [0031hrs] an enemy destroyer was sighted to port ahead approximately 400m distant. To vigorously oppose the attack the destroyer was rammed with hard port rudder and was destroyed. With the ramming the ship suffered the following damage:

On the port side the hull side of the forward batterie and of the infirmary from Frame 96 to 109 was torn with a breadth of 3.5m. The deck beams of the above mentioned frames were all bent aft, the light walls of the interior arrangements were partly destroyed. The forecastle deck from Frame 106 to 111 was pushed in for a length of 5m and was bent up.

The first port side boom is lost, the net harness and the net are damaged.

The forward part of the enemy destroyer, which drifted aft, caused damage to the following:

The port I 15cm cannon, which was facing directly forward, was torn aft with great violence. The carriage with shield struck the hard aft position with full force. Through the sudden impact of the gun the right sighting telescope, the shafts for elevation and training and the lateral training drum were smashed. In addition the right carriage side was pushed in. The two target bearing discs were rent off. Further the left trunnion broke, so that the barrel lay slightly tilted in the cradle. The gun is unusable for combat and is to be replaced.

The port sounding boom is broken. The port combat signal boom in bent.

The leak was sealed in the usual manner with exercise mats and timber. With the good weather water did not come over [the ship]. Only a few splashes penetrated the infirmary.

With dawn it was attempted to haul up the net which was hanging down. However, this was not possible because of the great weight of the net hanging down.[29]

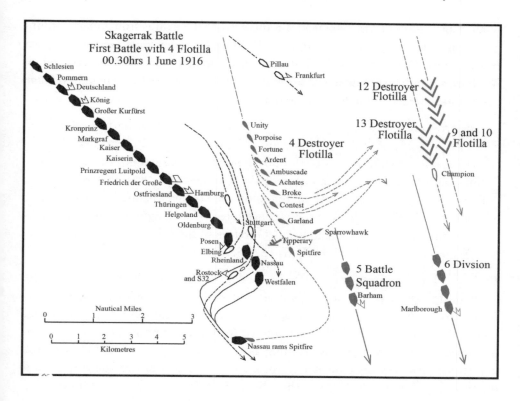

Skagerrak Battle
First Battle with 4 Flotilla
00.30hrs 1 June 1916

Schlesien
Pommern
Deutschland
König
Großer Kurfürst
Kronprinz
Markgraf
Kaiser
Kaiserin
Prinzregent Luitpold
Friedrich der Große
Ostfriesland   Hamburg
Thüringen
Helgoland
Oldenburg
Posen
Elbing
Rheinland
Rostock
and S32
Stuttgart
Westfalen
Nassau

Pillau
Frankfurt

Unity
Porpoise
Fortune
Ardent
Ambuscade
Achates
Broke
Contest
Garland
Tipperary
Spitfire
Sparrowhawk

4 Destroyer
Flotilla

12 Destroyer
Flotilla

13 Destroyer
Flotilla

9 and 10
Flotilla

Champion

5 Battle
Squadron
Barham

6 Division

Marlborough

Nassau rams Spitfire

Nautical Miles
0   1   2   3

0 1 2 3 4 5
Kilometres

Because of the damage to *Nassau*'s hull she could only run at 15 knots until the hole was made watertight, and she tried in vain to regain her position in the line between *Westfalen* and *Rheinland*.

The torpedoboot travelling behind *Rostock*, *S32*, suffered two direct hits. One shell went through the main steam pipe, the other detonated beneath the command bridge and *S32* lay unmanoeuvrable near a burning British ship, aboard which heavy detonations could be observed aft. Nevertheless, about 0130hrs *S32* could again use an engine after filling a boiler with sea water and could make her way east to seek protection under the Danish coast.

Meanwhile, Vizeadmiral Schmidt turned his battleships not engaged with the enemy onto course W by S, to avoid torpedo attack. After a short time course was resumed SE ¾ S but scarcely had *Westfalen* and *Rheinland* resumed this course than they had to open a violent fire to ward off British destroyers to port. After *Tipperary* had been brought to a stop the commander of *Broke*, Commander Allen, turned back onto course south, followed by *Sparrowhawk*, *Contest*, *Achates*, *Ambuscade*, *Ardent*, *Fortune* and *Porpoise*. Within a short time *Broke* sighted a large warship with two funnels and a large boats crane off to starboard, travelling on a parallel course to his Flotilla. When *Broke* showed the recognition signal the reply was the illumination of many searchlights and a deluge of incoming shells. The German small cruiser *Rostock* was 1000m abeam the head of the I Squadron and at 0040hrs opened fire at a range of 16 to 14hm. At 0050hrs *Westfalen* joined in the firing on *Broke*, whilst *Rheinland* took the destroyer second in line under fire. As recorded by *Westfalen* she only maintained fire for 45 seconds, but this was long enough to cause devastating damage to the Flotilla Leader.

> A destroyer of a very large type, 4 funnels, and a high mast forward was sighted on the port side of *Westfalen*, direction 215°, range 14hm. Fire opened. Turn away 8 points to starboard, A.K. [Utmost Power], after 45 seconds the destroyer sinks with burning bridge and forecastle. The destroyer was painted black, flying an English ensign in the foretop, on the bow was painted in white the number 93.[30] The bridge outline was occupied by a recognition signal lamp. The destroyer did not come to firing. Duration of the firing: 45 seconds.
> Munitions usage: 13–15cm Spgr; 13–8.8cm Spgr.[31]

Broke was hit nine times and suffered a total of 47 dead and 36 wounded. On the lower bridge all men had been killed or wounded and the helm was jammed as *Broke* was turning to port, and the starboard engine telegraph was also jammed. Under these circumstances *Broke* continued to turn and rammed her next astern, *Sparrowhawk*, who was likewise turning away to port. *Broke* cut halfway into the unfortunate *Sparrowhawk* on her starboard bow just forward of the bridge, and the two ships became locked together. Some men from *Broke* were thrown onto *Sparrowhawk* and some from the latter jumped across to the Flotilla Leader. Whilst stuck in the precarious position the next astern of *Sparrowhawk*, *Contest*, rammed

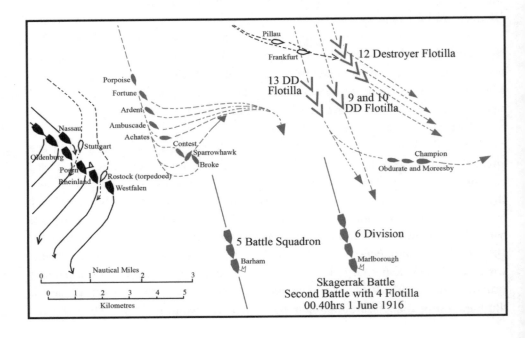

Skagerrak Battle
Second Battle with 4 Flotilla
00.40hrs 1 June 1916

Sparrowhawk aft and cut about 2 metres off the stern. *Sparrowhawk* suffered six dead and was later abandoned and sunk by *Marksman*.[32]

Several of the British destroyers had the opportunity to launch torpedoes against the German line, and one of them found a victim. *Rostock* had received two shell hits and was attempting to pass through the German battleline to the disengaged side, when she was rocked by a heavy explosion. The torpedo struck to port on the bulkhead between compartments X and XI, that is the IV and V boiler rooms. These two rooms immediately filled with water as did the wing passages and because the torpedo was a shallow runner the upper bunker also filled so that there were 930 tonnes of water in the ship. The bows sank by 1.45m and there was a list of 5° to port, but nevertheless at first *Rostock* could follow the line at 17 knots. However, when *Rostock* was about 50nm west of Horns Reef it was observed that the boilers were salting and beginning to boil over. The cause of this was never found. The auxiliary machinery soon failed and the turbines had to be stopped, whereby torpedoboot *S54* took her in tow at a speed which at times reached 10 knots and it looked as if *Rostock* would reach harbour safely. Towards 0300hrs the torpedobootes *V71* and *V73* arrived to assist. Nevertheless, towards 0445hrs what appeared to be two enemy cruisers were sighted, however actually it was *Dublin*, and as the airship *L11* reported further enemy forces in the immediate vicinity Kapitän zur See Feldmann decided to save his crew and abandon ship. The torpedobootes were called alongside and the crew was disembarked, then scuttling charges were detonated in the torpedo room and beneath the turbines. On the orders of the I FdT, Kommodore Michelsen, three torpedoes were fired at the ship to hasten the sinking, which occurred stern high at 0525hrs. During the battle *Rostock* suffered 11 dead, and two others who died later in hospital, six wounded and one missing. She was struck by shellfire a total of seven times; once on the poop deck, once athwart ships above the turbine room, once through the forth funnel, once on the belt amidships, once on deck behind the first funnel and twice on the forecastle. Five hits were from starboard and two were from port.

One of *Rostock*'s crew related his experiences:

The night was a pure witches' coven. All around flames of the heavens and powerful detonations with flaming phenomena were visible. It thundered and crashed from all sides. Enormous impacts appeared alongside us and showered the deck with water. The powerful, dark monsters of our ships ran through the night and water with Utmost Power (AK). Once there was an especially strong firelight ahead of us on the horizon for a long time. As we later learned it was our battleship *Pommern* which through a detonation was sunk with man and mouse.

At 1215 [NB Summer time is used throughout this account, i.e. 1215 is 2315 hrs, etc.] a vessel with 3 funnels and one mast was illuminated by us and shot at. It must be a so-called Destroyer Leader (perhaps *Tipperary*). *Tipperary* was later sunken. What effect was obtained by us cannot be determined, as other ships fired on her at the same time.

At 1221 a torpedo track came in sight to port, but the ship escaped the danger of the torpedo shot through a turn to hard starboard.

1240–1245 battle at approximately 30hm with 2 enemy ships. The right vessel was shot into flames by us. During this fire fight his searchlights lit up like starry eyes in the sky.

0140 battle with several destroyers at a range of 12–14hm. The right one burnt with high flames for a long time. Several detonations were observed.

0142 once again a torpedo track came in sight, as a surface runner. This time our destiny befell us. A turn away was not possible while we had to breakthrough the battleship line at the same time. It was a strange feeling to see the torpedo approaching in the searchlight beam. Now a tremendous crash and a powerful detonation! The torpedo had hit. The whole ship quivered. We are all on deck. All kinds flew through the air. The wireless antenna came down. At the same time we received 3 artillery hits, and splinters flew around. The fire bell calls the people back to their guns. Before us stands the mighty stern of a battleship of the *Nassau* class, so near, that we could almost climb aboard it, at a combined speed of 26 knots. I fire across the stern of the ship in front of us, whilst he shoots close over us with his 28cm guns. It is a wild state of things! What has happened? The torpedo has hit the bulkhead between the oil boiler room and the next coal boiler room. The two rooms immediately filled with water. The crews of both compartments found their deaths. The leak security (damage control) worked quickly. At first the engines and auxiliary machinery were still clear and we could run at 17 knots. The steam rudder, which at first had fallen out and was replaced by the hand rudder, is again clear. However, gradually sea water penetrates the pipes from the filled boiler rooms to the remaining boilers and the boilers start to cook (boil over). The auxiliary engines are quiet now and the electric lights go out. The engine receives water in the turbine and must temporarily be stopped, and the revolutions reduce more and more and eventually stop.

... Slowly the bow sank into the water, always deeper, in part the funnels went over, the stern rising out of the water, the screws pointing to the air, the ship rising steeply and slowly sank into the depths. We sent off our good, brave ship with three cheers, which had served as our home for 2½ years. Then we went with utmost power (A.K.) to the southeast, as the smoke of the enemy cruisers came threateningly closer. The torpedobootes *V71*, *V73* and *S54* had taken us about 0610. At 0625 *Rostock* sank to the sea bottom about the latitude of Horns Reef.

In total we had fired 500 shots and had 13 dead and 8 wounded. All others were rescued.

... After we made fast in Wilhelmshaven we were heartily welcomed. The entire population took an active part. The accommodation of the crew was taken care of, since our home, the beloved *Rostock*, was lost.[33]

After the collision of *Broke*, *Sparrowhawk* and *Contest* Commander Hutchinson of *Achates* took command of the 2 Division and led *Ambuscade*, *Ardent*, *Fortune*, *Porpoise* and *Garland* away to the east, and after covering 3 nautical miles returned to course south to reconnect with his own battle fleet. Because of her damaged bow *Contest* could not maintain speed and lost contact with the other boats, whilst these themselves again approached the German line.

At 0100hrs *Westfalen* exchanged recognition signals with two cruisers of the II AG and gave way to them as they passed ahead. Ten minutes later enemy destroyers came in sight and *Westfalen* regardless made the recognition signal, then opened fire and turned away to starboard at Utmost Power. In the beam of the searchlight the number 30 (*Fortune*) was recognized on the bow of a destroyer. The first salvo swept away the bridge and the mast crashed over. After only 28 seconds duration fire was ceased, after *Westfalen* had expended 7–15cm projectiles and 8–8.8cm. Next astern,

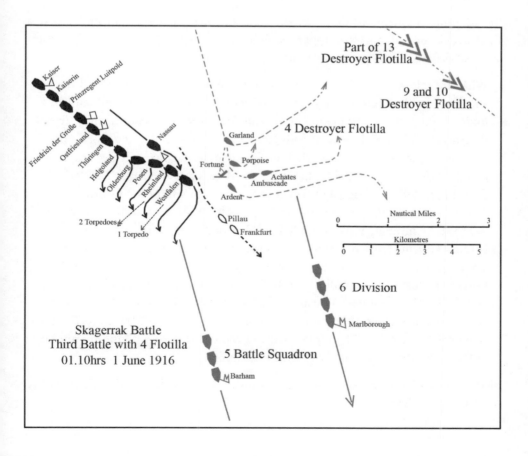

Rheinland, also opened fire on this target, and her medium artillery opened fire at a range of 1500m. Straddling salvos and hits were observed, before *Rheinland* had to cease fire as a German small cruiser now stood in the line of fire. As *Rheinland* turned hard away to starboard at 0113hrs a torpedo was observed to pass just 50m away.

The battleships *Posen*, *Oldenburg* and *Helgoland* also took the first three destroyers under fire at ranges of 8hm to 16hm. Kapitän zur See Lange, commander of *Posen*, reported:

> 0110hrs. 3 enemy destroyers approach from port aft, the first was illuminated, taken under fire and destroyed. Number on the forecastle *G30*. Thereon change target onto the second boat, which was likewise shot up. The third boat escaped under strong smoke development. Combat range 16–8hm. The burning and in sinking condition boat *G30*, which slacked aft, was then taken under fire by SMS *Oldenburg*. The Navigation and Torpedo Offizieres had observed that in the moment she was illuminated by searchlights *G30* had launched two torpedoes. I turned to starboard, and the torpedoes missed.
>
> The second destroyer fired with artillery until he was destroyed.[34]

At the same moment, 0110hrs, as she took the British destroyers under fire, a shell struck the port forward upper searchlight of *Oldenburg*, causing insignificant material damage, but a great cost in life.

> With the following destroyer attack 3 destroyers were effectively fired upon, and of them 2 were quickly illuminated with our searchlights and vanished under strong flame development in the fire. About 1.10am a shell from destroyer *G30*, which was already burning, exploded on the port upper searchlight, and splinters wounded the Commander Kapitän zur See Höpfner, killed 3 Offizieres (Kapitänleutnant Rabius, Leader of the Light Artillerie, II Searchlight Offizier, Signal Offizier) and 4 men. In addition 3 Offizieres and 9 men including the helmsman, and the Watch Offizier standing in the lee near the helmsman, were wounded. Both stood outside the conning tower, because steering from inside was not possible under the prevailing conditions. Splinters penetrated through the vision slits to the inside of the Artillerie Direction Position, wounding the R.W. [Direction Indicator] Unteroffizier and the Bg [Rangefinder] Measurer. Outside the conning tower the two masts were shot through and the exterior of the Bg was damaged, but nevertheless remained serviceable. The replacement of the fallen went without disruption of the ship's direction and Artillerie Direction.[35]

SMS *Helgoland* did not get many opportunities to fight during the night, as her combat report shows:

With the numerous attacks by enemy forces during the night SMS *Helgoland* only had two opportunities to fire on the enemy destroyers, and about 0107 hrs fired on boat No.30, which despite being shot on by the forward ships continued the attack on *Helgoland*, despite already being damaged. She was taken under fire with the medium artillerie and was shot into flames with 6 salvos. Range 24hm.[36]

The fire of the German battleships forced *Achates* and *Ambuscade* away to the east, whereby the latter launched a third torpedo, and therefore the German guns concentrated on *Ardent*. Soon she was on fire inside her hull. *Garland* and *Ardent* had each fired one torpedo from a favourable position 18hm to port ahead of the leading German ship, whilst *Fortune* and *Porpoise* had been under fire. As *Ardent* turned away to port and passed by *Fortune* the latter was already on fire, however, as related she kept up a defiant fire on the German battleships. *Porpoise* was also hit by German gunfire. A shell struck the base of the aft funnel causing a torpedo flask to explode, which ruptured the main steam pipe. The rudder and engine telegraph were put out of action but *Porpoise* found shelter behind smoke and steam emitting from *Fortune*, and finally she made off to the north by west at slow speed. There were two dead and one wounded. Later she joined *Garland* and *Contest* and made her way home.

After *Achates* and *Ambuscade* made off they believed German cruisers were following them and steered away to the north. In all probability the ship they thought was enemy was in fact *Black Prince*. During the day battle this armoured cruiser had lost contact with the 1 and 2 Cruiser Squadrons soon after the loss of *Defence*, and had subsequently fallen behind the British battle fleet with the coming of darkness and therefore found herself amongst the destroyer Flotillas. As related above it is believed she exchanged fire with *Rheinland*, and is thought to have been fired on by *Markgraf* previously. Suddenly *Black Prince* could make out a line of large warships, which she obviously mistook for her own fleet. The head of the German line was still warding off the 4 Destroyer Flotilla when soon after 0100hrs *Nassau*, who was to port of the line, and *Thüringen*, sighted a ship with four funnels to port ahead. When the recognition signal was given the stranger did not reply, but turned away to starboard and ran off. A searchlight was illuminated and an enemy cruiser could be recognized in its beam just 10hm distant. Almost immediately *Thüringen*, commanded by Kapitän zur See Küsel, opened fire and of the ten heavy, 27 medium and 24 light artillery shells fired under the direction of I Artillerie Offizier, Kapitänleutnant Franz, scarcely a shot could miss. *Black Prince* did reply to the fire with two salvos of her own, but with shells raking her from stem to stern she was soon on fire with flames leaping as high as the mast tops. At 0107hrs *Ostfriesland* joined in firing and at 0110hrs *Nassau* also opened fire. At 0115hrs the Fleet flagship, *Friedrich der Große*, also began to fire.

The *Ostfriesland* combat report recorded:

About 1.07am a vessel suddenly came in sight to port, seemingly on an intersecting course. At approximately 18hm *Thüringen* illuminated (searchlights) and it could be made out as a cruiser of the *Hampshire* class. Almost at the same moment *Ostfriesland* opened fire with the medium artillerie and illuminated searchlights. The cruiser turned away to starboard and passed *Ostfriesland* just 10hm away, and therefore was fired on by *Ostfriesland* with the medium artillerie for only 40 seconds. After the third salvo he was in flames and blew up 4 minutes later. *Thüringen* and *Friedrich de Große* also fired on him.

With the beginning of the battle the enemy cruiser fired 2 salvos, which went over the poop, and impacted behind the ship.[37]

Nassau related a similar story:

0110hrs. Enemy cruiser with 4 funnels in sight to port ahead. The enemy cruiser turns to a passing battle and seemingly a torpedo shot. Taken under fire from 1.10am to 1.12am. Very good fire and detonation effect observed at a range of 14 to 8hm. The ship sank under the development of a violent flash flame through an explosion. The enemy cruiser had 4 thin, raked, high funnels, vertical masts, vertical bow (perhaps *Cressy* class, the crow's nest was clearly made out).

Because of the cruiser battle and two instances of torpedoboat defence the connection to the I Squadron was not found. With the attempt to connect to the line, *Nassau* had to turn 8 points to starboard, while to port ahead a small cruiser stationed for torpedoboat defence also had to turn to starboard. Thereby there was a danger of collision with a ship of the III Squadron or Fleet flagship through reverse movement. Thereby attempted to close with the II Squadron.[38]

The war diary of *Friedrich der Große* related the grim picture of a fiery funeral pyre as follows:

1.15am. An enemy armoured cruiser comes in sight at approximately 320°, and briefly after that the next ahead (*Ostfriesland*) illuminates him and opens fire, and was also illuminated from here and taken under fire with the heavy and medium artillerie. (range 12–8hm) After 46 seconds the ship had obtained several medium and heavy hits, and two heavy detonations in the aft and forecastle were observed, the ship burned completely and sank. The cruiser belonged to the *Duke of Edinburgh* or *Aboukir* class. S.M.S. *Friedrich der Große* had suffered no damage or losses.[39]

Kapitänleutnant Friedrich Oldekop was also serving aboard *Friedrich der Große* and witnessed the demise of *Black Prince*.

> The clock shows 1.15hrs. Ahead of us *Thüringen* illuminates her searchlights. In the searchlight beam is a powerful ship. But somehow it appears to lie unfavourably, to be covered in smoke and flames. The guns speak sparingly. It comes straight towards us. Now our searchlights illuminate a powerful shape (*Black Prince*). The forecastle is high. It glides just as a ghost. Now our barrels flash. The whole salvo sits well. Medium and heavy artillerie at 800 metres. Just as a fuse flying into a powder keg, so sprayed out the sparkling flames; from hatches, shot holes, windows; flames, embers and smoke. The guns thunder once again.
>
> There was a primeval detonation. Debris was thrown whirling into the air; all burned. Powder, air, metal and iron. The entire ship's hull in incandescent. Flames spray from the iron mass.
>
> The enemy is destroyed. Forty eight seconds. Twice debris was thrown up over there, then as the cruiser came astern we saw nothing more. No fire, no smoke, just gurgling waves. So goes the night, attack after attack.[40]

Black Prince was left a glowing pyre, an overwhelming spectacle to all who witnessed it and as the German line passed several detonations were observed, followed by a single, powerful explosion which sent the ship to the depths, taking her entire compliment with her. At this moment *Nassau* loomed from the dark ahead of the III Squadron as she manoeuvred to avoid the wreck and *Kaiserin* had to sheer away to avoid a collision with her. *Nassau* could only rejoin the line later behind *Hessen*.

With the massive explosion aboard *Black Prince* the Royal Navy lost its fifth large warship for the day due to exploding munitions. *Indefatigable*, *Queen Mary*, *Defence* and *Invincible* had all exploded before the eyes of their compatriots. Why did the British ships have a propensity for blowing up? It has been said that during the battle the crews had stock piled ammunition in the working chambers and handling rooms of these ships in an effort to increase the rate of fire from their main armaments. At the Dogger Bank Battle Vice Admiral Beatty had estimated the German rate of fire superior to the British in the ratio of 5:2, in favour of the German dreadnoughts. It was suggested that the trail of munitions led down to the magazines. However, at the Dogger Bank Battle the German Panzerkreuzer (Battlecruiser) *Seydlitz* was hit by shellfire and had one of her munitions chambers completely burnt out, with approximately 6000kg of cordite burning in just a few short seconds. *Seydlitz* did not blow up, as the cordite just burnt. However, it was not uncommon for ships engaged in combat to blow up. At the Battle of the Nile (also known as Battle of Aboukir Bay) in 1798 the French flagship *Orion* exploded, as did the French battleship *Achille* at the Battle of Trafalgar in 1805. In comparatively modern times the Russian battleship *Borodino* blew up at the Battle of Tsushima and the British cruiser *Good Hope* was destroyed by a magazine explosion during the Battle of Coronel on 1 November 1914. However, there was another reason British ships had exploded. Other British capital ships and cruisers had blown up without being under fire; in October 1914 the dreadnought battleship *Audacious* was finally lost to a catastrophic magazine explosion after being mined in Lough Swilly off Ireland; the battleship *Bulwark* blew up in Sheerness in November 1914; the cruiser *Natal* exploded in Cromarty Firth in December 1915 and finally the dreadnought battleship *Vanguard* blew up and sank in Scapa Flow in July 1917. The reason for these ten large warships blowing up is probably the use of unstable cordite. The standard British cordite RDB contained 52% collodion (guncotton), 42% nitroglycerine and 6% petroleum jelly, whereas the German cordite, RP C/12 contained 64% nitrocellulose (guncotton), 29.77% nitroglycerine, 5.75% centralite (to reduce smoke), 0.25% magnesium oxide and 0.1% graphite. Therefore the

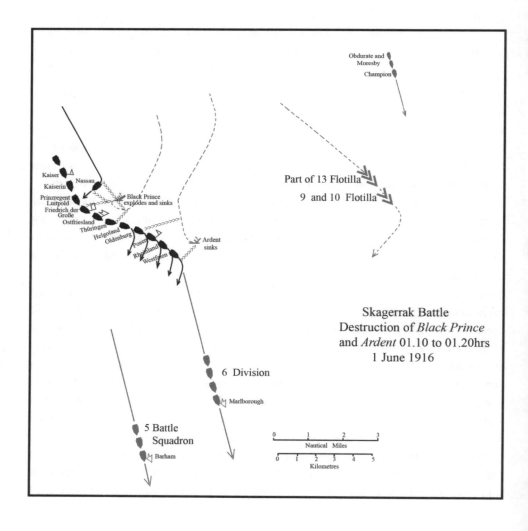

Skagerrak Battle
Destruction of *Black Prince*
and *Ardent* 01.10 to 01.20hrs
1 June 1916

British cordite contained about 12% more nitroglycerine than the German, which caused it to burn much more violently in the cannon, and detonate in the magazines. In 1927, after studying RP C/12, the British changed their cordite formula, but this did not entirely solve the problem, as the loss of *Hood* and *Barham*, both of which blew up, later proved.

Whilst part of the German battle line was busy engaging *Black Prince* the destroyer *Ardent* approached the Germans from the port bow. *Westfalen* was alert and illuminated a searchlight which picked out the destroyer at a range of 800m, and on her bow the pennant number 78 could be discerned. Nevertheless, it seems *Ardent* was not entirely certain as to the identity of the ships before her as she first flashed the British recognition signal, as recorded by *Westfalen*.

01.25hrs. To the port side of *Westfalen* at 310° and a range of approximately 800m one enemy destroyer was sighted, and was immediately taken under fire. A turn away 8 points to starboard was made. In the searchlight beam the number 78 was recognised on the bow. The destroyer – a new modern type – morsed with a searchlight the recognition signal, the letters 'u.a'. The duration of the shooting was 4 minutes and 10 seconds. On the destroyer first the bridge, then the forecastle, were totally destroyed. He ran on but after a boiler or steam explosion sank. The destroyer did not answer the fire of *Westfalen*. Munition use: 22–15cm Spgr., 18–8.8cm Spgr.

After the attack course was again taken SE by S, speed 16 knots.[41]

Ardent was left a floating wreck as the German line swept past in the dark, and soon sank with the loss of 78 crew, however, the Commander, Lieutenant-Commander Marsden, was rescued by *Marksman* after being in the water five hours.

At 0110hrs Kommodore Heinrich, aboard *Regensburg* at the end of the line, sighted a burning ship ahead and at 0125hrs ordered the accompanying torpedobootes, *S53*, *S54* and *G88*, to investigate. On the way *S54*, Kapitänleutnant Karlowa, came across the heavily damaged *Rostock* and remained with her, whilst *S53* and *G88* pushed on ahead and found the badly damaged *Tipperary*, which was aflame from stem to stern. At 0130hrs *Regensburg* passed *Rostock* and exchanged recognition signals with her. As *Tipperary* disappeared in a thick cloud of steam and smoke *S53* rescued nine British crewmen. *Tipperary* did not sink for some time and many more of the crew were rescued by *Sparrowhawk*, before she was sunk. Then as *S53* turned to return to her own main body a second vessel was sighted to port ahead, which when challenged did not answer the recognition signal. As *S53* readied a torpedo the ship signalled in Morse: 'Here is *Elbing*; am helpless. Please come alongside.' Before the torpedoboot could execute this request a third ship came in sight to starboard, which in the glare of the searchlight was recognized as a British destroyer with four funnels. Neither a torpedo fired from *S53* at 600m range, nor one from *G88* at 300m hit, even though one was seen to pass directly beneath the destroyer.

The torpedobootes opened artillery fire, which however, was not answered. The destroyer was *Broke*, which was already heavily damaged with 42 of her crew dead, 6 missing, 14 badly wounded and 20 lightly wounded. *Broke* was hit twice more, but then to the surprise of the British the German bootes turned away after a few salvos and allowed the destroyer to escape certain destruction by making off to the north. Apparently the Germans thought that *Broke* would surely sink and wanted to return to *Elbing* as quickly as possible. With that the German torpedobootes sighted a third destroyer which appeared to be abandoned. Whilst *S53* continued on to *Elbing* the *G88* attempted to quickly dispatch this latest find, which was in fact *Sparrowhawk*. Suddenly *G88* found herself under fire from two groups of more destroyers and as she had torpedoes remaining and already had her speed reduced she made away from this battle, and thereby lost contact with *Elbing* and *S53*.

Previously Vizeadmiral Scheer had ordered *S52*, *V28* and *S51* to go to the damaged cruiser *Lützow*, but only *S52* had carried out this order but was unsuccessful in finding the ship because *Lützow* was to starboard aft of the German Main Body. At around 0117hrs *S52* came across two groups of British destroyers on the opposite course, heading south. The port group opened fire at short range and the accompanying cruiser, *Castor*, turned to ram the torpedoboot. *S52* developed strong smoke clouds, made off at high speed and reported the incident by wireless at 0132hrs. A split boiler tube then caused *S52* to reduce speed to 21 knots and therefore she made for the safety of the Danish coast.

During these encounters with the 4 Flotilla the head of the German line was just four miles astern of *Marlborough*'s Battleship Division, due to the fact that *Marlborough* had her speed reduced due to a torpedo hit and had gradually fallen astern so that there was now a six nautical mile gap to the other columns. The British battleships had observed the glare of searchlights in the low smoke cover and the shooting of star shells, which only the Germans had, as well as gunfire, all to the NW and clearly a battle was raging. The battle of the light forces was so close that from time to time *Vanguard*, last ship of the 4 Battle Squadron, twice believed she had observed an attack on the 2 Battle Squadron to port, and *Thunderer*, last ship of the 2 Battle Squadron, could easily have intervened with gunfire. However, none of the British battleships opened fire, even though the range was short, giving as their reason they did not wish to betray their presence. The 5 Battle Squadron, without *Warspite*, was even closer to the fighting, and the light cruiser *Birmingham*, to starboard abeam of *Marlborough*, had German shells falling about her from time to time. At about 0040hrs the last ship of this squadron, *Malaya*, saw, in the light of shell explosions and the burning fire light of *Tipperary*, a ship of the *Nassau* class steering the same course as the British fleet.[42] However, Captain Boyle of *Malaya* did not pass on this important piece of information. If he had then Admiral Jellicoe might not have been so firm in his belief that the actions taking place astern of him were between his destroyers and German torpedobootes attempting to breakthrough. Nevertheless, at 2350hrs Commodore Hawksley reported that he had been in action with German small cruisers, and at 0030hrs and 0038hrs there were reports from the 2 Light Cruiser Squadron about contact with German battle cruisers and small cruisers. Admiral Jellicoe apparently dismissed these reports as he believed they were intervening to assist the torpedobootes in their breakthrough the British rearguard. In reality it was the High Sea Fleet that was breaking through to the east.

The British 4 Flotilla had had a difficult time of it and played no further part in the battle. However, to the east and SE of the German line there remained a mass of British destroyers. Whilst firing on the 4 Flotilla, many 'overs' had impacted about the adjacent 13 Flotilla, and even the 9 and 10 Flotillas, convincing Captain Farie, leader of the 13 Flotilla aboard *Champion*, that his flotilla had been discovered and he had been taken under fire. Therefore he suddenly turned *Champion* away to port without signal, but only *Obdurate* and *Moresby* followed. The remaining boats of the 13 Flotilla, *Nerissa*, *Termagant*, *Nicator*, *Narborough*, *Pelican*, *Petard* and *Turbulent*, continued on their previous course, and finally, without realizing their error attached themselves behind the destroyers of the 9 and 10 Flotillas, *Lydiard*, *Liberty*, *Landrail*, *Morris*, *Laurel* and *Unity*. At 0030hrs several large warships were sighted to starboard and aboard *Lydiard* they believed them to be the 5 Battle Squadron, which in fact was not too far away. Commander Goldsmith therefore turned *Lydiard* onto course SE at 0040hrs to put himself and the following destroyers on the same course as these ships and then increased speed to 30 knots, and attempted to put himself on the eastern flank of what he considered to be the 5 Battle Squadron. He would have succeeded in pushing past this line if he had not had an extended line himself.

At 0140hrs *Pelican* and *Narborough* sighted two ships to starboard, which they believed to be light cruisers, and challenged them with the recognition signal. At the same moment *Petard* and *Turbulent*, the last two destroyers, sighted the German ships 400 to 500 metres about six points to starboard. *Petard* also challenged by showing a lantern which immediately betrayed her as a British destroyer. She was in a good position to launch a torpedo but unfortunately had expended her outfit of torpedoes during the day battle. Therefore, *Petard* had to turn away but was caught in the searchlights of the German battleships and was caught in a violent fire. The first shell hit put the stern gun and its entire crew out of action, the second hit put a hole in the aft ship; the third hit destroyed an oil pipe and started a fire of considerable size. The next hit showered the entire midships area with splinters. After the sixth hit, out of nineteen shots fired, the destroyer succeeding in escaping.

The war diary of *Westfalen* reported:

The forward most destroyer (bow number 66)[43] ran across the bows of *Westfalen* and was fired on by the starboard batterie with 3 salvos at close range. The

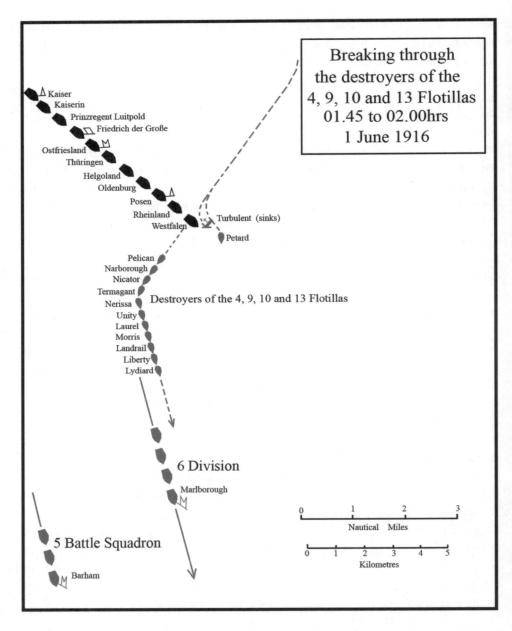

Breaking through
the destroyers of the
4, 9, 10 and 13 Flotillas
01.45 to 02.00hrs
1 June 1916

Kaiser
Kaiserin
Prinzregent Luitpold
Friedrich der Große
Ostfriesland
Thüringen
Helgoland
Oldenburg
Posen
Rheinland
Westfalen
Turbulent (sinks)
Petard
Pelican
Narborough
Nicator
Termagant
Nerissa
Unity
Laurel
Morris
Landrail
Liberty
Lydiard
Destroyers of the 4, 9, 10 and 13 Flotillas

6 Division
Marlborough

0   1   2   3
Nautical   Miles

0   1   2   3   4   5
Kilometres

5 Battle Squadron
Barham

following destroyer turned, apparently out of fear of being rammed, onto the
same course as *Westfalen* and ran close ahead of the ship so that only a small
turn to starboard brought him abeam and he could be fired upon by the port
batterie. On the first destroyer Number 66 the first salvo went in the stern and
so brought the engine to a stop…. Munition use:

13–15cm Spgr.
6–8.8cm Spgr.

On the other destroyer the same occurred with a hit in the stern being obtained at the beginning, and the stern gun crew were thrown overboard. A boiler explosion sank the boat after shooting lasting 5 minutes. Munition use

29–15cm Spgr.

16–8.8cm Spgr.

So, with shooting to both sides at almost the same time both destroyers were sunk [*Petard* did not sink in fact]. Both destroyers were of a specially large type with 4 funnels, the forward one raked and remarkably thin and high, a high mast with a large triangular top, apparently of the *Botha* class. They did not answer the fire of *Westfalen*.[44]

Rheinland was also reported to have opened fire on *Turbulent* after initially turning away to port. However, *Turbulent* did not immediately sink and was still capable of steaming when she was sighted to port by *Ostfriesland* and *Thüringen*. The latter fired a star shell and opened fire at 0147hrs. The first salvo hit and caused a large fire forward and after firing 18–15cm and 6–8.8cm fire was ceased on orders from *Ostfriesland* at 0149hrs.

About 0200hrs *Turbulent* was sighted by the torpedobootes *V71* and *V73*, which were at the rear of the German line with *Regensburg*. The torpedobootes closed on the British destroyer and rescued thirteen men, and then *V71* fired a torpedo, which however, ran under the target. A second torpedo hit and *Turbulent* soon sank.

Previously, at around 0045hrs, *Champion*, *Obdurate* and *Moresby* had turned away to the east before German gunfire, and *Faulknor* and the 12 Flotilla had followed this move. *Champion* moved away to the NE and only at 0120hrs had taken course to the south with her Flotilla. However, around this time *Frankfurt* and *Pillau* came across *Menace* and *Nonsuch*, the last two boats of the 12 Flotilla. *Menace* put her rudder hard over to avoid being rammed, whilst *Nonsuch* stood off to the east in an attempt to launch a torpedo. However, with these moves these boats were separated from their Flotilla. Likewise, *Pillau* lost contact with *Frankfurt*.

The 4 Flotilla had lost four destroyers sunk, five damaged and only had three undamaged boats remaining and had been dispersed. The 9, 10 and greater part of the 13 Flotilla had been broken through and had suffered losses too, so that only *Champion* and 12 Flotilla remained to the east of the German fleet. This eastern group were still well positioned to attack but apart from these the way to Horns Reef was clear for the Germans. Admiral Jellicoe had thought it impossible for the German battleships to break through his concentration of destroyer flotillas in his rear, but this is exactly what had occurred. The German Official History commented:

All the conditions of position, lighting and weather were favourable for a night attack by destroyers. The ease with which these English attacks were repulsed, and the small number of destroyers that actually came within sight of the fleet, had scarcely allowed Vizeadmiral Scheer to recognise the full extent of the danger which threatened the German van. True the German shore stations had also carefully monitored the wireless traffic of the enemy during the battle, but it had taken them longer to decipher and evaluate the messages than the British Admiralty. That the British Fleetchief had stationed all his Flotillas as rearguard during the night march, and that the German van constantly pushed into this hornets' nest, remained unknown to Vizeadmiral Scheer, along with other facts, which were of great significance during the day battle, and were only known after returning to port. The small success and comparative high losses of the British destroyers in view of all the facts are surprising. Personal bravery among the British Flotilla Chiefs and commanders was in no way lacking, and were fully recognised in the German Fleet. All attacks of the British destroyers, just as Kapitän zur See Redlich, commander of *Westfalen* and himself an experienced specialist in this area, said in his report, showed a lack of training in approaching [the enemy] and in recognising the position and counter manoeuvres of the attacked ships. All attacks were individual and while the boats were still closing, and if this is not the tactics of the British destroyers, then the destroyers always approached too close, so that they were sighted before they could turn to the passing battle and were fired upon. Kommodore Michelsen, the I FdT, observed the attacks from *Rostock*, and said that the attacks were made at a recognised interception angle, but with an audacity which apparently was only explicable by ignorance of the correct form of attack. The great losses were due to this. He had not observed an attack from a position ahead. The interception angle was usually very acute, the night shooting range of the British torpedoes was obviously very low, certainly not over 1500m. Several times *Rostock* escaped torpedoes that apparently had run that far. Several German commanders and the Chief of the VI Flottille noticed that as the British destroyers used light oil to fire their boilers it readily caught fire when hit and the fires were difficult to extinguish. On the British side they gave the reason for failure as being the Flotillas were too big. They did not attempt to hold contact and make a mass attack from both sides ahead.... Searchlight discipline, star shell use and fire direction had reached an advanced state during the long peacetime training of the I Squadron, especially in counter fire.[45]

Even as the British destroyers were having targets dropped in their laps, the German torpedobootes, which had been directed to search for and attack the Grand Fleet, were having no luck. With the breaking off of the day battle the German Flottilles had lost contact with the British Battle Squadrons, and had no accurate information as to their whereabouts. It only remained for the torpedobootes to search all the sectors from ENE to SW, and therefore there was a considerable splintering of the

German torpedoboote forces. Further, it was a mistake to allocate the sector ENE to ESE to the II Flottille, which were the largest and fastest of the Flottilles, and were in possession of almost all their torpedo weapons. Furthermore, they were ordered to return home via the Skagerrak and Kattegat if required, to Kiel, so that after their 'blow in the air' was complete at 0108hrs they began their rearmarch.

In the next sector, ESE to SE there were only the two bootes of the 12 Half Flottille, *V69* and *V46*. The third boot of this group, *S50*, had fallen out around 2152hrs. At around 2345hrs these bootes observed a battle to starboard at long range, however, they did not advance towards this action. The 11 HF, the torpedobootes with just one torpedo remaining each, began the night battle in the company of *Rostock*, and with the Leader Boot of the VI Flottille were stationed near the gap of the III Squadron. Kommodore Michelsen, aboard *Rostock*, still had the combat ready bootes of the IX Flottille, *V30*, *S34*, *S33*, *V26*, *S36* and *G42* of III Flottille, held as a reserve and when at 2237hrs the van reported enemy forces these bootes were deployed to the sector SSW to SW. Therefore it came about that the sectors with the greatest prospects of success were allocated to the bootes that were coal fired. Of these the VII Flottille, under Korvettenkapitän von Koch, had encountered the British 4 Flotilla towards 2300hrs and after that advanced on course SSE ½ E. Then around 0055hrs the 14 HF attached themselves and went onto course SE by E at a speed of 16 knots. As towards 0100hrs a third group of three bootes attached themselves some ships were sighted in battle with enemy destroyers, to starboard ahead, and therefore the Flottille remained back so as not to cause confusion with the enemy boats. Later a violent fire was seen to starboard at great range, followed by a powerful explosion, however the enemy main body was not sighted.

The V Flottille, under the command of Korvettenkapitän Heinecke, were favourably positioned. At around midnight they advanced S ½ W from the German Main Body in four groups: *G11*; 9HF, *V1*, *V4*, *V6*, V2 and *V3*, then 10HF: *G8*, *G7*, *V5*, *G9* and *G10*. Just as the VII Flottille the fires of these boats were strongly clinkered and they made abundant smoke, so that their speed was limited to 18 knots. The advance of this Flottille was relatively slow. Just as the other Flottilles they had been ordered to close on the Main Body at 0300hrs, but because of a position error they had barely been engaged in the advance when the western wing of the reconnaissance line, *V2*, *V4* and *V6*, and *G9* and *G10* turned to the SE, whilst the other two groups remained on their courses until 0130hrs. As the group *V2*, *V4*, *V6*, *G9* and *G10* were close to the German Main Body there was a chance they would become involved in the battle between the German Main Body and the British 4 Flotilla. At about 0053hrs a torpedo, probably from this battle, had passed beneath *G11*. At 0104hrs *G9* and *G10* sighted what they believed was a light cruiser with four funnels, more probably *Rostock* than the enemy, which, however, disappeared to the south before further identification could take place. Finally, about 0120hrs, the Flottille boot group were fired on by one of their own small cruisers. At 0140hrs these bootes united with those of the IX Flottille. These bootes had advanced to the SW by S at 2237hrs under the leadership of Korvettenkapitän Tilleßen, but just as the other boats had not made contact with the enemy and at about 0100hrs had turned for Horns Reef.

Therefore Admiral Jellicoe had been saved from one of his greatest fears, a night encounter with the German torpedobootes, or even worse, a night battle with the German battleships. Not only was the night training of the Grand Fleet virtually nonexistent, the night cruising formation chosen by Admiral Jellicoe would have been disadvantageous, as confirmed by Jellicoe, and could only have led to further British heavy losses.

Chapter 9

1 June and Disengagement

awn on the morning of 1 June 1916 was not until around 0355hrs, but already by 0330hrs the first vestiges of sunrise were discernible on the eastern horizon. The weather had deteriorated slightly. The wind had freshened to a south-westerly at strength 3 to 4, it was very hazy and overcast, visibility was reduced to 2–3 nautical miles and there was light rain. The swell was strength 3. The German line had remained intact throughout the night and only *Nassau* had lost her place after ramming the destroyer *Spitfire*, and had finally placed herself behind *Hessen* at 0220hrs. Similarly at 0049hrs *Schlesien* and *Schleswig-Holstein* had to sheer out of line to avoid their next ahead, *Pommern*, which had reduced speed. They were able to rejoin the line behind *Derfflinger* and *von der Tann* and took up their old positions at 0200hrs. *Schlesien* reported:

00.49am. Because of avoiding manoeuvres of the ships ahead the ship ahead, *Pommern*, reduced speed and goes astern. As a result, the line is compressed and *Schleswig-Holstein* approaches very close from astern. During this manoeuvre *Pommern* disappears from view. Finally *Schlesien* returns to the commanded course SE by S and again tried to connect with the Main Body.

01.30am. *Nassau* in sight.

01.40am. *Derfflinger* and *v.d. Tann* in sight. *Schlesien* and *Schleswig-Holstein* connect to the Panzerkreuzer. Several times gunfire was observed ahead.

02.00am. *Schlesien* and *Schleswig-Holstein* place themselves ahead of the Panzerkreuzer, behind the Main Body.[1]

After the last British destroyer attack the leading ship, *Westfalen*, had resumed her course SE by S, towards Horns Reef. After their futile advance to the west the IX and V Flottilles had closed on the Main Body and by 0300hrs the group *V2*, *V4* and *V6* of the 9 HF were to starboard abeam *Westfalen* and *Rheinland* steaming for the head of the line, whilst *Stuttgart* was to starboard as flank cover. Other bootes, including the VII Flottille were expected to port. Nevertheless, there was still a British unit, the 12 Destroyer Flotilla, between the Germans and Horns Reef. This Flotilla had been forced away to the NE and only turned back to the south at 0120hrs, the distance to the Grand Fleet then totalling 30 nautical miles. Still further to the NE was the cruiser *Champion* with her two destroyers of the 13

Flotilla, *Obdurate* and *Moresby*. They turned south at 0105hrs. These formations were now approaching the German line. Ahead was the Flotilla Leader *Faulknor*, under the command of Captain Stirling, followed by the 1 Division consisting of *Obedient*, *Mindful*, *Marvel* and *Onslaught*, whilst on her starboard quarter was the 2 Division, consisting of *Maenad*, *Narwhal*, *Nessus* and *Noble*. To port aft was the 2 Half Flotilla of *Marksman*, *Opal*, *Menace*, *Munster* and *Mary Rose*. These destroyers represented the most modern and powerful the Grand Fleet possessed. At 0243hrs *Obedient* sighted enemy ships to starboard, which *Faulknor* sighted two minutes later. Captain Stirling turned onto a parallel course and ordered the 1 Division to attack. At 0256hrs he also gave a contact report to Admiral Jellicoe: 'Urgent. Priority. Enemy's Battleships in sight. My position 10 miles astern of 1st B.S.'[2] However, at 0250hrs *Obedient* reported that the enemy were out of sight and therefore the 1 Division were ordered to take station astern of *Faulknor*. Captain Stirling then took *Faulknor* around 180° onto a NW course, followed by the remainder of the Flotilla and ordered them to attack, in what would be a passing battle.[3] The German ships were almost immediately sighted again, still steering SE.

The 16-point turn by *Faulknor* led the 1 Division back towards the 2 Half Flotilla, and in taking avoiding action the leader *Marksman* lost contact with her four destroyers. Nevertheless, conditions favoured the British destroyers as it was sufficiently light enough to hamper the use of searchlights, but was still dark enough to veil the destroyers in the haze, and make them a difficult target. The German line was also expecting the arrival of their torpedobootes and the leading ships were exchanging recognition signals with the IX and V Flottilles. *König* sighted British destroyers at 0247hrs and at 0307hrs opened fire briefly, before they disappeared, and just after 0300hrs *Markgraf* sighted a destroyer but held fire until the recognition signal was given, whereon the destroyer turned away. *Kronprinz* could make out destroyers, but was uncertain as to their identity, and did not open fire, even as next astern *Großer Kurfürst* did. *Großer Kurfürst*'s war diary recorded:

> Six enemy destroyers with four funnels attacked in tight formation at high speed. The range was certainly about 14–16hm, direction 290°. Therein the ship immediately turned away to starboard and thereby fired on the first, second and last boats with the medium and light artillerie. The RW (Direction Indicator) equipment was out of action. The boats turned away to starboard, the single observation was a torpedo going close ahead past the bow.
>
> A hit on the last boat [was observed], and shortly afterwards an explosion with a flash fire approximately 20hm away in a NE by N direction.[4]

Nessus was hit by a 15cm shell which put a boiler out of action. At the same time the German battleships began to turn away. For their part the British destroyers began firing their torpedoes, with *Faulknor* firing two at 0302hrs and 0303hrs, *Obedient* fired two at 0304hrs and 0309hrs, *Marvel* firing two at 0304hrs and two more at 0307hrs and *Onslaught* firing two at 0308/0309hrs, and a further two at 0311/0312hrs. All of these torpedoes were fired at reasonably close range, reported as between 2700m and 1500m.

When these torpedoes reached the German line one ran close ahead of *Großer Kurfürst*'s bow, whilst a second detonated approximately 100 metres behind the stern of *Kronprinz*. Two more torpedo tracks were sighted from *Markgraf* through the director telescope. The ship was turned away and one torpedo passed about 30 metres away, and the second appeared to pass beneath the ship without detonating. SMS *Hessen*, under the command of Kapitän zur See Bartels, opened fire at 0307hrs, before turning to evade a torpedo. Then at 0310hrs the German line was rocked by a series of tremendous explosions in quick succession. One, or perhaps two, of the torpedoes fired by *Onslaught* had struck SMS *Pommern*, Kapitän zur See Bölken. The explosion of the torpedo is thought to have detonated a 17cm magazine, which set off a chain of explosions, culminating in a large explosion which broke the ship into two in the middle. Flames spread over the entire ship and climbed mast high. Ship debris was hurled through the early morning air and *Hannover* had to sheer out of line to starboard to avoid the floating stern section of the ship. This soon capsized so that the propellers and rudder climbed into the air. Whilst the Official German History says 844 men were lost, other German sources say there were 839 fatalities.

The war diary of *Schlesien* recorded:

3.10am. *Pommern* blows up. Apparently through double torpedo shot. Two columns of fire next to one another were seen going over mast height. The wreck of *Pommern* or the drifting about wreck parts were not seen, as we turned away.

3.15am. Three enemy destroyers attacked from port. *Schlesien* turned away and took two under fire, and on one destroyer a hit was irreproachably seen. According to several witness statements the boat immediately sank. It was already so clear that shooting could be done without searchlight beams. Shortly after the destroyer attack a torpedo coming from port was seen onboard, which passed ahead with an interception angle of 15° to the ship's course. The torpedo was apparently fired by the attacking destroyer.

3.20am. A wreck was passed to starboard. It was apparently the bow or stern of a sunken ship towering out of the water.

3.41am. A strong shock was felt in the ship. The cause is apparently running over a wreck.

During the night various burning ships were sighted, the nationality of which could not be made out. Also gunfire was often observed ahead.[5]

Seekadett Günther Schütz was aboard *Hessen*, next astern of *Pommern*, and wrote:

Then suddenly something terrible happened, something that always will remain in my memory. I stood on deck, watching the battle through my glasses, when I heard a fearful noise, and I looked in the direction from which it had come. Now I looked in the direction of our next ahead, who was about 700m away from us, who was lifted high and then sank bow first. Only part of the aft ship could be seen for a short time out of the water. We immediately turned hard to starboard to avoid the pieces of the wreck and through this manoeuvre our ship remained undamaged. A huge piece of armour was blown off the ship, which stood vertically from the water and then vanished in the sea, beneath a towering column of water. At this moment some probably thought that we would share a similar fate. When comes the torpedo that would push us beneath the waves, or the mine that would blow us to a thousand pieces? However, we were lucky, we passed through the danger just as if immune. There had been some disquiet, but now there was more the danger of death, although we had just escaped death. We wondered who the unlucky ship was, and whether the crew had been rescued.[6]

As *Hannover* manoeuvred to starboard a torpedo ran close astern to port. *Hannover* turned further to starboard with hard rudder and 'three times Utmost Power ahead', and then two minutes later a powerful vibration was felt through the ship as though she had run over a wreck. The ships behind *Pommern* were undecided as to whether she had met her fate at the hands of a mine or submarine when suddenly *Nassau*, *Schlesien* and *Schleswig-Holstein* could make out the faint outlines of three or four destroyers in the smoke and haze to port. They were immediately taken under fire, but quickly vanished. Nevertheless the danger had been recognized and all ships turned away eight points to starboard. Soon after a torpedo passed close ahead of *Nassau*'s bow, and another close behind the stern, the third and fourth torpedoes to endanger this ship on this night. *Schlesien*, Kapitän zur See Friedrich Behncke, also gave way to a torpedo. At 0312hrs *Schleswig-Holstein* was able to take a destroyer under fire at a range of 15hm. Whilst the forward three destroyers had turned away, the last one was hit with a square salvo, which immediately produced fires. The destroyer *Onslaught* was hit by a 17cm shell which burst against the port side of the chart house and fore bridge, igniting a box of cordite, causing a fire in the chart house, completely wrecking the fore bridge and destroying nearly all navigational instruments. The captain was mortally wounded and *Onslaught* took station behind *Mindful*, before eventually being detached home.

At about 0320hrs the destroyers *Maenad* and *Narwhal* closed for an attack and launched one and two torpedoes respectively at a range of 27hm. The torpedoes were without result and *Maenad* turned back with tubes swung out to starboard and fired her last two torpedoes at a range of 37hm. These also missed. Of the other destroyers of the Flotilla, none launched any torpedoes.

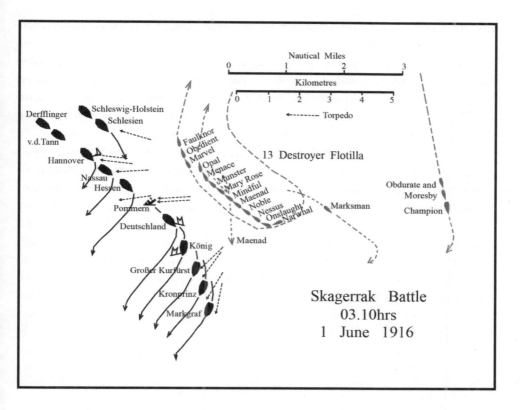

The gunfire between the German line and the 13 Flotilla caught the attention of the light cruiser *Champion* and the destroyers *Obdurate* and *Moresby*, which were nearby to the east. This force turned to the west at around 0315hrs and was soon joined by *Marksman* and *Maenad*. At 0325hrs this group turned onto a southerly course and at this moment ships were sighted to the south. *Champion* questioned *Marksman* as to the identity of the sighted vessels and received the reply that they were German. Nevertheless, at 0334hrs *Champion* suddenly broke off and turned to the east, and only the last destroyer, *Moresby*, sighted four ships, apparently of the *Deutschland* class. *Moresby* turned to port and carried out an attack at a range of 34hm. At the end of the German line *von der Tann* sighted a torpedo and turned away to starboard to avoid it at 0342hrs.

Meanwhile, at the head of the German line a strange incident occurred. The head of the German line was far enough away that they could not see any of the British destroyers making the attack at the rear, and therefore they held their hitherto course. The starboard group of torpedobootes, *V2*, *V4* and *V6* of the V Flottille were engaged in steaming for the head of the line to starboard. Their position was approximately 200m abeam *Westfalen* and *Rheinland* when at 0315hrs, just five minutes after *Pommern* was torpedoed, a violent detonation occurred on *V4*. The foreship to the aft edge of the forecastle was entirely torn away and for a brief time floated astern. At that time no enemy vessels were in sight and the detonation was attributed to a drifting mine. The torpedoboot *V2* immediately went alongside the stern of *V4*, which was towering from the waves and together with *V6* took aboard the survivors and wounded, which was no simple task in the rising seas. Seventeen men were killed and two were badly wounded. The wreck of *V4* was sunk with artillery fire and then finally with a torpedo from *V6*. Whether due to an accident or drifting mine the cause of *V4*'s sinking was never established.

Despite the intentions of Admiral Jellicoe the High Sea Fleet had slipped behind the Grand Fleet and continued its course to Horns Reef, where Vizeadmiral Scheer expected he would continue the battle with the British on the morning of 1 June. Naval battles continuing over two days was the norm, and the side that had gained the upper hand on day one usually pressed their advantage on day two and made the victory complete. In the Skagerrak Battle neither side did this. Although Vizeadmiral Scheer had never intended to engage the entire Grand Fleet, he had not shirked the issue and was fully prepared to continue the battle at Horns Reef. However, Admiral's Jellicoe and Beatty had misjudged the German intentions and the thrice repeated contact report of Captain Stirling, about the latest engagement with the German battleships, had failed to get through, probably because of the jamming work done by the German wireless stations. Jellicoe, with his preponderance in numbers of two to one, had already lost his last opportunity of coming to grips with the High Sea Fleet, as they proceeded to Horns Reef. He assumed the Germans were behind him, and were steering to the south, even though the Admiralty had advised him of Vizeadmiral Scheer's request for airship reconnaissance over Horns Reef at first light, and that Scheer was steering directly for Horns Reef. Admiral Jellicoe believed the German Squadrons must surely come in sight at dawn, which was towards 0400hrs, however at 0315hrs he ordered that the Battle Squadrons should turn to the north at 0330hrs. According to Jutland dispatches his order ran: '03.15. At 3.30 a.m. 2nd B.S. alter course to starboard to North. 4th B.S. will follow round. B.F. will form single line–head in 5th organisation. Admiral.'[7] It is strange that Admiral Jellicoe was ordering a change of course to the north even before it became daylight, and was therefore giving up any chance of encountering the High Sea Fleet before dawn, and in effect was giving up the battle and turning for home.

In his book *The Battle of Jutland* Commander H. Frost was critical of Admiral Jellicoe on this point.

> We remember Jellicoe's statement, as expressed in his book, that when at 10.00pm he had turned south, it had been his intention at dawn to head for Horns Reef. At 04.00 dawn had arrived and the time had come to carry out his intention; but he now decided that would be impracticable until his destroyers had been assembled. His book is very clear and explicit on that point.

The difficulties experienced in collecting the Fleet (particularly the destroyers), due to the above causes, rendered it undesirable for the Battle Fleet to close the Horn Reef at daylight, as had been my intention when deciding to steer to the southward during the night. It was obviously necessary to concentrate the Battle Fleet and the destroyers before renewing the action.

Therefore, the discussion concerning the failure of Jellicoe to receive Stirling's three messages is interesting only from a communication viewpoint, for Jellicoe clearly shows that, regardless of what information he received of the Germans, he had no intention of proceeding toward Horns Reef.

It is clear that at 3.12 his decision had been made, for at that time he informed all commanders that he would alter course to north at 3.30. All detached forces were ordered to 'concentrate and close'. The *Iron Duke*'s predicted position for 3.30 was Latitude 55° 07', Longitude 6° 21'.

That was the first order given by Jellicoe to concentrate the Fleet. As concentration of the Fleet was necessary, in his opinion, before renewing the action and carrying out his intention to steer toward Horns Reef, it is remarkable that he had not long previously issued orders to the Grand Fleet to concentrate at dawn. It will be noted that the Germans had little trouble in concentrating their forces, although their cruisers and destroyers were at least as widely scattered as these of the British. The German destroyers, however, had been ordered well in advance to concentrate at 3.00, while no such instructions had been issued to the British Flotillas. The German system of command through the first and second leaders of destroyers [I and II FdT] was vastly more effective than the British system of placing their flotillas directly under Jellicoe and Beatty, for in practice Hawksley's command proved to be only nominal.[8]

On 1 June 1916 at this latitude dawn was at about 0400hrs, Middle European Time. Nautical twilight occurs when the sun is 12 degrees below the horizon, therefore beginning at about 0315hrs in the east. Therefore Admiral Jellicoe had made his decision as the first traces of twilight were occurring, without giving himself any opportunity of surveying the horizon under anything like reasonable conditions. It should be said that not everybody was happy about this performance:

The general tenor of the 'Jutland Controversy', as it took shape in the summer of 1916, was that Jellicoe had been over cautious and too defensively minded, and had not done all that was possible to bring the enemy to battle; he had thrown away the heaven sent opportunity of annihilating the High Sea Fleet that Beatty's gallant work had presented to him. Some extremists (Cecil Lambert, the Fourth Sea Lord, was one of them) even asserted that Jellicoe had 'run away' on the morning of 1 June![9]

Nevertheless, there seems to have been a general confusion about the British disposition and actions, even into the 1980s. The otherwise creditable author Campbell had this to say:

> Jellicoe's intention on the evening of 31 May had apparently been to close Horns Reef if the German Fleet were not encountered at daylight, but the absence of destroyers prevented this, though it was increasingly doubtful if the enemy were in the vicinity. Definite information on the High Sea Fleet reached Jellicoe at about 0510hrs in a signal from the Admiralty timed at 0429hrs. This gave the deciphered text of Scheer's 0330hrs position signal, which had been passed to the Operations Division at 0400hrs, and stated that at 0330hrs the German Main Body had been in 55°33'N, 6°50'E, steering 133° at 16 knots. It was now certain that Scheer had taken the Horns Reef route and that there was no chance of resuming the action with the German Battle fleet.

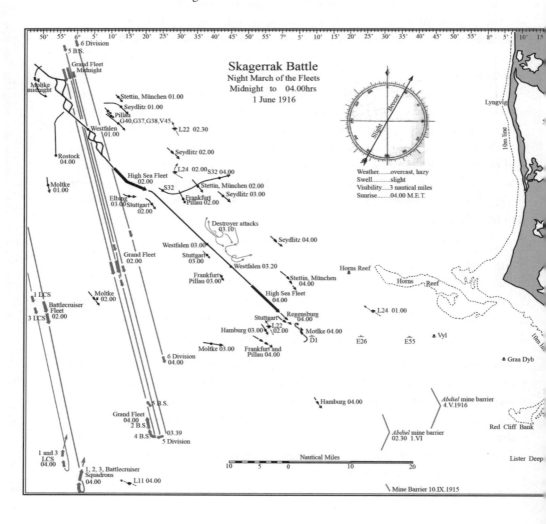

Skagerrak Battle
Night March of the Fleets
Midnight to 04.00hrs
1 June 1916

Weather......overcast, hazy
Swell..........slight
Visibility.....3 nautical miles
Sunrise........04.00 M.E.T.

Accordingly at 0513 Jellicoe signalled his ships to form divisions in line ahead...[10]

It seems that Campbell had confused his times and orders here and he seems to have ignored that Jellicoe signalled his intention to turn north at 0315hrs. With this order he was effectively abandoning any chance of regaining contact with the High Sea Fleet.

Likewise Vice Admiral Beatty's desire to reconnoitre to the SW was precluded by the order at 0322hrs to turn north, and to conform and close. The British Admirals were supposing that the German fleet was to the north, west or south west, but in reality at 0330hrs they were only 16 nautical miles west of the Horns Reef light vessel, about 30 nautical miles NE of *Iron Duke*. Because of *Marlborough*'s reduced speed, due to the torpedo hit, Vice Admiral Burney's 6 Battleship Division was 12 nautical miles behind the other battleship columns and was only 15 nautical miles SW of the German van. Only with daybreak did Admiral Jellicoe realize that *Marlborough*'s Division was missing, and *Revenge*, *Hercules* and *Agincourt* increased speed to 17 knots to rejoin the fleet, whilst *Marlborough* had to further reduce speed to 12 knots. At 0339hrs the 2 and 4 Battle Squadrons, and 5 Division, turned back to the north, with *King George V* as fleet guide. At 0344hrs the 5 Battle Squadron, *Barham*, *Valiant* and *Malaya*, also turned north. Finally at 0355hrs the Battle Cruiser Fleet, 15 nautical miles WSW of the Fleet, turned north. In the early morning light *Marlborough* sighted the light cruiser *Fearless*, which had lost contact with her destroyers, and was now called alongside the damaged battleship to transfer Vice Admiral Burney to *Revenge*, so that about 0435hrs he could again take over command of the 6 Division. *Marlborough* was detached to the Tyne and docking, and *Fearless* was assigned as her escort.

The Leader of Airships, Fregattenkapitän Strasser, ordered airship reconnaissance for early on 1 June and accordingly the airships *L11*, *L13*, *L17*, *L22* and *L24* ascended between midnight and 0230hrs and set course to their allocated positions in weather that was more suitable than on the previous day. However, the visibility was still low and this made things difficult for the airships. Both *L22* and *L24* sighted searchlights and gunfire and explosions between 0100hrs and 0200hrs as they approached the battlefield. At 0255hrs *L24*, under the command of Kapitänleutnant Koch, reported that he had been fired on without effect by several vessels in square 069 epsilon. He reported later that the enemy forces consisted of a destroyer flotilla and half a dozen submarines. At this time the British forces were well to the south of this position and perhaps Kapitänleutnant Koch had observed a night action between surface forces. This was the first of several highly inaccurate and even fanciful reports by Kapitänleutnant Koch, with one timed at 0400hrs saying twelve capital ships had been sighted in Jammer Bay, off the northern and coast of Denmark, and another at 0415hrs saying *L24* had been chased away by two light cruisers. Unfortunately,

Vizeadmiral Scheer had faith in these reports and believed Admiral Jellicoe had divided his forces and some of these were sighted in Jammer Bay.

On the other hand *L11*, under the command of Korvettenkapitän Schütze, made contact with the Grand Fleet and doggedly maintained this contact despite heavy anti-aircraft fire from the British ships. The report of *L11* ran in part:

On June 1 at 1.30, after midnight *L11* went up at Nordholz with the following orders: As fourth airship to cover the flank of High Sea forces, course NW by W via Helgoland. Full crew on board, fresh south-westerly wind, visibility limited owing to ground fog and later to a fog-like atmosphere high up extending over 2 or at most 4 nautical miles. Helgoland was not visible through the fog. At 5am clouds of smoke were seen north of the ship in Square 033 beta and were made for. At 5.10 it was possible to make out a strong enemy unit of twelve large warships with numerous lighter craft steering north–north–east full speed ahead. To keep in touch with them *L11* kept in the rear and sent a wireless report, circling round eastwards. At 5.40am east of the first unit the airship sighted a second squadron of six big English battleships with lighter forces on a northerly course; when sighted, they turned by divisions to the west, presumably to get into contact with the first unit. As this group was nearer to the Main Fleet than the first one, *L11* attached itself to it, but at 5.50 a group of three English battle cruisers and four smaller craft were sighted to the north-east, and, cruising about south of the airship, put themselves between the enemy Main Fleet and *L11*. Visibility was so poor that it was extremely difficult to keep in contact. For the most part only one of the units was visible at a time, while, apparently, the airship at an altitude of 1,100–1,900 m [3600 to 6200 feet] was plainly visible to the enemy against the rising sun.

At 5.15, shortly after sighting the first group of battleships, the enemy opened fire on the airship from all the vessels with antiaircraft guns and guns of every calibre. The great turrets fired broadsides; the rounds followed each other rapidly. The flash from the muzzles of the guns could be seen although the ships were hidden by the smoke. All the ships that came in view took up the firing with the greatest energy, so that *L11* was sometimes exposed to fire from 21 large and numbers of small ships. Although the firing did not take effect, that and the shrapnel bursting all around so shook the ship's frame that it seemed advisable to take steps to increase the range. The firing lasted till 6.20am. At that time the battle cruisers bearing down from S.W within close distance of *L11* forced her to retire to NE to avoid their fire. At the same time the visibility became worse and the enemy was lost to view.

L11 again took a northerly course and went as low down as 500 metres [1600 feet], in the hope of better visibility. It was impossible to see beyond 1 to 2 nautical miles, and as under these conditions no systematic plan for keeping in contact could be made, north and south course was followed so as to keep between the enemy and our own Main Fleet. The enemy did not come in sight again.

At 8am the Commander-in-Chief of the High Sea Fleet dismissed the airship, and *L11* returned. On the way back the ship came across a number of our own torpedo-boats exchanging bases, and messages were given for further transmission. The airship remained close to those boats as far as Sylt. Landed at Nordholz at 2pm.[11]

Airship L11 had at first sighted Vice Admiral Beatty's forces and was taken under fire by them, notably *Indomitable* and then the 3 LCS. As *L11* circled away to the east to evade the fire she discovered Admiral Jellicoe's forces and was then was taken under fire by *Marlborough*, *Hercules*, *Colossus*, *Revenge*, *Thunderer*, and *Benbow*, many of whom used their heavy calibre weapons, together with many destroyers. Although *L11* and Korvettenkapitän Schütze had done an excellent job under extremely difficult circumstances, including poor visibility and heavy counter fire, her reports were not fully appreciated by Vizeadmiral Scheer, who was influenced by *L24*'s imaginary reports. He later wrote:

These events prove that the English Naval forces made no effort to occupy the waters between the scene of battle and Horns Reef.

It was only during the night that there was opportunity for the ships to report on the number of prisoners they had on board and to gather from them some idea of the enemy's losses. Then I learned that the *Warspite*, which we had observed to be badly damaged in the battle, was sunk. Among other vessels reported sunk were the battle cruisers *Queen Mary*, *Indefatigable*, and *Invincible*. This was all news to me, and convinced me that the English losses were far more considerable than our own.

On arriving at Horns Reef at 5am I decided to remain there and await the *Lützow*. I had not then heard of her fate. From 11.30pm on, the vessel had been able to do 13 knots. The last report from her was at 1.55am – transmitted by escort boat *G 40* – stating that she was making very slow way, that the means of navigation were limited, that the gun power was reduced to a fifth, course south, station 016 epsilon. At 5.30am came a message that the *Lützow* had been abandoned at 4am.

After that I had no difficulty in drawing my own conclusions. As the enemy did not come down from the North, even with light forces, it was evident that he was retiring, especially as nothing more could be seen of him notwithstanding that his destroyers were about until dawn....

At 4am 50 nautical miles west of Bovbjerg, *L24* sighted a flotilla of enemy destroyers, was fired at and returned the fire with bombs, then got away further north, and at 5am discovered a unit of twelve ships in Jammer Bay, steaming rapidly to the south. It was impossible to keep in contact for further reconnaissance as there was a bank of cloud as low down as 800 m.

From the Main Body itself no signs of the enemy were visible at daybreak. The weather was so thick that the full length of a squadron could not be made out. In our opinion the ships in a south–westerly direction as reported by *L11* could only have just come from the Channel to try, on hearing the news of the battle, to join up with their Main Fleet and advance against us. There was no occasion for us to shun an encounter with this group, but owing to the slight chance of meeting on account of visibility conditions, it would have been a mistake to have followed them. Added to this the reports received from the battle cruisers showed that the I Reconnaissance Group would not be capable of sustaining a serious fight, besides which the leading ships of Squadron III could not have fought for any length of time, owing to the reduction in their supply of munitions by the long spell of firing. The *Frankfurt*, *Pillau* and *Regensburg* were the only fast small cruisers now available, and in such misty weather there was no depending on aerial reconnaissance. There was, therefore, no certain prospect of defeating the enemy reported in the south. An encounter and the consequences thereof had to be left to chance. I therefore abandoned the idea of further operations and ordered the return to port.[12]

After *Lützow*'s last battle contact escorting torpedobootes drew a veiling smoke screen around the damaged cruiser and there was some respite, however a life and death struggle began to save the ship. By 2113hrs there was 1038 tonnes of water in the ship and at 2215hrs there were 2395 tonnes. At first *Lützow* ran at 13 knots but speed had to be reduced to 7 knots because of water pressure on the forward bulkheads.

Towards 0100hrs the pumps began to lose further ground in the fight against flooding. The forward drainage group of pumps had failed, and the midships group was unable to cope with the vast quantities of water that were flooding into the ship. Water began to penetrate the forward (No. VI) oil fired boiler room. 'The forecastle, the fore part of the ship, was rent apart by several hits and showed holes which a railway locomotive could comfortably have driven through.'[13] There were four gaping holes below the armoured belt and now the huge holes in the forecastle deck were admitting vast amounts of water above the armoured deck, which was freely flooding. At 0200hrs Korvettenkapitän Paschen relates that the battle to save the ship was slowly being lost:

I still held out hope for the ship, but as about 2am in the morning the Commander called the senior Offizieres to a conference, and the First Offizier reported 7500 tonnes of water in the ship, and gave his view that at the longest we could remain afloat until 8am in the morning. The news was a bitter blow. Our beautiful ship! However, it must be so; the forecastle was now 2 metres under water, that through the open casemates water entered the battery in streams, and poured through the ragged deck into the Between Deck. The large forward oil boiler room had to be abandoned, to save the men.[14]

The last figures from damage control indicated that there were 4209 tonnes of water below the armoured deck, and 4142 tonnes above, giving a total of 8351 tonnes, but this was still increasing. Shortly after 0200hrs an attempt was made to steer the ship stern first, but this failed because the propellers were already too far out of the water. Likewise an attempt to tow the battle cruiser with torpedobootes was abandoned. Kapitän zur See Harder ordered 'Fires out' and gave the order to abandon ship. The II AO wrote:

The bridge was full of lookouts. The commander intended to take the ship in the direction of Helgoland, so that with the danger of capsizing or being sunk whilst under attack, there would be a greater chance to rescue the crew. It was the honourable duty of every German commander. The chance of reaching harbour had long gone.

Towards midnight the men from turret 'Alsen' were rescued by half swimming over the forecastle. About 1 o'clock the water was already in the casemate. Around 3 o'clock the drain means of the midships group could no longer master the water. There was 8000 tonnes of water in the forecastle. The ship's movement became more unstable. The jack staff forward was under water, the stern towered high from the water. A towing attempt with torpedobootes failed. On orders from the commander all wounded were taken aft. The Torpedo Offizier took a patrol through the ship several times. The crew, which had battled so outstandingly, must now quit the ship. They mustered on the aft deck. Three cheers for the Highest Warlord and the German Fatherland were brought out by the commander. The wounded, and then the crew, were transferred to the four torpedobootes. The Torpedo Offizier and II Artillerie Offizier went through the ship one more time, and then disembarked. The last to leave the battle cruiser *Lützow* was the commander.[15]

There was still one tragic episode aboard *Lützow*. Six men were trapped in the forward diesel-dynamo room and could not be freed. They are mentioned in a letter by an unnamed Offizier:

The forecastle sank continually deeper and the stern always came higher. Towards 3 o'clock in the morning it was clear that the ship could no longer be held. We stopped and called the torpedobootes along side. Then all men went aft, wearing life vests, but thankfully they were not needed. The men transferred to the torpedobootes after the wounded had been taken across. I myself went through the compartments with another Leutnant to ensure everyone, including the wounded, was out. Then I climbed over on the last boot, *G38*, and with us the commander. He was the last to quit the beautiful ship. It cut into my heart to have to quit our beautiful ship. It also pulls at my heart when officially or otherwise they begin to complain. With one torpedo shot from our boot the ship went to rest. Slowly it lay over on the side and capsized. At the same time I had to think of the 6 poor stokers that were still alive when the ship sank. They sat in the forward diesel–dynamo switch room, just as a diving bell, and could not get out. They had called me once, as I had a connection with them, and reported that the water was slowly rising in their room. It was held by pumps at a certain height. They maintained courage and optimism until the last. They were still trapped.[16]

The four torpedobootes that had remained with *Lützow*, *G40*, *G38*, *V45* and *G37* were now called alongside. Three lay contiguously aft, to starboard.

The survivors assembled on the quarter deck. Above them fluttered the battle flag, shot to pieces by the enemy shells. Where there was no longer any Offizieres, the senior Unteroffizier took command. Still it was a black night. Only in the east the hesitating twilight appeared heralding the new day. The address of the Commander was short and concise. He concluded with the request that we be proud of S.M.S. *Lützow* and her crew today for their selfless and extraordinary service for the Fatherland. Then three cheers were carried for the ship and the Supreme Warlord.

'And now go to the bootes!' The last words of the Commander were almost paternal, sounding out of the dark. They touched the deepest senses of all of his subordinates.[17]

Kapitän zur See Harder was the last to leave the ship.

On the orders of the Commander the torpedoboot *G38* fired a torpedo to scuttle the cruiser, but the draught aft was reduced and the torpedo ran under the sinking ship; a second struck amidships and the great cruiser lay slowly over to starboard and capsized at 0247hrs.

The Commander of the escorting torpedoboot *G40*, Kapitänleutnant Beitzen, wrote in his war diary:

I passed on an FT message to the flagship of the BdA – *Lützow* can only run at slow speed, navigational means limited. Square 016 epsilon, course south. Artillerie limited to one third. *G40*.

Lützow sheered out hard to starboard and went astern. During the trip it was observed that the cruiser gradually went deeper by the bow and water came over the forecastle. My assumption, that the cruiser could run no more was confirmed. Morse message from *Lützow*, that the Commander would attempt to travel stern ahead. *G40* placed herself to the side behind the cruiser (previously on the bow).

Morse message from *Lützow*, come alongside. I gave the Morse message to the other bootes. I lay to starboard aft on *Lützow*, allowing three transfer stations, which I had prepared, to be deployed and took approximately 500 people on board. At the same time a Morse signal was made to the other three bootes: come alongside. *G37* lay on *G40*, *V45* behind *G40*; after depositing on *G37*, *G38* came alongside *G40*. *G40* took more of *Lützow* crew and gave a part to *G37* and *G38*. Finally aboard *G40* there remained from the *Lützow* crew 260 people, including 30 wounded, which were looked over by the Flottille physician on *G40*. *G38* had the Commander onboard and scuttled the cruiser. I remained with *G40* in the immediate vicinity. After the second explosion the cruiser sank at 2.45am in square 014 epsilon. During the sinking I brought out three Hurrahs for His Majesty the Kaiser and his proud cruiser *Lützow*, which the crew of *Lützow* and *G40* enthusiastically joined in. As the senior commander I took the leadership of the 4 bootes *G40*, *G38*, *G37* and *V45*.

The German Main Body was approximately in the direction of Horns Reef. To seek a rendezvous with our own forces I therefore went onto course SE by S at 25 knots.[18]

However, the ordeal for the crew of *Lützow* was not yet over, as the German torpedoboats twice ran into enemy forces. At 0320hrs about 35nm NW of Horns Reef light vessel two British destroyers came in sight in the early morning twilight. They were *Garland* and *Contest*, apparently looking for the other destroyers of the 4 Flotilla. The German torpedoboats were greatly hampered in the employment of their weapons by the presence of so many extra men from the sunken Panzerkreuzer: aboard *G40* were 260, including 30 wounded, aboard *G38* was Kapitän zur See Harder with 15 Offizieres and 50 men, including 12 badly wounded, *G37* had 500 men aboard and *V45* had 215 men. Kapitänleutnant Beitzen decided to immediately attack, hoping to dispose of the enemy with shallow running torpedoes and a rapid fire from his artillery.

To starboard ahead (SSE) 2 English destroyers were sighted, course west at high speed. Intention: to be recognised as late as possible show the bow to the enemy, and the English recognition signal, which was known. Tube to starboard, clear for a shallow shot, guns directed but for the time being not opening fire, in order to get as close as possible and, if possible, open a sudden rapid low trajectory fire from all guns on the destroyer, and destroy him. I hold 2 points to starboard ahead. Through the high speed the destroyers were so quickly upon us that a torpedo shot could not be fired owing to the interception angle.

At 1200m rapid fire was opened from all guns, which was replied to without result by the destroyers. As the range quickly increased (passing speed 60 knots) I turned onto the old course and continued speed.[19]

Only *V45* could fire a torpedo at a range of 30hm at 0330hrs, which missed.

Just one hour later at about 0420hrs, further British forces were sighted 15 nautical miles NW of Horns Reef. This time it was the light cruiser *Champion* and the destroyers *Obdurate, Maenad, Marksman* and *Moresby*. Kapitänleutnant Beitzen wrote:

> 4 points to starboard an English cruiser and 4 destroyers in line ahead come in sight on the opposite course.
>
> Situation: The route of the bootes to the south to SE is blocked. If the enemy intended he could also cut off the way east without difficulty. A further turn away to the NE to NW is without chance as with the higher speed and considerable superiority of the enemy it could be expected the bootes would be shot up without the expectation of a successful reply.
>
> Therefore the intention: Forestall the enemy and proceed ruthlessly to the attack. The position was favourable, 4 points ahead on the opposite course. Range 4000m. The weather was somewhat hazy. I expected the enemy forces to come at *G40* from the eastern direction whilst I expected they had their combat strength reduced from the night battles.
>
> I gave orders through the boot: Attack, all tubes to starboard, utmost power. At 2500m a torpedo was fired from the forward starboard tube, interception angle 90 degrees. The shot missed, but was successful in that the attacked cruiser, because he saw the attack, the launch of the torpedo or else the bubble track, turned away and ran off to the west at highest speed. The way to the SE was free. When I realised this situation I gave orders to the Artillerie Offizier: rapid fire on the aft most destroyer. Course SE. The boat still delivered 'Utmost Power' (AK). The cruiser and destroyers replied to the fire. *G40* received a hit in the aft turbine. A report arrived on the bridge that the port turbine had failed. Great steam danger in the port turbine room, which must be abandoned. At first I hoped that *G40* could run with the starboard turbine alone at 25 knots, but the exhaust steam slide valve was not tight, as the pipes had been destroyed by the hit. The port turbine room was entered with gas masks on, and all valves were closed. For 10 minutes the boat could run at 26 knots. Owing to the strong steam loss and gradual loss of water the speed reduced to 17 knots, then later 10 knots and the vacuum fell to zero.[20]

The *V45*, under Kapitänleutnant Laßmann, also launched two torpedoes at a range of 25 to 22hm and opened a lively fire. The bold attack had succeeded but *G40* had been hit and soon had to be taken under tow by *G37*, whilst Kapitänleutnant Metger aboard *G38* took over command of the small German unit. The hit to *G40* had caused a 1.5m diameter hole in the starboard side, so Kapitänleutnant Beitzen assembled all the *Lützow* men on the port side, giving the torpedoboat a list and moving the hole above water, where it was sealed with hammocks. The steel hawsers used for the tow proved too weak for the job and broke a total of seven times. One after another *G37*, *V45*, *G38* and then *G37* again towed the boat. One of the *Lützow* crew, Vizesteuermann Schreyer, who had great experience in merchant shipping, came up with the idea of using the torpedobootes anchor chains as a towline. This worked and *G40* was successfully brought home. When the II FdT learned of the plight of the bootes he turned back with *Regensburg* and *S30*, *S34* and *S33*, and the *Lützow* crew were transferred to the cruiser by *V30* from between 1400 to 1416hrs and then the remainder were taken aboard between 1500 and 1600hrs, in total some 1177 men.

Just as there had been a life and death struggle aboard *Lützow* to try and save the ship a similar struggle was being played out aboard *Seydlitz*. At around 2200hrs on 31 May the ship's leadership was able to appraise the extent of damage due to the numerous hits and obtain an impression of the buoyancy capabilities of the ship.

The munitions chambers of C turret had been flooded when that turret was hit and flaws in the watertight integrity meant that water had penetrated into the shell chamber of D turret, and flooded it to a depth of approximately 1 metre. The bunkers of compartment XIII and wing passage were flooded. In the area of the torpedo hit the torpedo bulkhead was holding firm. In the forecastle beneath the armoured deck only the wing passage in compartment XIV made water. Altogether there was about 2000 tonnes of water in the lower ship and the draught forward had increased by about 1.8m.

The water mass did not constitute a danger to the ship if water could be kept out of the forward upper ship. This was not to be, however, as the large shell holes in the decks allowed water to enter above the armoured deck because the speed of the ship brought water over the forecastle. Because of the destruction of interior bulkheads and decks the water freely flooded the forecastle. A heavy shell hit in compartment VIII on the citadel armour allowed an upper bunker to flood and the hole in the armour of the port No.4 15cm casemate threatened to become a serious danger. It was estimated that there was 1000 tonnes of water in the forecastle, above the armoured deck. The large hole in the forecastle was inaccessible and could not be sealed. The fight against flooding was limited to sealing rooms not already affected and sealing shot holes above water as much as possible. Wooden mats, hammocks and wedges were used for the most part. When the swell reached a leaky position the mats were soon loosened and washed away.

The broadside torpedo room in compartment XIV could be held through continuous pumping through the main drainage pipe. In compartment XIII the rooms below the armoured deck, despite all attempts at sealing, gradually began to fill with water which penetrated through the armoured deck via shot through ventilation ducts and the lack of water tightness between the torpedo–bulkhead and the armoured deck owing to the torpedo hit. This important compartment possessed no connection with the main drainage system. Boiler room V also leaked but could be held.

The bow of the ship continued to sink deeper. The speed had to be reduced from 20 knots to 15, then 12 knots because the bow wave came over the forecastle and the oblique position of the fore deck made the control of the ship more and more difficult. A critical moment arrived, as the water on the batterie deck came over the transverse bulkhead of the citadel armour, compartment XIII/XIV, and penetrated the rooms of compartment XIII above the armoured deck. The water was penetrating into the armoured midships. The available portable leakage pumps could not master the quantities of water or failed after a short time. The broadside torpedo room made water but use of the pumps and drainage system stemmed the tide and caused the water level to fall. However, the remainder of the forecastle gradually filled.

Conditions were difficult for the crew. One of the ship's physicians, Marine-Oberstabsarzt Dr Robert Amelung, wrote after the battle:

On 24th January 1915 the battle had continued three hours, so that perhaps our fight would end around 8pm. It was considered that the battle would conclude with the coming of darkness. There was a general desire in the dressing room to make an end. However, again and again 'battle to starboard', or 'battle to port' sounded throughout the ship, and so the night went on…. There was a feeling of reassurance in the dressing station. But we were premature in our assumptions, and more and more frequently the call was given throughout the ship, 'battle to starboard', or 'battle to port', and gradually an increasing number of wounded arrived and sometimes there was battle to both sides…. All that could be seen of the overwhelming enemy line was the flash of guns of the heaviest calibre, from port, ahead and from starboard…. Towards 1am the guns thundered again and then gradually it became quieter and quieter. We learned that we were on a southerly course – homewards! The heat in the two dressing stations was unbearable as they were overflowing with men and had been without ventilation for several hours. On the port side the small hatch to the batterie deck could sometimes be opened for a little cooling, so that compared to the starboard side the temperature was somewhat reduced. However, many times this small hatch had to be closed immediately our guns crashed out, and the bandaged, prone men would spring up in the assumption that the din was caused by a penetrating enemy shell and in the next moment they would be forced to evacuate the dressing station by a flash fire or poison gas. In fact a little later a loud crash followed by blinding flames and a thick gas cloud did appear through the hatch, and all had to don their gas masks and shortly after go through the bulkhead door to compartment V. As I automatically slipped on my gas mask, at the same moment a man appeared in the gloom. As he stepped forward dizzily I could see his blacked arm, his right hand had been severed and his forearm was a bloodied, badly bleeding stump. The vibrations had caused the electric light bulbs to fail and only the emergency lighting with candles gave a sparse light. Immediately I quickly placed a bandage packing over the bleeding stump and a rubber binding over his upper arm. For myself I was still not burnt nor affected by gas and only had a scratch on the neck. We could remain in the dressing station and continue our work … we sent above to the galley where tea was being prepared. The men there were afraid to see the swollen bodies of their badly burnt comrades, who suffered hour by hour until life was finally extinguished. They questioned me about how the wounded were behaving, and the answer was always the same, they were simply model. Individuals would groan and sigh, however there was never a wail, they remained humble. A brilliant, shining example was Pastor Fenger, who with one of the first hits on the starboard VI casemate was wounded in the face and body and remained the sole survivor from the casemate. He would not move from the heat of the starboard side to the more pleasant port side dressing station, and on account of his low and weak pulse I pressed him to do so. He said he did not consider himself as one of the wounded but rather as a clergyman with the wounded, and he moved painfully around the men, consoling them and sometimes giving out wine….[21]

At 0645hrs on 1 June the torpedo central position had to be quit owing to the great water pressure on the bulkhead. *Seydlitz* tried to increase speed to connect to the end of the II Squadron but with the speed over 15 knots water came over the forecastle, so that speed was gradually reduced, at first to 10 knots, then to 7 knots. *Derfflinger* and *Posen* ran past on the starboard side.

At around 0840hrs in Square 158 beta, the two gyro compasses fell out so that *Seydlitz* requested the Leader of the II AG to dispatch a cruiser to navigate her through the Amrum Bank passage. The magnetic compass had suffered a deviation change and was unreliable. All *Seydlitz* charts were lost or damaged, by the blood of those wounded in the conning tower, or were underwater. Whilst five minesweepers took over antisubmarine security *Pillau* arrived and followed in the wake of the Panzerkreuzer. At 0940hrs the ship had a draught forward of 13 metres and a trip through the Amrum Passage was thought impossible, but steering to the west of Amrum Bank was abandoned and a renewed attempt was made to the east of the bank.

Briefly after a request had been sent for two pump steamers and material to seal the leaks the ship became stuck fast towards 1000hrs abeam Hörnum–Sylt in a depth of 13.5 metres. To bring the bow as high as possible the middle and port aft trim cells and the port wing passage were flooded, whereby at the same time the list to starboard would also be reduced. With these measures, and the rising tide, the ship came free again.

At 1125hrs *Seydlitz* passed through the Amrum passage but by 1312hrs the situation was becoming critical and the starboard list had changed to a port list because of bunkers flooding, increasing to 8°. Stability was considerably reduced. At 1600hrs *Seydlitz* was steering stern ahead along the coast in water 15m deep. Towards 1800hrs the starboard aft wing passage was flooded, to reduce the list. Now more than 5300 tonnes of water were in the ship and the list still amounted to 8° to port. Shortly after this the two pump steamers from the Imperial Dockyard at Wilhelmshaven, *Boreas* and *Kraft*, came alongside. *Boreas* sucked from starboard from compartment XIII, above the armoured deck; *Kraft* was to pump out the magazine of turret A, however it was impossible to get her pumps to suck.

Between 1800 and 1900hrs *Pillau* made a futile attempt to tow *Seydlitz* over the stern and she continued going stern ahead. *Pillau* continued to pilot the ship and at dawn on 2 June she was taken in tow by two dockyard tugs. However, the wind freshened to strength 8 from the NW and the sea began to run unpleasantly for the ship. Therefore *Pillau* made a lee for the ship, *Boreas* pumped from the forward port casemate and *Kraft* calmed the rough seaway by laying an oil slick.

At 0845hrs on 2 June *Seydlitz* anchored in the vicinity of the outer Jade light vessel and *Pillau* and minesweepers were detached. The auxiliary hospital ship *Hansa* came alongside and took off the wounded, although Pfarrer Fenger was disappointed he could not remain aboard until the ship reached Wilhelmshaven. A tug took the dead who could be reached to Wilhelmshaven. With high water *Seydlitz* weighed anchor and moved to Schillig Roads, but the powerful cross currents caused the ship to ground from 1620 to 2100hrs. Around midnight *Seydlitz* passed through the net barrier off the Jade going sideways.

About 0425hrs on 3 June the cruiser anchored in Vareler Deep off Wilhelmshaven and as the dock could only take a draught on 10.5m work began on sealing and lightening the ship. At 1530hrs on 6 June *Seydlitz* entered the southern lock with a draught of 14m and the work continued there until 13 June, when the ship was moved to the large floating dock. The saving and return to Wilhelmshaven of *Seydlitz* was a feat which all involved could truly be proud of.

As related previously the torpedoboot *S32* had been struck by two British shells at around 0022hrs (see page 193) which left the hapless boat unmanoeuvrable. Three men had been killed and one stoker was badly wounded. During the battle with the British forces she had fired a total of 24 shots, and soon after observed eight detonations on a British ship, probably *Tipperary*. Only at 0130hrs could slow speed be taken up after a boiler was filled with sea water and *S32* proceeded at first to the east, then SE. At 0225hrs *S32* sighted a British cruiser in the SSW, which passed just 1.5 nautical miles away. At first a speed of only 3 to 7 knots could be made with the available steam, but at 0250hrs this could be increased to 13 knots. Soon after, at 0255hrs, four British destroyers with four funnels were sighted in the south. When only 1.5 nautical miles distant the destroyers turned away and ran off to the SSW. *S32* has been extremely lucky and after gaining the Danish coast was able to proceed safely home.

With his turn to the north just after 0330hrs on the morning of 1 June Admiral Jellicoe had given up any chance of further engaging the High Sea Fleet, and had resigned himself to sweeping the area north for stragglers, both his own and perhaps German. Admiral Jellicoe did not learn of the sinking of *Indefatigable* and *Queen Mary* until a signal sent by Vice Admiral Beatty timed at 1101hrs. Incredibly Admiral Jellicoe replied with: 'Was cause of sinking mines, torpedoes or gunfire?'[22] to which Beatty replied: '*Indefatigable* sunk 10 minutes after engaging enemy by shell exploding magazine. *Queen Mary* sunk same cause. *Invincible* sunk, probably from same cause, possible might have been torpedo.'[23] What this serves to illustrate is Jellicoe's paranoia about mines and torpedoes. Even as the Grand Fleet was making its turn to the north the High Sea Fleet was still 35 nautical miles to the NE. Vizeadmiral Scheer had expected to renew the battle off Horns Reef at around daybreak.

As about 0419hrs Admiral Scheer received the report of the airship [*L24*] that numerous enemy forces, including twelve large units, had been sighted in Jammer Bay, he saw it as a solution to the puzzle as to where the British battle fleet had been after the breaking off of the day battle. No longer did it seem strange that the German Flottilles had found no attack opportunities during the night and that, much to everybody's surprise, with daybreak no English squadrons were in sight of the German Fleet. Obviously the British battle fleet, or at least the greater part of it, with their known timidity before night torpedoboot attack, had withdrawn in a northerly direction soon after the coming of darkness and awaited the dawn of the new day in the area east of Hanstholm.[24]

With the chance of further encounters gone Vizeadmiral Scheer gave the order for the I AG to run in at 0424hrs, followed at 0454hrs for the remainder of the fleet to run in via the channel east of Amrum Bank. However, they still had to run the gauntlet of British submarine weapons. At about 2132hrs the previous evening Admiral Jellicoe had given the minelayer *Abdiel* orders to carry out her minelaying operation and the destroyer recorded the message was received at 2205hrs. The destroyer proceeded at high speed to Horns Reef to lay a barrier west of the barrier laid by her on 4 May 15 nautical miles SW by W of Vyl light vessel. This barrier consisting of 80 mines was across the line of retreat of the German fleet and might be taken as evidence that Admiral Jellicoe suspected that the night route the Germans would take would be via Horns Reef. Unnoticed by any German forces *Abdiel* reached the commencement point for this mine barrier at 0224hrs and had completed the barrier by 0300hrs. The mines were 4.5 metres below the low water mark and there was only 10 nautical miles between the two barriers, so there were good prospects of the German forces running onto a mine. Unobserved the

British destroyer distanced herself from the mined area with at first a northerly course, and then westerly, at a speed of 30 knots.

Also at this time the British submarines *E55*, *E26* and *D1* were off Horns Reef. They had departed Harwich on 30 May and were deployed in a line running due west from Vyl Light at distances of 4, 12 and 20 nautical miles. Another group, the destroyer *Tallisman* and submarines *G2*, *G3*, *G4* and *G5* had received orders to position themselves along 4°E longitude 80 nautical miles NW of Borkum Reef, and had arrived in position by midday of 31 May. Nevertheless, neither group saw anything of the German forces.

As the High Sea Fleet approached *Abdiel*'s barrier of 4 May the Minesweeper Flottilles awaiting the battle squadrons did not suspect a mine barrier and as floating mines were an almost daily occurrence they were not taken as a warning. The IV AG and most of I Squadron passed the mines safely, whilst *Derfflinger* and *von der Tann* steamed to port abeam making for the head of the Main Body to join with *Moltke*. At 0620hrs *Ostfriesland*, travelling as number seven and immediately ahead of the Fleet flagship, ran onto a mine. The author Campbell, writing in 1986, stated that no detailed damage report of *Ostfriesland*'s damage survived, however in the early 1990s Russia returned over 90 tonnes of documents to Germany, including a report about damage to *Ostfriesland*.

About 6.20am a mine with a lever arm detonated on the starboard side, and a piece of the arm was later found on deck.

A violent vibration was felt through all parts of the ship. The engines, which before had made 66 revolutions, were stopped on orders from the bridge.

At 6.21am the heeling pendulum indicated a list of 1 degree to starboard, which slowly increased and about 6.24am totalled 2½ degrees to starboard. The draught aft was 8.71 metres, forward 9.02 metres. Already around 6.21, through leak- and torpedo telephones, and through direct speaking tubes, came the first clear reports that the fore- and aft ship, and the large rooms inside the torpedo bulkhead were not hit.

Around 6.23 followed the report: 'Chamber 19 (magazine of turret B) filling with water, water approximately 0.25m high', and at the same time the report from the starboard forward boiler room, that water was penetrating the boiler room from the starboard protective bunker frames 70/80.

All rooms received the message: 'Leak Compartment XI starboard'

The mine had detonated to starboard frame 78 somewhat above the forward edge of the bilge keel. From the reports it followed that the torpedo bulkhead had kept the main effect of the detonation from the ship's interior, and although damaged the torpedo bulkhead was not destroyed, or otherwise chamber 19 and the chambers lying above it would have immediately filled with water. One man was killed when a shell fell on him, and there were two badly wounded.

The ship went with 'slow speed', which after the reports from the leak service was gradually increased to 'Great speed' [Große Fahrt].

In order to obtain as perfect a picture as possible on the spot through personal inspection, the First Offizier[25] sent the Leakage Ingenieur to the position of the leak.[26]

In munitions chamber 19 the torpedo bulkhead was bent and damaged and water was penetrating the chamber in small amounts. The bulkhead was bulged inward and had a small tear in it. Water also penetrated the starboard forward boiler room in small amounts. The wing passage and protective bunker between frames 70 and 90 was full of water and the list increased to 4° so that counter flooding was effected to port. Later, at around 0824hrs, the torpedo bulkhead gave way somewhat so that the water in munitions chamber 19 climbed, but pumps could hold it to a depth of 90cm. Speed was gradually increased to 15 knots but at around 1220hrs an enemy submarine was believed to have been sighted, and the ship was turned 8 points to port out of line. The consequence of the turn was that the torpedo bulkhead further gave way, so that projectile chamber 17 and the chamber 11 to the rear, and chamber 14 on the lower platform deck slowly filled with water. Therefore *Ostfriesland* reduced speed to LF (slow speed), whilst there was a list 4¾° to starboard. Eventually 400 tonnes of water entered the ship. At 1425hrs the Outer Jade light vessel was passed at a speed of 8 knots and at 1815hrs *Ostfriesland* ran into the northern lock of the III Entrance and subsequently made fast to berth A4.

At 0628hrs Vizeadmiral Scheer gave the following III Squadron the order to hold their course as he reckoned that with a density of just ten mines per nautical mile there was little chance of one of the following battleships striking one. Nevertheless two minutes later *Kaiserin* reported one mine in sight to port, and one in sight to starboard.

At 0758hrs the first of many reports began arriving with Vizeadmiral Scheer about the events of the previous day and night. *Westfalen* reported: 'Have last night sunk 5 attacking destroyers, apparently *Botha* class, a sixth shot into flames. Five observed boat numbers: 60, 93, 30, 78, 606.'[27] The numbers probably indicate: 60-H6C was *Tipperary*; 93- was H98, *Broke*; 30 was *Nestor*; 78 was *Ardent* and 606 was *Petard*, whose pennant number was G66. More reports followed, including from torpedobootes who reported their number of British prisoners taken. Torpedoboot *G11* said she had 56 men from *Nomad* aboard, *S16* reported that she had two survivors from *Indefatigable* aboard, *S73* reported eight survivors from *Tipperary*, and then at 1220hrs Vizeadmiral Hipper mentioned *Queen Mary* had been sunken. At 1016hrs the FT Station at Neumünster reported that the British Main Body was approximately 20 nautical miles WSW of Horns Reef steering north at 20 knots.

Shortly after 1400hrs the German battleships began arriving in the outer Jade. Previously the II Squadron had detached to the Elbe River shortly after midday, and began anchoring on Altenbruch Roads at around 1425hrs. In the Jade five ships of the I Squadron took up picket duty on Schillig Roads: *Posen*, *Nassau*, *Westfalen*, *Thüringen* and *Helgoland*. Four battleships of the III Squadron anchored on Wilhelmshaven Roads in battle ready condition: *Kaiser*, *Kaiserin*, *Prinzregent Luitpold* and *Kronprinz*. The remaining capital ships entered Wilhelmshaven harbour to either replenish coal and ammunition, or for repairs. At 1600hrs Vizeadmiral Scheer gave the following message of thanks to his forces:

> In proud gratitude for the safe leadership of the units and the devoted work of the crews of the Fleet I give my warmest appreciation, in particular my faithful feelings for those who sacrificed their blood and lives for the Fatherland. Germany and our Kaiser above all![28]

After turning onto a northerly course at 0339hrs Admiral Jellicoe continued north searching for his light cruisers and destroyers, which had been scattered during the night action with the German battleships. At 0513hrs he ordered his squadrons to resume cruising formation, that is in columns, abreast of one another. At 0531hrs the cruiser *Dublin* reported she had sighted a cruiser and two destroyers, *Rostock* with *V71* and *V73*. Then at 0540hrs Admiral Jellicoe signalled Vice Admiral Beatty that: 'Enemy fleet has returned to harbour. Try to locate *Lützow*.'[29] Having found nothing himself, at 0703hrs Admiral Jellicoe turned his fleet to the SE for a short time, resuming his northerly course at 0816hrs. After loitering at the scene of the previous day's engagement the British forces finally abandoned their pointless search and began the long trip home. However, some of their number were not yet out of the woods.

The badly damaged armoured cruiser *Warrior* had been taken in tow by the seaplane carrier *Engadine*, and the group had covered about 100 nautical miles and was approximately 160 nautical miles east of Aberdeen early on the morning of 1 June. Nevertheless, *Warrior* was slowly sinking and the engine rooms had flooded and the main deck was 2 feet under water. The ship had a 6° list and with the increasing swell water was washing over her upper deck. At 0815hrs *Engadine* was ordered to take off *Warrior*'s crew and despite the heavy seas she successfully rescued the remaining crew, including wounded. *Warrior* was then abandoned and *Engadine* took course for the Firth of Forth, nothing more being seen of the armoured cruiser.

At 0904hrs the destroyer *Marksman*, which had the crippled *Sparrowhawk* in tow,[30] signalled to Admiral Jellicoe: 'Hawser parted. Shall I sink *Sparrowhawk*?', to which the answer was given: 'Is salvage impossible?' At 0915hrs the laconic reply was given: '*Sparrowhawk* has been sunk having received orders from Senior Officer 1 Battle Squadron.'[31]

On the morning of 1 June the damaged battleship *Warspite* was approaching the coast, without a destroyer escort and alone. When about 100 nautical miles ENE of the May Island at about 1035hrs she was attacked by *U51*, under Kapitänleutnant Rumpel. Because of the rough seas and swell it had been difficult for *U51* to

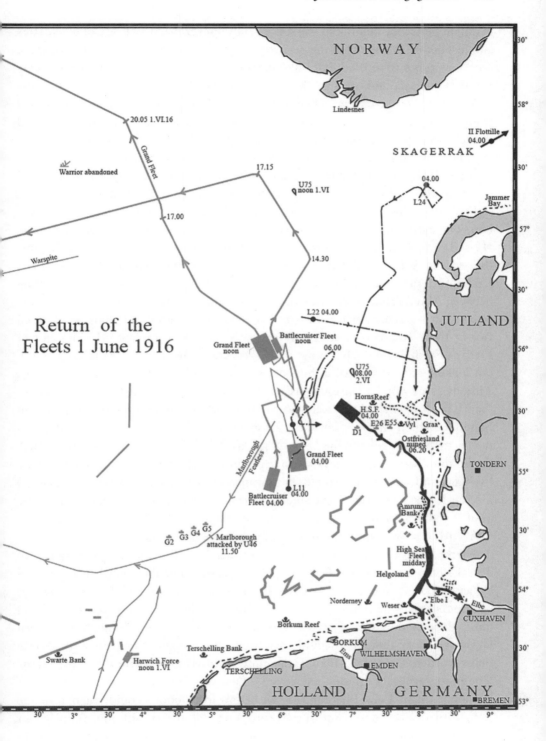

NORWAY

Lindesnes

SKAGERRAK

II Flottille
04.00

20.05 1.VI.16

Grand Fleet

Warrior abandoned

17.15

04.00

L24

Jammer
Bay

U75
noon 1.VI

17.00

Warspite

14.30

L22 04.00

JUTLAND

Return of the
Fleets 1 June 1916

Grand Fleet
noon

Battlecruiser Fleet
noon

06.00

U75
08.00
2.VI

HornsReef

H.S.F.
04.00

E26 E55   Vyl   Graa

D1

Ostfriesland
mined
06.20

TONDERN

Marlborough

Fearless

Grand Fleet
04.00

L11
04.00

Battlecruiser
Fleet 04.00

Amrum
Bank

G5
G4

G2   G3

Marlborough
attacked by U46
11.50

High Sea
Fleet
midday

Helgoland

Norderney

Weser   Elbe I   Elbe

CUXHAVEN

Borkum Reef

BORKUM

Swarte Bank

Harwich Force
noon 1.VI

Terschelling Bank

WILHELMSHAVEN

EMDEN

Ems

TERSCHELLING

HOLLAND   GERMANY

BREMEN

maintain periscope depth, but she successfully approached to a range of 600 metres and just before the bow shot the periscope dipped beneath the waves. Nevertheless, both bow tubes were fired, but only one torpedo quit the tube, and unfortunately this broke surface and betrayed the attack. *Warspite* immediately turned away to the NW with a zigzag course and made off. *Warspite*'s log recorded: '1 torpedo passed from aft-forward starboard at a distance of about 5 yards.' Kapitänleutnant Rumpel did not take up the pursuit, believing his target had been of the pre-dreadnought *Canopus* class, and that countermeasures would now be increased.

When *Warspite* reported the attack by wireless destroyers from the east coast put to sea to meet and screen the badly damaged ship. Even as the first destroyers were sighted, at 1242hrs, the periscope of another U-Boot was sighted close ahead of the bow. The battleship immediately went to full speed ahead, but because of damage *Warspite* was being steered from the aft position in the engine room and by the time the order to turn arrived there it was too late to successfully ram the U-Boot. It was *U63*, under the command of Kapitänleutnant Schultze, which had been operating between May Island, North Carr light vessel and Bell Rock, but was now on the return journey as the starboard engine had fallen out. At around 1230hrs she sighted two or three vessels on a northerly course when about 40 nautical miles east of Firth of Forth. With the heavy swell *U63* repeatedly lost sight of the leading vessel, but looking around sighted a ship abeam, one of the destroyers going to *Warspite*. Although this ship had already passed, *U63* immediately turned to the attack, but then loud propeller noises were heard, and with a look around Kapitänleutnant Schultze sighted *Warspite*, obviously closing to ram his U-Boot. The battleship was just 50 metres distant and the U-Boot quickly dived, and at 50 metres depth struck the bottom. Rising again quickly to a depth of just 7 metres *U63* was taken under a lively fire and was depth charged, but escaped at a depth of 27 metres, and later 35 metres. It was a relieved, but unlucky, *Warspite* that stopped and signalled for the pilot at 1600hrs, before entering the Firth of Forth.

At 1015hrs on 1 June the deciphering station at Neumünster reported that a damaged British battleship stood approximately 100 nautical miles north of Terschelling, course WSW. It was *Marlborough*, which had previously been sighted by airship *L11*, and had taken the latter under fire. At 1130hrs *Marlborough* believed she had sighted two submarines about eight miles away to the west, and most probably they were G-Class boats of *Tallisman*'s group, although the official German history thought it could have been *U64*. A short time later Vizeadmiral Scheer ordered the 3 U-Boot Half Flottille to advance against the battleship. The most favourably positioned for an attack was *U46*, under the command of Kapitänleutnant Leo Hillebrand. Even before instructions could reach *U46* she sighted two vessels one point to starboard, one a destroyer with four funnels, but actually the light cruiser *Fearless*, the other a battleship of the *Iron Duke* class, in reality *Marlborough*. The battleship was observed to be laying deep in the water with a starboard list and was proceeding on a zigzag course a 10 to 12 knots, with a general course of SW. Immediately the four bow tubes were made ready and at 1200hrs the U-Boot was in a firing position, 3000 metres away, interception angle 70°. However, aboard *Marlborough* the keen lookouts must have seen the torpedo launch as she immediately turned away six to eight points (90°) and the torpedo passed 20m to port. As the battleship had turned away the U-Boot commander thought further shots pointless, and unfortunately he also considered it chanceless to pursue *Marlborough* on the surface because of the rising SW seas, even though the damaged battleship's speed was obviously reduced. A wonderful opportunity to further damage the Grand Fleet had been squandered and later that afternoon eight destroyers of the Harwich Force arrived as an antisubmarine screen.

Apart from the damaged vessels making for east coast harbours the remainder of the Grand Fleet had returned to Scapa Flow by noon on 2 June. From a German perspective the Battle of Jutland was over, but on the British side of the North Sea the fight had just begun.

Chapter 10

The Outcome

From a German perspective the Skagerrak Battle was an obvious victory. The newspapers trumpeted the headline 'Victory in the Skagerrak', and why wouldn't they? It had never been Vizeadmiral Scheer's intention to engage the full strength of the Grand Fleet, which had approximately twice the number of capital ships as his High Sea Fleet, but when he found himself confronted by Admiral Jellicoe's fleet he did not shirk the issue and repeatedly turned his ships to attack, and overall the Germans inflicted twice the loses as they received. Writing about their arrival in Wilhelmshaven Fähnrich zur See Mardersteig, a survivor of the sunken *Lützow*, said:

> With slow speed *Regensburg* steered closely past *Derfflinger*. From the command bridge of the battle cruiser sounded the loud call: 'For the comrades of our flagship, *Lützow*, three cheers!' Like a relieved proclamation from the throats of a thousand rough sailors: 'Hurrah-Hurrah-Hurrah!' The answer from *Lützow*'s crew was not long in coming. 'A triple cheer for our courageous *Derfflinger*; Hurrah-Hurrah-Hurrah.' A deep silence came over the crew of *Regensburg* as they realised they had witnessed the last meeting of the two large crews from the Skagerrak Battle.
>
> After an hour's cruise the III harbour entrance of Wilhelmshaven was reached. People dressed for celebrations lined the dykes and banks. After passing through the lock *Regensburg* made fast in the large harbour basin. The crew of *Lützow* went ashore, lined up and numbered and then marched to the Wilhelmshaven barracks. The IV Artillerie Offizier, Leutnant zur See Schulz, said there were more than a thousand men. The Technical Divisions under the guidance of a Marineingenieuraspiranten, followed. They marched in step and on all lips was the song '*Lützow*'s bold, audacious hunt.' Who could have prevented that? The residents of Wilhelmshaven clearly heard it. There were people everywhere and in an instant the news of the fate of the battle cruiser *Lützow* spread.[1]

Indeed cheering crowds welcomed the High Sea Fleet home, and there were great celebrations throughout Germany, with school children being given a holiday. It was bright, cheering news in a war year that had brought the draining battle at Verdun, and would soon bring the Russian Brusiloff offensive and the Somme. The navy had proved that it could fight and win and for the second half of 1916 this was the one bright spot for Germany in a period of great concern.

Vizeadmiral Scheer gave the following report to the Kaiser:

> The success achieved is due to the eagerness in attack, the efficient leadership through the subordinates, and the admirable deeds of the crews full of an eminently warlike spirit. It was only possible owing to the excellence of our ships and arms, the systematic peacetime training of the units, and the conscientious development on each individual ship. The rich experience gained will be carefully applied. The battle has proved that in the enlargement of our Fleet and the development of the different types of ships we have been guided by the right strategical and tactical ideas, and that we must continue to follow the same system. All arms can claim a share in the success. But, directly or indirectly, the far reaching heavy artillery of the great battleships was the deciding factor, and caused the greater part of the enemy's losses that are so far known, as also it brought the torpedo-boat flotillas to their successful attack on the ships of the Main Fleet. This does not detract from the merits of the flotillas in enabling the battleships to slip away from the enemy by their attack. The big ship – battleship and battle cruiser – is therefore, and will be, the main strength of naval power. It must be further developed by increasing the gun calibre, by raising the speed, and by perfecting the armour and the protection below the water-line.
>
> Finally, I beg respectfully to report to Your Majesty that by the middle of August the High Sea Fleet, with the exception of the *Derfflinger* and *Seydlitz*, will be ready for fresh action. With a favourable succession of operations the enemy may be made to suffer severely, although there can be no doubt that even the most successful result from a high sea battle will not compel England to make peace. The disadvantages of our geographical situation as compared with that of the Island Empire and the enemy's vast material superiority cannot be coped with to such a degree as to make us masters of the blockade inflicted on us, or even of the Island Empire itself, not even were all the U-Bootes to be available for military purposes. A victorious end to the war at not too distant a date can only be looked for by the crushing of English economic life through U-Boot action against English commerce. Prompted by the convictions of duty, I earnestly advise Your Majesty to abstain from deciding on too lenient a form of procedure on the ground that it is opposed to military views, and that the risk of the boats would be out of all proportion to the expected gain, for, in spite of the greatest conscientiousness on the part of the Chiefs, it would not be possible in English waters, where American interests are so prevalent, to avoid occurrences which might force us to make humiliating concessions if we do not act with the greatest severity.[2]

There are several points of great interest in this report. Vizeadmiral Scheer says the big gun was arbiter in the battle and after the battle he advocated building battleships of 38,000 tonnes armed with 38 and 42cm cannon, and 38,000 tonne battle cruisers armed with 8 × 38cm cannon. He makes the point that the *torpedobootes* enabled the battleships to slip away, not torpedoboats and battle cruisers, therefore further dispelling claims by other authors that he threw his battle cruisers into a combined attack. The pragmatic Vizeadmiral further says: 'even the most successful result from a high sea battle will not compel England to make peace', giving Britain's geographic advantage and huge weight of numbers as reasons. This contrasts with Churchill's pro Jellicoe propaganda that he 'was the only man who could lose the war in one afternoon'. Then he advocates the use of an unrestricted U–Boot campaign as the most effective way the Navy, that is surface and U–Boot forces, can be employed to crush British *economic* life, as opposed to a hunger blockade. It will be remembered that Vizeadmiral Scheer had been pushing for this unrestricted U–Boot campaign in early 1916 (see page 24). Of course many of Vizeadmiral Scheer's comments have been misleadingly quoted and taken out of context by his detractors.

What was the reason it was popularly believed in Germany that the Skagerrak Battle had been a victory? It was because the High Sea Fleet had inflicted twice as much damage and casualties as it had received. The British suffered 14 ships sunk for a total loss of 112,920 tons, and 6094 casualties, whilst the Germans lost 11 ships sunk for a total of 60,314 tons and 2551 casualties. Unambiguous statistics. The British lost three battle cruisers, capital ships, and three valuable armoured cruisers. Sometimes it is said that the armoured cruisers were of little value in a fleet action, and this is true, but they were very valuable for protecting Britain's trade routes. The presence of just one armoured cruiser would have prevented the annihilation of two convoys by German surface forces in October and December 1917.

The British reaction was at first somewhat different. The first newspaper reports admitted the German claims of victory. The *Manchester Guardian* of 3 June 1916, in one of the first reports printed, wrote:

> The battle which was fought on Wednesday and the night following off the coast of Jutland is much the most important naval action of the war. Since the object of fleets in action is, as a rule, simply the annihilation of the opposing forces, the result of an engagement may be judged roughly by the loss in ships. The British report announces the loss of three battle cruisers, three armoured cruisers, and a number of destroyers. The German report, which gives a fairly accurate account of the British losses (except that it names battleship *Warspite* in place of battle cruiser *Invincible*), states that the Germans lost one battleship (a pre-Dreadnought) and also one light cruiser, while another light cruiser and some torpedo craft are missing.... Omitting small craft, therefore, it appears that

the British lost three battle cruisers and three powerful armoured cruisers to one German battleship, one battle cruiser (not admitted by the Germans), and two light cruisers. We need not exaggerate the significance of these figures, and they are subject to revision.... What matters most, however, is not the actual loss of ships, heavy though that is, but something quite different, which we should not seek to evade: that, on the present evidence, the Germans had rather the better of us in this engagement in the precise way in which they have from the first aimed at circumventing us and in which it has been one of our fundamental objects to thwart them. In a word, the whole German High Sea Fleet succeeded in engaging a section of the British Fleet and handling it severely before the main British forces came on the scene.... The object in war is to oppose superior strength to the enemy. The Germans therefore, decline battle with the whole of the British Fleet, but seek to engage any part of it which is definitely inferior to the strength which they can put against it. On Wednesday they succeeded in both aims.

However, it did not take long before the tone had changed. Also in the *Manchester Guardian* of 3 June 1916: 'In the first British Admiralty statement the battle was presented as an undeniable German success; the corrected report from Sir John Jellicoe issued early this morning puts a more favourable complexion on the affair.'

How could the British Government and Admiralty admit that the fleet that had been built up at such a tremendous cost, had been defeated in battle? Put simply they couldn't. The development of the Dreadnought type and following arms race had cost the British a huge amount, and the 'we want eight, and we won't wait' campaign of 1909 had involved the British public to the extent of drawing on public subscriptions. Therefore, the British press and Government began to spin a web of deceit aimed at disguising the outcome of the battle. It was easy to sell their point of view to the British public who preferred to hear about German defeats rather than British losses. On 8 June 1916 a paper reported an address given by First Lord of the Admiralty Balfour:

At a luncheon given in London yesterday by the Imperial Chamber of Commerce Mr. Balfour, the First Lord of the Admiralty, delivered a speech on the Battle of Jutland. 'We have not yet,' he said, 'received from authentic sources a connected account of the whole action. Admiral Jellicoe's despatch giving his views upon it has not yet been received; indeed it could not be received yet. The difficulty of writing such a dispatch, of collating from innumerable sources the relative facts, would take all the time of a man left heavily burdened with the work of our Grand Fleet, and until that despatch comes I neither mean myself to discuss the details – or any details – of the battle nor to encourage such discussions in others. Still less do I propose to quarrel with the German newsmongers over their account of the comparative losses of the two sides.[3]

However, the British were hampered by the reluctance of Admiral Jellicoe to put out a report about the action and neither Beatty's nor Jellicoe's reports were published until 6 July. In the meantime the cracks continued to appear and the *Manchester Guardian* of 5 June 1916 wrote:

> The weekly dispatch said: 'Bring Jellicoe down to Whitehall with the wisdom of twenty-two months' war, and let him advise his old chief out of his hard earned knowledge. Give the fleet over to younger men. Beatty would need no instruction....

The spin campaign assumed all kinds of arguments to discredit the German Navy, none of which hold any water, and yet they are continued 100 years after the event. Many British sympathizers maintain that the Grand Fleet held the field after the battle. This of course is not true in a naval battle as both sides must return to port at some juncture after the battle, and by the afternoon of 1 June 1916 neither side remained on the place of the engagement. The Grand Fleet would never again return to the waters where the battle was fought, and in fact never again sallied forth with the intention of drawing the High Sea Fleet into battle, as they had done on 4–5 May 1916. On the other hand by 1918 the German heavy ships were regularly at sea in the area the battle had been fought, acting as support for minesweeping forces.

Sometimes the Skagerrak battle is referred to as a 'tactical victory' for the Germans, but a 'strategic victory' for the British. During the war the Russian Captain 1st Rank von Schoultz served as a liaison officer aboard the battleship *Hercules*, and was present at the Battle of Jutland. In his book *With the British Battle Fleet* he wrote:

> Was the Battle of Jutland a strategic victory for the British, as some naval writers maintain? I must admit that personally I cannot associate myself with this view. Naval history knows no such thing as a strategic victory ... but a victory, as such, can only be won tactically ...[4]

He also wrote:

> On the 3rd June I talked with some of the officers of our own, and other ships about the battle. Their views about the battle itself and its various stages differed strikingly; not only in details but even as to the general course of the action and its geographical position. All, however, were clearly convinced that it could not be regarded as a victory for us.[5]

Even more confusing are views such as that ascribed to Admiral Usborne, who is quoted as saying: 'In chess you may lose innumerable pieces, but provided you checkmate the king you are the winner.' This is akin to saying the allies must have won all the battles of World War One, since ultimately they won the war. According to this line of reasoning Napoleon must have lost the battle of Austerlitz!

Often, it is said that the British losses didn't matter so much as they were quickly and easily replaced. However, the replacements for the British battle cruisers lost during the battle, *Renown* and *Repulse*, were inferior ships to those lost, as First Lord of the Admiralty Geddes confirmed:

> In spite of the numerical superiority of the British Force the position cannot either now, or in the immediate future, be considered as satisfactory. Although a certain amount of additional protection has been worked into the British ships since Jutland, a repetition of the loss of our battle cruisers by the explosion of their magazines is only less possible than was then the case and has not been prevented.
>
> The armour protection of *Repulse* and *Renown* calls for serious consideration. With a belt of only 6 inches they are dangerously liable to destruction by a *single hit* and in view of their high-speed and powerful armament it is considered that, as soon as the new shell has been supplied to all battle cruisers, no time should be lost in fitting the additional protection which is now in course of preparation for them.[6]

Another fabrication disseminated by the spin doctors was that after the Skagerrak Battle the High Sea Fleet remained bottled up in Wilhelmshaven. Nothing could be further from the truth. In August 1916 the High Sea Fleet carried out an operation against the British coastal town of Sunderland. On 19 August it looked as if there would be another Fleet battle, but then Admirals Jellicoe and Beatty reversed course for 2 hours because of U-Boot contacts. Then Admiral Scheer received an erroneous report from an airship that an isolated British force, including battleships, lay to his south and he abandoned the coastal bombardment to chase this phantom force. In the end there was no fleet contact, but the British lost two light cruisers to U-Bootes. A further operation in the North Sea was conducted by the High Sea Fleet from 18 to 20 October 1916.

In October 1917 the III and IV Squadrons of the High Sea Fleet went to the Baltic to participate in the capture of the Baltic Islands. This operation was essential to force Russia to the negotiating table and bring about at separate peace in the east, to free up men and equipment for an offensive on the western front. With the Baltic Islands captured the Russian capital of St Petersburg was threatened and the Russians accordingly began negotiations.

In early 1918 the Finnish provisional government requested German assistance to free themselves from the grip of Russia and the Bolsheviks. A 'Special Unit' of battleships and other vessels arrived off Eckerö in the Aaland Island group on 5 March 1918 and despite the presence of Swedish naval forces quickly occupied the islands. On 3 April Hangö was taken by troops supported by German battleships and on 11 April naval forces arrived off Helsingfors, the Finnish capital, and the city was liberated from Bolshevik forces. The capture of the Baltic Islands and the liberation of Finland were historically and politically very important events, and showed what a valuable commodity the High Sea Fleet was, able to execute the will of the German Government.

In April 1918 the High Sea Fleet conducted an advance through the North Sea to the latitude of Stavanger, in Norway, to attack an allied convoy and hopefully isolate a battle squadron and bring it to battle. However, once again faulty intelligence meant this operation was a blow in the air. Nevertheless, the Panzerkreuzer *Moltke* suffered engine damage and had to be towed right across the entire North Sea, but the British Grand Fleet, now under the command of Admiral Beatty, failed to intervene.

Through part of 1917 and all of 1918 the heavy ships of the High Sea Fleet, battleships and Panzerkreuzer, were active in the North Sea supporting minesweepers in their daily work. After the Skagerrak Battle the British ceased their efforts to engage the Germans and began a widespread minelaying campaign in an attempt to blockade the German North Sea coast. Therefore the German minesweepers were constantly at work searching for and removing mine barriers. It was essential to have mine free routes to allow the Fleet to put to sea and also to allow the U–Bootes free passage. Therefore the British countered with a number of raids by light forces on the minesweeping forces. This required the minesweepers to be covered by heavy forces and not one minesweeper was lost to British surface forces. By 1918 the heavy German covering forces were operating almost daily in the area where on 31 May 1916 the Skagerrak Battle had been fought.

One author once claimed that the indirect result of the Skagerrak Battle was the declaration of unrestricted U–Boot warfare and that this provoked the United States to enter the war on the side of the Entente powers. This is incorrect. The first German unrestricted U–Boot campaign had taken place in 1915, from 1 February until 30 August, and had been rescinded after American threats. At a conference held on 4 March 1916 Chancellor Bethmann-Holweg stated that reopening the unrestricted U–Boot war would cause a break in relations with the USA, and perhaps also Holland and Denmark, and that only when an honourable peace seemed chanceless for Germany and continuing the war would totally exhaust Germany should the difficult decision for unrestricted warfare be considered as the ultimate solution. A renewed 'limited' campaign began in February 1916, but after the sinking of the liner *Sussex* the German Government cancelled plans to renew an unlimited campaign. Vizeadmiral Scheer was a strong advocate of unlimited U–Boot warfare and was adamant in his insistence on this type of warfare. In his post Skagerrak report he was simply reiterating his view that this was the best way of carrying the war to Britain.[7] So, a return to unlimited U–Boot warfare was planned even before the Skagerrak Battle; it was inevitable, and was only a question of timing.

Such a campaign offered a better prospect of success than did any of the alternatives open to Germany. Whether a victory would result was by no means certain, but everything in war is uncertain. As Scheer had been striving by every means to gain the Kaiser's permission for submarine warfare, his expression reflected no change in his views or in his plans. As far as we can determine, the battle had no effect on Scheer's strategic handling of the High Sea Fleet other than to cause an interlude in his active operations until August.[8]

As early as 1904 the British planned a close blockade of the German coastline in the event of war, but this plan changed in 1912 to one of an 'observational blockade' between Norway and Holland, and then just on the eve of the war the plan changed yet again to a distant blockade between Norway and Scotland. It is often claimed that the Grand Fleet was instrumental in the success of this blockade, but in fact they played little or no part in maintaining it. As Vizeadmiral Scheer has stated, because of Britain's geographical position it was easy for them to mount a blockade against Germany, and it was carried out with the most modest of sea forces, the 10 Cruiser Squadron, which consisted of armed merchant ships. However, the naval contingent represented only a small part of the blockade strategy. The main effort was a political campaign to coerce and even force the neutral countries from trading with the Germans. This campaign gathered momentum as the war dragged on but after the entry of the United States to the war in April 1917 more and more neutral countries were dissuaded from dealing with Germany, mainly through the massive influence the US had on neutral countries, particularly in South America. Therefore, the blockade of Germany was more a political campaign than a naval one, and could have been accomplished without the Grand Fleet.

Nevertheless, some in Britain were dissatisfied with the performance of the distant blockade. Churchill wrote on 7 July 1917:

The policy of distant blockade was not adopted from choice, but from necessity. It implied no repudiation on the part of the Admiralty of their fundamental principle of aggressive naval strategy, but only a temporary abandonment of it in the face of unsolved practical difficulties and it was intended, both before and after the declaration of war, that every effort should be made to overcome those difficulties. It was rightly foreseen that by closing the exits from the North Sea into the Atlantic Ocean, German commerce would be almost completely cut off from the world. It was expected that the economic and financial pressure resulting from such a blockade would fatally injure the German power to carry on a war.[9]

He continued:

A number of profoundly important changes have taken place in the naval situation since these plans were made. The submarine attack upon commerce ruptures the basis upon which the policy of 'distant blockade' and still more the policy of 'distant blockade and nothing else' stand. The sinkings by submarines have already affected, and will continually affect, our power to carry on the war. They are perhaps at this moment the main cause of the prolongation of the struggle. It is absurd, for this and many other reasons, to speak of carrying on this war as if time might not be a decisive factor against us. It has also been proved, that the economic pressure of *our distant blockade upon Germany is not in itself sufficient to prevent the enemy from carrying on the war* by land or to force him to come out and fight at sea. He rightly prefers to remain in his defended waters, enjoying the command of the Baltic, neutralising and containing Allied forces at least four times the strength of his own fleet, while ravaging all our sea communications with his submarines.... It must here be observed that the policy lately adopted of scattering mines, and sowing minefields a considerable distance out at sea, which are subsequently left unwatched and unguarded, is open to question. The enemy cannot be prevented from sweeping good broad channels through these minefields, which he charts carefully, and thereafter traverses with very little risk, either with submarines or surface vessels. We, on the other hand, are naturally shy of approaching our own minefields, and we do not know what channels he has swept through them. Our movements are therefore hampered, which is especially serious for the stronger fleet, while the enemy is not only 'not prevented from' moving, but has his coast largely protected for him by our agency. A minefield which is not watched and guarded is a barrier only to those who lay it....

The pressure of the blockade has not caused the enemy either to make peace or to come out and fight at sea, and there is no evidence that he will do so. The submarine attack on our commerce imposes a time limit on our power to continue the war.[10]

Mr. Churchill was convinced that the close blockade needed to be reinstituted, and this would have given the Grand Fleet a more meaningful role.

There is no doubt that the greatest naval threat to Britain during World War One came from the U-Boot campaign that began in February 1917. But this campaign cannot be viewed as a standalone event, rather it must be seen as the sharp end of the naval war conducted overall by the High Sea Fleet. Many writers are fond of dividing Germany's naval campaign into two parts. They say the first part was the campaign of the surface fleet, which they deleteriously suggest faded away after the Skagerrak Battle, and that the second part was the U-Boot campaign. This is a prejudiced view, and the overall German effort must be looked at as a homogeneous effort, for without the surface fleet there would have been no U-Boot campaign.

If the British forces had won a comprehensive victory in the Skagerrak Battle and annihilated the High Sea Fleet, what would the consequences have been? To begin with there would not have been a U-Boot campaign. If the German surface fleet had been annihilated a close blockade of the German coastline could have been mounted, with light forces and mines, which would have prevented the German U-Bootes from putting to sea. The main U-Boot bases were Emden, Wilhelmshaven, Kiel and Helgoland, and all of these could have been blockaded and shut down. There would also have been no materiel base for the U-Boot service to draw its technical and seaman personnel from.

Writing on 23 October 1918 Admiral Beatty was convinced that the power of the German naval forces lay with the High Sea Fleet, and he saw a removal of this threat as paramount:

> The power behind the submarine warfare of the enemy is the High Sea Fleet. Remove that power and the submarine menace would completely collapse. The removal of the High Sea Fleet would allow the whole of the forces of the Grand Fleet being set free to tackle the submarine menace at its source, i.e. the enemy bases.
>
> The bases could be ringed in by mine barriers, obstructions and nets, which could be guarded by comparatively light patrols, which could be continuous and of sufficient strength as circumstances required. The removal therefore of the High Sea Fleet means the removal of the one naval menace – the submarine....
>
> During four years of war the enemy has built up a huge submarine fleet. In four years of peace he can do all [this] and more than this, and with the High Sea Fleet in being, and assuredly stronger than ever, Germany will again menace the sea power of Great Britain.[11]

A defeat of the High Sea Fleet would have been a great blow to the morale of the Imperial Navy and its remaining personnel.

The British Navy could have entered the Baltic Sea, and therewith could have supported the Russian Navy. With the Baltic in allied hands Germany's trade with Sweden would have been cut off, particularly the vital trade in iron ore, which supported the German war effort. Germany could not have invaded the Baltic Islands and there would have been no threat to St Petersburg, the Russian capital. In all probability Russia, with allied support, would have remained in the war, bringing about a quicker end to the war. The British and French would not have had to wait for American involvement and reinforcements. On the other hand there would have been no liberation of Finland.

With the removal of the German fleet a great part of the light forces of the Grand Fleet, destroyers and light cruisers, could have been used for anti-submarine operations, such as there would have been.

A British weekly naval appreciation of May 1917 wrote:

The success of the German submarine attack, which is an offensive operation of the first magnitude, partly depends on the latent power of the German High Sea Fleet. Not only does the latter immobilise a large number of destroyers, and cruisers, from the direct protection of trade, but it makes attack on the enemy submarines in close vicinity to the enemy ports, an extraordinarily difficult operation. For this reason, the German High Sea Fleet will tend to adopt a strictly defensive attitude during the present phase of the war.[12]

There was another intangible result of the Skagerrak Battle. The spell cast by the Battle of Trafalgar had truly been broken, and never again would American or Japanese sailors be overawed by the spectre of British naval tradition. Their self belief was enhanced and from this point onwards they believed themselves the equals of any navy. The sequel was that with the Washington Naval Treaty of 1922 Britain conceded parity with the United States, and Britain's 'two power standard' was gone forever. As it was Britain had already scrapped many of the ships she had saved at Jutland by Fabian tactics, for reasons of economy, and many more were scrapped under the terms of the treaty. Under the terms of the treaty Japan came in a comfortable third.

There was a choice: to fight or not to fight. Ours, in the place of the Admiralty, would have been to fight. Theirs was not to fight. That decision fastened upon the British Navy an incubus of which it will not rid itself for many a year. Every British commander with an instinctive willingness to assume risks, which is the very foundation of naval and military greatness, will be confronted with a formidable library purporting to prove by every form of skilful plea and clever argument that Jellicoe won the World War without 'leaving anything to chance.[13]

Finally some observations should be made on the various commanders, from a German perspective. These are only generalizations about their performances on the day, not their overall careers. It may be timely to remember a famous remark made by Napoleon; when a commander was highly recommended to him he replied: 'Yes, but is he lucky?'

Vizeadmiral Scheer performed very well on the day and not only saved his fleet from annihilation at the hands of a force almost twice the size of his, he also took the initiative for the entire battle. Not only was Vizeadmiral Scheer a pugnacious fighter, he also had political savvy, evidenced by his desire not to appear as if he had retreated from the enemy. Towards 2000hrs he returned to attack the centre of the British line, hoping that his bold tactic would throw Admiral Jellicoe off balance, and he was proved correct when his torpedobootes forced Jellicoe to turn away. His firm resolve to force his way through the British forces during the night to the more favourable battle ground near Horns Reef, before battle could recommence in the morning, showed courage and determination.

Vizeadmiral Hipper also displayed great resolve and courage. At the beginning of the battle he was quite prepared to fight Vice Admiral Beatty's forces on a northerly course, even though outnumbered by two to one, including British battleships of the latest type armed with 15 inch cannon. This course took him away from the support of the Vizeadmiral Scheer's battleships but Hipper did not flinch. Only when Beatty manoeuvred to try and cut Hipper off did the latter turn southwards. Vizeadmiral Hipper then gave a creditable performance and kept his superior well informed of his movements until *Lützow* had his wireless installation destroyed. After his flagship was badly damaged he sought to transfer to another ship, but delays in doing this meant he played no further meaningful part in the battle. Vizeadmiral Hipper's only mistake was to attempt to take his damaged Panzerkreuzers to the head of the line during the night, which allowed the I AG to become separated.

Kontreadmiral Behncke carried out his role as commander of the III Squadron with firm resolve and he did not flinch as his flagship, *König*, came under heavy fire at the van of the German line. Kontreadmiral Behncke was of tall and slim build and was nicknamed 'the Sheik'. When the conning tower of *König* was struck by a heavy shell Behncke was wounded in the head.

Kontreadmiral Boedicker, commander of the II AG, put in a poor performance. Whilst at first he carried out his role of reconnaissance adequately, after his II AG came under heavy fire from the British 3 Battle Cruiser Squadron, and *Wiesbaden* was disabled, he seems to have lost his nerve and spent much of the remainder of the battle circling his ships in the lee of the fleet. During the night he frequently refused battle with British light forces and the commander of *Pillau* gave a veiled criticism of this. After the battle he received some criticism but seems to have avoided disciplinary action as the Fleet leadership persevered with him in positions of responsibility.

Kommodore von Reuter was commander of the IV Reconnaissance Group, which consisted of older small cruisers of the *Stettin* and *Bremen* classes, with the even older *Frauenlob* as the final member. The latter was capable of just 21 knots, slower than many of the battleships involved in the battle, so Kommodore von Reuter's group was of limited combat value. Nevertheless, cometh the hour, and cometh the man, and so it was when von Reuter ordered his reconnaissance group to engage the much more powerful 2 Light Cruiser Squadron at 2330hrs. Although outgunned by the more powerful British squadron the IV AG gave a creditable performance but lost *Frauenlob*. Kommodore von Reuter had displayed a willingness to fight, so essential for a naval commander.

The I FdT, Kommodore Michelsen, performed well on the day, and showed great maturity when Vizeadmiral Scheer gave him responsibility for all the torpedobootes at 2115hrs and he allowed the torpedobootes under the II FdT to continue to operate as ordered by their chief. Likewise, although initially opposed to the scuttling of his flagship, *Rostock*, he listened to the valid arguments of others and was therefore able to save the crew by a timely evacuation.

Kommodore Heinrich was II FdT, and held equal authority with the I FdT. He was an extremely talented commander and during the battle showed good intuition and knew what was required and when, as evidenced by his 1952hr and 1954hr orders to the VI and IX Flottilles: 'Torpedoboote ran!', or attack the enemy. This order therefore ensured the torpedoboote Flottilles were excellently placed to carry out Vizeadmiral Scheer's similar order of 2021hrs, and their timely attack forced the British battleship squadrons to turn away. His Flottille commanders, Korvettenkapitän Max Schultz and Korvettenkapitän Goehle, gave him excellent support. Kommodore Heinrich performed well all day.

The other Admirals, including Vizeadmiral Schmidt and Kontreadmiral Mauve, all did a good job but had little opportunity to distinguish themselves.

Admiral Jellicoe acted in accordance with his inherently flawed Grand Fleet Battle Orders. It is impossible to cover all battle situations with a set of rigid orders and they served to restrict the initiative and performance of his subordinates. Jellicoe had overestimated the strength of the German ships and the effectiveness of the torpedo and mine weapons. His strict adherence to his preconceived conception of the battle cost him any chance of success.

Vice Admiral Beatty performed well on the day. He was known to be headstrong and impetuous and he was willing to fight. After the preliminaries he neatly delivered the High Sea Fleet to Jellicoe. Beatty has been criticized for not keeping his chief informed of his movements but Beatty was hampered in that the wireless installation aboard his flagship had been disabled, and he was frequently let down by his signal staff. He kept up a constant pressure on the head of the German line, even into the evening, and took full advantage of better visibility.

Rear Admiral Hood was a bright and enthusiastic leader who handled his 3 Battle Cruiser Squadron excellently. He was favoured by Jellicoe's decision to send him on ahead and when he appeared on the battlefield it was from an unexpected direction as far as the Germans were concerned and Hood made the most of it. He swept aside the II AG, badly damaging *Wiesbaden*, and then attacked the I AG. He inflicted serious damage to *Lützow* before the latter caught him and destroyed his flagship inside two minutes, Rear Admiral Hood forfeiting his life.

Rear Admiral Evan-Thomas commanded the 5 Battle Squadron and handled his ships very capably. Although left behind at first, because of Beatty's poor signalling, he caught up and saved Beatty from being overwhelmed. His ships fought bravely against the High Sea Fleet, even though *Warspite* was eventually forced to retire. Caught out of position by the deployment of the Grand Fleet his squadron nevertheless continued to make a contribution.

Of the cruiser commanders Commodores Goodenough and Le Mesurier preformed good work, both in reconnaissance and fighting ability.

Rear Admiral Arbuthnot, commander of the 1 Cruiser Squadron, was a keen sportsman, but was outspoken. When he sighted the crippled *Wiesbaden* he boldly charged across the bows of Vice Admiral Beatty's battle cruisers to get to grips with what he believed was his natural opponent, the enemy reconnaissance forces. Unfortunately his impetuous rush brought him within sight of the I AG and *Lützow* destroyed his ship within three minutes. Arbuthnot's headstrong attitude had led to his demise.

Some of the squadron commanders in the Skagerrak Battle, such as Vice Admiral Burney, commander of the 1 Battle Squadron, were described by Marder as:

> a hard task master of the old school – orthodox, unimaginative, in no way out of the ordinary – he appeared to one officer as 'a piece of wood'. He was not one who would ever take the initiative or depart from the most rigid interpretation of the battle orders. His contemporaries would not have chosen him to lead the battle line at Jutland. Nor did the commander of the 2 Battle Squadron, the colourless Vice Admiral Jerram possess much initiative or dash.[14]

At about 2145hrs Vice Admiral Jerram ordered the 4 Light Cruiser Squadron, under Commodore Le Mesurier, not to attack the head of the German battleship line, which they had sighted. Nevertheless, the light cruisers were astute enough to ignore the order and carried out a torpedo attack. Vice Admiral Jerram wrote: 'I should like to mention specially that about 9 p.m. I negatived an attack with Whitehead torpedoes ordered by *Caroline*, as I was certain that the vessels seen on our starboard beam were our own battle cruisers.'[15]

Vice Admiral Burney refused to report action taking place astern of his 6 Division, as the German battleships broke though, to Admiral Jellicoe, as he believed the commander in chief could see it for himself.

The quality of the officers and men of the Royal Navy was second to none. They were astute, loyal and were excellent in their technical ability and seamanship. The Offizieres and Matrosen of the Imperial Navy had similar attributes. The loss of around 8500 men in a single day's battle was a terrible loss of fine young men even by World War One standards. But this was a different era; the loyal men thought they were doing their heartfelt duty for their country and people. They were perfectly willing to lay down their lives for King, Kaiser and country. In those days warfare was looked upon as a legitimate extension of politics, and all the European countries engaged in wars all over the globe, to further their political and economic objectives. Today we revile such policies, and yet some countries still promulgate this course of action, and still believe might is right. The men who fought in the Skagerrak Battle could not be criticized for doing their duty.

On 1 June 1916 all across the North Sea the bodies of men who had given their lives during and after the battle were being committed to the deep in the traditional manner of the seaman, wrapped in their hammocks and weighted. On the other side of the North Sea solemn burial ceremonies were being conducted at the Wilhelmshaven Naval Cemetery. We should never forget these brave men who gave their all in the battle that was Skagerrak-Jutland.

Notes

Chapter 1

1. N162-5, Nachlaß Hipper.
2. N162-5, Nachlaß Hipper
3. *Der Krieg zur See-Nordsee Band 5*, page 27.
4. *Germany's High Sea Fleet in the World War*, by Admiral Scheer, page 97.
5. N162, Nachlaß Hipper.
6. Kommodore Köthner.
7. N162-5, Nachlaß Hipper.
8. RM92/3457, *Seydlitz* war diary.
9. N162-5, Nachlaß Hipper.
10. N162-5, Nachlaß Hipper.
11. *Germany's High Sea Fleet in the World War*, by Admiral Scheer, page 123.
12. M.Dv.Nr.352. *Der Artillerieoffizier eines Großkampfschiffes im Kriege 1914/18*, by Korvettenkapitän Mahrholz.
13. A4, A5, A8, A10, A12, A13, A14, A16 and A19.
14. Drifter *Moss* suffered six dead.
15. RM3/2983.
16. ADM137-2069.
17. H.H. Frost, *The Battle of Jutland*, page 74.

Chapter 2

1. *Germany's High Sea Fleet in the World War*, page 134.
2. *Germany's High Sea Fleet in the World War*, page 134.
3. N162-5, Nachlaß Hipper.
4. BA–MA 162, Nachlaß Hipper.
5. RM52/143.
6. War Light Vessel A of the Jade.
7. The British used Greenwich Mean Time (GMT, now Zulu), the Germans Middle Europe Time (MEZ), with some of the German reports using summer time. GMT one hour behind MEZ, summer time one hour ahead. To avoid confusion MEZ has been used throughout, although this may be different from standard British works.
8. Korvettenkapitan Richard Foerster, I Artillerie Offizier, *Seydlitz*, in *Auf See unbesiegt*.
9. Letter by an unnamed Offizier from Neusalz am Oder (now in Poland) dated 8 June 1916.
10. I FdT, or I Leader of Torpedobootes. It should be said the I FdT and II FdT held equal authority.

Chapter 3

1. Reported as P.S. in RM56/50, II Flottille KTB, but as P.L. in German official history.
2. Probably the fire of 5 Battle Squadron, but time may be in error.
3. Z.0. (Z, zero) follow the leader.
4. RM92/2358, SMS *Elbing* war diary.
5. Hermann Jung, *Skagerrak*.
6. Der Krieg in der Nordsee Band 5.
7. Leutnant zur See H. Kienast: Mit Admiral Hipper auf der *Lützow*.
8. 'SMS *Lützow* in the Skagerrak Battle', in Marinerundschau 1926, by KK Paschen.
9. Der Krieg in der Nordsee Band 5.

10. In Dienstschrift Nr. 10, The Artillerie Offizier of a Capital Ship in the war 1914/18. Berlin 1930.
11. Commander H.H. Frost: *The Battle of Jutland* (1936)
12. 22½° degrees, 1 point equals 11¼°.
13. 'SMS *Lützow* in the Skagerrak Battle', in *Marinerundschau* 1926, by K.K. Paschen.
14. Gabel, or Fork. Referred to by the British as the 'ladder 'system, where each shot was fired at a slightly different range, giving an extended line for the fall of shot, making observation easier.
15. Rate of change.
16. In Diensrschrift Nr. 10, *The Artillerie Offizier of a Capital Ship in the War 1914/18*. Berlin 1930.
17. *Jutland Dispatches*, page 132.
18. 'SMS *Lützow* in the Skagerrak Battle', in *Marinerundschau* 1926, by K.K. Paschen.
19. 'SMS *Lützow* in the Skagerrak Battle', in *Marinerundschau* 1926, by K.K. Paschen.
20. In *Kiel and Jutland* by Korvettenkapitän von Hase. (First published as *Two White Peoples*.)
21. In Diensrschrift Nr. 10, *The Artillerie Offizier of a Capital Ship in the War 1914/18*. Berlin 1930.
22. 'At it Seydlitz'.
23. In *The Sea Battle off the Skagerrak on 31 May 1916*, by Korvettenkapitän Richard Foerster, page 139.
24. Leutnant zur See Harry Habler, who later perished aboard *U154*.
25. In 'Auf Felde unbesiegt', *The Sea Battle off the Skagerrak on 31 May 1916*, page 139, by Korvettenkapitän Richard Foerster.
26. Jutland Dispatches page 140.
27. 'SMS *Lützow* in the Skagerrak Battle', in *Marinerundschau* 1926, by KK Paschen.
28. 'SMS *Lützow* in the Skagerrak Battle', in *Marinerundschau* 1926, by KK Paschen.
29. *Jutland Official Dispatches*.
30. In *Kiel and Jutland* by Korvettenkapitän von Hase.
31. In *The Sea Battle Off the Skagerrak on 31 May 1916*, by Korvettenkapitän Richard Foerster.
32. Approximately 24 knots, according to *Warship Monographs, Queen Elizabeth class*, John Campbell, Conway Maritime Press 1972.
33. RM92/3256, *Pillau* KTB.
34. RM 92/3736 *von der Tann* KTB.
35. Battle report SMS *von der Tann*.
36. In Diensrschrift Nr. 10, *The Artillerie Offizier of a Capital Ship in the War 1914/18*. Berlin 1930.
37. In *The Sea Battle off the Skagerrak on 31 May 1916*, by Korvettenkapitän Richard Foerster.
38. Korvettenkapitän Goehle.
39. RM52/143. II FdT KTB.
40. RM56/97. IX Flottille KTB.
41. *The Battle of Jutland*, H.H. Frost, page 233.
42. 'SMS *Lützow* in the Skagerrak Battle', in *Marinerundschau* 1926, by K.K. Paschen.

Chapter 4
1. The dead reckoning positions of ships of this era were liable to error, which could only be rectified by taking a secure position fix on a land object. As quoted the difference in the positions of *Southampton* and *Champion* was over 25 nautical miles, when it was more like 10. This did not matter to Beatty, who had the ships in visual range, but Jellicoe had *Champion* 15nm further south than she was.
2. From Nachlaß Seekadett Günther Schütz Schütz, held by the MOV.
3. RM92/2759, *Kaiser* KTB, titled 'SMS *Kaiser* in the Battle Off the Skagerrak'. K.K. Studt served as First Offizier of *Karlsruhe*, First Offizier *Regensburg*, Navigation Offizier *Kaiser*, and finally commander of *U155*.
4. RM92/2759, *Kaiser* KTB, titled 'SMS *Kaiser* in the Battle off the Skagerrak'. K.K. Studt.
5. RM92/2759, *Kaiser* KTB, titled 'SMS *Kaiser* in the Battle off the Skagerrak'. K.K. Studt.
6. RM92/3324, *Prinzregent Luitpold* KTB.
7. RM92/2798, *Kaiserin* KTB.
8. RM92/3378. *Rheinland* KTB.
9. *Memories and Experiences of the Years 1914–1918*, by Kurt Goebell.

10. From RM92/2307, *Derfflinger* KTB.
11. In Dienstschrift Nr. 10, *The Artillerie Offizier of a Capital Ship in the War 1914/18*. Berlin 1930.
12. Kapitänleutnant Schumacher, II Artillerie Offizier *Lützow*.
13. N162/5, Nachlaß Hipper.
14. 'The Sea Battle off the Skagerrak', by Korvettenkapitän Foerster, In *Auf See unbesiegt*.
15. *Der Krieg in der Nordsee*, Volume 5, page 265.
16. 'Have at the enemy.'
17. RM92/3457, *Seydlitz* KTB.
18. *The Battle of Jutland*, H.H. Frost, page 161.
19. RM92/2759, *Kaiser* KTB.
20. *Nomad*.
21. RM92/3324, *Prinzregent Luitpold* KTB.
22. RM92/2798, *Kaiserin* KTB.
23. RM92/2435, Friedrich der Große KTB.
24. Copy of a Report by Kapitänleutnant Friedrich Oldekop.
25. RM92 3/3243, *Ostfriesland* KTB.
26. RM92/3607, *Thüringen* KTB.
27. RM92/2659, *Helgoland* KTB.
28. RMRM92/3219, *Oldenburg*.
29. RM56/73. Flottille VII KTB.
30. Range Difference Indicator – rate of change, opening or closing.
31. RM92/3256, *Pillau* KTB.
32. RM92/3256, *Pillau* KTB.
33. RM51/335, Leader of II Reconnaissance Group KTB.
34. RM92/3337, *Regensburg* KTB.
35. RM56/66, VI Torpedoboote Flottille KTB.
36. RM56/50, II Flottille KTB.
37. Der Krieg in der Nordsee Band 5.
38. *The Battle of Jutland*, H. H. Frost, p. 296.
39. RM92/2759, *Kaiser* KTB.
40. RM3/4717, report by Oberheizer Zenne, made shortly after the battle aboard the Norwegian submarine tender *Ellida* in Tonsberg.
41. *Germany's High Sea Fleet in the World War*, Reinhard Scheer, pages 151–152.

Chapter 5
1. Naval Staff Appreciation, page 81.
2. Der Krieg in der Nordsee, Band 5, page 283.
3. *Memories of the Battle off the Skagerrak*. Korvettenkapitän Viktor Habedanck, I Artillerie Offizier SMS *Kronprinz*.
4. *Battle cruiser Lützow's Battle and Sinking in the Skagerrak Battle*, by Kapitänleutnant Schumacher, II AO.
5. 'SMS *Lützow* in the Skagerrak Battle', in Marinerundschau 1926, by Korvettenkapitän Paschen.
6. Battle cruiser *Lützow's Battle and Sinking in the Skagerrak Battle*, by Kapitänleutnant Schumacher, II AO
7. *Kiel and Jutland*, by Korvettenkapitän von Hase
8. RM92/2759, *Kaiser* KTB, titled 'SMS *Kaiser* in the Battle off the Skagerrak'. Korvettenkapitän Studt.
9. RM92/3324, KTB *Prinzregent Luitpold*.
10. RM92/2898, KTB *König*.
11. RM92/2435, KTB *Friedrich der Große*.
12. Der Krieg in der Nordsee Band 5.
13. 'SMS *Lützow* in the Skagerrak Battle', in *Marinerundschau* 1926, by K.K. Paschen.
14. *On Board SMS Lützow*, by Seaman Fritz Loose.
15. 'SMS *Lützow* in the Skagerrak Battle', in *Marinerundschau* 1926, by K.K. Paschen.

16. 'SMS *Lützow* in the Skagerrak Battle', in *Marinerundschau* 1926, by K.K. Paschen.
17. Kiel and Jutland, by Korvettenkapitän von Hase.
18. RM92/2898, KTB *König*.
19. RM3/4717, Report by Oberheizer Zenne, made shortly after the battle aboard the Norwegian submarine tender *Ellida* in Tonsberg.
20. Admiral Scheer's Staff included: Kpt.z.S. v. Levetzow (Chief of Operations Dept), Kpt.z.S. v. Trotha (Chief of Staff), Korvkpt. Reimann, Korvkpt. Wilke, Frgkpt. Quaet-Faslem, Kptlt. Bindseil, Chief Ingenieur Schützler, Kptlt. Heusinger v. Waldegg, Korvkpt. Franz, Korvkpt. Meyer.
21. Navigation NCO.
22. With Scheer on the Command Bridge, Kapitän zur See von Trotha. In *Auf See unbesiegt*.
23. RM56/55, KTB III Flottille.
24. *The Battle of Jutland*, by H. Frost, page 328.

Chapter 6
1. RM92/2983, *Lützow* KTB.
2. RM3/3449, *Lützow* trials report.
3. RM92/2983, *Lützow* KTB.
4. Chronicle of the Battlecruiser '*Lützow*'. Fähnrich zur See Mardersteig (unpublished).
5. With Admiral Hipper on the '*Lützow*', by Leutnant zur See Harald Kienast.
6. The Battle of Jutland, H. Frost, page 335.
7. *The Grand Fleet, 1914–1916*, pages 316–317.
8. *Germany's High Sea Fleet in the World War*, Admiral Scheer, page 155.
9. *Der Krieg zur See 1914–918, Nordsee V*, page 311.
10. Commander H.H. Frost: *The Battle of Jutland* (1936)
11. RM52/143, II FdT KTB.
12. Kapitänleutnant Gautier.
13. RM56/55, III Flottille KTB.
14. RM56/55, III Flottille KTB.
15. *Germany's High Sea Fleet in the World War*, by Admiral Scheer, page 156.
16. *Kiel and Jutland*, Korvettenkapitän Georg von Hase, page 107.
17. RM92/2307, *Derfflinger* KTB.
18. RM92/3003, *Markgraf* KTB.
19. 'SMS *Lützow* in the Skagerrak Battle', in *Marinerundschau 1926*, by Korvettenkapitän Paschen.
20. Stabsärzte Florus Gelhaar died on 12.6.1916 aboard the hospital ship *Sierra Ventana*.
21. Hans Behrens, in *Das Volksbuch vom Skagerrak* by F.O. Busch.
22. On the Bridge of S.M.S. *Lützow* in the Skagerrak Battle. A letter by Oberleutnant zur See Wolfgang Schönfeld, Signal Offizier of *Lützow*.
23. Either Leutnant zur See Joachim Schulz, or Leutnant zur See Joachim Schmidt.
24. *Chronicle of the Battlekreuzer Lützow*, by Fähnrich zur See Mardersteig. (unpublished)
25. Description of my experiences and activity aboard SMS *Derfflinger* during the battle 31.5.1916, by Zimmermannsgast Schwendler.
26. *Kiel and Jutland*, Korvettenkapitän Georg von Hase.
27. Korvettenkapitän Viktor Habedanck, I Artillerie Offizier SMS *Kronprinz*.
28. RM92/2759, *Kaiser* KTB, titled 'SMS *Kaiser* in the Battle Off the Skagerrak'. Korvettenkapitän Studt.
29. *Kiel and Jutland*, Korvettenkapitän Georg von Hase, page 109.
30. Combat simulations.
31. Despos 18, A304: Admiral Scheer. Nr. 28, copies of correspondence Scheer-Hollweg, from Nachlaß Hollweg, 19.5.1919, Weimar.
32. Despos 18, A304: Admiral Scheer. Nr. 28, copies of correspondence Scheer-Hollweg, from Nachlaß Hollweg, 15.1.1920, Weimar
33. *The Battle of Jutland*, H. Frost, page 328.
34. Slow speed.

35. RM92/2798, *Kaiserin* KTB.
36. RM92/3003, *Markgraf* KTB.
37. *Der Krieg in der Nordsee*, Volume V, page 321.
38. The signal for 'Torpedoboote Ran!', indicated by the forked red pennant Z.
39. Utmost Power.
40. RM56/66, VI Flottille KTB.
41. *Der Krieg in der Nordsee*, Volume V, pages 325–326.
42. RM56/55, III Flottille KTB.
43. Grand Fleet Battle Orders.
44. *Der Krieg in der Nordsee*, Volume V, page 330.
45. Figures according to *Dienstschrift Nr. 11, The Employment of the Torpedo Arm in the Battlecruiser Battle on the Dogger Bank and in the Skagerrak Battle.* MDv 352 II.
46. RM56/73, VII Flottille KTB.
47. *The Battle of Jutland*, H. Frost, page 343.

Chapter 7
1. *Der Krieg in der Nordsee*, Volume V, page 337.
2. RM92/3517, *Stettin* KTB.
3. RM51/335, II AG KTB.
4. RM92/3256, *Pillau* KTB.
5. RM56/62, V Flottille KTB.
6. *Jutland Dispatches*, page 466.
7. *Kiel and Jutland*, Korvettenkapitän von Hase, page 118.
8. In *Auf Felde unbesiegt*, 'The Sea Battle Off the Skagerrak on 31 May 1916', by Korvettenkapitän Richard Foerster, page 148.
9. RM92/2619, *Hannover* KTB.
10. Seekadett Günther Schütz, Crew of January 1916, about the Skagerrak Battle on board SMS *Hessen*.
11. RM92/3819, *Westfalen* KTB.
12. Jellicoe to Admiralty, 12 June 1916.
13. *The Grand Fleet, 1914–1916*, Admiral Jellicoe, page 373.
14. *The Battle of Jutland*, H. Frost, page 411 ff.
15. *Der Krieg in der Nordsee*, Volume V, page 355.

Chapter 8
1. V1 to S24 had one oil fired boiler and three coal fired boilers.
2. RM56/73, war diary of the VII Flottille.
3. RM52/115, I FdT war diary.
4. *Jutland Dispatches*, page 472, *Duke of Edinburgh* to *Shannon* at 2217hrs: 'Your masthead light is burning.'
5. See page 20.
6. Jutland Dispatches, page 475.
7. *Room 40, British Naval Intelligence 1914–18*, by Patrick Beesly, page 161.
8. Quoted in *From the Dreadnought to Scapa Flow*, Volume III, Arthur Marder, page 152.
9. IV AG war diary.
10. RM92/2358, *Elbing* combat report.
11. *Tipperary, Spitfire, Sparrowhawk, Garland* and *Contest*.
12. RM92/2358, *Elbing* war diary.
13. The crew of *Frauenlob* had previously crewed *Danzig* until she was mined. The Imperial Navy suffered from a constant shortage of trained crew.
14. RM47/4753.
15. *The Last Eight*, by Oberleutnant zur See a.D. Stolzmann.
16. RM3/4249. Survivors' reports.
17. RM92/3457, *Seydlitz* war diary (KTB).

18. In 'Auf Felde unbesiegt', *The Sea Battle Off the Skagerrak on 31 May 1916*, by Korvettenkapitän Richard Foerster.
19. RM92/3457, *Seydlitz* war diary (KTB).
20. *The Battle of Jutland*, H. Frost, page 467.
21. 13 Flotilla: *Obdurate, Moresby, Nerissa, Narborough, Nicator, Pelican, Petard*. 10 Flotilla: *Termagant, Turbulent*.
22. 9 Flotilla: *Lydiard, Liberty, Landrail, Laurel*. 10 Flotilla: *Morris*.
23. Destroyers *Marksman, Obedient, Mindful, Marvel, Onslaught, Maenad, Narwhale, Nessus, Noble, Opal, Nonsuch, Menace, Munster* and *Mary Rose*.
24. RM3/3378, *Rheinland* KTB.
25. H6C was *Tipperary*.
26. RM3/3819, *Westfalen* KTB.
27. RM92/2358, *Elbing* combat report.
28. RM92/3274, *Posen* war diary.
29. RM92/3119, *Nassau* war diary.
30. *Broke*'s pennant number was '98'.
31. RM92/3819, *Westfalen* KTB.
32. See also page 138.
33. Account by Kapitänleutnant Knobloch, I AO of *Rostock*.
34. RM92/3274, *Posen* KTB.
35. RM92/3219, *Oldenburg* combat report.
36. RM92/2659, *Helgoland* combat report.
37. RM92/3243, *Ostfriesland* combat report.
38. RM92/3119, *Nassau* KTB.
39. RM92/2435, *Friedrich de Große* KTB.
40. Report by Kapitänleutnant Friedrich Oldekop, from SMS *Friedrich der Große* (Fleet flagship).
41. RM92/3819, *Westfalen* KTB.
42. Jutland Dispatches, page 39.
43. *Petard*.
44. RM92/3819, *Westfalen* KTB.
45. *Der Krieg zur See-Nordsee Band 5*, page 387.

Chapter 9
1. RM92/3406, *Schlesien* KTB.
2. Further contact reports were sent by Captain Stirling at 0308 and 0313hrs, but the *Jutland Dispatches* say only the 0313hrs was received by *Marksman*.
3. This tactic as suggested by German report, see p. 125.
4. RM92/2572, *Großer Kurfürst* KTB.
5. RM92/3406, *Schlesien* KTB.
6. Seekadett Günther Schütz, about the Skagerrak Battle on board SMS *Hessen*.
7. *Jutland Dispatches*, page 478.
8. *The Battle of Jutland*, H. Frost, page 494.
9. *From Jutland to Scapa Flow*, volume 3, A. Marder, page 200.
10. *Jutland* by N.J.M Campbell, page 308.
11. *Germany's High Sea Fleet in the World War*, Admiral Scheer, page 164.
12. *Germany's High Sea Fleet in the World War*, Admiral Scheer, pages 163–166.
13. *Onboard SMS Lützow*, by Seaman Loose.
14. 'SMS *Lützow* in the Skagerrak Battle', in *Marinerundschau 1926*, by Korvettenkapitän Paschen.
15. *Battlecruiser 'Lützow's' Battle and Sinking in the Skagerrak Battle*, by Kapitänleutnant Ernst Schumacher.
16. A letter written by an unknown Offizier of SMS *Lützow* shortly after the Skagerrak Battle, Neusalz, a/Oder 8 June 1916.
17. *Skagerrak*, by Hermann Jung, commander of A turret.
18. RM56/149, 1 Half Flottille KTB.

19. RM56/149, 1 Half Flottille KTB.
20. RM56/149, 1 Half Flottille KTB.
21. *Experiences of a Ship's Doctor in the Skagerrak Battle*, by Marine-Oberstabsarzt Dr. Amelung, in Auf See unbesiegt.
22. *Jutland Dispatches*, page 511.
23. *Jutland Dispatches*, page 514.
24. *Der Krieg in der Nordsee*, volume V, page 411.
25. Korvettenkapitän Franz Pfeiffer.
26. Secret report number 372, SMS *Ostfriesland*.
27. *Krieg in der Nordsee*, volume V, page 541.
28. *Krieg in der Nordsee*, volume V, page 418.
29. Jutland Dispatches, page 488.
30. See page 194.
31. *Jutland Dispatches*, page 500.

Chapter 10
1. Unpublished report by Fähnrich zur See Mardersteig.
2. *Germany's High Sea Fleet in the World War*, by Admiral Scheer, page 168.
3. *Manchester Guardian*, 8 June 1916.
4. *With the British Battle Fleet*, Captain 1 Rank von Schoultz, page 186.
5. *With the British Battle Fleet*, Captain 1 Rank von Schoultz, page 154.
6. CAB/24/62, 31.8.1018.
7. See page 239.
8. *The Battle of Jutland*, H. Frost, page 511.
9. CAB24/18, Printed for the War Cabinet July 1917, signed W. Churchill, 7 July 1917.
10. CAB24/18, Printed for the War Cabinet July 1917, signed W. Churchill, 7 July 1917.
11. CAB/24/68.
12. CAB/24/14.
13. *The Battle of Jutland*, Commander H Frost, page 516.
14. *From Dreadnought to Scapa Flow*, volume 3, by A. Marder, page 39.
15. *Jutland Dispatches*, page 108.

Appendices

The High Sea Fleet

Chief of the High Sea Forces: Vizeadmiral Scheer
Chief of Staff: Kapitän zur See Adolf von Trotha
Leader of Operations Department: Kapitän zur See Magnus von Levetzow

Main Body

Ship	Commander	I Offizier	I Artillerie Offizier
Friedrich der Große	Kapitän zur See Fuchs	Korvettenkapitän Batsch	Korvettenkapitän von Nostitz und Jänckendorf

I Squadron

Vizeadmiral Ehrhard Schmidt
I Admiral Staff Offizier: Korvettenkapitän Wolfgang Wegener
2 Admiral: Kontreadmiral Engelhardt

Ship	Commander	I Offizier	I Artillerie Offizier
Ostfriesland	Kapitän zur See Natzmer	Korvettenkapitän Pfeiffer	Korvettenkapitän Stricker
Thüringen	Kapitän zur See Küsel	Korvettenkapitän Roedenbeck	Kapitänleutnant Franz
Helgoland	Kapitän zur See von Kameke	Korvettenkapitän Stever	Korvettenkapitän Richter
Oldenburg	Kapitän zur See Höpfner	Korvettenkapitän Vollmer	Kapitänleutnant Hermann
Posen	Kapitän zur See Lange	Fregattenkapitän Reichardt	Korvettenkapitän Werther
Rheinland	Kapitän zur See Rohardt	Korvettenkapitän von Gorissen	Kapitänleutnant Frömsdorf
Nassau	Kapitän zur See Klappenbach	Korvettenkapitän Helf	Kapitänleutnant von Richthofen
Westfalen	Kapitän zur See Redlich	Korvettenkapitän Hans von Laffert	Korvettenkapitän Hinsch

II Squadron

Kontreadmiral Mauve
I Admiral Staff Offizier: Korvettenkapitän Kahlert
2 Admiral: Kontreadmiral Freiherr von Dalwigk zu Lichtenfels

Ship	Commander	I Offizier	I Artillerie Offizier
Deutschland	Kapitän zur See Meurer	Korvettenkapitän Blothuis	Kapitänleutnant Faber
Pommern	Kapitän zur See Bölken	Korvettenkapitän von Goeffel	Korvettenkapitän Elle
Schlesien	Kapitän zur See Behncke	Korvettenkapitän Becker	Korvettenkapitän Punt
Hannover	Kapitän zur See Heine	Korvettenkapitän von Sechow	Korvettenkapitän Herrmann
Schleswig-Holstein	Kapitän zur See Varrentrapp	Korvettenkapitän Klehe	Korvettenkapitän Aßmann
Hessen	Kapitän zur See Bartels	Korvettenkapitän Schulze-Jena	Kapitänleutnant Korndörfer

III Squadron

Kontreadmiral Paul Behncke
I Admiral Staff Offizier: Korvettenkapitän Freiherr von Gagern
2 Admiral: Kontreadmiral Nordmann

Ship	Commander	I Offizier	I Artillerie Offizier
König	Kapitän zur See Brüninghaus	Korvettenkapitän Bendemann	Kapitänleutnant Meusel
Großer Kurfürst	Kapitän zur See Goette	Korvettenkapitän Brökelmann	Korvettenkapitän Dollmann
Markgraf	Kapitän zur See Seiferling	Korvettenkapitän Teichmann	Korvettenkapitän Schumann
Kronprinz	Kapitän zur See Feldt	Korvettenkapitän Tietgens	Korvettenkapitän Habedank
Kaiser	Kapitän zur See Freiherr von Keyserlingk	Korvettenkapitän Karcher	Korvettenkapitän von Hugo
Prinzregent Luitpold	Kapitän zur See Heuser	Fregattenkapitän Schubart	Korvettenkapitän Lohmann
Kaiserin	Kapitän zur See Sievers	Korvettenkapitän Dombrowsky	Korvettenkapitän Wehner

Reconnaissance Forces

Commander (BdA): Vizeadmiral Hipper
I Admiral Staff Offizier: Korvettenkapitän Raeder

I Reconnaissance Group (I AG)

Ship	Commander	I Offizier	I Artillerie Offizier
Lützow	Kapitän zur See Harder	Fregattenkapitän Hillebrand	Korvettenkapitän Paschen
Derfflinger	Kapitän zur See Hartog	Korvettenkapitän Fischer	Korvettenkapitän von Hase
Seydlitz	Kapitän zur See von Egidy	Korvettenkapitän von Alvensleben	Korvettenkapitän Foerster
Moltke	Kapitän zur See von Karpf	Korvettenkapitän von Rebensburg	Kapitänleutnant Schirmacher
von der Tann	Kapitän zur See Zenker	Korvettenkapitän Scheibe	Korvettenkapitän Mahrholz

II Reconnaissance Group (II AG)

Leader: Kontreadmiral Boedicker
Admiral Staff Offizier: Kapitänleutnant Stapenhorst

Ship	Commander	I Offizier	I Artillerie Offizier
Frankfurt	Kapitän zur See Thilo von Trotha	Kapitänleutnant Hoppenstedt	Kapitänleutnant Kraus
Pillau	Fregattenkapitän Mommsen	Korvettenkapitän Berrenberg	Kapitänleutnant von Blanquet
Elbing	Fregattenkapitän Madlung	Kapitänleutnant Werber	Kapitänleutnant Witzell
Wiesbaden	Kapitän zur See Reiß	Kapitänleutnant Berger	Kapitänleutnant Wende

IV Reconnaissance Group (IV AG)

Leader: Kapitän zur See and Kommodore von Reuter
Admiral Staff Offizier: Korvettenkapitän Heinrich Weber

Ship	Commander	I Offizier	I Artillerie Offizier
Stettin	Fregattenkapitän Rebensburg	Kapitänleutnant Zores	Kapitänleutnant Pierstorff
München	Korvettenkapitän Böcker	Kapitänleutnant von Koblinski	Kapitänleutnant Bornebusch
Frauenlob	Fregattenkapitän Hoffmann	Kapitänleutnant Schroeder	Kapitänleutnant Scherzer
Stuttgart	Fregattenkapitän Hagedorn	Kapitänleutnant Mertens	Oberleutnant zur See Croll

Torpedoboote Flottilles of the I FdT (Leader of Torpedobootes)

I Leader of Torpedobootes: Kapitän zur See and Kommodore Michelsen
Admiral Staff Offizier: Korvettenkapitän Junkermann

Ship	Commander	I Offizier	I Artillerie Offizier
Rostock	Fregattenkapitän Feldmann	Kapitänleutnant Gerlach	Kapitänleutnant Knobloch

I Torpedoboote Flottille

Chief: Kapitänleutnant Conrad Albecht

1 Half Flottille: Chief Kapitänleutnant Conrad Albecht
G39 Oberleutnant zur See von Loefen
G40 Kapitänleutnant Richard Bietzen

G38 Kapitänleutnant Metger
S32 Kapitänleutnant Froelich

II Torpedoboote Flottille

Chief: Fregattenkapitän Schuur
B98 Oberleutnant zur See Meese

3 Half Flottille Chief: Korvettenkapitän Boest
G101 Kapitänleutnant Schulte
G102 Kapitänleutnant von Varendorf
B112 Kapitänleutnant August Claußen
B97 Kapitänleutnant Leo Riedel

4 Half Flottille Chief: Korvettenkapitän Dithmar
B109 Kapitänleutnant Hahndorff
B110 Kapitänleutnant Vollheim
B111 Kapitänleutnant Schickhardt
G103 Kapitänleutnant Fritz Spieß
G104 Kapitänleutnant von Bartenwerffer

III Torpedoboote Flottille

Chief: Korvettenkapitän Hollmann
S53 Kapitänleutnant Friedrich Götting

5 Half Flottille Chief: Kapitänleutnant Gautier
V71 Oberleutnant zur See Ulrich
V73 Kapitänleutnant Delbrück
G88 Kapitänleutnant Scabell

6 Half Flottille Chief: KKapitän Theodor Riedel
S54 Kapitänleutnant Karlowa
V48 Kapitänleutnant Friedrich Eckoldt
G42 Kapitänleutnant von Arnim

V Torpedoboote Flottille

G11 Kapitänleutnant Adolf Müller

9 Half Flottille Chief: Kapitänleutnant Hoefer
V2 Kapitänleutnant Hoefer
V4 Kapitänleutnant Barop
V6 Oberleutnant zur See Berebdt
V1 Oberleutnant zur See Röthig
V3 Kapitänleutnant von Killinger

10 Half Flottille Chief: Kapitänleutnant Klein
G8 Oberleutnant zur See Rodenberg
G7 Kapitänleutnant Weineck
V5 Oberleutnant zur See Tils
G9 Kapitänleutnant Anschütz
G10 Oberleutnant zur See Haumann

Torpedoboote Flottilles of the II FdT

II FdT: Kapitän zur See and Kommodore Heinrich
Admiral Staff Offizier: Kapitänleutnant Mejer

Ship	Commander	I Offizier	I Artillerie Offizier
Regensburg	Fregattenkapitän Heuberer	Kapitänleutnant Schepke	Kapitänleutnant von dem Borne

VI Torpedoboote Flottille

Chief: Korvettenkapitän Max Schultz.
G41 Kapitänleutnant Boehm

11 Half Flottille Chief: Kapitänleutnant Rümann	12 Half Flottille Chief: Kapitänleutnant Lahs
V44 Kapitänleutnant von Holleuffer	*V69* Kapitänleutnant Stecher
G87 Kapitänleutnant Karstens	*V45* Kapitänleutnant Laßmann
G86 Kapitänleutnant Grimm	*V46* Kapitänleutnant Krumhaar
	S50 Kapitänleutnant Recke
	G37 Kapitänleutnant Wolf von Trotha

VII Torpedoboote Flottille

Chief: Korvettenkapitän von Koch
S24 Oberleutnant zur See Otto Schniewind

13 Half Flottille Chief: Kapitänleutnant von Zitzewitz	14 Half Flottille Chief: Korvettenkapitän Cordes
S15 Oberleutnant zur See Schmidt	S19 Oberleutnant zur See Rode
S17 Kapitänleutnant von Puttkamer	S23 Kapitänleutnant von Killinger
S20 Kapitänleutnant Benecke	V189 Kapitänleutnant Mootz
S16 Kapitänleutnant Walther Loeffler	
S18 Kapitänleutnant Haushalter	

IX Torpedoboote Flottille

Chief: Korvettenkapitän Goehle
V28 Kapitänleutnant Lenssen

17 Half Flottille Chief: Kapitänleutnant Ehrhardt	18 Half Flottille Chief: Korvettenkapitän Tillessen
V27 Oberleutnant zur See Buddecke	*V30* Oberleutnant zur See Ernst Wolf
V26 Kapitänleutnant Köhler	*S34* Kapitänleutnant Andersen
S36 Kapitänleutnant Fischer	*S33* Kapitänleutnant von Wünch
S51 Kapitänleutnant Dette	*V29* Kapitänleutnant Steinbrinck
S52 Kapitänleutnant Ehrentraut	*S35* Kapitänleutnant Ihn

U-Bootes

Leader: Fregattenkapitän and Kommodore Hermann Bauer
Admiral Staff Offizier: Korvettenkapitän Friedrich Lützow

Ship	Commander	I Offizier	I Artillerie Offizier
Hamburg	Korvettenkapitän von Gaudecker	Kapitänleutnant Heinemann	Kapitänleutnant Mohr

1 U-Half Flottille
U74 Kapitänleutnant Weisbach
U72 Kapitänleutnant Krafft
UB21 Kapitänleutnant Hashagen
UB22 Oberleutnant zur See Putzier
UB27 Kapitänleutnant Dieckmann
U75 Kapitänleutnant Curt Beitzen

2 U-Half Flottille
U51 Kapitänleutnant Rumpel
U52 Kapitänleutnant Walther
U53 Kapitänleutnant Rose

3 U-Half Flottille
U47 Kapitänleutnant Metzger
U24 Kapitänleutnant Schneider
U43 Kapitänleutnant Jürst
U44 Kapitänleutnant Wagenführ
U46 Kapitänleutnant Leo Hillebrand

4 U-Half Flottille
U32 Kapitänleutnant Freiherr Spiegel von und zu Peckelsheim
U67 Kapitänleutnant Nieland
U63 Kapitänleutnant Otto Schultze
U66 Kapitänleutnant von Bothmer
U70 Kapitänleutnant Wünsche

U-Flottille Flanders
UB6 Oberleutnant zur See Neumann
UB10 Oberleutnant zur See Salzwedel
UB12 Oberleutnant zur See Kiel
UB17 Oberleutnant zur See Wenninger
UB18 Oberleutnant zur See Steinbrinck
UB19 Kapitänleutnant Becker

UB23 Oberleutnant zur See Voigt
UB29 Oberleutnant zur See Pustkuchen
UC1 Oberleutnant zur See Ramien
UC6 Oberleutnant zur See Ehrentraut
UC10 Oberleutnant zur See Nitzsche

Naval Airship Department

Commander: Korvettenkapitän Peter Strasser

L9 Hauptmann z.D. Stelling
L11 Korvettenkapitän Schütze
L13 Kapitänleutnant der Reserve Prölß
L14 Kapitänleutnant der Reserve Böcker
L16 Oberleutnant zur See Peterson
L17 Kapitänleutnant Ehrlich

L21 Kapitänleutnant der Reserve Max Dietrich
L22 Kapitänleutnant Martin Dietrich
L23 Kapitänleutnant von Schubert
L24 Kapitänleutnant Robert Koch

The Grand Fleet

Admiral Jellicoe
Chief of Staff: Vice Admiral Madden

2 Battle Squadron

Vice Admiral Jerram
Rear Admiral Leveson

1 Division		2 Division	
King George V	Captain Field	*Orion*	Captain Backhouse
Ajax	Captain Baird	*Monarch*	Captain Borrett
Centurion	Captain Culm–	*Conqueror*	Captain Tothill
Erin	Seymour	*Thunderer*	Captain Fergusson
	Captain Stanley		

Attached: *Boadicea* Captain Woollcombe

4 Battle Squadron

Vice Admiral Sturdee
Rear Admiral Duff

3 Division		4 Division	
Iron Duke	Captain Dreyer	*Benbow*	Captain Henry Parker
Royal Oak	Captain MacLachlan	*Bellerophon*	Captain Breuen
Superb	Captain Edmond	*Temeraire*	Captain Underhill
Canada	Parker	*Vanguard*	Captain Dick
	Captain Nicholson		

Attached: *Blanche* Captain Casement

1 Battle Squadron

Vice Admiral Burney
Chief of Staff: Captain Grant
Rear Admiral Gaunt

5 Division		6 Division	
Colossus	Captain Pound	*Marlborough*	Captain Ross
Collingwood	Captain Ley	*Revenge*	Captain Kiddle
Neptune	Captain Bernard	*Hercules*	Captain Clinton–Baker
St Vincent	Captain Fisher	*Agincourt*	Captain Doughty

Attached: *Bellona* Captain Dutton

3 Battle Cruiser Squadron

Rear Admiral Hood

Invincible	Captain Cay
Inflexible	Captain Heaton–Ellis
Indomitable	Captain Kennedy

Attached: *Chester* Captain Lawson
Canterbury Captain Royds

1 Cruiser Squadron

Rear Admiral Arbuthnot

Defence	Captain Ellis	*Duke of Edinburgh*	Captain Blackett
Warrior	Captain Molteno	*Black Prince*	Captain Bonham

2 Cruiser Squadron

Rear Admiral Heath

Minotaur	Captain D'Aeth	*Cochrane*	Captain Leatham
Hampshire	Captain Savill	*Shannon*	Captain Dumaresq

4 Light Cruiser Squadron

Calliope Commodore Le Mesurier

Constance	Captain Townsend	*Royalist*	Captain Meade
Caroline	Captain Crooke	*Comus*	Captain Hotham

Destroyer Flotillas

12 Flotilla	11 Flotilla	4 Flotilla
Faulknor Captain Stirling	*Castor* Commodore Hawksley	*Tipperary* Captain Wintour
Marksman Commander Sulivan	*Kempenfelt* Commander Sulivan	*Broke* Commander Allen
Obedient Commander Campbell	*Ossory* Commander Dundas	*Achates* Commander Hutchinson
Maenad Commander Champion	*Mystic* Commander Allsup	*Porpoise* Commander Colville
Opal Commander Sumner	*Moon* Commander Irvin	*Spitfire* Lt-Cmmdr Trelawny
Mary Rose Lt-Cmmdr Homan	*Morning* Star Lt-Cmmdr	*Unity* Lt-Cmmdr Lecky
Marvel Lt-Cmmdr Grubb	Fletcher	*Garland* Lt-Cmmdr Goff
Menace Lt-Cmmdr Poignand	*Magic* Lt-Cmmdr Wynter	*Ambuscade* Lt-Cmmdr Coles
Nessus Lt-Cmmdr Carter	*Mounsey* Lt-Cmmdr Eyre	*Ardent* Lt-Cmmdr Marsden
Narwhal Lt-Cmmdr Hudson	*Mandate* Lt-Cmmdr Lawrie	*Fortune* Lt-Cmmdr Terry
Mindful Lt-Cmmdr Ridley	*Marne* Lt-Cmmdr Hartford	*Sparrowhawk* Lt-Cmmdr
Onslaught Lt-Cmmdr Onslow	*Minion* Lt-Cmmdr Rawlings	Hopkins
Munster Lt-Cmmdr Russell	*Manners* Lt-Cmmdr Harrison	*Contest* Lt-Cmmdr Master
Nonsuch Lt-Cmmdr Lyon	*Michael* Lt-Cmmdr Bate	*Shark* Commander Jones
Noble Lt-Cmmdr Boxer	*Mons* Lt-Cmmdr Makin	*Acasta* Lt-Cmmdr Barron
Mischief Lt-Cmmdr Ward	*Martial* Lt-Cmmdr Harrison	*Christopher* Lt-Cmmdr Kerr
	Milbrook Lt-Cmmdr Naylor	*Owl* Commander Hamond
		Hardy Commander Plowden
		Midge Lt-Cmmdr Cavendish
		Ophelia Lt-Cmmdr Crabbe

Attached: *Oak* Lieutenant-Commander Faviell
Abdiel Commander Curtis

Battle Cruise Fleet

Vice Admiral Beatty
Chief of Staff: Captain Bentick

Lion Captain Chatfield

1 Battle Cruiser Squadron

Rear Admiral de Brock

Princess Royal	Captain Cowan
Queen Mary	Captain Prowse
Tiger	Captain Pelly

2 Battle Cruiser Squadron

Rear Admiral Pakenham

New Zealand	Captain Green
Indefatigable	Captain Sowerby

5 Battle Squadron

Rear Admiral Evan–Thomas

Barham	Captain Craig
Valiant	Captain Woollcombe
Warspite	Captain Phillpotts
Malaya	Captain Boyle

1 Light Cruise Squadron

Commodore Alexander–Sinclair

Galatea	Cdore Alexander–	*Inconstant*	Captain Thesiger
Phaeton	Sinclair	*Cordelia*	Captain Beamish
	Captain Cameron		

2 Light Cruiser Squadron

Commodore Goodenough

Southampton	Cdore Goodenough	*Nottingham*	Captain Miller
Birmingham	Captain Duff	*Dublin*	Captain Scott

3 Light Cruiser Squadron

Rear Admiral Napier

Falmouth	Captain Edwards	*Birkenhead*	Captain Reeves
Yarmouth	Captain Pratt	*Gloucester*	Captain Blunt

Destroyer Flotillas

1 Flotilla
Fearless Captain Roper
Acheron Commander Ramsey
Ariel Lt-Cmmdr Tippet
Attack Lt-Cmmdr James
Hydra Lieutenant Glossop
Badger Commander Fremantle
Goshawk Commander Moir
Defender Lt-Cmmdr Palmer
Lizard Lt-Cmmdr Brooke
Lapwing Lt-Cmmdr Gye

13 Flotilla
Champion Captain Farie
Nestor Commander Bingham
Nomad Lt-Cmmdr Whitfield
Narborough Lt-Cmmdr Corlett
Obdurate Lt-Cmmdr Sams
Petard Lt-Cmmdr Thomson
Pelican Lt-Cmmdr Beattie
*Nerissa*Lt-Cmmdr Legge
Onslow Lt-Cmmdr Tovey
Moresby Lt-Cmmdr Alison
Nicator Lieutenant Mocatta

9 and 10 Flotillas
Lydiard Commander Goldsmith
Liberty Lt-Cmmdr King
Landrail Lt-Cmmdr Hobart
Laurel Lieutenant Stanistreet

Moorsom Commander Hodgson
Morris Lt-Cmmdr Graham
Turbulent Lt-Cmmdr Stuart
Termagant Lt-Cmmdr Blake

Seaplane Carrier: *Engadine* Lieutenant-Commander Robinson

Index

Abdiel, 25, 178, 231, 232, 266
Acasta, 96, 98–9, 100, 111
Achates, 190, 193, 197, 199
Acheron, 267
AG I, 5–8, 11–12, 14–15, 17–18, 20–1, 25, 27, 29, 35, 36–8, 43, 46–7, 51, 64, 68, 72, 78, 80–2, 84, 89, 93, 96, 99, 116, 121, 126–7, 128, 133, 136, 145, 148–9, 151–2, 154, 162–3, 166, 179, 231, 249–51, 261
AG II, 6–8, 10, 13–15, 17–18, 21, 27, 29, 32, 36–7, 43, 46–7, 63, 82, 93–101, 104, 133, 161, 166, 177, 180–1, 197, 229, 249–50, 256, 261
Agincourt, 104, 116, 134, 137, 142, 151, 157, 219, 265
Aircraft;
    291, 10
    503, 16
    505, 10
    508, 10
    541, 10
    553, 10
Ajax, 137, 265
Alexander-Sinclair, Commodore, 42–3, 267
Alyssum, 4
Ambuscade, 14, 190, 193, 197, 199
Amelung, Marine Oberstabs Arzt Dr, 228, 258
Andersen, Kapitänleutnant. 263
Anschütz, Kapitänleutnant, 262
Arabis, 4–6
Ardent, 14, 193, 197, 199, 203, 233
Arethusa, 4, 6 ,42, 183
Ariel, 267
Arnim, Kapitänleutnant, 123, 262
Aßmann, Korvettenkapitän, 260
Australia, 14

B97, 4–5, 97, 262
B98, 97, 262
B109, 4, 42, 93, 262
B110, 4, 42, 97, 262
B111, 4–5, 262
B112, 4–5, 97, 262
Badger, 267
Barham, 44, 63, 65–6, 72, 78, 82–4, 103, 134, 137, 203, 219, 267
Barop, Kapitänleutnant, 262
Bartels. Kapitän zur See, 213, 260
Bartenwerffer, von Kapitänleutnant, 262

Battle Cruiser Squadron 1, 39, 41, 45–6, 96–7, 99–100, 111–12, 115, 137, 266
Battle Cruiser Squadron 2, 36, 39, 46, 82, 87, 96, 99, 111, 115, 128, 137, 266
Battle Cruiser Squadron 3, 28, 93, 95–6, 98–9, 104, 111–14, 119, 127–30, 137, 160, 249–50, 265
Battle Squadron 1, 28, 150–1, 234, 251, 265
Battle Squadron 2, 28, 35, 39, 150, 156–7, 160, 170, 186, 204, 219, 251, 265
Battle Squadron 3, 13
Battle Squadron 4, 150, 160, 204, 219, 265
Battle Squadron 5, 19, 28, 39, 44–7, 62–6, 71–2, 75, 80–7, 96, 100, 102, 108, 130, 157, 168, 178, 188, 204–205, 219, 250, 266
Bauer, Fregattenkapitän, 30, 38, 264
Bayern, 2–3, 39
BdA, 17–18, 33, 36–7, 126, 224, 261
Beatty, Vice Admiral, 10, 12, 14, 24, 28, 39–51, 57, 62, 66–7, 71, 81–104, 108, 111–15, 127–8, 150, 160, 162, 168–79, 201, 216–19, 221, 231, 234, 242–4, 247–51, 266
Becker, Korvettenkapitän, 260
Behncke, Kapitän zur See Friedrich, 214, 260
Behncke, Kontreadmiral Paul. 12, 25, 29, 72, 87, 89, 101, 118, 249, 260
Beitzen, Kapitänleutnant Curt, 264
Beitzen, Kapitänleutnant Richard, 224–6
Bellerophon, 116, 137, 140, 265
Bellona, 265
Benbow, 116, 137, 221, 265
Bendemann, Korvettenkapitän, 260
Benecke, Kapitänleutnant, 263
Berger, Kapitänleutnant, 261
Berrenberg, Korvettenkapitän, 261
Bethmann-Hollweg, Chancellor, 28
Biarritz, 15
Birkenhead, 267
Birmingham, 71, 76–8, 182, 204, 267
Black Prince, 104, 189–90, 199, 201, 203, 266
Blanche, 265
Blanquet, Kapitänleutnant von, 261
Blothuis, Korvettenkapitän, 260
Boadicea, 20, 35, 265
Böcker, Korvettenkapitän, 38, 261
Böcker, Kapitänleutnant der Reserve, 264
Bode, Kapitänleutnant Gustav, 114

Boedicker, Kontreadmiral/Vizeadmiral, 17–21, 37, 47, 93, 96, 99, 101, 104, 133, 151, 161, 180, 249, 261
Boehm, Kapitänleutnant Hermann, 263
Boest, Korvettenkapitän, 262
Bölken, Kapitän zur See, 213, 260
Boreas, 230
Borne, Kapitänleutnant von dem, 263
Bornebusch, Kapitänleutnant, 261
Bremen, 249
Brock, Rear Admiral, 266
Broke, 190, 193–4, 197, 204, 233
Brökelmann, Korvettenkapitän, 260
Brüninghaus, Kapitän zur See, 260
Buddecke, Oberleutnant zur See, 263
Burney, Vice Admiral, 104, 188, 219, 251, 265
Buttercup, 4

Calliope, 109, 162, 170, 266
Canada, 116, 137, 265
Canterbury, 93, 98, 104, 266
Caroline, 168–70, 174, 251, 266
Castor, 161–2, 168, 180–1, 204
Centurion, 40, 137, 265
Champion, 67, 71, 189, 205, 207, 211, 215, 226, 267
Chester, 93–6, 100, 104, 265
Christopher, 96
Cleopatra, 9–12, 21, 42
Cochrane, 266
Collingwood, 116, 137, 157, 265
Colossus, 116, 134–7, 143, 157, 221, 265
Comus, 6, 162, 169–70, 266
Conqueror, 116, 265
Conquest, 9, 11, 21, 119
Constance, 162, 266
Contest, 190, 193–4, 197, 199, 225
Cordelia, 42, 267
Cordes, Korvettenkapitän, 263
Croll, Oberleutnant zur See, 261
Cruiser Squadron 1, 39, 95, 100, 104, 107, 119, 251, 266
Cruiser Squadron 2, 177, 266
Cruiser Squadron 3, 10, 13, 245

D1, 232
D4, 22, 25
D6, 25
Dalwigk zu Lichtenfels, KA Freiher von, 73, 166, 172, 260
Danzig, 182
Defence, 95, 100, 104, 106–108, 111, 115, 124, 199, 201, 266
Defender, 99, 267
Delbrück, Kapitänleutnant, 262
Derfflinger, 6–7, 12–13, 18, 20–1, 36, 48, 50–2, 59–61, 78, 80, 82, 87, 96, 100, 106, 114–15,

119, 126, 133, 135–40, 145–8, 151, 163–4, 166, 176–7, 211, 229, 232, 238–9, 261
Dette, Kapitänleutnant, 253, 263
Deutschland, 72, 166, 215, 260
Dithmar, Korvettenkapitän, 42, 262
Dollmann, Korvettenkapitän, 260
Dombrowsky, Korvettenkapitän, 260
Dublin, 76, 168, 182, 186, 195, 234, 267
Duff, Rear Admiral, 265
Duff, Captain, 267
Duke of Edinburgh, 35, 100, 104, 135, 200, 266

E5, 8
E22, 22, 24
E23, 31
E24, 12
E26, 22–4, 232
E29, 22
E31, 25, 27
E34, 25
E41, 14
E53, 25
E55, 22, 24–5, 232
Eckoldt, Kapitänleutnant Friedrich, 123, 262
Egidy, Kapitän zur See, 36, 187, 261
Ehrentraut, Kapitänleutnant, 263
Ehrentraut, Oberleutnant zur See, 264
Ehrhardt, Kapitänleutnant, 153, 263
Elbing, 14, 20, 37, 42–3, 45, 93, 95, 100, 180–2, 186, 189, 191, 203–204, 261
Elle, Korvettenkapitän, 260
Engelhardt, Kontreadmiral, 259
Erin, 265
Evan-Thomas, Rear Admiral, 44–5, 62, 66, 72, 82, 87, 91, 108, 111, 250, 267

Faber, Kapitänleutnant, 260
Falmouth, 44, 111, 127, 160, 170, 267
Farie, Captain, 189, 205, 267
Faulknor, 158, 207, 212
I FdT, 4, 6, 10–11, 29, 32, 38, 71, 123, 133–4, 159, 174–5, 195, 208, 217, 249–50, 262
II FdT, 8, 10–12, 33, 37, 67–8, 97, 132–3, 150–2, 159, 175–6, 217, 227, 249–50, 263
Fearless, 188, 219, 236, 267
Feldmann, Kapitän zur See. 195
Feldmann, Fregattenkapitän Otto, 38, 262
Feldt, Kapitän zur See, 260
Fenger, Pfarrer, 62, 229–30
Fischer, Kapitänleutnant Franz, 153, 263
Fischer, Kapitänleutnant Wolfgang, 139
Fischer, Max. Korvettenkapitän. 261
Foerster, Korvettenkapitän, 52, 54, 61, 66, 165, 187, 261
Fortune, 190, 193, 197, 199
Frankfurt, 14, 37, 43, 63, 93, 95, 100, 104, 157, 179–80, 207, 222, 261

Franz, Kapitänleutnant, 199, 259
Frauenlob, 13, 38, 182–6, 249, 261
Friedrich der Große, 18, 25, 74, 76, 91, 109, 111, 121, 132, 149–51, 199–201, 259
Froelich, Kapitänleutnant, 262
Frömsdorf, Kapitänleutnant, 259

G7, 209, 262
G8, 209, 262
G9, 209, 262
G10 209, 262
G11 162, 209, 233, 262
G37, 96, 126, 133, 151, 159, 224–7, 263
G38, 126, 133, 224–7, 262
G39, 126, 133, 177, 188, 262
G40, 126, 133, 224–7, 262
G41, 4, 24, 97, 151–2, 159, 263
G42, 4, 123, 151, 159, 209, 262
G85, 4
G86, 151–2, 263
G87, 151, 263
G88, 123, 134, 151, 154, 203–204, 262
G101, 4, 68, 96, 262
G102, 4, 96, 262
G103, 4, 96–7, 262
G104, 4, 68, 96–7, 262
G193, 11–12
G194, 11–12
G class British submarines:
    G1, 25
    G2, 25
    G4, 25
    G5, 25
Gagern, Korvettenkapitän Freiherr von, 260
Galatea, 27, 35, 36, 42–3, 267
Garland, 14, 180, 190, 197, 199, 225
Gaunt, Rear Admiral, 265
Gautier, Kapitänleutnant, 262
Gelhaar, Florus Marine Stabsärtze, 138
Gerlach, Kapitänleutnant, 262
Gloucester, 95, 267
Goehle, Korvettenkapitän, 68, 96, 151–3, 159, 250, 263
Goette, Kapitän zur See, 260
Goodenough, Commodore, 67, 71–2, 93, 103, 135, 170, 250, 267
Gorissen, Korvettenkapitän von, 259
Goshawk, 25, 267
Götting, Kapitänleutnant Friedrich, 262
Graudenz, 13
Grimm, Kapitänleutnant Conrad, 151, 263
Großer Kurfürst, 72, 75, 78, 83, 104, 135, 141–2, 150, 212–13, 260

H class British submarines:
    H5, 21
    H7, 9
    H10, 21

Habedank, Korvettenkapitän, 260
Habler, Oberleutnant zur See Harry, 54
Hagedorn, Korvettenkapitän, 38, 186, 261
Hahn, Kapitän zur See Max, 2
Hahn, Oberingenieur, 184
Hahndorff, Kapitänleutnant, 262
Hamburg, 32, 38, 161, 181–2, 186, 189, 264
Hampshire, 31, 161, 200, 266
Hannover, 73, 92, 166–7, 177, 213–14, 260
Harder, Kapitän zur See, 36, 126, 223–5, 261
Hartog, Kapitän zur See/Kommodore, 4–5, 11, 18, 36, 126, 136, 148, 261
Hase, Korvettenkapitän von, 51, 61–2, 106, 114, 135–6, 140, 145–8, 164, 261
Haumann, Oberleutnant zur See, 262
Haushalter, Kapitänleutnant, 263
Hausser, Kapitänleutnant, 106
Hawksley, Commodore, 180, 205, 217
Heath, Rear Admiral, 266
Heine, Kapitän zur See, 260
Heinecke, Korvettenkapitän, 176, 209, 262
Heinemann, Kapitänleutnant, 264
Heinrich, Kapitän zur See/Kommodore, 33, 36–7, 67–8, 97, 132–3, 150, 159, 174, 176–7, 203, 250, 263
Heinrich, Prinz von Preußen, 3
Helf, Korvettenkapitän, 259
Helgoland, 76, 92, 109, 111, 143, 198–9, 234, 259
Hercules, 104, 116, 137, 141, 157, 219, 221, 242, 265
Hermann, Kapitänleutnant, 259
Hessen, 72–3, 166–7, 201, 211, 213, 260
Heuberer, Fregattenkapitän, 37, 263
Heuser, Kapitän zur See, 260
Hillebrand, Fregattenkapitän Leo, 236, 264
Hillebrand, Fregattenkapitän Otto, 261
Hinsch, Korvettenkapitän, 259
Hoefer, Kapitänleutnant, 262
Hoffmann, Fregattenkapitän Georg, 38, 186, 261
Hollmann, Korvettenkapitän, 123, 133, 151, 154, 176, 262
Hood, Rear Admiral, 93, 95, 98, 111, 150, 265
Höpfner, Kapitän zur See, 198, 259
Hoppenstedt, Kapitänleutnant, 261
Hugo, Korvettenkapitän von, 260
Hydra, 267

Ihn, Kapitänleutnant Friedrich, 70, 153, 263
Inconstant, 42, 267
Indefatigable, 48, 50–7, 65, 75–6, 81, 84, 173, 201, 221, 231, 233, 266
Indomitable, 95, 98, 119, 162, 164, 167, 221, 265
Inflexible, 95, 97–8, 112, 128, 157, 162, 265
Invincible, 95, 98, 112–15, 124, 127, 201, 221, 231, 240, 265
Iron Duke, 109, 111, 116, 119, 137, 141, 157, 159–60, 169–71, 217, 219, 236, 265

Jackson, Captain, 33, 71
Jellicoe, Admiral, 14, 18, 25, 27–8, 33, 39–40,
  48, 66, 71, 93, 102–108, 111, 127–9, 135,
  137, 150, 156, 158–60, 169–74, 178–80, 188,
  204–207, 210, 212, 216–21, 231, 234, 238,
  240–3, 248, 250–1, 265
Jerram. Vice Admiral, 39, 150, 156, 169–70, 251,
  265
Johnke, Maschinisten, 184
Jung, Kapitänleutnant Hermann, 45
Junkermann, Korvettenkapitän, 262

Kahlert, Korvettenkapitän, 260
Kaiser Wilhelm II, 3, 185, 225, 234, 239, 246,
  251
Kaiser, 2, 6, 25, 29, 73–5, 84, 91, 99, 104, 107,
  116, 135, 137, 142, 149–50, 162, 234, 260
Kaiserin, 25, 29, 72, 76, 84, 91, 109, 149–50, 201,
  233–4, 260
Kameke, Kapitän zur See von, 259
Karcher, Korvettenkapitän, 260
Karlowa, Kapitänleutnant, 123, 203, 262
Karpf, Kapitän zur See Johannes von, 2, 36,
  186, 261
Karstens, Kapitänleutnant, 263
Keyserlingk, Kapitän zur See Freiherr von, 260
Killinger, Kapitänleutnant von, 263
Killinger, Kapitänleutnant Manfred, 262
King George V, 111, 135, 137, 168–71, 219, 265
Klappenbach, Kapitän zur See, 259
Klehe, Korvettenkapitän, 260
Klein, Kapitänleutnant Friedrich, 262
Knobloch, Kapitänleutnant, 262
Koblinski, Kapitänleutnant von, 261
Koch, Korvettenkapitän von, 157, 175, 180, 209,
  263
Koch, Kapitänleutnant, 219, 264
Köhler, Kapitänleutnant Hans, 70, 263
König Albert, 6, 38
König, 6, 25, 29, 38, 72–8, 82–3, 89, 101, 107,
  109, 111–12, 116, 118–19, 124, 135, 137, 141,
  149–50, 154, 174, 177, 212, 249, 260
Korndörfer, Kapitänleutnant, 260
Kraft, 230
Kraus, Kapitänleutnant, 261
Kronprinz, 25, 29, 75, 84, 104, 142, 149–50,
  212–13, 234, 260
Küsel, Kapitän zur See Hans, 199, 259

L9, 14, 21, 264
L11, 195, 219–22, 236, 264
L13, 219, 264
L14, 104, 264
L16, 264
L17, 219, 264
L19, 24
L21, 14, 104, 264

L22, 219, 264
L23, 104, 264
L24, 219, 221, 231, 264
Laertes, 9–10, 21
Laffert, Korvettenkapitän von, 259
Lahs, Kapitänleutnant, 96, 262
Landrail, 205, 267
Lange, Obermatrosen, 88, 165,
Lange, Kapitän zur See Richard, 191, 198, 259
Lassoo, 9, 11–12
Laurel, 9, 62, 205, 267
Laverock, 9–10
Lenssen, Kapitänleutnant, 263
Leveson, Rear Admiral, 265
Levetzow, Kapitän zur See Magnus von, 2, 259
Liberty, 9, 205, 267
Light Cruiser Squadron 1, 25, 42, 71, 82
Light Cruiser Squadron 2, 46, 67, 71–2, 75–6,
  78, 82, 84, 135, 158, 168, 170, 182, 186, 205,
  249, 267
Light Cruiser Squadron 3, 71, 160, 221, 267
Light Cruiser Squadron 4, 14, 30, 157, 162, 168,
  170, 251, 266
Light Cruiser Squadron 5, 9, 11, 19, 21
Lion, 44, 48, 50–1, 57–62, 67, 70–6, 80–7, 100,
  102, 104, 111, 128, 138, 162, 164, 166, 170,
  266
Loefen, Oberleutnant zur See von, 126, 262
Loeffler, Kapitänleutnant, 263
Lohmann, Korvettenkapitän, 260
Löwe, Kapitänleutnant, 66
Lützow, 7, 10, 12, 17–18, 20–1, 29, 36–7, 45–51,
  57–9, 66, 72, 78, 80, 82, 84, 87–8, 96, 99,
  104–106, 111–15, 124–8, 133, 137–9, 151,
  159, 174, 204, 221–7, 234, 238, 249–51, 261
Lydiard, 205, 267

Madden, Vice Admiral, 265
Madlung, Fregattenkapitän, 37, 191, 261
Maenad, 212, 214–15, 226
Magic, 181
Mahrholz, Korvettenkapitän, 15, 46, 52, 55, 64,
  81, 261
Malaya, 52, 63, 65, 75, 80, 82, 86–9, 109, 137,
  187–8, 204, 219, 267
Mandate, 266
Manners, 266
Mardersteig, Fähnrich zur See, 126, 139, 238
Markgraf, 6, 75, 78, 84, 104, 108, 116, 119, 124,
  135–6, 142, 149–50, 162, 199, 212–13, 260
Marksman, 195, 203, 212, 215, 226, 234, 266
Marlborough, 102, 104, 108, 116, 128–9, 134–7,
  151, 157, 160, 188–9, 204, 219, 221, 236–7, 265
Marne, 181, 266
Martial, 266
Marvel, 158, 212, 266
Mary Rose, 212, 266

Mauve, Kontreadmiral, 29, 72, 124, 166, 168, 177, 250, 260
Medusa, 9–12
Meese, Oberleutnant zur See, 262
Mejer, Kapitänleutnant, 263
Menace, 207, 212, 266
Mertens, Kapitänleutnant, 261
Mesurier, Commodore, 250–1, 266
Meteor, 9
Metzger, Kapitänleutnant, 264
Meurer, Kapitän zur See Hugo, 260
Michael, 266
Midge, 266
Milbrock, 266
Mindful, 158, 212, 214, 266
Minion, 266
Minotaur, 170, 266
Mischief, 266
Moltke, 2, 6–7, 10, 13, 20, 29, 36, 48, 50–1, 54–5, 62–5, 78, 80, 88, 135, 145, 163, 166, 177, 179, 181, 186–8, 232, 244, 261
Mommsen, Kapitän zur See, 37, 261
Monarch, 116, 119, 129, 137–8, 265
Mons, 266
Monsey, 266
Moon, 266
Moorsom, 67, 267
Mootz, Oberleutnant zur See, 263
Moresby, 67, 205, 207, 212, 215, 226, 267
Morning Star, 266
Morris, 9, 70, 205, 267
Möve, 6
Müller, Kapitänleutnant Adolf, 262
Müller, Obermaschinist Max, 182, 185
München, 38, 161, 182, 186, 261
Munster, 212, 266
Mystic, 266

Napier, Rear Admiral, 127–8, 160, 267
Narborough, 67, 205, 267
Narwhal, 212, 214, 266
Nassau, 25, 77, 92, 109, 119, 166, 169, 189–93, 196, 199–204, 211, 214, 234, 259
Natzmer, Kapitän zur See von, 259
Neptune, 14, 116, 134, 137, 265
Nerissa, 67, 70, 205, 267
Nessus, 212
Nestor, 67, 91–3, 233, 267
New Zealand, 14, 48, 50–1, 55, 62, 65, 80, 111, 128, 141, 162, 164–7, 266
Nicator, 67, 205, 267
Noble, 212, 267
Nomad, 67–8, 91–3, 233, 267
Nonsuch, 100, 207, 266
Nordmann, Kontreadmiral, 260
Nöthig, Kapitänleutnant, 259
Nottingham, 67–8, 71, 76, 182, 267

Oak, 266
Obdurate, 67, 70, 205, 207, 212, 215, 226, 267
Obedient, 158, 212, 266
Ossory, 266
Oldekop, Kapitänleutnant, 91, 201
Oldenburg, 76, 92, 109, 198, 259
Onslaught, 158, 212–14, 266
Onslow, 67, 99, 119, 267
Opal, 42, 266
Ophelia, 96, 266
Orion, 116, 119, 137–8, 201, 265
Orvietto, 15
Ostfriesland, 25, 72, 76, 92, 109, 111, 119, 124, 149, 199–200, 207, 232–3, 259
Owl, 266

Pakenham, Rear Admiral, 266
Paris, 15
Pelican, 67, 205, 267
Petard, 62, 66–8, 205, 207, 233, 267
Peterson, Oberleutnant zur See. 264
Pfeiffer. Korvettenkapitän. 259
Phaeton, 27, 35–6, 42–3, 267
Pierstorff, Kapitänleutnant, 261
Pillau, 4, 14, 37, 43, 93–5, 100, 161, 164, 179–80, 207, 222, 229–30, 249, 261
Pommern, 162, 166–7, 195, 211, 213–15, 260
Poppy, 4
Porpoise, 190, 193, 197, 199
Posen, 76–7, 92, 166, 169, 191, 198, 229, 234, 259
Princess Royal, 45, 48, 50–2, 59–62, 67, 71, 75, 87, 96, 108, 111, 128, 162, 164–6, 266
Prinzregent Luitpold, 75, 78, 84, 91, 109, 135, 149–50, 161, 234, 260
Punt, Korvettenkapitän, 260
Puttkamer, Kapitänleutnant von, 263

Queen Elizabeth, 28, 47, 82, 84, 147
Queen Mary, 48, 50–4, 60–2, 70, 82, 115, 173, 201, 221, 231, 233, 266

Raeder, Korvettenkapitän, 45, 261
Rebensburg, Fregattenkapitän Friedrich, 38, 261
Recke, Kapitänleutnant, 263
Redlich, Kapitän zur See, 124, 190, 208, 259
Regensburg, 8, 11, 14, 32, 37, 51, 67–70, 91, 97–8, 132–3, 151, 157, 159, 176, 203, 207, 222, 227, 238, 263
Reichardt, Fregattenkapitän, 259
Reiß, Kapitän zur See, 37, 261
Renown, 243
Repulse, 243
Reuter, Kapitän zur See/Kommodore, 13, 21, 38, 160–1, 180, 249, 261
Revenge, 116, 129, 137, 139–41, 157, 188, 219, 221, 265

Rheinland, 2, 77, 92, 169, 189–90, 193–4, 198–9, 207, 211, 215, 259
Richter, Korvettenkapitän, 259
Richthofen, Kapitänleutnant von, 259
Riedel, Kapitänleutnant Leo, 262
Riedel, Flugmeister, 16
Riedel, Korvettenkapitän Theodore, 123, 262
Rode, Oberleutnant zur See, 263
Rodenberg, Oberleutnant zur See, 262
Roedenbeck, Korvettenkapitän, 259
Rohardt, Kapitän zur See, 259
Rostock, 11, 20, 22, 27, 29, 32, 38, 71, 99, 105–106, 123, 132–4, 153, 158–62, 174–6, 186, 189–90, 193–7, 203, 208–209, 234, 249, 262
Royal Oak, 116, 137, 140, 151, 265
Royalist, 168–70, 174, 266
Rümann, Kapitänleutnant, 263

S15, 175, 180, 263
S16, 57, 93, 175, 180, 233, 263
S17, 93, 175, 263
S18, 11, 175, 180, 263
S19, 175, 263
S20, 93, 175, 263
S23, 175, 180, 263
S24, 175, 180, 263
S32, 123, 189, 193, 230, 262
S33, 151, 159, 209, 227, 263
S34, 96, 151, 159, 209, 227, 263
S35, 68, 90, 151, 153, 263
S36, 67, 151, 153, 159, 209, 263
S50, 96, 151, 159, 168, 176, 209, 263
S51, 13, 151, 153, 159, 204, 263
S52, 68, 96, 151, 153, 159, 204, 263
S53, 151, 191, 203–204, 262
S54, 123, 151, 154, 195–6, 203, 262
Scheer, Vizeadmiral, 1–3, 10, 12–14, 18, 21, 24–5, 28, 32, 39, 47, 71–104, 109, 121–53, 157–60, 174, 177–9, 188–9, 204, 208, 216, 218, 220–1, 231, 233–4, 236, 238–40, 243–5, 248–50, 259
Scheibe, Korvettenkapitän, 261
Schepke, Kapitänleutnant, 263
Scherzer, Kapitänleutnant, 261
Schickhardt, Kapitänleutnant, 262
Schirmacher, Kapitänleutnant, 54, 261
Schlesien, 92, 166–7, 211, 213–14, 260
Schleswig-Holstein, 166–7, 211, 214, 260
Schmidt, Bootsmannsmaat, 185
Schmidt, Vizeadmiral Ehrhard, 72, 76, 150, 166, 177, 193, 250, 259
Schniewind, Oberleutnant zur See Otto, 263
Schroeder, Kapitänleutnant, 261
Schubart, Fregattenkapitän, 260
Schulte, Kapitänleutnant, 262
Schultz, Korvettenkapitän Max, 11, 151–2, 236, 250, 263

Schutze, Kapitänleutnant, 264
Schumacher, Kapitänleutnant Ernst, 105
Schütz, Seekadett Günther, 72, 167, 213
Schumann, Korvettenkapitän, 260
Schuur, Fregattenkapitän, 5, 96, 262
Schwendler, Zimmermannsgast, 140
Seydlitz, 6–8, 10, 12, 14, 17–18, 20, 25, 29, 31–2, 36, 45, 48, 50–4, 60–2, 66, 72, 78–9, 82, 85, 87, 89, 96, 100, 119, 126, 135, 141, 145, 163–6, 177, 179, 181, 186–8, 201, 227, 229–30, 239, 241
Shannon, 266
Shark, 96–9, 123, 151, 266
Sievers, Kapitän zur See, 260
Southampton, 33, 66, 71, 75–8, 111, 135, 168, 170, 182, 186, 267
Sparrowhawk, 190, 193–7, 203–204, 234, 266
Spieß, Kapitänleutnant Fritz, 262
Spitfire, 190, 192, 211, 266
Squadron I, 1, 5–7, 10–12, 15, 17, 25, 29, 32–3, 38, 72–3, 76, 93, 124, 150, 153, 159, 164, 166, 169–70, 177, 181, 186, 189, 194, 200, 208, 232, 234, 259
Squadron II, 2, 15, 17, 25, 29, 32–3, 38, 72–3, 78, 92, 124, 147, 150, 157, 161–2, 166–8, 177–8, 180, 200, 209, 233, 260
Squadron III, 2, 7, 10, 12, 15, 17–18, 25, 29, 32–3, 38, 72–3, 82, 93, 101, 121, 134, 136, 149–50, 154, 159, 177, 200–201, 209, 233–4, 243, 249, 260
Squadron IV, 243
St Vincent, 46, 137, 141, 265
Stecher, Kapitänleutnant, 263
Steinbrinck, Kapitänleutnant Erich, 153, 263
Steinbrinck, Oberleutnant zur See Otto, 20, 23–4, 264
Stettin, 38, 160–1, 182, 186, 249, 261
Stever, Korvettenkapitän, 259
Stirling, Captain, 189, 212, 216–17, 266
Stosch, Oberleutnant zur See von, 115
Stralsund, 19, 21
Stricker, Korvettenkapitän, 259
Sturdee, Vice Admiral, 265
Stuttgart, 38, 161, 182, 186, 189, 191, 211, 261
Superb, 116, 137, 265

Teichmann, Korvettenkapitän, 260
Temeraire, 116, 137, 151, 265
Termagant, 70, 205, 267
Thunderer, 116, 186, 204, 221, 265
Thüringen, 76, 92, 109, 199–201, 207, 234, 259
Tietgens, Korvettenkapitän, 260
Tiger, 48, 50–1, 54–5, 62, 74–5, 79, 82–6, 111, 128, 162, 164, 266
Tillessen, Korvettenkapitän, 263
Tils, Oberleutnant zur See, 262
Tipperary, 180, 189–95, 203–204, 230, 233, 266

Tirpitz, Großadmiral von, 3, 147
Torpedo Bootes Flottille I, 11–12, 262
Torpedo Bootes Flottille II, 3–4, 6, 8–9, 29, 37, 70, 97, 133, 151, 157, 159, 168, 174, 176, 209, 262
Torpedo Bootes Flottille III, 38, 123, 128, 132–4, 151, 154, 159, 176, 209, 262
Torpedo Bootes Flottille V, 38, 158, 162, 168, 174–6, 209, 211–12, 262
Torpedo Bootes Flottille VI, 3–12, 24, 32, 133, 150–4, 157, 159, 208–209, 250, 263
Torpedo Bootes Flottille VII, 38, 92, 157–9, 174–6, 180, 209, 211, 263
Torpedo Bootes Flottille IX, 3, 6, 8–9, 29, 37, 67–8, 91, 96, 132–3, 150–4, 157, 159, 174–6, 180, 209–12, 250, 263
Torpedo Bootes Half Flottille 1, 27, 38, 123, 133, 126, 168
Torpedo Bootes Half Flottille 3, 68
Torpedo Bootes Half Flottille 4, 42
Torpedo Bootes Half Flottille 9, 25
Torpedo Bootes Half Flottille 11, 97, 151–2, 157, 159
Torpedo Bootes Half Flottille 12, 96–7, 133, 159, 174, 209
Torpedo Bootes Half Flottille 13, 29
Torpedo Bootes Half Flottille 17, 153, 159
Torpedo Bootes Half Flottille 18, 153, 159, 174, 177
Trotha, Kapitän zur See Adolf von, 2, 121, 259
Trotha, Kapitän zur See Thilo von, 37, 261
Trotha, Kapitänleutnant von Wolf, 263
Turbulent, 66–7, 205, 207, 267
Tyrwhitt, Commodore, 9–11, 19–23

U22, 30
U24, 30, 264
U32, 30, 35–6, 39, 264
U43, 30, 35, 264
U44, 30, 264
U46, 30–1, 236, 264
U47, 30, 264
U51, 30, 234, 264
U52, 30, 264
U53, 264
U63, 30, 236, 264
U64, 236
U66, 30, 35, 39, 264
U67, 30, 264
U70, 30, 264
U72, 30–1, 264
U74, 30–1, 264
U75, 30–1, 264
UB6, 16, 21, 264
UB10, 16, 21, 264
UB12, 16, 264
UB17, 264

UB18, 16, 19–20, 23, 264
UB19, 264
UB21, 30, 264
UB22, 30, 264
UB23, 264
UB27, 30–1, 264
UB29, 16, 20, 23–4, 264
UC1, 16, 264
UC5, 16
UC6, 16, 264
UC7, 6,16
UC10, 16, 264
Ulrich, Oberleutnant zur See, 262
Undaunted, 9–12
Unity, 190, 205

V1 (British Submarine), 21
V1, 209, 262
V2, 209, 211, 215–16, 262
V3, 263
V4, 209, 211, 215–16, 262
V5, 209, 262
V6, 209, 211, 215–16, 262
V26, 68, 70, 151, 153, 159, 209, 263
V27, 68, 70, 96, 151, 263
V28, 18, 62, 67, 96, 151–3, 159, 204, 263
V29, 68, 70, 151–2, 263
V30, 151, 159, 209, 227, 263
V43, 4
V44, 4, 151, 263
V45, 18, 126, 133, 151, 159, 224–7, 263
V46, 96, 151, 159, 209, 263
V47, 16
V48, 123, 129, 151, 158, 168, 262
V67, 16
V68, 16
V69, 18, 96, 151, 159, 209, 263
V71, 134, 151, 195–6, 207, 234, 262
V73, 123, 134, 151, 195–6, 207, 234, 262
Valiant, 63, 65–6, 72, 75, 80, 82–7, 108, 137, 158, 219, 267
Vanguard, 116, 137, 151, 202, 204, 263
Varrentrapp, Kapitän zur See, 260
Vindex, 9, 25
Vollheim, Kapitänleutnant, 42, 262
Vollmer, Korvettenkapitän, 259
von der Tann, 2, 6–7, 15, 20–1, 36, 46, 48, 50–1, 55–7, 62–5, 80–2, 88, 96, 100, 135, 141, 145, 163, 176–7, 211, 215, 232, 261

Warrior, 95, 100, 104, 107–108, 111, 234, 266
Warspite, 63–4, 82, 85, 87, 107, 108–109, 111, 124, 204, 221, 234, 236, 240, 250, 267
Wegener, Korvettenkapitän, 259
Wehner, Korvettenkapitän, 260
Weineck, Kapitänleutnant, 262
Wende, Kapitänleutnant, 261

Werber, Kapitänleutnant, 261
Werther, Korvettenkapitän, 259
Westfalen, 6, 78, 124, 166, 169, 171, 177, 179,
    189–90, 193–4, 197, 203, 205–208, 211, 215,
    233–4, 259
Wiesbaden, 32, 93, 95, 99–100, 104, 111, 116,
    119, 121–2, 129–30, 132–7, 143, 146, 151,
    154, 249, 250, 261
Wintour, Captain, 189, 266

Witting, Leutnant zur See, 165
Wolf, Oberleutnant zur See Ernst, 263

Yarmouth, 267

'Z' Flottille Flanders, 16–17
Zenker, Kapitän zur See, 36, 81, 261
Zitzewitz, Kapitänleutnant von, 263
Zores, Kapitänleutnant, 261